Teaching the Learning Disabled Adolescent: Strategies and Methods

Gordon Alley and Donald Deshler
University of Kansas

LOVE PUBLISHING COMPANY
Denver · London

Copyright © 1979 Love Publishing Company
Printed in the U.S.A.
ISBN 0-89108-094-5
Library of Congress Catalog Card Number 78-78030
10 9 8 7 6 5 4 3 2 1

ACKNOWLEDGMENTS

In the process of writing this book, numerous people made contributions. We are indebted to our colleagues and students who reviewed the manuscript during its formative stages or contributed to our conceptualization by their input. Specifically, we thank Edward L. Meyen for supporting our participation over the past four years in research and program development activities related to the LD adolescent. Staff members of the Kansas Child Service Demonstration Center (Lawrence High School) Steve Carlson, Jerry Keimig, Carol Ann Buller and Karen Lyerla have carefully implemented many of the ideas in this text in a school setting, and their feedback allowed us to refine and modify our work, especially in its latter stages. Many students and teachers devoted long hours to critiquing our work and making suggestions for changes, particularly Fran Clark, Patty Lee, Nancy Lowrey, Carmen Mayer, and Daryl Mellard, Ed Pieper, and Mike Warner.

For assistance in typing the manuscript, we wish to thank Cindy Bauer, Mina Carr, Sheryl Saathoff, Pam Sletner, and Bonnie Ward.

Finally, we appreciate the tremendous support and encouragement of our parents and families — Eva, Steve, Melissa, Carol, Reed, Jill, and Todd.

G.R.A.
D.D.D.

CONTENTS

FIGURES

TABLES

LEARNING DISABILITIES IN ADOLESCENTS: A PERSPECTIVE

Programming for Learning Disabled Adolescents

An Alternative Approach

An Overview

1

Formally, the history of the learning disability field began in 1963. The Association for Children with Learning Disabilities (ACLD) was formed at a conference by the Fund for Perceptually Handicapped Children. As an organization, ACLD was interested in children who evidenced specific disorders in spoken and written language and perceptual-motor functioning. The next few years were marked by the publication of several key documents (for example, *The First Annual Report of the National Advisory Committee on Handicapped Children* in 1968 and the three task force reports funded by the National Society for Crippled Children and Adults and by the National Institute of Neurological Diseases and Blindness) and by much organizational growth (for example, the Division for Children with Learning Disabilities [DCLD] was organized within the Council for Exceptional Children).

These publications and national organizations did much to generate public interest in individuals with learning disabilities, to initiate school programs, to support the funding of special projects (for example, Child Service Demonstration Centers), and to formulate teacher training programs in the area of learning disabilities. However, the fact that ACLD and DCLD both chose to use "children" in their names suggests a primary interest in helping preschool and elementary school children. Hammill (1978) has indicated, however, that some parents and professionals have shown sustained interest in the older learning disabled student:

> From the start some parents and professionals have balked at this neglect of the older student. At every convention they would justifiably complain that the program contained little or nothing of interest to them. Although they had contributed their fair share to the organizational efforts to make government officials, public school administrators, and teachers aware of the unique instructional requirements of individuals with

specific learning disabilities, often they were forced to watch with resignation as programs were initiated only at the elementary levels. Time was on their side, however; children in elementary schools eventually became adolescents. With each passing year the ranks of those interested in adolescents with specific learning disabilities have become larger and increasingly more vocal.

Only now, twelve years after the founding of the learning disabilities movement, are the problems of young adults with specific learning disabilities beginning to receive a fair proportion of attention. (p.30)

As the learning disability field has evolved over the past one and a half decades, several factors and events have increased interest in the needs of the learning disabled adolescent and adult. Among these are the following:

1. The passage of the Education for All Handicapped Children Act of 1975, PL 94-142, was a long-awaited event in the struggle for equal educational opportunity for handicapped individuals. While this law has many key features, there is one of particular concern to older learning disabled individuals. Specifically, the act indicates that if a state education agency or a local education agency is to continue to receive funds under this act and other specified acts, such recipients must guarantee, by September 1, 1978, the availability of a free, *appropriate* education to *all* handicapped individuals between the ages of three and eighteen. By September 1, 1980, the states and their school districts must make the same guarantees for all handicapped individuals ages three to twenty-one. Thus, the educational concerns of the older learning disabled individual are guaranteed under the law.

2. A fundamental *assumption* in the learning disability field, as well as in education as a whole, has been that educational efforts are most productive if they are focused on the young child. Recently however, the efficacy of early childhood programs has been questioned. Rowher (1971), in a review of several Head Start programs, concluded that " . . . even the demonstrable benefits produced by some small scale programs often disappear over time; gains observed in treatment groups relative to control groups at the end of pre-school programs diminish by the end of the first or second grades of formal schooling" (p. 318). While the empirical support of such concerns is equivocal, the problem of diminishing benefits warrants examination and has caused some experts to reconsider whether early childhood is, in fact, the prime time for educational intervention. For example, a Stanford Research Institute report, *Compensatory Education in Early Adolescence* (1974), speaks of maturational deficiencies in describing the poor performance of some

3

high school students. This report notes that intensive educational efforts with certain older pupils may be as effective as early intervention with other segments of the population, because in adolescence some students experience accelerated cognitive development.

3. Another assumption that dominated the learning disability field during its formative years was that learning disabled children could be "cured." In redefining learning disability, Kass (1974) suggested that one of the conditions of learning disability is that it obtains at maturity. Similarly, Rogan and Lukens (1969) stated that a learning disability is characterized by persistence or chronicity. They also noted that the disability may manifest itself in changing ways as the pupil matures and school demands change. The question of how manifestations of a disability vary as a function of chronological age is a critical one. Deshler (1978) has concluded in a review on the characteristics of learning disabled adolescents:

> By adolescence there is a high probability that learning disabled students will experience the indirect effects of a learning handicap as manifested by poor self-perception, lowered self-concept, or reduced motivation. Disability in a basic learning process may be the root problem, but it must be considered not only by itself but also in relation to other problems that it may precipitate. . . .
>
> Maturation and/or compensation tends to refine and integrate many psychological, perceptual, and motor functions. Consequently, problems of incoordination, hyperactivity, distractability, and poor attention may manifest themselves in more subtle or controlled ways in older students. (p. 68)

4. Over the years, the field of learning disabilities has gained considerable visibility in the popular press. As the problems encountered by learning disabled students are described in the media, adults have recalled similar difficulties they encountered as children in an era before the concept of learning disability existed. Ironically some of the adults, who apparently once had or still have a learning disability, are quite successful and well adjusted in their personal and occupational life. Some have even been in highly visible positions; for example, the late Nelson A. Rockefeller noted the difficulties he had in reading. Such examples have had several effects. First, parents and professionals have been reassured that the learning disabled can succeed in life situations and that concentrated efforts in school programming for the learning disabled may enhance successful adjustments. Second, these examples have shown that it is average or above-average functioning that distinguishes the learning disabled adolescent from secondary students

demonstrating generalized learning problems (Meyen & Schiefel-busch, 1977). Deshler (1978) suggests that research and program-matic efforts in the field should shift from a total concentration on weaknesses to an exploration of strengths in an effort to better understand the learning disabled adolescent:

> Few researchers or authors have emphasized areas of strength in learn-ing disabled adolescents. Most characteristics are defined in terms of weakness and do not consider integrities that are available for compen-sating for the deficit or circumventing it. (p. 70)

5. The fact that learning disabled adolescents are defined primarily in terms of the impact of their specific disability upon academic functioning and educational opportunities does not mean that the population of learning disabled adolescents is to be found only in school settings. They may be found in state or local agencies such as social rehabilitation services programs, employment opportunity centers, detention homes, group homes, vocational-technical pro-grams, or in private sector settings such as trade schools, labor unions, or unskilled occupations. The relationship of reading prob-lems and other specific disabilities to dropping out of school and having contact with the courts is currently a topic of much interest (Murray, 1976). The number of juvenile delinquents who are also learning disabled has been estimated as 25 percent of the adjudicated population *(Congressional Record,* March 7, 1977). Because an estimated 700,000 young people each year leave secondary schools before they graduate (Anderson, 1970), interventions that take place outside of school settings are also relevant to learning disability in adolescents.

6. The demands of the secondary curriculum are much different from the demands of the elementary curriculum. The secondary cur-riculum is based on content acquisition. It is assumed that by the time students have reached the secondary schools, they have mastered the skills emphasized at the elementary level — reading, writing, spelling, mathematics, and spoken language — well enough to use these skills as tools in acquiring further information. Unfortunately, many learning disabled adolescents have not mastered these skills well enough to compete with their peers in junior and senior high school without supportive services. Not only do secondary cur-riculums demand the basic skills of decoding and computation taught in the elementary school, but also they demand a much broader set of skills in listening, thinking, speaking, reading,

5

writing, mathematics, and personal/social skills. For example, in reading, students are expected to demonstrate vocabulary development, comprehension, reading speed, and various content and study skills, not merely skills in decoding and recognizing words. As educators have come to recognize the types of demands placed on the learning disabled adolescent, they have acknowledged the need for different intervention strategies than those typically used with learning disabled students in elementary schools. Not only do academic demands change in secondary schools, but also the support and individual attention given to students by teachers diminishes. Deshler (1978) notes how such a change in the school structure can be devastating to the learning disabled adolescent:

> One goal of adolescence is independence of action, both in and out of the classroom. Successful social adjustment and successful classroom performance depend, in part, on the degree to which a student can function autonomously. Typically, secondary students do not have the close interaction with, and supervision by, teachers that they enjoyed in the elementary grades. The imposed structure and organization that provided direction to students in elementary school is reduced to a subtle, more flexible structure in high school.
> In elementary school many of the study assignments and test reviews are conducted under the watchful eye of the teacher. Secondary level students are expected to assume more responsibility for such activities and to impose their own structure. For many youngsters with a learning disability, the absence of structure and organization and an inability to function independently can prove devastating. (p. 57)

7. Determining the effects of a learning handicap on an individual is difficult, if not impossible. Nevertheless, there is evidence that students with learning disabilities experience significant problems in social adjustment, social perception, self-concept, and motivation. Authors who have written about learning disorders in adolescents have stressed the concomitant emotional and personality difficulties that beset these individuals (Gordon, 1969; Griffin, 1971; Rosenthal, 1973; Silver, 1974). These accompanying difficulties warrant the full attention of those involved in educating learning disabled adolescents because of the potentially heavy toll a history of prolonged failure can take. Such problems potentially are a greater hindrance to success and adjustment in life than is failure to master certain academic concepts.

A review of factors and events that have directed the attention of parents and professionals to the needs of the learning disabled adolescent in recent years suggests three general conclusions. First, the characteristics of these adolescents indicates that, while their disability is not "cured," they are capable of succeeding in school and postschool settings. Second, due to the change in demands of the secondary school curriculum from skill to content acquisition and to the negative effects of prolonged failure on learning disabled adolescents, there is evidence that new intervention procedures will be required to meet their needs adequately. Third, the passage of PL 94-142 demands that the educational community step up to the challenge of providing services appropriate to the needs of the learning disabled adolescent.

PROGRAMMING FOR LEARNING DISABLED ADOLESCENTS

The past few years have witnessed a dramatic growth in interest in programming for learning disabilities at the secondary level. The pressures put on secondary schools since the mid-1970s to develop programs for the learning disabled adolescent have been tremendous. Unlike programming in other areas of special education, such as mental retardation, deafness, blindness, programming for learning disabilities has had to be done in an extremely short period and at a time when the entire field of special education is quite visible in the community. The demands of PL 94-142 for the provision of "equal educational opportunities" for all students and the expectations of parents of learning disabled adolescents has led to the development of programs based on limited and sometimes no theory or research data.

In our eagerness to help an age group that has been denied services for years, we have often come to hasty and sometimes shortsighted decisions. While youngsters in need of help at the secondary level cannot wait for research to provide answers to crucial questions, neither should they be expected to endure educational programs and service alternatives that have been conceived on limited knowledge and questionable assumptions. For example, many secondary programs for learning disabled adolescents are merely extensions of the same service models used for elementary children. While some components of these models may be valid, they should not be applied in blanket fashion to older populations. To make the same assumptions about secondary students as are made about elementary children is to ignore the critical changes that occur in the developmental process, as well as the curricular and setting differences of the secondary schools. Likewise, to approach all secondary learning disabled students with the alternative, watered-down curriculum traditionally used with mentally retarded populations would be to deny the potential these adolescents have for normal functioning and adjustment.

AN ALTERNATIVE APPROACH

This book describes an alternative approach to meeting the needs of many learning disabled adolescents currently placed in special support programs at the secondary level. The approach, called a *learning strategies model*, is designed to accomplish the following goal: To teach learning disabled adolescents strategies that will facilitate their acquisition, organization, storage, and retrieval of information, thus allowing them to cope with the demands of the secondary curriculum and the demands of social interaction.

The learning strategies model has been developed in light of current assumptions and knowledge about the psychoeducational characteristics of learning disabled adolescents. Specifically, these youngsters are viewed as having the potential for successfully adjusting to the demands of the secondary curriculum. Further, the learning strategies approach has been designed to promote independence of action by these adolescents both in and out of the classroom and to facilitate the transfer and generalization of strategies across tasks and settings. Much of the theoretical rationale for this approach is derived from cognitive psychology. The concepts and methodology presented in this text are being developed and evaluated through the Kansas Child Service Demonstration Center (funded by the Bureau of Education for the Handicapped under Title VI-G) at Lawrence High School, Lawrence, Kansas. The need for thorough and systematic research to determine the efficiency of this approach for learning disabled adolescents is evident. The ideas underlying this approach are being presented as ones that appear to have strong face validity. Practitioners and researchers are encouraged to share, with the authors, data that relate to the application of this approach with learning disabled adolescents.

AN OVERVIEW

The remainder of this text covers two major areas. The first part outlines the specific components of the learning strategies approach, including rationale, target population, skill areas taught, administrative placement issues, activities within the resource room, roles of the teacher of the learning disabled and the regular class teacher, and the use of materials. In addition, other models for serving learning disabled adolescents are described in detail and evaluated. The second part present specific learning methods for these students in the following areas: reading, writing, mathematics, thinking, social interaction, listening, and speaking. Chapters 3 through 9 discuss (1) specific characteristics of the learning disabled adolescent population,

(2) informal and formal assessment procedures for tapping deficits in each area, and (3) specific learning strategies for each skill area. The appendix lists and analyzes materials available for use in a learning strategies model.

REFERENCES

Anderson, L. E. (Ed.). *Helping the adolescent with the hidden handicaps*. Belmont, Calif.: Fearon/Lear Siegler, 1970.

Compensatory education in early adolescence. Menlo Park, Calif.: Stanford Research Institute, 1974.

Congressional Record, Vol. 123, No. 39. Washington, D.C.: U.S. Government Printing Office, March 7, 1977.

Deshler, D. D. Psychoeducational aspects of learning disabled adolescents. In L. Mann, L. Goodman, & J. L. Wiederholt (Eds.), *Teaching the learning disabled adolescent*. Boston: Houghton Mifflin, 1978.

Gordon, S. Psychological problems of adolescents with minimal brain dysfunction. In D. Kronick (Ed.), *Learning disabilities: Its implications to a responsible society*. Chicago: Developmental Learning Materials, 1969.

Griffin, M. How does he feel? In E. Schloss (Ed.), *The educator's enigma: The adolescent with learning disabilities*. San Rafael, Calif.: Academic Therapy Publications, 1971.

Hammill, D. D. Adolescents with specific learning disabilities: Definition, identification, and incidence. In L. Mann, L. Goodman, & J. L. Wiederholt (Eds.), *Teaching the learning disabled adolescent*. Boston: Houghton Mifflin, 1978.

Kass, C. E. Construction of a model of learning disability with attention to system - theoretic approaches. *Proceedings of the International Federation of Learning Disabilities*. Speech presented at the first meeting of the International Federation of Learning Disabilities, Amsterdam, The Netherlands, 1974.

Meyen, E. L., & Schiefelbusch, R. L. *Institute for research in learning disabilities with an emphasis on adolescents and young adults*. Washington, D.C.: Bureau of Education for the Handicapped, U.S. Office of Education, Department of Health, Education and Welfare, 1977.

Murray, C. A. *The link between learning disabilities and juvenile delinquency: Current theory and knowledge*. Washington, D.C.: U.S. Government Printing Office, 1976.

Rogan, L. L., & Lukens, J. E. Education, administration and classroom procedures. In N. G. Haring (Ed.), *Minimal brain dysfunction in children* (NINDS Monograph No. 2, U.S. Public Health Service Publication No. 2015). Washington, D.C.: U.S. Government Printing Office, 1969.

Rowher, W. D., Jr. Prime time for education: Early childhood or adolescence? *Harvard Educational Review*, 1971, *41*, 316-341.

Rosenthal, J. H. Self-esteem in dyslexic children. *Academic Therapy*, 1973, *9*, 27-39.

Silver, L. B. Emotional and social problems of children with developmental disabilities. In R. E. Weber (Ed.), *Handbook on learning disabilities*. Englewood Cliffs, N.J.: Prentice-Hall, 1974.

2

LEARNING STRATEGIES: AN APPROACH FOR THE LEARNING DISABLED ADOLESCENT

What is a Learning Strategies Approach?

What is the Rationale of a Learning Strategies Approach?

For What Target Population of LD Adolescents is the Learning Strategies Approach Most Appropriate?

What Skill Areas are Valued in a Learning Strategies Approach?

What Administrative Arrangement is Most Conducive To a Learning Strategies Approach?

What are the Major Components and Activities of a Learning Strategies Resource Room?

What are the Roles of the Learning Disabilities Teacher and the Classroom Teacher under a Learning Strategies Approach?

What Factors in a School Setting Support a Learning Strategies Approach?

Other Models for Serving LD Adolescents

2

This chapter describes in detail a learning strategies approach to teaching the learning disabled adolescent (hereafter referred to as the LD adolescent or LD student). Specifically, we will address the following questions:

What is a learning strategies approach to teaching LD adolescents?

What is the rationale underlying a learning strategies approach?

For what target population within this group is the learning strategies approach most appropriate?

What specific skills are dealt with in a learning strategies approach?

What administrative arrangement is most conducive to a learning strategies approach?

What are the major components and activities of a learning strategies resource room?

What are the roles of the learning disabilities teacher and the regular classroom teacher under a learning strategies approach?

What factors in a school setting are critical to the support of a learning strategies approach?

In the latter part of the chapter, other models currently used in teaching LD adolescents are described and analyzed. This discussion is based on a nationwide study of major programs for LD adolescents.

WHAT IS A LEARNING STRATEGIES APPROACH?

Learning strategies are defined as techniques, principles, or rules that will facilitate the acquisition, manipulation, integration, storage, and retrieval of information across situations and settings. A learning strategies model of instruction for LD adolescents is designed to teach students *how* to learn rather than to teach students specific content. For example, under a learning strategies model, the teacher of LD students would teach them some *techniques* for organizing material that has to be memorized for a history test, rather than teaching them the actual history content. Thus, while learning to use organizational strategies to improve comprehension and retention of history concepts, students are also learning a skill that may facilitate acquisition of information in other subject areas.

In short, a learning strategies approach identifies specific strategies, techniques, and rules that the student can use in coping with the demands of the secondary curriculum. Even more important, the learning techniques that students master will help them adjust to a world in which there is a constant flood of new and highly technical information and rapid change. While coping with the demands of a school curriculum is important for some practical reasons, such as the acquisition of a diploma that will facilitate access to future opportunities, in the final analysis it is more important that students have the ability to apply appropriate strategies in life that will allow them to cope with demands in the job market and in family and personal adjustments.

Rowher (1971) maintains that the effectiveness of schooling practices should be judged by the degree to which they help the student adapt to "extraschool tasks." The specific skills needed in extraschool activities are:

> . . . the tasks of seeking, finding, inquiring, and remembering information; the tasks of extending, transferring, and creating new information; the tasks of communicating information, thoughts, and feelings to oneself and to others as well as of comprehending such communications from others; the tasks of understanding and accurately predicting future events; and the tasks of acquiring tactics and strategies for reading chosen goals and for enjoying the journey, either alone or in concert with others. . . . These tasks all demand that the individual develop well-honed cognitive skills and coordinate them with his actions. (p. 320)

Therefore, the adage "Give me a fish, and I can eat for a day. Teach me to fish, and I can eat for a lifetime" summarizes the goal of this approach. The intent is to teach students skills that will allow them not only to meet immediate requirements successfully but also to generalize these skills to other situations over time.

WHAT IS THE RATIONALE
OF A LEARNING STRATEGIES APPROACH?

The philosophical underpinnings of the learning strategies approach are found in four conditions: the transience of knowledge and events, the failure of current educational practices, the teachability of learning strategies, and the compatibility of learning strategies with the concept of "least restrictive environment."

Transitory Knowledge and Situations

Our technological society is marked by a high level of transience, novelty, and diversity. Knowledge becomes increasingly perishable as advances proliferate at a geometrically progressive rate — a condition that has come to typify industrialized nations in the twentieth century. Futurist Alvin Toffler (1970) has clearly described the magnitude of the information explosion in this century by comparing the rate at which book titles have been generated in recent decades with the rates of book production in previous centuries:

> Prior to 1500 . . . Europe was producing books at the rate of 1000 titles per year. . . . By 1950 the rate had accelerated so sharply that Europe was producing 120,000 titles a year. By the mid-sixties, the output of books on a world scale . . . approached the prodigious figure of 1000 titles per day. . . . The computer . . . with its unprecedented power for analysis and dissemination of extremely varied kinds of data in unbelievable quantities and at mind-staggering speeds has become a major force behind the latest acceleration in knowledge acquisition. (p. 30-31)

"Thus, given this rapid accumulation, change, and dissemination of knowledge, today's 'fact' may in all likelihood become tomorrow's misinformation" (Toffler, 1970, p. 403). Futurists, however, voice concern about other components of the transient nature of life in the twentieth century. Specifically, the increased temporariness in everyday life is reflected in relationships with other people. Groups of people, things, places, institutional or organizational environments, and the flow of ideas and information in schools and in society seem increasingly fragile and impermanent.

Such conditions in today's world have not gone unnoticed by educators. Speaking of the rapid changes in the American culture, Clark, Klein, and Burks (1972) have noted some poignant implications for the development of high school curriculums:

> Our American cultural scene is changing rapidly, so rapidly that much of the curriculum soon becomes out of date unless it is continually revised. Changing employment practices make it necessary to reevaluate our provisions for general and vocational

education. The new technical and service industries continually call for increased numbers of highly trained workers. (p. 28)

Schools not only must consider the demands of today's world, but also anticipate the nature of tomorrow's world. Regardless of the specific directions that our society takes, it seems evident that the general climate will be one characterized by rapid information accumulation and a movement away from permanence. Thus, the future will require individuals who can make critical judgments; negotiate their way through novel situations; acquire, manipulate, and apply information across different situations and settings; and identify new relationships in a rapidly changing society. In short, schools must not merely teach students to memorize static information, but also teach them to manipulate information and to discard or refine old ideas. Toffler (1970) concludes that students must "learn how to learn" (p. 414).

Clark, Klein, and Burks (1972) have further elaborated on the role of secondary schools in the future, relative to the thrust of its efforts:

1. The first responsibility of the school is to teach boys and girls how to think and to give them tools to think with. (p. 133)
2. Modern curricula should emphasize using subject matter as a tool of thinking. Boys and girls should learn to think by actually solving problems by both inductive and deductive reasoning. (p. 139)
3. Subject matter is valuable for teaching processes, principles, attitudes, ideals, appreciations, and skills. To teach these important learnings does not depend so much on what subject matter one teaches as *how* one teaches it. (p. 132)

Therefore, the central education mission of schools in the future is to teach students skills for coping and adapting to inevitable change. Roger's statement (1976) on the role of a college education seems applicable to secondary schools as well:

It is my view that a college education was never for the sole purpose of teaching one how to make a living. We can no longer expect to educate someone in four years for a lifetime of employment. Instead we can give the student basic skills and try to prepare him or her to be adaptable to the changes that are going to take place. (p. 6)

Failure of Current Practices

The relevance and effectiveness of current educational practices have come under increasing criticism in recent years. Declining college entrance scores and poor job performance, coupled with inadequate reading, writing, speaking, and problem-solving skills of high school graduates, have given genesis to negative reactions.

Data from a series of nationwide studies conducted from 1965 to 1975 by the National Assessment of Education Progress (NAEP) project provide some support for the critics of current educational practices. The NAEP administered a variety of tests to develop profiles of nine-, thirteen-, and seventeen-year-old students. Here are some of the major conclusions of these studies:

1. Thirteen-year-olds can read, write, add, subtract, divide, and multiply — if told to do so. But by themselves they don't use these skills to solve everyday problems. In essence, they do not realize the potential uses of the skills and facts they have learned.
2. Thirteen-year-old students have not been taught (or have not learned) to use skills to aid them in gathering information. Specifically, their knowledge of reference materials and how to use them is superficial. Ninety-four percent of those surveyed knew that a dictionary is used to find the meanings of words, but only 78 percent of them could take the first three letters of a word and figure out from the guide words on the dictionary page where the word they were looking up would be.
3. Seventeen-year-olds can read, write, and compute in well-structured situations, but they were found to have difficulty in applying their knowledge in new situations.
4. Seventeen-year-olds don't do well on problems that require more than one step and can't organize their thoughts in writing. Furthermore, they had writing problems if they were not told specifically what to do.

Engelmann (1969) notes that by the time students reach the eighth grade many of them "lack comprehension and interest; they can't generalize, and they can't follow instructions." He has attempted to delineate the causes for these failures in junior and senior high schools. Among the causes, he names the following:

1. *Basic language skills were not taught.* During the first few grades, several children fail to master the basic language skills on which most of their instruction is built. For example, children may not be taught the differences between familiar and unfamiliar words, or they may be given tasks to do ("Draw a line around the top man") without being taught the meaning of key words (*draw, line,* and *top*). Furthermore, children are not taught to follow instructions. Instead of carefully breaking down tasks and sequentially presenting information, teachers often present the material in one lump sum in a

lecture. Many unwarranted assumptions are made about children's basic language concepts; teachers proceed to talk, assuming that students understand and can follow everything that was said.

2. *The teachers shifted the focus of the learning situation from solving problems to learning certain behaviors.* Because students are often reinforced for making "appropriate appearances" of learning, they often fail to learn strategies to solve problems that generalize across settings. Many behaviors — for example, getting assignments in on time, writing neatly, or looking busy — are often misinterpreted by students as being the most important ones in surviving the school game. Instead, the emphasis of instruction should be on the acquisition of effective solution strategies.

> A solution strategy begins with understanding that the goal is to solve the problem confronting you, not to go through a behavioral ritual. To solve a problem, you must know both where you are starting from and where you would end if you discovered an adequate solution. . . . You follow *rules* [italics added]. The rules are important for one reason only. They allow you to dispose of obstacles. . . . When a solution strategy is employed, rules take on a special meaning, because they specify the types of moves that are being made in attacking a problem. . . . To learn a rule is to learn how to attack a whole class of problems. . . . The children studied grammar, but they were never taught the basic language strategies . . . [Children are not taught] what the obstacles are and how to remove them because they haven't been taught to think of a problem in terms of steps essential to its solution. (Entelmann, 1969, pp. 17-19)

3. *The teachers did not teach basic principles.* Many of the children who fail in school do so because they have not been taught the importance of explaining a phenomenon in terms of basic principles. Children are seldom given exercises in which they are to answer *why* questions, using basic principles (for example, "When a light is turned on in a room, the pupils in your eyes get smaller. Why?"). In addition, instruction often emphasizes the learning of specific pieces of information first rather than general principles. Engelmann (1969) maintains:

> We have to *begin* [italics added] with the principle that covers most of the cases. . . . If you don't teach the child the basic principles of science, he may never learn them. They are the most logical starting place. . . . When a child learns a principle, he can use it as a criterion for distinguishing between different kinds of problems. . . . The child must see that the purpose of a principle is to explain a specified class of phenomena. This can be done most economically by first teaching the principle, then showing how the principle applies to a range of tasks. (pp. 19-20)

4. *The teachers did not show the children how to use what they had learned.* Oftentimes children are expected to learn facts and complete

lessons for the sake of learning them. The application and generalization of this learning are seldom valued. Even when principles
are taught, they often are not applied to a broad array of situations
and settings. Children must be taught *how* to use what they have
learned as much as they are taught the original piece of information
or principle.

In summary, current educational practices seem to promote a system
that teaches students to learn specific pieces of information and skills quite
well but minimizes the acquisition of principles that will facilitate problem-
solving and application of skills to a variety of tasks in different situations
and settings.

Teachability of Learning Strategies[1]

The research done on cognitive learning in children at such research
centers as the Wisconsin Research and Development Center for Cognitive
Learning and the Stanford Research Institute has created an empirical base
in educational psychology from which to take a learning strategies approach
in instructing LD adolescents. This research has taken a variety of forms,
but enough has been done to allow us to draw some implications for instructional practices in school settings. Our purpose is to give a few examples of
the research to show the potential strength of strategies in facilitating
learning. In discussing developmental changes that occur in children,
Rowher (1971) has concluded that early adolescence is the prime time for
instruction of learning strategies. His research indicated that attempts to
help students increase their learning skills through training are more
appropriate in the adolescent than in the younger child; however, younger
children have been found able to learn and apply strategies to advantage also.
    Some of the learning strategies that have increased performance include
verbal mediation, clustering, and visual imagery. These will be briefly
discussed below.
    Verbal mediation as a learning strategy involves the use of language in
a meaningful way to facilitate the storage and retrieval of information.
Flavell, Beech, and Chinsky (1966) found that students at the second-grade
level used naming and rehearsal techniques to facilitate recall. Verbal
labeling has been found to increase performance, particularly in short-term
memory tasks, such as using mnemonic devices (Hagen, 1971). Rowher
(1971) found that performance on a paired associate task was facilitated by

---

[1] Information in this section was compiled with the assistance of Ms. Fran Clark, doctoral
student in Special Education, University of Kansas.

the introduction of a verbal mediator that required the student to make a meaningful association between the two words. For example, if the pair of words was *corn* and *Vermont,* the mediator might be "Corn will not grow in Vermont." Whimbey (1976), believing that the ability to score well on tests is a skill that can be learned, used the verbal mediation strategy of "thinking aloud," coupled with immediate feedback, to develop students' problem-solving skills. Following training, the students raised both GRE and LSAT scores.

Clustering as a learning strategy involves grouping or categorizing material to be learned. Miller (1956) has postulated that memory span is defined by a fixed number of chunks of information, but that memory span may be extended by organizing material into larger and larger chunks, each chunk with more information. Students' ability to use clustering as a learning strategy depends on their ability to discover the organizational structure or categories to be learned (Mandler, 1967). In a study designed to examine the effectiveness of repetition and category organization among graduate students, Winne, Hauck, and Moore (1975) presented selected category labels, followed by five category members, using four repetition conditions. Students who were presented with new members of a previously mentioned category learned more material in the time allowed than did other subjects. The authors suggested that the increase in learning resulted from the review of the category label and category members as each new member was coded and stored. Thus, use of the clustering strategy and a repetitive activity designed to review that cluster facilitated recall.

Imagery as a learning strategy involves making associations between stimulus items and then generating a visual image of the items or an interaction between the items. Paivio (1969) has found imagery to be more important in learning and memory than verbal mediation. Lesgold, McCormick, and Golinkoff (1975) found that imagery training facilitated recall of phrase content and concluded that its effects are in the areas of organization and storage of information. These positive results of imagery strategies were supported by Kerst and Levin (1973). Both student-generated and experimenter-generated strategies (imagery and sentences) facilitated recall, both immediately and over time (one week later). No differences were found in results when students produced their own strategies or when a strategy was provided for them, though greater variability was found in the student-generated strategies. The authors concluded that students who may be unable to produce their own learning strategy may benefit from having a strategy provided.

While the research that has been done in empirical psychology seems to underline the potential effectiveness of strategies to facilitate learning, retention, and application of information, these data should be interpreted in light of the following observations by Levin (1976): (1) The potential effectiveness of a strategy is dependent on the nature of the task and the materials. What constitutes an appropriate strategy in one context may be completely inappropriate in another. (2) A strategy is most effective if the learner generates his own, rather than having one imposed on him by the experimenter. Self-generated strategies usually better meet the individual learning style of the student. In the absence of self-generated strategies, however, those given by the teacher can serve as effective models. (3) A strategy that works effectively for one student in a given setting may not work for another student under similar circumstances.

Finally, only limited research in the learning and application of strategies has been conducted with LD populations. While caution must be exercised in the overgeneralization of findings from empirical psychological research done on populations that are not learning disabled, preliminary research findings on LD populations supports previous research (for example, Warner, 1977).

Compatibility with the Concept of "Least Restrictive Environment"

PL 94-142 specified that the placement procedures followed by schools must assure, to the maximum extent appropriate, that handicapped students are educated with students who are not handicapped. Furthermore, special classes, separate schooling, or other removal of handicapped students from the regular educational environment occurs *only* when the nature or severity of the handicap is such that education in regular classes with the use of supplementary aids and services cannot be achieved satisfactorily.

The learning and adjustment problems encountered by many LD adolescents are such that students can and should be placed in regular classrooms and given support service in a resource room setting. This seems particularly true for the mildly to moderately disabled adolescent. A study by Deshler, Lowrey, and Alley (1979) to determine the percentage of mildly to moderately learning disabled adolescents and the percentage of severely learning disabled adolescents being served in programs across the country indicated that 89 percent of the LD adolescent population fell in the mild to moderate category and only 11 percent in the severe category. If LD students are placed in regular classes, they will be expected to meet many of the same curriculum demands placed on all students. They must be able to learn, integrate, manipulate, and express large amounts of content information. In addition, students need skills to facilitate their interactions with peers and teachers in academic and nonacademic situations. The learning strategies approach has been developed in light of the demands placed on the student by the secondary school curriculum and setting. This seems particularly true for the mildly to moderately disabled adolescent. A major concern of the learning strategies approach is to stress the generalization and transfer of skills learned in the resource room to tasks performed in the regular classroom.

FOR WHAT TARGET POPULATION OF LD ADOLESCENTS IS THE LEARNING STRATEGIES APPROACH MOST APPROPRIATE?

A limited amount of research has been conducted on the efficacy of different curriculum models for different populations of LD adolescents. At present, programming decisions are being made primarily on the basis of observational data and previous experiences with other handicapped populations at the secondary level. However, data collected in a national survey of secondary learning disabilities programs by Deshler, Lowrey, and Alley (1979) provide some insight into the types of youngsters that may best be served under a learning strategies approach. The characteristics of youngsters who appear to benefit from a learning strategies approach seem to fall into the following categories:

1. These students read above the third-grade level. This is significant, because reading authorities (Harris, 1970) have indicated that during the first three grades in school students master the basic reading skills necessary for breaking the code. Students who have mastered reading skills through the third-grade level have the prerequisites for an instructional shift from decoding to comprehension, speed, and vocabulary development. With a reading foundation, students are in a position to learn techniques that will facilitate their comprehension of larger amounts of material. Obviously, the higher the student's reading level, the more readily the student can utilize strategies, such as skimming, scanning, SQ3R, and REAP.

2. Reading skill may be one dimension for differentiating students who can best benefit from a strategies approach, but it is not a sole indicator, nor does it exclude other indicators. Another critical indicator seems to be the student's ability to deal with symbolic as well as concrete learning tasks. While concrete representations, such as pictures, have been found to facilitate learning greatly (Levin, 1976), many of the task demands of a secondary curriculum are abstract and must be dealt with symbolically. For example, in

chemistry, students must be able to understand and manipulate symbolic language to deal with this problem: $CO_2 + Br \rightarrow$. Typical classroom situations require students to deal with abstract concepts and symbolic representations. Most lectures require well-honed listening skills that go beyond the concrete level of information acquisition. Thus, some students whose reading skills are below third-grade level still are able to benefit from a strategies approach that teaches them to listen more effectively, to solve problems in social situations, to differentiate relevant from irrelevant information, to apply a principle to mathematics data, to isolate a variable, or to accomplish a variety of other tasks that are not dependent on the student's reading ability, but that are a function of the student's ability to deal with symbolic representations.

3. Most students demonstrate at least average intellectual ability, scoring in the 85-115 IQ range.

In short, the learning strategies approach seems to be most effective with a target group of LD adolescents who have normal IQs, possess reading skills above the third-grade level, and can deal with symbolic language. These conditions are not all necessary, nor are they necessarily exhaustive. The need for additional documentation to verify the best match between instructional approach and learner attributes is evident. The needs of adolescents with learning disabilities are extremely varied and complex. It is unlikely that any one curriculum approach or instructional model will satisfy the diverse needs of this population. Instructional attempts and learner attributes must be carefully noted and described so that we may reach a better understanding of the relationship between the two.

WHAT SKILL AREAS ARE VALUED IN A LEARNING STRATEGIES APPROACH?

Strategies are taught to students in seven skill areas under the learning strategies model. The seven skill areas are reading, writing, mathematics, thinking, social interaction, speaking, and listening. These areas are emphasized because the authors suspect that a variety of strategies and techniques are needed beyond the traditional approaches to teaching reading and mathematics skills in most learning disability services if students are to meet the demands of the secondary curriculum. Not only is the number of skill areas greater with this model, but the emphasis within each area helps the LD adolescent better meet the demands of the secondary curriculum and arrive at postsecondary adjustment.

TABLE 2.1
Reading Skills

Subskill Areas

	Vocabulary Development	Word Recognition	Reading Comprehension	Reading Rate	Study Skills
Instructional Goals	Denotation of words	Sight-word recognition	Syntax	Skimming skills	Awareness of differing content area/text reading demands
			Semantics		
	Multiple meanings of words	Structural analysis	Comprehension of individual written elements (phrase, sentence, paragraph, etc.)	Scanning skills	
					Previewing material
	Morphology	Use of context clues			
	Connotations of words	Dictionary usage		Spontaneous reading flexibility	Increasing reading efficiency through application of strategies
			Reading at various levels of comprehension		
					Reviewing material
					Summarizing material

Tables 2.1 through 2.7 present overviews of each area.[2] In many cases, breakdown and organization are arbitrary, but each area has been designed to best reflect an array of possible skills needed by LD students in secondary and postsecondary settings. Each area has been conceptualized along two dimensions: subskill area and instructional goal. The subskill areas represent the major components of a skill area; for example, reading has been subdivided into five subskill areas — vocabulary development, word recognition, reading comprehension, reading rate, and study skills. The instructional goals are the components in each subskill area around which short-term instructional plans can be developed.

---

[2] These tables (except 2.3) were devised by the staff of the Kansas Child Care Service Demonstration Center (Lawrence, Kansas) for the purpose of implementing a learning strategies approach in Lawrence High School.

TABLE 2.2
Writing Skills

Subskill Areas

	Attitude	Content	Craft
Instructional Goals	Emotional blocks to writing	Description writing	Organizing ideas
			Vocabulary
		Relationship writing	Building sentences
			Writing questions
			Notetaking
	Motivation to write	Explanatory writing	Summarizing
			Punctuating
			Capitalizing
		Personal views	Spelling
			Neatness
			Monitoring performance

WHAT ADMINISTRATIVE ARRANGEMENT IS MOST CONDUCIVE TO A LEARNING STRATEGIES APPROACH?

Since a major goal of a learning strategies approach is to teach students techniques that will allow them to cope better with the demands of the regular classroom, a resource room model is the most conducive administrative arrangement. The resource room is advocated for the following reasons:

1. A major assumption underlying this approach is that LD adolescents can, with appropriate support services, benefit from the offerings available through the regular class curriculum. The talents and strengths of the LD adolescent should not be minimized. While these students may lack some basic skills in reading, mathematics, writing, and other areas, they should not be denied the opportunity to acquire the information available through the regular curriculum. Cognitively, LD adolescents have the ability to acquire, appreciate, and use this information. Many LD students are highly creative and exhibit skills far beyond their reading

24

TABLE 2.3
Mathematics Skills

Subskill Areas

	Number System & Numeration	Computation	Problem Solving
Instructional Goals	Numeration 1. Digits — Numbers 2. Sets and subsets	Operations 1. Addition 2. Subtraction 3. Multiplication 4. Division	Measurement
			Money
			Time
	Place-value system		Geometry
			Functions (miles per hour, A = πr^2, etc.)
			Relationships (=,<,>, etc.)
	Complex numerals and numbers 1. Fractions 2. Decimals 3. Percentages	Axioms 1. Communitive properties 2. Associative properties 3. Distributive properties 4. Additive inverse 5. Multiplicative inverse	Deductions (Estimates, identifying variables, etc.)
			Transformations (Changing money from dollars to cents, etc.)
			Maps and graphs
			Computer uses
			Mathematical aids
	Concepts	Combining Concepts	Applying Concepts

grade level. Pulling such students out of the regular class altogether and providing them with an alternative curriculum (often a watered-down one) in a self-contained class would be a disservice to many LD adolescents. It should be emphasized, however, that LD adolescents' chances of benefiting from the regular curriculum will be greatly reduced if they and the classroom teachers do not receive sufficient support services from the resource room teacher and other ancillary personnel.

2. Placement in a resource room for only part of the school day allows LD adolescents to interact with more peers in varied settings and under different circumstances. Given that LD adolescents will spend most of their life in employment and social situations with nonhandicapped

TABLE 2.4
Thinking Skills

Subskill Areas

Instructional Goals	Time Management	Organizing	Problem-Solving
	Setting priorities	Awareness of importance of organization	Entry point/attention area
	Goal setting		Observation
	Awareness of time traps	Perception of organization	Description
		Manipulation of information	Attribute listing
	Planning		Developing concepts
	Time recording	Reorganization of information	Differentiating and defining
	Evaluating and modifying plan	Organization for single tasks	Comparing and contrasting
			Brainstorming
		Organization for multiple tasks	Offering alternatives
			Hypothesizing
			Hypothesis testing
			Explaining
			Generalizing
			Predicting
			Challenging assumptions
			Morphological analysis
			Synetics
			Vertical and lateral thinking

peers, it is important for them to gain skills and experiences that will facilitate this interaction. It is believed that LD students can gain more skills in social interactions in a resource room than in a relatively sheltered, self-contained classroom.

3. A resource room model offers greater opportunities for the transfer and generalization of skills than most self-contained classroom models. Deficits are identified and worked on in the resource room within the context of the demands of the regular class situation. For example, if

TABLE 2.5
Social Interaction Skills

Subskill Areas

Self-Awareness	Social Relationship
Awareness of behavior	Seeking out friends
Awareness of personal values	Alliance with peer groups
Awareness of societal values	Knowledge of peer group "tone"
Perception of the environment	Knowledge of social conventions
Separation of motives, values, goals from peers — Self-identity	Perception of the situational gestalt
Expression of opinion/feeling to self	Nonverbal communication
Realistic goal setting	Cooperative behavior
Decision making	Acceptance of others
Personal problem solving	Consideration of others
Acceptance of responsibility	Active/empathic listening
	People-pleasing behaviors
	Assertiveness
	Self-disclosure
	Romantic relationships/Popularity
	Social problem solving

Instructional Goals (vertical label)

students lack the ability to organize materials for studying for a test, a technique for facilitating performance in this area can be worked on in the resource setting and *applied* in the regular class setting. This generalization is essential if students are to improve their ability to cope with existing circumstances. The risk of teaching "splinter skills" or irrelevant skills is greater the further students are removed from the least restrictive setting.

4. When the learning disabilities teacher can operate out of a resource model, that teacher has an opportunity to work with regular class teachers in a support role. This function is important, as the learning

TABLE 2.6
Speaking Skills

Subskill Areas

	Word Finding	Syntax	Oral Speaking
Instructional Goals	Naming	Use of correct structures	Appropriateness to setting
	Word power (verbiage and modifiers)		Error detection
			Spontaneous speech
	Abstract concepts	Use of transition	Formal speech
	Social community concepts		Elaboration by expansion
	Convergent concepts	Use of complex structures	Elaboration by analogy/example
	Divergent concepts		Assessing and adjusting to listener reaction

disabilities teacher is in a position to influence the teaching style and habits of the regular class teacher, as well as to gain a keener appreciation of the skills and talents of the regular classroom teacher that may be used to advantage on behalf of LD adolescents. Through continued interaction and cooperative planning, the climate within the school on behalf of LD adolescents can be enhanced.

WHAT ARE THE MAJOR COMPONENTS AND ACTIVITIES OF A LEARNING STRATEGIES RESOURCE ROOM?

The major activities in a resource room teaching learning strategies are: (1) diagnosing student deficits and determining the nature of intervention required, (2) gaining student cooperation, (3) teaching strategies under controlled conditions, (4) applying strategies to controlled materials, (5) transferring strategies to classroom requirements, (6) grouping students for instruction, and (7) cooperative planning. Each of these will be discussed in turn.

TABLE 2.7
Listening Skills

Subskill Areas

Understanding	Listening Comprehension	Critical Listening	Appreciative Listening
Words	Relationship of details to main idea	Recognizing absurdities	Listening to visualize
	Following directions	Recognizing propaganda	Listening for rhythms of speech
Concepts	Sequencing	Correcting others	Recognizing tone and mood
	Listening for details	Finishing stories	Appreciating speaker's style
	Active listening (formulating questions or answers)	Distinguishing fact from opinion	Interpreting character from dialogue
Sentences	Summarizing what has been heard	Distinguishing emotive from report language	Understanding effect on listener of speaker's vocal qualities and gestures
		Detecting bias — prejudice	Understanding effect of audience on listener's reaction
		Evaluating speaker's argument	
Large linguistic elements		Drawing inferences and making judgments	
		Recognizing repetition of same idea in different words	

Instructional Goals

Diagnostic Assessment

To understand how best to program for students in a secondary setting, teachers must first gather data from three important sources. Specifically, students must be assessed to determine their particular learning style, strengths, and deficits; the demands of the classes in which students are currently enrolled or experiences they expect to encounter must be inventoried; and the style of teaching of the students' regular classroom teachers must be determined. All three factors must be carefully considered when educational plans are formulated for LD students.

A variety of formal and informal assessment procedures can be followed to obtain these data. The following informal procedures can be used to advantage by the learning disabilities teacher. The general direction that diagnosis for programming takes should initially be determined by the data received from referring teachers. These data are often most beneficial because they indicate how the student is failing to meet specific curriculum requirements. These data should be confirmed and added to in a variety of ways. First, the learning disabilities teacher should confirm whether student deficits have been observed in other classes or under different circumstances than those observed by the referring teacher. This confirmation can be gained by observing students in other classes or situations or by having other teachers respond to queries concerning the students in their classroom. Second, students should be carefully interviewed to determine their perception of their own areas of difficulty. This step is crucial in working with adolescents because they often articulate problems that go undetected in the referral process or even by the most observant teacher. Furthermore, an interview can do a great deal to enlist the support and trust of the student.

After all data have been collected, priorities for instruction must be established. In many instances, students may have a broad array of deficits, and it is essential to work from a set of preestablished priorities. Various factors should be considered in establishing priorities for instruction, among them (1) the student's previous instructional history in learning disabilities; (2) the age and grade of the student (priorities are probably different for a seventh-grader and a twelfth-grader who have basically the same profiles); (3) the immediate demands of the classroom situation; (4) the long-term demands of adjustment in employment and social situations. In essence, the teacher must say, "Given the limited time I have available to work with these students and given these deficits, which disabilities are of most importance to address?"

Specific assessment procedures for each of the seven skill areas will be discussed in Chapters 3 through 9. There are, however, some general considerations that are important to bear in mind in doing diagnostic work with LD adolescents.

1. Make observations unobtrusively.

LD adolescents are sensitive to their difficulties and to people and events associated with those difficulties. Most students in junior or senior high school know who the learning disabilities teacher is and what the teacher does. If the teacher comes into a regular classroom to make an observation, it may be very upsetting to LD students because they may be sensitive about being associated with the resource room group. The influence of the peer group is strong under such circumstances. It is essential, therefore, to gather observational data as unobtrusively as possible. Sometimes the learning disabilities teacher may have to ask the regular class teacher to make certain observations for him/her. In other cases, it may be necessary to observe the student in nonacademic settings.

2. Be aware of previous testing.

By the time LD students have reached junior or senior high school, many of them have taken a large number of tests, some tests more than once. Look at these data for two reasons. First, testing is *very* time-consuming. Tests should not be repeated unless it is totally necessary. Second, LD adolescents often do not perform well on tests because it is boring to repeat the same task time and time again, or because it is highly frustrating to be repeatedly placed in a failure situation.

3. Motivate students.

Students should be motivated to perform well on formal and informal tests so that accurate performance profiles may be obtained. Spend a few minutes at the beginning of the assessment session explaining that you do *not* intend to grade the students but rather to obtain some information that will better help you make plans for them. This approach should help you enlist the students' cooperation. Planned breaks during the testing session can help remotivate as well as rest the students. Finally, give students general reinforcement throughout a testing session; for example, when a change is being made from one subtest to another, students might be commended for how hard they are trying and what a good job they are doing. Remember, however, that the examiner is *never* to give direct feedback or reinforcement for performance on a specific test item.

4.   Keep students informed.

It is very important for LD adolescents to be given a general idea about the kinds of testing that will be done and the anticipated length of the testing session. This information helps to reduce uncertainties and fears that often develop in the minds of students when they go through much testing. Drake and Cavanaugh (1970) speak of the predominant feeling among LD adolescents of being "mentally subnormal." Such unjustified feelings may be dissipated by simply explaining the specific nature of activities planned. Keeping students informed of actions to be taken also helps develop a trust between teacher and students.

Two important factors influence the degree of success that LD students experience in school situations after diagnostic assessment. The first factor deals with the motivation and commitment that students have to improve their performance. The second relates to the selection, teaching, application, and transfer of given strategies.

Gaining Student Cooperation

If LD adolescents are to be taught successfully, they must be closely involved in the learning process and must be committed and motivated to change their behavior. Prior to any intervention with LD adolescents, it is important to explain to students *why* they are spending time in the resource room. The teacher must explain *what* deficits will be worked on and what strengths will be used. This step is important for two reasons. First, it provides students with a clear understanding of what their deficits are and thus does not put them in a position of guessing the reasons for their being there. Often, LD students incorrectly conclude that they are totally inadequate. Second, by stressing abilities that the students have and by indicating how one plans to work with them in the intervention, a teacher can show students that he or she is aware of and values their strengths. In addition to explaining why the students are in the resource room and what deficits will be worked with, it is important to explain *how* one plans to proceed and what the anticipated goal is. This action further helps put students' minds at ease and gains their cooperation for intervention. The students should be encouraged to ask any questions they might have about proposed activities in the resource room. There are four important steps that the teacher should work through with each LD student.

Step 1.   Understand and affirm the problem.

LD students should first demonstrate awareness that a problem exists in a certain area by articulating what the problem seems to be. This step rests on each student's ability to understand and conceptualize the problem as it was described by the teacher and to assume responsibility for solving the problem. Unless students have clear understanding of their deficits and how those deficits affect their schoolwork, they are unlikely to give the problems their total commitment and motivation. One way to check students' understanding of the ramifications of their deficits is to ask them to give specific examples of how their performance in school is hindered by the ways they are currently dealing with the curriculum.

Step 2.   Establish the value of mastery of the deficit.

While students may be able to understand their problems, they may not recognize the importance or relevance of the target skill and value its acquisition enough to take steps to master it. The teacher can help make students aware of situations in which the target skills can be used to the students' advantage. It is best, however, if students discover these situations by themselves or through leading questions put by the teacher. It is also important for the teacher to convince students that the deficits can be mastered. Oftentimes students will give the impression that they don't value mastery of the deficit when in reality they are saying, "I don't think that *I* can do it."

Step 3.   Set goals.

Once students indicate that they value mastery of their deficits, teacher and students *jointly* establish overall goals for performance. It is important that the teacher assist each student in this goal-setting so that the goals established will be realistic. Drake and Cavanaugh (1970) speak of the tendency of LD adolescents to experience "time-panic." They define time-panic as a feeling that overtakes adolescents when they realize how much they have to learn. Being highly motivated, students also may experience time-panic when they realize that the time to learn it is very short. Often-times feelings of time-panic are precipitated in students by their setting *unrealistic* goals for performance. By working together, the teacher and students can establish goals (relative to amount and time) that are consistent with students' potential. Instead of setting unrealistic goals, some students set unchallenging or meaningless goals for performance. These goals are often the product of the student's history of failure. By setting goals together, the teacher can show students that they will be given the support they need to meet the higher goal. The goals and subsequent objectives set should be ones that will put enough pressure or tension on both students and teacher to elicit maximum work and effort, but not so much pressure as to cause anxiety in the learning situation.

Step 4.   Decide on performance standards.

The standard for performance should be set by the teacher. The authors believe that the teacher must do this for two reasons: First, the teacher has the necessary knowledge of curriculum and learner characteristics to establish appropriate standards. Second, a major responsibility of teaching is to orchestrate an appropriate match between the needs and characteristics of the student and the demands of the curriculum. This responsibility should not be abdicated by the teacher. It is, however, essential that the performance criteria and the expectations of the teacher be *clearly* specified and communicated to the students. Students should be allowed to ask questions for clarification so that the expectations of students and teacher are consistent.

Teaching the Strategies

It is important that LD teachers follow a particular sequence of activities in teaching LD students strategies so that they can be used eventually in the regular classroom. Students are first taught the strategy in isolation before they are asked to apply it to controlled materials and later to transfer it to regular class assignments.

First, the teacher should ask students to perform tasks that demonstrate the deficit or difficulty that they have. As an example, let us assume that one student is a laborious reader who does not vary his reading attack with different types of materials. Thus, given a history chapter to read, the student merely opens his book to the first page and slowly works his way through the assignment — word by word. In this case, the teacher would give the student a history book and ask him to read a given section within a specified time. After the student is well into the assignment, the teacher would stop the student and point out to him the manner in which he approached the task. The purpose of this is to make the student aware of the inefficient or ineffective habit that he is currently practicing. It is important for the student to understand his current approach so that he can clearly see the difference between that approach and the new strategy or technique that will be taught to him. The teacher can repeatedly refer back to the student's "old" way during intervention — the student will have an understanding of what the teacher means as a result of this step.

The next step is to *explain* to the student the "new" or replacement strategy. In our example, the learning disabilities teacher may decide that an appropriate strategy for the student with his history chapters would be use of the SQ3R method. After briefly explaining the technique and its purpose, the teacher should demonstrate how to apply it as an alternative strategy in reading the history assignment. In the demonstration, the teacher should carefully point out the advantages of using the new strategy over the old one. The demonstration and comparison should not be a long lecture, but rather a short, intensive explanation related to the student's previous behavior. The student should be encouraged to ask questions at any time to help him understand the strategy.

Before being asked to apply the strategy, the student must learn what the strategy or technique is to an automatic level. In our example, the teacher would have the student memorize the five steps in SQ3R so that he could say them from memory and briefly describe the meaning of each. These new strategies must be learned to an automatic level so that they will be readily applied in habitual fashion to various tasks. Students have practiced incorrect or inefficient strategies for years — if the new one is to replace the incorrect one, it must be practiced to an automatic level.

A variety of techniques and aids might be used to help the student learn and apply the new strategy. For example, the steps of the strategy might be listed on a 3″ x 5″ card that the student could easily refer to. In our example, it might be most effective for the student to put each of the five steps of SQ3R on a separate card and then practice the steps in flash card fashion. It is important that the student vocalize the strategy during this phase.

In summary, the purpose of teaching a strategy in isolation is to show students how it is different from their previous approaches to learning and to have them memorize the strategy step by step so that they can apply each step in the strategy in the correct order. This entire process should not take a great deal of time.

Applying the Strategy to Controlled Materials

As soon as students demonstrate a basic understanding and mastery of the steps or procedures involved in a given strategy, the teacher may choose high-interest, low-vocabulary materials that are written on the students' reading level and are relatively content free. The Croft materials, for example, might be used to give students practice in applying organizational strategies. The appendix lists materials that have been found effective in teaching different learning strategies to LD students.

The major purpose of taking students out of their classroom textbooks at this point is to give them an opportunity to apply the strategy with many repetitions (since chapters or sections in these materials are relatively short) and to apply the strategy in materials that are conducive to their learning a given skill without making a lot of additional demands on them.

As students initially apply a strategy to controlled materials, they should vocalize each step of the strategy. As soon as they demonstrate familiarity with the sequence of steps, they need no longer vocalize the strategy. Students may also use cues (on 3″ x 5″ cards, for example) to remind them of steps they are to follow. These cues should be removed as soon as students can function without them. Records should be kept on students' progress with these materials. When criterion is reached and maintained and the teacher is satisfied that students have mastered the new strategy and abandoned the old one, the teacher must plan for the *transfer* and *generalization* of that strategy back to the regular classroom material (in our example, the history book).

Transferring the Strategy to Classroom Work

So much of the work that is done with LD students in resource rooms ignores the importance of teaching students specifically how to transfer skills learned and applied to controlled or "special education" materials back to the curriculum materials and assignments required in the regular classroom. When no attention is given to the question of transfer, students' performance usually falls off markedly once they are placed back in the regular classroom or given regular classroom materials. When students are unable to perform well with classroom materials, they once again fail and the hopes and expectations they have gained from the instruction given in the resource room are dampened. Once dampened, student motivation and faith are much more difficult to rekindle. The demands made on students outside of the resource room are markedly different; consequently, it should *never* be assumed that students can transfer or generalize skills by themselves. Therefore, to facilitate transfer and generalization, students are next asked to apply the strategies they have learned to curriculum materials from their classroom.

Classroom materials are used for the purpose of teaching application of strategies and not for the purpose of tutoring the content (acquisition of the content is viewed as a separate activity from the acquisition and application of a given strategy). Allowing students to apply a given strategy to actual classroom material is important for two reasons: First, the classroom textbook is *not* a controlled material, and thus the demands it places on students are much greater than the demands of controlled materials. For example, the reading level is higher, the chapters are longer, and the content is much more difficult. Therefore, students should have the support of the learning disabilities teacher in learning how to apply the strategy under almost totally new circumstances. Second, application of the strategy to these materials affords students more opportunity to practice the strategy and to practice with the material to which they previously applied a less efficient strategy.

Grouping for Instruction

To provide LD students with additional practice and repetition of a newly learned skill, Alley (1977) has suggested that instructional grouping be used. Further, he has suggested that grouping arrangements are vitally important in planning for the instruction of LD adolescents. The grouping alternatives are as follows:

1. Monads — individual, student-directed settings, such as cubicles and individual work centers.
2. Dyads — one-to-one teacher-directed settings. This arrangement includes peer teaching.
3. Personal groups — groups of three or four students in a teacher- or student-directed setting.
4. Small groups — groups of five to fifteen students in a teacher- or student-directed setting.
5. Large groups — groups of fifteen to thirty-five students, generally in a teacher-directed setting.

In explaining the nature and advantages of different groupings of LD adolescents for instruction, Alley (1977) states:

> The nature of a specific method or material chosen by the teacher may well determine the size of the group.
> Instructional grouping is also determined by the content of the material. The learning disabled student is first introduced to the desired coping skill by using remedial materials in a dyad group. Later, when practicing the coping skill, the student should use materials that are identified with the regular curriculum. This approach

helps to process from the special education setting to the regular class. To systematically generalize skills which have been taught by the learning disabilities teacher into the group instructional setting of the regular class, the two teachers must engage in cooperative lesson planning.

Another consideration is that the teacher is restricted in grouping options by the skills which are required of a student before using a material, a teaching method, or a coping skill. It is suggested that the student be taught in the dyad when he or she is introduced to a new coping skill. There, the teacher has the greatest control over the learning process. After the skill has been modeled by the learning disabilities teacher and the student has initially met the criterion through a series of successive approximations, the student should be integrated into a monad, personal group or small group for practice on the skill. All these groups should be considered as instructional options. The placement of the student in a specific group for practice will depend on the motivation and feedback unique to each group. The final practice group should approximate the regular class size in which the coping skills are to be applied. When mastery has been achieved in one or more of the practice groups, the student is prepared to generalize to the setting of the regular classroom. (pp. 43-44)

Cooperative Planning

One factor alluded to by Alley (1977) in the grouping of students for instruction was that of cooperative planning. Cooperative planning is a most critical link in the learning strategies model. Without effective cooperative planning between the learning disabilities teacher and the regular classroom teacher, the probability of an LD adolescent being successfully integrated into and maintained in the regular classroom is greatly reduced.

Cooperative planning is an educational programming and monitoring arrangement on behalf of students. It is a process involving two or more professionals. This process taps the expertise of each professional involved and forms a collective effort on behalf of LD students that bridges the gap between activities and goals of the regular classroom and activities and goals of the resource room.

To make cooperative planning work effectively, one must be aware of several factors that relate to its operation within a secondary setting. First, cooperative planning must be viewed as a process that depends on direction and input being provided by *each* professional involved. Too frequently, the interchange between ancillary personnel (in this case, the learning disabilities teacher) and the regular class teacher consists of the specialist telling the regular class teacher what to do and what to change. Cooperative planning is *not* a one-way street. Both teachers must recognize that each one alone cannot meet the needs of the LD student, but that through cooperative planning their collective efforts have a much greater chance of meeting the youngster's needs.

Second, cooperative planning assumes that each professional involved has some unique knowledge and expertise that can be brought to bear on the needs of the LD student. A major purpose of cooperative planning is to tap the expertise of each professional. For example, if a history teacher and a learning disabilities teacher are working together on behalf of an LD student, the history teacher can best specify what the most important concepts and objectives are in a given history unit, whereas the learning disabilities teacher is skilled in modifying and adapting various materials and instructional techniques for teaching those content items most effectively. When the teachers work together, the LD student has a better chance of learning the appropriate content in a way that best suits that student's needs. In short, cooperative planning is a process in which each professional maintains and applies an area of expertise on behalf of a given student, but at the same time gains an awareness and appreciation of what others can do for the LD student.

Third, cooperative planning usually requires that participants be willing to change their teaching practices to a certain degree, based on the plans they have made for the LD student. Any changes or modifications made by the teachers must be consistent with their values and needs as professionals. Without a willingness to change, they are unlikely to make much progress through cooperative planning. Let us consider an example of a learning disabilities teacher and a vocational education teacher working together to plan for an LD student who is placed in a vocational education class. Given that the LD student has a depressed reading level, it would be desirable for the student to have reading materials approximating the student's reading level. The learning disabilities teacher may take this opportunity to discuss with the vocational educator the notion of readability by pointing out that one may get a rough estimate of the difficulty of materials by analyzing sentence length and number of difficult words in a passage. The intent is not to have the vocational educator gain a thorough knowledge of all readability formulas and their application, but rather to learn enough about them to be able to modify instruction for the LD student. Since cooperative planning is not a one-way street, it may also be possible for the learning disabilities teacher to learn from the vocational education teacher some information about the specific demands and goals of the vocational class that would help the special teacher prepare the LD student for placement in the least restrictive environment.

Cooperative planning between special and regular educators must take place at various phases in programming for LD students. Beginning with the *referral* of a student for special services, it is essential that the observations and concerns of the regular class teacher be carefully considered. The way in which a given deficit is manifested in the classroom is of the utmost concern. To insure that the instruction offered in the resource room is consistent with the demands of the curriculum, the learning disabilities teacher should consult with each classroom teacher about the unique goals, requirements, and teaching style of that teacher. Such knowledge allows the special teacher to individualize instruction by taking into account the classroom teacher as well as the LD student in facilitating the youngster's maintenance in the regular class.

When it is time for the LD student to be phased back into the regular class setting, the intensity and frequency of cooperative planning must increase, to provide a proper level of support for *both* the LD student and the regular class teacher. The learning disabilities teacher should carefully review with the classroom teacher the things that have been learned about the LD student during his or her placement in the resource room. This information would include an explanation of the student's learning style (for example, the student learns things better through an inductive rather than a deductive approach), learning and performance habits (the student best demonstrates comprehension of material through multiple choice tests rather than essay tests), and response or lack of response to various strategies or techniques. The purpose of describing the strategies that have been found successful with the student is to outline a *specific* program for the teacher to follow in the regular classroom to insure that the student applies those strategies within that setting. In addition, the classroom teacher will be asked to observe carefully the student's performance and to provide feedback to the learning disabilities teacher for modification of the strategies taught to the student that will help the student adjust to classroom demands.

There are some important factors to consider during this stage of cooperative planning. First, resource room instruction must be individualized for the classroom teacher as well as the LD student. While the learning disabilities teacher may find that a given procedure works well for the student on a one-to-one or small group basis in the resource room, the classroom teacher may find the procedure impossible to carry out and monitor in a classroom of thirty-five youngsters. Consequently, the LD teacher may have to modify the procedure for use by the classroom teacher. If the strategy can be modified so that it assists not only the LD student, but also all the other students in the classroom, it will have a higher probability of being followed up and used by the teacher. For example, if the LD student was taught a set of elaborate preorganizing strategies, through cooperative planning the regular class teacher may be encouraged to provide an overview and outline of each class lecture for the whole class, even though the teacher may not be willing to follow up on the specific techniques as closely as the special teacher did. However, it is important that the class teacher be made aware of all techniques taught to the student in the resource setting so that the teacher has a full understanding of what the student should be applying in the regular classroom.

40

Second, it is important that in this phase of cooperative planning the learning disabilities teacher be as specific as possible in describing given procedures to the classroom teacher. Ample opportunity should be given for the teacher to ask questions about the procedures and to request specific assistance.

Finally, it is most important that the learning disabilities teacher follow up with the teacher on a regular and frequent basis to prevent the student from lapsing into old habits and to help the student sustain himself or herself in the regular class. After a few weeks, the follow-up contacts can be reduced if the student is progressing appropriately, but the class teacher should be encouraged to contact the learning disabilities teacher as soon as difficulties are noted.

Perhaps the most common concern voiced by teachers about cooperative planning is, "We can't find the time to do it." While the practical limitations are not to be minimized, it is important to pursue every possible option, since cooperative planning is crucial to the success of maintaining the LD student in the regular classroom. The following are some options for cooperative planning:

1. Most cooperative planning takes place during planning periods, study halls, lunch periods, and before and after school. To make the most efficient use of this limited time, have specific questions carefully prepared and materials well organized before the session begins. Parkinson's Law, "Work expands so as to fill the time available for its completion," seems most applicable to cooperative planning. In other words, if we allot one hour for a session, planning will probably take that much time. On the other hand, in a well-planned, twenty-minute session teachers can often accomplish the same amount.

2. In addition to standard times for planning, the learning disabilities teacher should seek out short periods of time during the day that are convenient to the schedules of both teachers. For example, the learning disabilities teacher could be available. Often, teachers or a twenty-minute quiz or assignment given to the class. The test or assignment can be monitored periodically while the teachers talk in the hall.

3. The use of a checklist on which the regular class teacher specifies possible meeting times often reveals several options not previously considered. This list should specify the amount of time needed for the meeting (remember Parkinson's Law!) and times that the

learning disabilities teacher could be available. Often, teachers overlook short segments of slack time that can be put to effective use.

4. Finally, the use of written communication should not be overlooked in cooperative planning. It is often assumed that cooperative planning must be done orally — when this approach is taken, the options for cooperative work are greatly limited. Through the use of an NCR form (carbonless paper that produces multiple copies of communications), the teachers can keep in close contact with each other in monitoring and following up on LD students. In addition to overcoming scheduling problems, written communications provide a record of progress and decisions that can be used to evaluate the effectiveness of the instructional procedures used. Some commercially prepared packages, such as the Instructional Based Appraisal System (IBAS) distributed by Edmark, Inc. (Meyen, 1976) provide highly structured communication systems to help teachers monitor student progress and facilitate communications.

WHAT ARE THE ROLES OF THE LEARNING DISABILITIES TEACHER AND THE CLASSROOM TEACHER UNDER A LEARNING STRATEGIES APPROACH?

Learning disabilities teachers who work in a learning strategies resource room fulfill three major roles. First, they serve as learning strategists to help pupils acquire coping skills. The major teaching role is to assess and teach to skill deficits so that the student masters sufficient strategies and principles for independent application. It is *not* to teach the content. Second, learning disabilities teachers must spend a significant portion of time working with other professionals in the school. They can best serve LD students if they do not spend all of their time in direct service to their students. Regular class teachers need sufficient support services through consultation, if youngsters are to be successfully mainstreamed into their classes. Third, learning disabilities teachers need to serve as advocates for LD students within the secondary school setting. Many curriculum offerings are not available to LD students because of entrance requirements, teacher attitude, teacher skill in dealing with the LD student in regular classroom settings, and so on.

Regular classroom teachers play a major role in the education of LD adolescents. They must assume major responsibility for delivery of the content material to the students. Classroom teachers, through cooperative planning with the learning disabilities teachers, must modify or adapt course requirements and delivery to accommodate the academic deficits of LD students. The skills taught to LD students in the resource room may be ineffectual without appropriate adaptation within the regular classroom. Classroom teachers may be required to modify their teaching style (e.g., in lecturing) to help LD students who must rely almost entirely on their listening skills to gain content from class sessions.

WHAT FACTORS IN A SCHOOL SETTING SUPPORT A LEARNING STRATEGIES APPROACH?

The success of a special education program within a given school setting is largely a function of the degree of support available to that service. The effective operation of a learning strategies model depends on several factors. While each factor may not be absolutely essential for successful operation of a learning strategies resource room, its absence has been found to detract greatly from successful operation. These factors include administrative support, paraprofessional assistance, planning periods, in-service programs, comprehensive curriculum and service options, and continuous curriculum revision.

Administrative Support

Beery (1975) has stated that if mainstreaming is to be successful in a school setting, the staff, beginning with the top administrator on down, must be committed to the concept. His idea has application in many areas. Certainly, any service model is less likely to meet with success in a school setting if the program does not have the backing of the principal and other key administrators. Since a learning strategies approach requires the involvement of several professionals and taps several resources within a school setting, administrative support is essential. In proposing operating procedures (for example, a referral procedure), the learning disabilities teacher would be well advised to secure the support of the principal for the procedure before proposing it to the entire staff. Similarly, administrative support is essential for successful implementation of other procedures and plans.

Paraprofessional Assistance

The learning disabilities teacher must have the support of a paraprofessional to carry out the functions of the learning strategies approach appropriately. Specifically, the teacher must have the time to spend in cooperative planning with other staff members as well as in planning and carrying out one-to-one and group instruction. Without at least one para-professional, the increased demands and reduced flexibility greatly reduce the teacher's effectiveness.

Planning Periods

The learning disabilities teacher needs a *minimum* of one planning period per day. Preferably two or three periods should be allotted so that the teacher not only can plan instruction, but also can provide indirect services to LD students by working with their classroom teachers and with the students in their regular classrooms.

In-service Programs

The successful implementation of a learning strategies approach depends on the degree to which the majority of a school staff is committed to and afforded the opportunity to upgrade its professional skills on behalf of exceptional students. To make appropriate accommodations to the needs of LD students in secondary schools, a total staff effort is required. The teacher alone cannot meet these students' needs. While many skills can be taught on a one-to-one basis through cooperative planning, schools must also engage in comprehensive staff development programs that deal with awareness-level instruction on exceptional students as well as on specific procedures for identifying and dealing with these students in the regular class. PL 94–142 has set a sizable portion of its funds aside for in-service training. These funds should be employed to their fullest in second-ary settings.

Comprehensive Curriculum and Service Options

Since the learning strategies approach is designed to meet some but not all of the needs of the LD student in a secondary setting, it is advanta-geous to have the additional supports within the school that help main-tain the student successfully. These supports are usually found in compre-hensive junior and senior high schools. Supports may take a variety of forms, but the broader the array of supports, the greater the probability of meeting the needs of LD adolescents. These supports include a broad range of curriculum options which permit LD students not only to choose from a comprehensive set of class offerings, but also to be matched with teachers who are interested in individualizing instruction for them. Another form of support for LD students may be ancillary personnel or services, such as counseling services or a peer tutoring system.

Continuous Curriculum Revision

Schools that are committed to a continuous program of curriculum revision are usually better prepared to support a learning strategies approach. If curriculums are evaluated on a regular basis, the possibility of changing them on behalf of exceptional students is increased. These changes may include having each teacher or academic department specify *minimum competencies* or objectives for each class, or consider the adoption of multiple forms of books, including one at a reduced reading level, when decisions are being made on the purchase of new texts. Learning disabilities teachers should seek every possible opportunity to be involved in curriculum projects in their schools or districts to advocate changes that would make the regular class curriculum more accommodating for LD students.

OTHER MODELS FOR SERVING LD ADOLESCENTS

As current learning disabilities practices are analyzed in secondary settings, one finds a variety of program options used in teaching LD adolescents. It is important to note, however, that these models (and the learning strategies model) are seldom applied exclusively in a school setting. Rather, a program within a given school will predominantly reflect one of these approaches, but the approach will be used in combination with components from other models. For example, the activities and components of the secondary learning disabilities service in one school may *primarily* reflect the functional curriculum approach (to be described later in this chapter), but some students may receive remediation of basic skill deficits.

The various models for serving LD adolescents are broadly diverse. Some of the following factors account for this diversity. First, the *philosophy* of the persons initiating the program may support a specific approach. For example, if the learning disabilities teacher describes LD students primarily in terms of their weaknesses, the philosophy may be to prepare students to "survive" in the world. On the other hand, if LD students are viewed primarily in terms of their strengths, the philosophy may be to prepare them for a broader range of experiences in the postschool world.

Second, the learning disabilities *staff capabilities* may favor the use of one approach over another. For example, many secondary school programs offer activities similar to those done in elementary learning disabilities resource rooms. This may be a reflection of the fact that most learning disabilities teachers received their training in a university program primarily designed to teach the elementary LD child. Third, the *attitude* of the school administration and staff may reflect a certain tolerance or preference for one model over another. Each approach makes a different set of demands on other school personnel (for example, the functional model is basically self-contained and thus does not require much of other staff members in a school setting, whereas a learning strategies approach does). Fourth, the *type of student* classified as learning disabled may cause a school to favor one approach over another. For example, if only the severely disabled students are referred and placed for service, the program may primarily reflect a functional approach. However, if the students referred are mildly disabled, the philosophy may be to tutor the students to support them in their classwork.

As each model in this section is discussed, it is important to note that there is little research data available to support or reject any of these approaches. The same applies to the learning strategies approach. It does appear reasonable to conclude, however, that no *one* approach meets the needs of *all* LD adolescents. Decisions as to which approach to use for an LD adolescent must be made in light of a variety of factors: the *age* of the student (a senior in high school and a seventh-grade junior high student with similar deficits may require drastically different approaches because of the amount of time they will be remaining in school), *severity* of the student's deficit (an LD student with no reading skills will demand different program offerings than an LD student with fifth-grade reading skills). The *previous services* that the LD student has received (a ninth-grade LD student who has received little or no remedial or special education service may benefit from some highly intensive remediation, whereas another ninth-grade LD student with a similar deficit but a long history of receiving remedial services is unlikely to benefit from more remediation), and the *support services* available (the attitude of the staff and staff capabilities within a given school setting and district can greatly influence the success or failure of a given approach for LD students).

The purpose of this section is to describe other approaches currently used to serve LD adolescents. The data on these approaches come from a nationwide study conducted by Deshler, Lowrey, and Alley (1979) to determine the state of the art in secondary LD service delivery. To obtain these data, a mailing was sent to secondary (junior and senior high) learning disabilities teachers in all fifty states. The teachers were asked to do the following: (1) describe the ten most salient characteristics of your learning disabilities program, (2) describe a critical incident in which you were successful in dealing with an LD student, and (3) describe a critical incident in which you were not successful in dealing with an LD student. Among other things, these data were analyzed to determine different program options currently used to serve LD adolescents. The data indicated that there are five predominant program options currently in use. For purposes of discussion, these have been labeled the basic skills remediation model, the functional curriculum model, the tutorial model, the work-study model, and the learning strategies model. All but the learning strategies model will be presented here. Each model, including its underlying assumptions, will be described. In addition, the authors will evaluate the relative strengths and weaknesses of each model.

The Basic Skills Remediation Model

This approach provides developmental or remedial instruction for basic academic skill deficits. Reading and mathematics deficits receive the most attention. The skills taught are usually at a level that approximates the student's achievement level. For example, if a sophomore in high school reads on a fourth-grade level, instructional tasks will be designed to teach basic reading skills typically taught at that grade level with the goal of sequentially improving the youngster's skills. The activities, materials, and objectives of intervention are similar to those found in learning disabilities resource rooms in elementary schools. Our study indicated that 51 percent of the programs followed this approach. Fifty-six percent of the programs making use of this model were junior high schools. The majority of the programs serviced over twenty students in categorical resource rooms.

Underlying Assumptions

The following assumptions underlie the basic skills remediation approach:

1. Prerequisite skills can be identified and sequenced.
2. Past skill instruction has been inappropriate or incompetently delivered.
3. Students will benefit from skill instruction in spite of a history of not benefiting from similar instruction in the elementary grades.

47

4. Skill instruction will be more valuable than other curriculum options in relation to school success.
5. Skill instruction will be more valuable than other curriculum options in relation to life success.
6. Attainment of functional literacy is vital for mobility in modern society.
7. Instruction in basic skills (primarily reading and mathematics) is sufficient and most important to the needs of students who must negotiate the demands of the secondary curriculum and postschool experiences.
8. Increased facility with skills will adequately reverse the pattern of school failure.

Strengths

The potential strengths of the basic skills remediation approach include the following:

1. Increased student competence in basic skills should enable students to perform better in content classes.
2. Increased literacy and skill abilities should facilitate extraschool learning and performance involving these skills.
3. Basic skill instruction should lead to functional literacy.
4. Instruction in basic skills may have particular relevance for the secondary student who has received no or poor special or remedial instruction in previous schools. *Intensive* instruction to correct key skill deficits may produce rapid gains.

Weaknesses

The potential shortcomings of the basic skills remediation approach include the following:

1. Instruction in basic skill deficits begins at the level at which the student is functioning and proceeds in a sequential fashion. Due to the limited time available for working with secondary LD students in a special setting, it is highly unlikely that enough progress can be made to substantially change the student's overall skill level and reduce the gap between grade level placement and level of functioning in basic skills. This seems particularly true if the LD

student has received years of such instruction in the elementary school (most LD students have). The hope that presenting such instruction "one more time" will make a difference may be overly optimistic. Furthermore, since the instruction usually follows a scope and sequence chart, the student rarely receives instruction in higher order skills. For example, under a basic skills approach, a high school student reading at the third-grade level will receive instruction in basic word attack and decoding skills, but is highly unlikely to receive instruction in comprehension, inference, or evaluation, which are high ranking skills on most scope and sequence charts. Such an approach ignores the demands of the high school curriculum. If a student's only skills in reading are decoding skills, he or she will be unable to cope with the reading requirements in secondary content areas.

2. The motivation of the LD student under this approach may be a problem because of overexposure to similar (in some cases, exactly the same) instruction during the elementary years. Further, many special materials for teaching basic skills use examples, stories, and illustrations that appeal to the second- and third-grade child but are insulting to the secondary student.

3. This approach focuses on a limited number of skill areas — usually reading and mathematics. While these areas are important, the secondary curriculum, as well as postschool adjustments, require student facility in many other skill areas. Specifically, the areas of written expression, listening, speaking, thinking, and personal-social skills *must* be considered if the LD adolescent is to benefit from the secondary curriculum and experience success in out-of-school situations.

4. The growth that the student experiences as a result of instruction often will not be enough to meet academic and postacademic demands.

5. The crucial issue of transfer of acquired skills to the specific requirements of the regular classroom is usually not addressed in this approach. Basic skill components are taught through the use of special materials within the resource room. Even when progress is noted in a given skill through the use of a special reading material, time is not spent in showing the student how that skill can be generalized to regular classroom material.

The Functional Curriculum Model

This approach emphasizes equipping students to function in society. The focus of instruction is on consumer information, completion of application forms, banking and money skills, and life-care skills such as grooming. In addition, this approach often attempts to relate academic content to career concepts. Guidance and counseling for self-identity and career-identity are stressed. The regular curriculum of the secondary school is deemed inappropriate, so a new curriculum is devised to meet the student's basic needs. Development of the curriculum and its delivery is primarily the responsibility of the learning disabilities teacher. This approach usually operates out of a self-contained model. Our study indicated that 17 percent of the programs surveyed followed a functional curriculum approach.

Underlying Assumptions

The following assumptions are basic to the functional curriculum approach:

1. LD adolescents are less functionally competent than their peers.
2. Survival skills are identifiable and stable over time.
3 LD students cannot succeed in a traditional program.
4. One person (the learning disabilities teacher) can adequately provide for all of the students' educational needs in the secondary setting.

Strengths

The potential strengths of the functional curriculum approach include the following:

1. Students are equipped to function independently, at least over the short term, in society.
2. Students may be better prepared to compete for specific jobs upon graduation from high school.
3. Instruction in the functional curriculum may have particular relevance for the high school junior or senior who is severely disabled. In a second phase of the study by Deshler, Lowrey, and Alley (1979), teachers were asked to specify program components that were most appropriate for mildly to moderately disabled students and those most appropriate for severely disabled students. The components that these teachers listed as best for severely

disabled students closely paralleled the aims of the functional curriculum approach. It should also be noted that when asked to estimate the incidence of severe and mild to moderate disability in a total LD population, teachers said 11 percent were severely disabled and 89 percent were mildly to moderately disabled.

Weaknesses

Potential shortcomings of the functional curriculum approach include the following:

1. This approach ignores the potential strengths and assets of LD adolescents. The concept of normal is denied for all practical purposes when LD students are presented with a curriculum that is primarily designed to help them survive and meet their most basic needs. In many instances, LD students are treated almost the same as mentally retarded individuals.

2. The assumptions that survival skills can be identified and that they are stable over time are highly questionable. The complex nature of our society is not conducive to the simple identification of a set of skills necessary for survival. The skills required for survival vary widely from setting to setting and change quickly over time. For example, one skill taught in almost every functional curriculum class for LD adolescents is how to write checks. This skill may soon be outdated, however, because of anticipated changes in the financial world. Specifically, there is mounting pressure to convert to a checkless society because of the overwhelming amount of paperwork involved in check processing and monitoring. In short, the identification of exactly what constitutes the curriculum under this approach is a difficult question to resolve in light of our rapidly changing, highly complex society.

3. Since this approach basically operates out of a self-contained model, LD adolescents are largely isolated from peer association and interaction. Allowing LD adolescents to associate only with others who are encountering difficulties in school and of denying them the opportunity to benefit from the strengths and skills of talented students in the regular classroom is potentially damaging to the development of LD adolescents. After leaving high school, LD students will not be isolated from their same age peers.

4. The learning disabilities teacher is expected to assume major (or complete) responsibility for curriculum development and delivery. Current teacher training programs in learning disabilities do *not* prepare their graduates to carry out these duties.

The Tutorial Model

This approach emphasizes provision of instruction in academic content areas. Areas of instruction are usually those in which the student is experiencing difficulty or failure. The teacher's major responsibility is to help keep the LD student in the regular curriculum and, therefore, the teacher operates out of a resource model. Our study indicated that 24 percent of the programs surveyed followed a tutorial approach. This approach was used in an equal number of junior and senior high schools.

Underlying Assumptions

The following assumptions are basic to the tutorial approach:

1. The learning disabilities teacher can deliver the content as well as certified content teachers.
2. Getting students through a particular content area is the most valuable intervention.
3. Student performance in other classes could not be improved through special education intervention.

Strengths

The potential strengths of the tutorial approach include the following:

1. LD students' immediate needs are addressed.
2. LD students are provided with the means of mastering the content of particular subjects.
3. This approach is readily accepted by the regular content area teachers and parents.

Weaknesses

The potential shortcomings of the tutorial approach include the following:

1. Tutoring an LD student in a given content area provides the student with a short-term solution, at best. Since the main objective is to teach specific content so that the student can respond to classroom assignments, little or no time is spent on dealing with the underlying problem. Thus, the student does not acquire skills that will generalize to other assignments within that subject are or across subject areas. For example, one reason that a student is having difficulty in biology is because she lacks proper study techniques. The tutorial approach would emphasize the teaching of the content of a specific chapter so that the student could pass an upcoming test (a short-term solution), rather than teaching the student some study techniques that would not only help her on the test but also would generalize across subject areas. Under the tutorial approach, withdrawal of support leaves the student in no better shape than at the time of referral.

2. The tutorial approach shifts responsibility for teaching the LD student from the regular class teacher to the content teacher. Content teachers learn that problems need not be dealt with in class and that there is little need to alter their instruction. The easiest solution when students do not learn in the content teacher's class is simply to give them to special education. Once the responsibility for instruction is assumed by the learning disabilities teacher, it is difficult for students to return to the regular class teacher.

3. A major limitation of the tutorial approach is the training of the teacher. Learning disabilities teachers at the secondary level are not trained to teach all subject areas in a comprehensive high school. They do not have the background to make content decisions about the nuances and points of emphasis within a given subject area. An LD student who may be a potential historian should not be taught history in a watered-down fashion just because he or she lacks the reading skills to gain information from the textbook.

The Work-Study Model

This approach emphasizes instruction in job- and career-related skills and on-the-job experience. Students typically spend half of the day on the job and the remainder of the day in school studying compatible material. The time spent in school is usually in a self-contained setting. The teacher serves as a work coordinator for the purposes of obtaining and supervising job placements for LD adolescents. Our study indicated that 5 percent of the programs surveyed followed this model for serving LD adolescents. Work-study programs were found only in senior high schools with enrollments of more than 750 students.

Underlying Assumptions

The following assumptions are basic to the work-study approach:

1. The regular curriculum is inappropriate for LD students; therefore, it is most desirable to train LD adolescents in job-related skills that can be applied in the world of work.
2. This approach is often quite motivating for LD students in that it represents a significant change from the routine and requirements of the typical classroom in which they have operated for many years. Since many student experiences in the classroom have involved failure, LD students welcome the opportunity to start anew and hopefully to succeed in some of their work-study experiences.

Weaknesses

Potential shortcomings of the work-study approach include the following:

1. While in theory the work-study model holds some promise for students who have difficulty with the traditional curriculum, in practice there are some serious limitations. The most notable limitation lies in job assignment options. Specifically, most job placements are in the food and restaurant industry. Thus, students are not exposed to different career clusters. There are further limitations placed on LD students within the job setting. For example, students working in a fast-food restaurant may *not* be exposed to the wide array of jobs available in that setting because of the goals of the business. Since mass production is a major goal in the fast-food business, students who cannot make change from a cash register quickly will *not* be trained to do so, but will be shifted to other jobs. Thus, students do not acquire training in areas in

which they have deficits; therefore, the range of students job-related skills is not expanded.

2. The work-study approach assumes that a trained special education work coordinator can most effectively place LD youngsters in jobs. In reality, the special educator usually does not have training or experience in a given vocational area; therefore, the educator often lacks access to a given job setting that a vocational educator has when it comes to making job placements. Consequently, the types of job assignments secured for LD students often are limited in nature.

The Learning Strategies Model

The learning strategies model, along with its underlying assumptions and strengths, was described earlier in this chapter. However, its potential shortcomings have not been presented. While professionals other than the authors of this text can probably evaluate the approach more objectively, these statements about potential shortcomings reflect some of our concerns.

1. This approach relies heavily on cooperative planning for its implementation. The structure of the high school is not conducive to cooperative planning. If it is to become a viable component of the high school structure, procedures must be developed to promote the work between regular and learning disabilities teachers.
2. The learning strategies approach has been implemented by only a small number of school programs. Consequently, limited data are available to determine its efficacy as a service delivery model to adolescents.
3. While a major goal of the model is to promote the transfer and generalization of strategies across settings and situations, data are not available to indicate that generalization does occur and maintain itself.
4. The learning strategies approach does not address the functional, tutorial, and basic skill needs of LD adolescents as directly as other models.

REFERENCES

Alley, G. R. Grouping secondary learning disabled students. *Academic Therapy*, 1977, *13*, (1), 37-45.
Beery, K. Mainstreaming: A problem and an opportunity for general education. *Focus on Exceptional Children*, 1974, *6* (6).

Clark L. H., Klein, R. L., & Burks, J. B. *The American secondary school curriculum*. New York: Macmillan, 1972.

Deshler, D. D., Lowrey, N., & Alley, G. R. Programming alternatives for learning disabled adolescents: A nationwide survey. *Academic Therapy*, 1979, *14*, (4).

Drake, C., & Cavanaugh, J. A. Teaching the high school dyslexic. In L. E. Anderson (Ed.), *Helping the adolescent with the hidden handicap*. Belmont, Calif.: Fearon, 1970.

Engelmann, S. *Preventing failure in the primary grades*. New York: Simon & Schuster, 1969.

Flavell, J. H., Beech, D. R., & Chinsky, J. M. Spontaneous verbal rehearsal in a memory task as a function of age. *Child Development*, 1966, *37*, 283-299.

Hagen, J. W. Some thoughts on how children learn to remember. *Human Development*, 1971, *14*, 262-271.

Harris, A. J. *How to increase reading ability*. New York: McKay, 1970.

Kerst, S., & Levin, J. R. A comparison of experimenter-provided and subject-generated strategies in children's paired associate learning. *Journal of Educational Psychology*, 1973, *65*, 300-303.

Lesgold, A. M., McCormick, C., & Golinkoff, R. M. Imagery training and children's prose learning. *Journal of Educational Psychology*, 1975, *67*, 663-667.

Levin, J. R., What have we learned about maximizing what children learn? In J. R. Levin & V. L. Allen (Eds.), *Cognitive learning in children: Theories and strategies*. New York: Academic Press, 1976.

Mandler, G. Organization and memory. In K. W. Spence & J. T. Spence (Eds.), *The psychology of learning and motivation: Advances in research and theory* (Vol. 1). New York: Academic Press, 1967.

Meyen, E. L. *Instructional based appraisal system*. Bellevue, Wash.: Edmark Assoc., 1976.

Miller, C. A. The magical number seven, plus or minus two: Some limits on our capacity for processing information. *Psychological Review*, 1956, *63*, 81-97.

Paivio, A. Mental imagery in associative learning and memory. *Psychological Review*, 1969, *76*, 241-263.

Rogers, D. The future in Texas. *DuPont Context*, 1976, *5* (2), 6-15.

Rowher, W. D., Jr. Prime time for education: Early childhood or adolescence? *Harvard Educational Review*, 1971, *41*, 316-341.

Toffler, A. *Future shock*. New York: Bantam Books, 1970.

Warner, M. M. Teaching learning disabled junior high students to use visual imagery as a strategy for facilitating recall of reading passages. Unpublished doctoral dissertation, University of Kansas, 1977.

Whimbey, A. Getting ready for the test or: You can learn to raise your IQ score. *Psychology Today*, 1976, *9* (8), 27-29, 84-85.

Winne, P. H., Hauck, W. E., & Moore, W. The efficiency of implicit repetition and cognitive restructuring. *Journal of Educational Psychology*, 1975, *67*, 770-775.

READING: STRATEGIES AND METHODS

Developmental Stages of Reading

Types of Readers at the Secondary Level

Characteristics of the LD Student with Mild to Moderate
Reading Disabilities

Reading Skills to be Taught to Students
with Mild to Moderate Reading Disabilities

Assessing Reading Deficits in LD Adolescents

Teaching Vocabulary

Increasing Reading Comprehension

Developing Reading Flexibility

Promoting Study Skills

Demands of the Curriculum

Motivation

3

Reading is a complex process. It is more than merely the decoding of printed symbols. It is, as Harris and Sipay (1975) state, ". . . the meaningful interpretation of written or printed verbal symbols" (p. 3). The interpretation ". . . can and should embrace all types of thinking, evaluating, judging, imagining, reasoning and problem-solving" (Gates, 1947, p. 3). The relationship between reading and cognition is clear. The product of reading and cognition is achievement.

Age and acculturation are interrelated criteria on which achievement is measured (Newland, 1977). Educators are well aware that the age of the student must be considered when assessing achievement levels. Ames (1968) considers overplacement in school the prime factor in student reading failure.

Acculturation is also important when judging student achievement. Children arrive at school with many different value systems. If the children are from culturally different homes, they may not have been exposed to the experiences that are valued by educators. As a result, they lack the experiences they need to learn to read (Woolman, 1965). This lack of experience continues to handicap students as they grow older. They fall farther and farther behind in reading. The cumulative effect is reading failure.

DEVELOPMENTAL STAGES OF READING

Before discussing the reasons for reading failure in adolescents, it is important to outline the stages of reading instruction from kindergarten to college. The National Committee on Reading lists five steps of reading development (Gray, 1925): (1) development of reading readiness; (2) beginning reading instruction; (3) rapid development of reading skills; (4) stage of wide reading; (5) refinement of reading.

58

Reading Readiness

The development of reading readiness is a process that begins almost at birth. It is a general maturation that permits the child to learn to read without undue difficulty. However, as may be expected with any similar, unstructured and informal program, the child will manifest uneven development of the readiness skills that are required for beginning reading. Children beginning school enter a readiness program that helps them attain all the readiness skills. Readiness programs consist of both individual and group activities, i.e., cutting, painting, show and tell, dramatizations, field trips, and group functioning (Harris & Sipay, 1975). The teacher may supplement these activities with reading readiness workbooks. Harris and Sipay caution kindergarten and first-grade teachers against the exclusive use of workbooks in the readiness program. Use of the workbook only will produce limited skills, which are not sufficient for beginning reading instruction.

Beginning Reading

Aukerman (1972) has reviewed over one hundred commercially prepared beginning reading programs. These programs have been categorized under six major approaches: (1) meaning-emphasis; (2) code-emphasis; (3) special alphabet; (4) programmed instruction; (5) language-experience; and (6) individualized reading (Harris & Sipay, 1975).

The meaning-emphasis approach uses preplanned, organized, developmental reading materials to teach children the association between the printed word and its spoken counterpart. Some persons refer to this method as the "look-say" approach. It is the most traditional method and familiar to most individuals (Harris & Sipay, 1975).

The code-emphasis approach focuses on developing the child's decoding skills. This approach can be delivered quite differently, depending on whether the teacher is using a phonic or a linguistic approach. Teaching the phonic approach as a total program of beginning reading is relatively new. Traditionally it has been used as a supplement to other approaches. These newer programs differ in the grouping of letters and groups of letters when decoding words. In contrast, the linguistic approach requires children to identify letter names rather than letter sounds. Then children are taught three-letter consonant-vowel-consonant (CVC) words in which each letter represents only one phonemic value, for example, cat, and man. Children then are taught to generalize these CVC patterns, using minimal phonetic contrasts — man, can, pan, Dan. Finally, children use the words in a meaningful sentence, such as, "Nan can fan Dan" (Harris & Sipay, 1975).

59

The sound-symbol relationships in English are not always regular. There have been several recent innovations of phonetically regular alphabets. The Initial Teaching Alphabet (ITA) (Pitman, 1961) contains forty-four graphemes that closely match the grapheme-phoneme correspondence required for a phonetically regular alphabet. Another system is Words in Color (Gattegno, 1968). Rather than increase the number of graphemes, as is done in the ITA, Words in Color uses forty-seven color hues and various spellings, which may make use of the same color in various words that represents the phonemes. The research investigations of these special alphabet approaches have not shown that they are superior to other approaches, especially when the skills developed through the use of the special alphabet are transferred to the traditional English alphabet (Dykstra, 1967; Hill, 1967; Lockmiller & DiNello, 1970; Wapner, 1969; Warburton & Southgate, 1969; Dunn, Pockanart, Pfost, & Bruininks, 1967).

The renewed interest in behaviorism has been evident in education. Skinner (1968) has suggested that the principles used in programmed instruction and computer-assisted instruction be used in teaching reading. The student is presented with material broken down into series of small, informational steps, to which the student must make an active response and, in turn, receive immediate feedback that either reinforces the correct response or corrects the initial error. Tests of the effectiveness of these programs are too limited to make a definitive statement regarding their benefits or weaknesses (Harris & Sipay, 1975).

Harris and Serwer (1969) clearly and succinctly describe the language-experience approach as one in which:

> . . . emphasis is placed on the teaching of reading in close correlation with the related language arts activities of listening, speaking, and writing. Children are encouraged to express their thoughts, ideas, and feelings, often stimulated by a specific experience guided and developed by the teacher. The verbal productions of the children are written down by the teacher in the early stages, and are used in the earliest reading materials. Pupil expression is encouraged through the use of a variety of media, such as painting, speaking and writing. Gradually the program moves from exclusive use of reading materials developed out of the oral language of the children, into a program of reading in which increasing emphasis is placed upon a variety of children's books. (p. 4)

Individualized programs are only in the developmental stage. Two popular programs are Individualized Developmental Reading and Individually Prescribed Instruction (Beck & Bolvin, 1969). These programs require children to work independently for long periods of time, and seem to be more feasible for children working above beginning reading levels (Harris & Sipay, 1975).

The studies comparing the aforementioned beginning reading approaches have not provided definitive evidence that one approach is superior to another. Rather, the critical interrelated factors of successful beginning reading have been shown to be (1) the skill of the teacher, (2) the strengths and weaknesses of the child, and (3) the conditions of the learning environment. When one considers this information, perhaps the best beginning reading approach is an eclectic one that uses all of the child's modes of learning — auditory, visual, kinesthetic, and tactile — to develop word recognition, while emphasizing reading comprehension in the total process (Harris & Sipay, 1975).

Rapid Development of Reading Skills

The third stage of reading instruction is critical for students who must cope with the many content areas they encounter in the secondary school curriculum. At the stage of rapid development of reading skills, students become more fluent and use vocal expression when reading orally. Contextual clues are now important in decoding unknown words. Concurrently, more emphasis is placed on comprehension during silent reading. In fact, it is at this stage, between second and third grade, that students' silent reading rate equals and then becomes superior to their oral reading rate. They also begin to use reading as a skill to obtain content information from textbooks in areas such as geography, science, and mathematics. This content reading is closely associated with the increase in recreational reading. Developmental reading programs are still the paramount activity in the classroom during this stage.

Wide Reading

The fourth stage of reading finds the student working with a broad range of materials. The "reading period" rapidly diminishes from the 90-120 minutes a day spent in the primary grades to three hours or less a week in sixth grade. Vocabulary study focuses on word meaning rather than decoding skills. Comprehension of material that is read silently is emphasized at this stage. Some time is given to practice to improve reading rate. Students are introduced to study skills that include organizing reading materials, summarizing information, and locating information in reading sources.
Reading is no longer a subject when students enter junior high school. The responsibility for teaching developmental reading and refining reading skills falls on the English teacher. The English teacher must understand the reading developmental program of the first six grades, analyze the reading problems of students who have not developed the necessary skills, and then

provide corrective help when it is needed. In addition, the English teacher must plan for recreational reading (Harris & Sipay, 1975). Recreational reading at the junior high school level is defined as ". . . a combination of rather intensive reading and discussion of selected 'classics' and individualized outside reading" (p. 79).

Refinement of Reading

Developmental reading programs are relatively new at the senior high school level. The focus of these reading programs is unclear. Two areas have been identified for teaching: (1) appreciation of literature and (2) increase in reading (Harris & Sipay, 1975).

Four areas of emphasis in teaching developmental reading in the secondary schools have been identified by various sources: (1) vocabulary building; (2) reading comprehension; (3) increased and fluctuating reading rate; and (4) study skills. These areas are discussed in detail later in this chapter.

TYPES OF READERS AT THE SECONDARY LEVEL

Most students are adequate readers when they reach the secondary schools (Gibson, 1970). This does not mean that all students have mastered the developmental reading skills presented in elementary schools. Rather, it means that these students are not in need of corrective reading instruction.

A second group of students entering secondary schools are poor readers. These students need to be retaught developmental reading skills previously covered in the elementary grades. However, these poor readers may have already received corrective reading instruction and still sustain reading skill deficits. At this point students may have been referred to and entered in classes for the learning disabled. These students are in need of both untaught developmental reading skills and the services offered by a learning disabilities specialist. They are judged to be reading at levels between the third and fifth grades on an individual reading diagnostic test. However, F. B. Davis (1970) states that the learning disabilities teacher in secondary school cannot reteach the reading skills normally taught in elementary school at grades one to three because these rudimentary skills will not prepare students for the content areas with which they must cope in secondary school and adult life. Tutoring secondary LD students in content areas also is not advocated. Murphy (1972-1973) laments:

In our findings, contrary to the many dedicated educators who continue to tutor reading, spelling and writing in junior high school and high school, it was learned that for most students tutoring in subject matter areas was too little too late. (p. 176)

But Frostig (1972), Fareed (1971), Palkes, Stewart, and Kahana (1968) believe that the judicious use of verbal instructions in how to cope with problems encountered in reading and how to develop a course of action can effectively alter the performance of students with learning disabilities at the secondary level. Thus, the teaching of learning strategies and student application of these skills to problem-solving in secondary school appears to be a viable methodological approach for the teacher of LD adolescents. This is the role of the learning disabilities teacher because there is no content teacher, including the English teacher, who is prepared to take the leadership in shaping this program (Herber, 1965). A detailed description of the students who are learning disabled in reading and the methods to teach them will be described later. These students are classified as having mild to moderate reading disabilities.

In addition to the adequate and the poor readers found in secondary school, there is a small group of hard-core reading disabled students. Goodman and Mann (1976) classify these students as "developmental learners." These learners range in reading achievement from illiteracy — those whose chronological age is over fourteen and who respond negatively to the question, "Can you read and write?" (Otto & Ford, 1967, p. 1) — up to low fourth-grade level. "Developmental learner" is not a good term for these hard-core LD students because they are so easily confused with students who are functioning adequately in developmental reading programs. We would suggest that these students be described as LD students with severe and profound reading disabilities. They function no higher than the third stage of reading instruction, that is, rapid development of reading. This would place their achievement at levels no higher than second or beginning third grade. These severely and profoundly disabled students have been found enrolled in learning disabilities classes or having received remedial reading services for a prolonged period during their enrollment in elementary school. These students also have not developed the reading skills required for the learning strategies approach nor have they benefited from traditional remedial reading approaches. These students, when they reach secondary schools, are in need of intensive clinical reading instruction, an approach that is beyond the scope of this chapter. However, this limitation does not hold for other skills, such as listening, speaking, and mathematics.

CHARACTERISTICS OF THE LD STUDENT WITH MILD TO MODERATE READING DISABILITIES

Students with mild to moderate reading disabilities have demonstrated competence through the stage of rapid development of reading skills. They probably have had difficulty reading and have manifested such problems as forgetfulness (especially if two or more instructions are given simultaneously), distractibility, and poor copying skills. None of these behaviors has been associated with sensory handicaps, motor dysfunctions, or cultural differences. These students have consistently performed within at least the average range of intelligence — IQ 85-115. In addition, LD students with mild to moderate reading disabilities generally have displayed reading difficulties — reversed letters and words, failed to attain adequate sight vocabulary, substituted words of similar phonetic characteristics, included words that were not part of the text, and omitted words from the text with greater frequency of reading hesitations and repetition of words than the adequate reader. With the help of remedial teaching in small groups or on a one-to-one basis, students have mastered the decoding skills required for subsequent reading skill development.

Poor readers, as they enter the secondary schools, manifest difficulty with oral reading as it relates to the substitution of words, weak comprehension, lack of expression, failure to observe punctuation or misinterpretation of punctuation, loss of place in reading, and word-by-word reading (Harris & Sipay, 1975). These students also have difficulty with silent reading, but not to the degree they have with oral reading. They read slower and do not adequately comprehend content. Lip movements are also frequently present.

In spite of these handicaps, the poor reader (1) learns to depend on context clues, (2) benefits from guessing, (3) rereads passages, (4) is less concerned than peers about expression, (5) is less self-conscious than peers, and (6) may read more slowly than peers, but be superior to them in comprehension on passages read silently (Harris & Sipay, 1975). Because the students have these difficulties, they generally read only required materials and rarely read supplemental or recreational materials.

Because these students may have been receiving remedial instruction, they have had little or no opportunity to develop reading skills in functional or recreational reading materials. They do not possess the readiness skills for developmental reading instruction, and they were probably receiving remedial reading instruction while the rest of their classmates were receiving developmental reading instruction.

READING SKILLS TO BE TAUGHT TO STUDENTS WITH MILD TO MODERATE READING DISABILITIES

The reading skills introduced in grades four, five, and six are the skills to be mastered in junior and senior high school learning disabilities classes (Harris & Sipay, 1975; Olson & Ames, 1972; Miller, 1973; Robinson & Rauch,

1966). As stated before, these skills are (1) vocabulary development, (2) word recognition, (3) reading comprehension, (4) reading rate, and (5) study skills.

One might well ask why these skills should be identified with learning disabilities instruction. They are developmental reading skills that are to be taught to all students in secondary schools. This is a salient and penetrating question that has begged a definitive, candid answer in the past. Miller (1973) has delineated the situation. Developmental reading generally has been offered to secondary students who wish to master these reading skills. Students who have enrolled in developmental reading programs have done so for no credit and on a voluntary basis. In most secondary schools the developmental reading program is viewed as a supplement to the curriculum and related only indirectly to the language arts program. Students receive instruction in study skills only if they, their school counselors, or parents have recognized the future benefits of such skills for these particular students.

Conversely, remedial instruction at the secondary level usually is required of LD students who are reading two or more years below their grade placement. Remedial instruction at this level is offered as an alternative to English. Student reading problems are pinpointed by a skilled diagnostician using individual reading skills tests. Therefore, the decision is generally not whether the student should be enrolled in a developmental reading program or in a learning disabilities class. Rather, the question is, is the student so disabled in reading as to require instruction in any or all of the areas of word knowledge, reading comprehension, reading rate, and study skills. This is determined by a learning disabilities teacher after a thorough diagnostic workup. Subsequently, team members at a case conference must agree that remedial instruction is appropriate for the student and should be included in the individual's educational program.

ASSESSING READING DEFICITS IN LD ADOLESCENTS

The learning disabilities teacher should evaluate the following:

1. Vocabulary development
    a. Word recognition — sight words
    b. Decoding words
        1. phonemic analysis
        2. structural analysis
        3. contextual clues — reading comprehension
        4. dictionary usage — study skills
    c. Word meaning
        1. denotative

    a. common experience with topic
    b. similar and contrasting words
    c. author definition provided
   2. connotative
    a. specialized or technical vocabulary
    b. figurative language
    c. word power

  2. Reading comprehension
   a. Types and purposes
   1. literal — recall/recognition
   2. inferential
   3. critical
   4. applied
   b. Conditions
   1. words
   2. phrases
   3. organization
    a. main idea
    b. facts
    c. reading directions
    d. visual imagery
    e. organizational patterns
    f. context clues
   4. sentences
   5. paragraphs

  3. Reading rate (flexibility)
   a. Skimming
   1. organizational
   2. locational
   3. survey
   b. Scanning
   1. Type I to find a point of emphasis (italics, block lettering, etc.)
   2. Type II to find an answer to a question
   3. Type III to identify organization or find a procedure
   c. Intensive study
   1. Types
    a. textbook/nonfiction
    b. fiction
    c. poetry
   d. Nature and type of material as it affects reading rate

The teacher should use both standardized and informal measures to assess LD student performance on these reading skills. Blanton, Farr, and Tuinman (1972) have edited a pamphlet that the learning disabilities teacher will find useful when selecting standardized measures. We are impressed with three standardized measures that have been evaluated by various reading experts. They are:

1. *SRA Achievement Series*, Science Research Associates.
2. *Gates-MacGinitie Reading Tests*, Teachers College Press.
3. *Iowa Silent Reading Tests*, Harcourt Brace Jovanovich.

These measures are survey instruments and will not pinpoint student competence among the reading subskills requiring remediation.

To pinpoint reading subskills, the teacher may choose standardized diagnostic measures or informal diagnostic measures. Many reading experts choose the *Diagnostic Reading Scales* (Spache, 1972), *Reading Diagnostic Scales* (Gates & McKillop, 1962), or the *Tests of Reading Skills Difficulty* (Durrell, 1955), among others. We do not dispute the benefits of these or similar standardized diagnostic measures for specific children. However, we prefer informal measures.

Voix (1968) has provided examples of informal measurement of reading subskills as these skills are related to content areas covered in the secondary curriculum. It seems that evaluating reading skills within the content areas is sound practice, especially if the LD students are to be mainstreamed for the greater part of a school day. This method of assessment lends itself to cooperative planning, which is so necessary between the learning disabilities teacher and the content area teachers.

In addition to using the informal measurements suggested by Voix, the teacher should confirm reading deficit findings by trial teaching with the methods and materials suggested later. If the instruments or methods used in identifying skill or subskill deficits do not provide directions for remediation, those identification tools are of little value to the teacher.

TEACHING VOCABULARY

Reading is a means of communication. It is only one of several essential skills for obtaining information. As such, reading is not only a perceptual task (for example, decoding individual words into spoken words), but also a cognitive task, which requires the student to " . . . reconstruct the written message into spoken message" (Ausubel & Robinson, 1969). Any attempt to separate word recognition skills from word meaning skills is artificial and may lead to student confusion. The same argument can also be made against artificially separating sentence structure from sentence meaning. A dependent relationship exists between verbal recognition and meaning (Ausubel & Robinson, 1969).

Learning disabled students with mild to moderate reading disability are defined as students who possess reading skills above the primary grade level, that is, above third grade. These students should have been taught phonics during second and third grades. Word recognition problems do occur in oral reading by secondary students (Schale, 1966). These problems evidenced by students reading above third-grade level generally involve recognition of long words, such as *government* and *hibernate*, rather than short words, such as *whose* and *down*. (These students must be retaught the phonics skills presumably covered in the second and third grades. Harris and Sipay [1975] provide a table that includes the skills to be retaught and the methods and materials to be used.) On the basis of Harris and Sipay's supposition, we will assume that students with mild to moderate reading disabilities have mastered primary phonics skills through remedial instruction and/or developmental teaching. Therefore, if a student encounters a word and does not "know" it, we may interpret this to mean that the student is able to decode the word, using (1) phonic skills and (2) letter-clustering, but does not understand its meaning in isolation or in context.

Teaching Denotative Meanings of Words

Learning disabled students must be taught the meanings of words used in reading passages. They will fail to understand the passage if some words (1) are not within their experience (Crawford, 1967), (2) are used infrequently by students (Deighton, 1959; Kaluger & Kolson, 1969), or (3) are used in a specialized or technical way that is different from the more common meaning; *compound* is such a word as in compound fracture, military compound, compound sentence, compound word, chemical compound, compound interest, compound leaf, compound microscope, compound number, and so on.

Meaning vocabulary should be taught by exposing students to many firsthand experiences with the words through illustrations, concrete examples of word meanings, and frequent use of the words in spoken language. It is especially valuable if the word can be used frequently in the context of assigned reading through the use of diverse methods of presentation. Deighton (1959, pp. 2-6, 15-16) gives eight examples of how to apply this method. They are, with minor modifications, as follows:

1. The new word is set off by underlining, quotation marks, or all capital letters to call attention to it.
   Examples: The "Confederacy" was then formed. The CONFEDERACY was then formed.
2. A brief explanation or definition of the word is given in parentheses or in a footnote.
   Example: The Confederacy (the government of the southern states) was formed.
3. A clause or phrase that explains the meaning of the word is inserted in the sentence.
   Example: The *Confederacy*, the government of the South, was formed.
4. A simpler synonym or substitute phrase is used to indicate the meaning.
   Example: The organization of the eleven southern states was formed.
5. Similes and metaphors may be used.
   Example: A "Washington of the South" was formed.
6. The meaning of the word may be shown in pictorial illustration.
   Example: A map.
7. A direct explanation of the word may be presented in a full sentence.
   Example: Confederacy — the eleven southern states seceding from the United States in 1860 and 1861.
8. The sentence can be written so that there is only one meaning the new word could possibly have.
   Example: The government of the seceding eleven southern states during the Civil War was called the Confederacy.

Harris and Sipay (1975) also offer six general methods for increasing vocabulary skills. They are as follows:

1. Word tests. Example: Look up words in dictionary, and write sentences using the words.
2. Study word parts — roots, prefixes, and suffixes, particularly those of Latin or Greek origin.
3. Teach dictionary skills by constructing vocabulary notebooks, studying origins of words, synonyms, antonyms, and homonyms, using informal materials, workbooks, programmed instruction, and audiovisuals.
4. Contextual clues.
5. Wide reading.
6. Discussion of denotative and connotative meanings, idioms, colloquialisms using the word (p. 446).

Other methods and materials have been suggested by Strang (1968), Kaluger and Kolson (1969), Thomas and Robinson (1972), Hafner and Karlin, (1967), and Mills (1963).

Teaching Word Meanings of Infrequently Used Words

The second reason why the LD student might not know a word is that the word is in the student's emerging vocabulary or is used infrequently by the student. Some words require less effort to understand than to use. The word *dossier* is a word that many teachers use, but it is seldom found in print or used spontaneously, except in limited contexts.

Deighton (1970) suggests three other conditions that may dictate why a student does not recognize and use some words. First, situations are not conducive to using the word. This may occur when only the text is used for instruction. The student's reading scope is limited to words that are used by a single author or authors of the text. The simple remedy for this is the use of a variety of materials in teaching and abundant reinforcement for recreational reading.

The second condition for infrequent word use and recognition difficulties is inadequate instruction by the teacher when the student is studying the word. The word must be presented across contexts and in a variety of circumstances. Simply asking the student to copy the definition as it is found in the dictionary or meet the competency requirement on a vocabulary test does not mean the student "knows" the word (Bruland, 1974). We are seeking word mastery. A technique that we have found to be of value is a word file. The word file is kept by each student and the teacher. The words are presented in daily assignments, and the student can look up the word in the file. During this period, the learning disabilities teacher and content area teachers observe to see if the student is using the word in writing and in speaking. When the student makes no use of the word file and uses the word in writing and speaking, the word card is transferred to the inactive portion of the file. At this point, only periodic checks are made to insure that the word is being maintained in the student's written and spoken vocabularies.

The final condition for infrequent word use and difficulties in recognition exists because of social circumstances during oral reading. The student's earlier attempts at word attack have often received punishing reactions from peers in the form of laughter, or depersonalizing comments such as "dummy" or "retard," or facial and other gestures. Similar negative peer and teacher reactions often occur when the LD student provides an inappropriate oral or written definition. As a result of such experiences, the LD student remains reticent in classroom discussions of vocabulary and tends not to provide definitions, either written or oral, when required to do so. This creates a circular problem — the more limited the vocabulary of the student, the more inaccurate the student will be in interpreting what is read. Several steps need to be taken if such adverse conditions arise in the classroom. Probably the best first step is to provide time each day for vocabulary development in both the learning disabilities class and the content area classes. As a part of this approach, the teacher must provide an accepting climate for the experimental use of new words and word meanings. Such an approach is mandatory in learning disabilities classes; however, time may not permit teachers to implement this approach every day across all content areas. The rule of thumb for content area teachers is to provide the time and accepting conditions cited above when working on vocabulary for unit study or specific lessons (Deighton, 1959).

As a second step, LD students should be instructed to make use of the two basic aids for deriving meaning from an infrequently used word. These two aids are the context in which the word is found (Dulin, 1969) and the dictionary. The major limitation on the use of context is that it is content specific. That is, the meaning of the word may be appropriate only in this one setting. The major limitation of using a dictionary is that the word may be accompanied by qualifying words that affect the meaning of the word in this specific context — "The area is hot, dry, and sparsely populated." The qualifying word, *sparsely*, if not considered with the key word, *populated*, will cause LD students to misinterpret the sentence, even though they have the correct dictionary meaning of the key word.

Crawford (1967) offers several instructional techniques for teaching LD students to identify qualifying words and their effects on word and sentence meaning. Thomas and Robinson (1972) have devised guidelines for LD students that will help them distinguish circumstances for using either context clues or the dictionary to arrive at the meaning of a word.

Do Rely on *Context Clues*	*Do* Rely on your *Dictionary* (*Don't* Rely on Context Clues)
1. When you have an "unmissable clue" — a direct explanation.	1. When you require a precise meaning. It *almost always* [italics added] takes the dictionary to pin the meaning down.
2. When you have highly revealing clues and the meaning you arrive at definitely "clicks" with the rest of the passage.	2. When the word is a key word, one crucial to your understanding, and full comprehension is important to you.
3. When, in view of your purpose for reading the selection, you need only a general sense of the meaning [previewing material or reading for the main idea].	3. When the [context] clues suggest several meanings — and you must know which.

4. When you don't know the nearby words [watch this carefully for qualifying words].

5. When you have encountered the word a number of times, realize that it is a common useful one which you will meet again and want to master it thoroughly. [Record it in your word file] for future reading. (p. 38)

Teaching Polysyllabic Words

Special problems exist when the LD student has difficulty decoding polysyllabic words that require the use of not only simple sound-symbol phonics, but also related syllabication skills. Polysyllabic words are of four types: (1) compound words, e.g., *shellfish, shipmate, pullman;* (2) known words to which a prefix and/or suffix has been added, e.g., *adverb, embattle, federalize, feminism, incandescent, inbreeding;* (3) words that can be divided into familiar syllables, e.g., *incarnate, respiration, subsidiarily;* (4) words that only dictionaries can be used to decode, e.g., *mnemosyne, Tchaikovsky, zygapophysis* (Olson & Ames, 1970). Olson offers the following three generalizations that the LD student can use when approaching similar polysyllabic words:

1. Prefixes and suffixes generally form separate syllables, i.e., *ad-verb.*
2. Syllables generally divide between two consonants or double consonants, *wel-come, poly-dac-tyl.*
3. Words ending in *le* usually take the consonant immediately before it and form the final syllable, i.e., *syl-la-ble.* (p. 135)

In conclusion, reading authorities differ on the methods to be used to develop vocabulary skills, but they agree that students must recognize a need to learn and retain the meanings of new, emerging, or infrequently encountered words. If students are either not interested in learning the words or cannot see the importance of these words, no method will be successful. If students do not see the importance of learning the words even after the purpose for such learning is explicitly described to them, they must be motivated through the use of positive reinforcers that are contingent upon their learning the words.

72

Teaching Connotative Meanings of Words
(Words with Technical or Multiple Meanings)

The above discussion of developing a vocabulary has dealt with obtaining denotative meanings of words. *Denotative* is defined by Tubbs and Moss (1974) as ". . . the primary association a word has for most members of a linguistic community" (p. 115). However, a word may have a primary denotative meaning and a secondary connotative meaning. The word *fox* is reported to have five meanings (Tubbs & Moss, 1974). "Sometimes the connotations of a word are the same for nearly everyone; sometimes they relate solely to one person's personal experience. To most of us the word 'fox' connotes guile or cunning. To a naturalist, a furrier, a chicken farmer, or a man who has just been bitten by a fox, the word 'fox' may have completely different connotations" (p. 115). We would add an additional connotative meaning for the word "fox" — "an attractive woman."

Connotatively, a word can mean whatever *one* or more members of the linguistic community " . . . choose it to mean — neither more nor less" (Carroll, 1965, p. 94). We can speak of connotations of words as they are found in the specialized or technical vocabulary of differing content areas (a topic that will be discussed later in this chapter), in the word power of politicians, who may choose words more for their magical power than for the content of the words — "new deal," "square deal," "great society" — and in figurative language — "no man is an island," "my word." Tubbs and Moss (1974) suggest two assumptions that will minimize oral communication problems. These assumptions apply to written communication, with slight modification: (1) acknowledge that the words of the author may or may not be meaningful to the reader, and (2) grant the possibility that the author's interpretation of a given word is not necessarily superior to the reader's interpretation. Perhaps the optimal method for meeting the two assumptions is to apply Bruland's (1974) five principles of vocabulary study:

1. Most words have more than one meaning.
2. Context determines which of a word's meanings fit a particular passage.
3. We never get all of a word's meaning in one encounter.
4. Meaning comes from experience.
5. We obtain clues to word meanings from context, structural analysis, and from phonics related to meaningful sounds in aural memory. (pp. 212-214)

Bruland's study brings us full circle in the methodology of developing the LD student's vocabulary skills.

INCREASING READING COMPREHENSION

Reading comprehension requires competence in both word recognition and word meaning. However, these skills are only two elements required for reading comprehension. Students must also be able to relate the ideas that are inherent in groups of written words. The reader must be primarily aware of the meaning conveyed by the writer.

The foundation of reading comprehension is even more than the relationship of ideas. According to Niles (1965), it also includes the conscious effort to read for some purpose and to relate the experiences of the reader to the reading passage. If the reader (1) cannot relate the ideas of the writer; (2) is unaware of the purpose for reading a particular passage; and/or (3) cannot relate experiences to the content, then comprehension of materials falls to a minimum or the reader stops reading. Most of us can relate these three problems in reading comprehension to our initial college course in statistics. We may have "passed" the course, but because we had difficulty (1) relating the ideas (probability to random assignment, F-tests to x^2, large samples to Z-scores), (2) reading for a purpose ("Why am I deriving these formulas? I am never going to use this information in the future."), and (3) relating our own experiences to the content ("This is unlike anything I have done before!"), our comprehension of statistics was minimal. However, when we *found a need* for statistics, we had to reread the information to solve the problem. Few individuals can solve applied problems in statistics without having a statistics text close at hand.

Analytical and Critical Reading Skills

In our estimation, Aukerman (1972) provides a good classification of reading comprehension. He divides reading comprehension into analytical skills and critical skills. Under analytical comprehension, we would include literal and inferential comprehension. Critical comprehension, as used by Aukerman, would include the sublevels described by Miller (1973).

The component skills of reading comprehension are provided by N. B. Smith (1963). She postulates nine skills required for comprehension that include both analytical and critical reading skills. Dechant (1973) suggests that the individual who is able to comprehend reading materials must possess twenty-one component skills. We have presented component skills of reading comprehension using rubrics from Aukerman's categories, for clarity to the reader.

Analytic Reading Comprehension	*Critical Reading Comprehension*
1. Identify main ideas.	1. Interpret figurative expressions.
2. Recognize significant details.	2. Evaluate character traits, reactions, and motives.
3. Recognize organizational patterns.	3. Recognize the writer's purpose.

Wallace and McLoughlin (1975) surveyed the levels and components of reading and concluded that LD students may be expected to have difficulty with components of analytical and critical reading. The reasons for the difficulties may be classified into four major areas (Wiener & Cramer, 1970). They are (1) defects within students; (2) deficiencies in reading skills; (3) disruptions that interfere with reading; and (4) experiential and cognitive differences. High school students with reading problems have provided self-reports that show that their manifest problems fall within the four areas of reading disabilities provided by Wiener & Cramer (Ephron, 1953). Defects within students are manifested by their concepts of themselves as poor readers, their poor retention skills, inability to concentrate, and nervousness, restlessness, and fatigue when reading. The behaviors stemming from deficiencies in reading skills are poor general vocabulary, poor spelling, difficulty in dealing with words and their contextual intent, and noted weakness in work analysis skills. Students who procrastinate and then cram when studying may be reflecting the disruptions that interfere with reading. Finally, experiential and cognitive differences are manifested in difficulties with multiple meanings of words, lack of nonlanguage referents, the tendency to give equal stress and value to every word, and the search for the one best way to read (Raygor, 1959).

Teaching Analytical Skills

Numerous reading experts focus on recognizing the logic in paragraphs as the primary skill in reading for comprehension. Paulsen and Larmer (1966) state that two of the three basic elements in any written composition are unity, which provides the parameters of the idea, and order, which provides the details that relate to the unity. When the paragraph is studied, the concept is the same, but the terminology is changed. The following are suggested methods of teaching the analytical skills required for comprehension.

Teaching LD Students to Recognize Topic Sentences

Determine if LD students can identify the topic sentence of a paragraph by a formal assessment measure, such as Sequential Tests of Educational

Progress, Series II, Reading (Educational Testing Service, 1969), or SRA Achievement Series (Science Research Associates, 1963), or by an informal measure. The topic sentence generally is the first sentence of the paragraph, but occasionally it may be found in the middle or at the end of the paragraph.

Worksheets of prepared paragraphs with multiple choices including the most appropriate topic sentence for each paragraph and three or four distractor sentences may be used for practice. Or the teacher might develop language experience paragraphs based on students' experiences and question students concerning the topic sentence.

Teaching LD Students to Locate Important Details

The next logical aspect of a paragraph is locating relevant facts and important details. These factors or details are related to the topic sentence. They answer the questions Who? What? Where? When? Why? and How?

Teaching LD Students to Recognize Organizational Patterns

LD students' ability to identify organizational patterns of paragraphs will greatly assist them in recognizing the important ideas presented by the writer. This skill is recognized by many authors as a major comprehension skill that should be developed by all readers (Bailey, 1975; Dechant, 1973; Fareed, 1971; Johnson & Myklebust, 1964; Kaluger & Kolson, 1969; Lerner, 1976; Niles, 1965; Paulsen & Larmer, 1966).

Within each organizational pattern the experts disagree on the number of categories. We will present the categories on which the experts have agreed. Dechant (1973), Niles (1965) and Paulsen and Larmer (1966) agree on four analytic, organizational patterns. They are (1) enumerative order, (2) time order, (3) following a sequence, and (4) using structural connectives.

1. Enumerative order is simply a listing of facts that are of similar importance (e.g., "The three major reasons for the energy crisis are (1) . . . , (2) . . . , (3), or facts arranged from the general to the particular, or vice versa (e.g., "Two animals that belong to the order of mammals are the dog and the cat," or "Dogs and cats are part of the order of mammals."). Dechant (1973) suggests that students may identify enumerative order by the cue words "part of" and "belong to."

2. Time order organization includes space concepts also. The chronological order of history is a good example of time order. Dechant (1973) suggests that the cue words "after" and "under" are examples of cues to the time order organization (e.g., "After the death of Lincoln, Andrew Johnson assumed the Presidency" or "The scrolls were found under the cliffs.")

3. The third organizational pattern, following a sequence, is closely associated with time order. We view it as a composite of the time order and enumeration categories of the functional organization pattern. Following a sequence is important in reading, especially in prevocational and vocational subjects, such as home economics and business.

4. The final organization pattern uses structural connectives (Paulsen & Larmer, 1966). They cite four categories of connectives that relate to organizational pattern. They are (1) word order, (2) punctuation, (3) word shifts, and (4) structural cues. The word order is related to the syntax of the sentences in the paragraph. The closer the syntax comes to subject-verb-object order the easier it is to read and the easier it is to determine the organization. Punctuation is also important in determining the organization. Probably the most difficult paragraph to organize is the one in which the author uses many word shifts. Paulsen and Larmer (1966, p. 57) provide sentences that are excellent examples of the effects of word shifts on meaning and organization (e.g., "When mother turned her head, baby drank her coffee," compared with a sentence with the word shift, "Mother turned her head when baby drank her coffee.") The structure signals provided by Paulsen and Larmer are similar to the cue words of Dechant, but they are not provided as cues to specific organizational style. The structure signals are "because," "however," "in the beginning," "next."

It is difficult to assess an LD student's ability to identify the organization of a paragraph. Probably one must improvise to determine if such a difficulty exists, through informal means based on samples of the student's summaries, outlines, and underlining and notetaking on longer passages. This is possible because generally the writer of the passage will follow a specific organization from one paragraph to the next.

How can one help LD students identify the functional organization of a paragraph? The obvious method is to teach application of the major organizational patterns and then have a group of students construct a chart of the patterns. Finally, students are provided with easy reading paragraphs in which to identify the pattern. The paragraphs should then become more and more difficult until the task becomes analogous to reading in the content areas.

If students cannot cope with the method described above, the task may be made easier by asking them to order their daily routines. Then proceed to sequence pictures that have been selected for different organizational patterns and ask for a story described in the pictures. See if the students can identify their "picture" story with one of the organizational patterns listed on the chart constructed by the students. Finally, provide the students with a series of cards containing one sentence on each card. These sentences should be constructed so that the organizational pattern is obvious and there are connectives between sentences. Students then order the sentences in the organizational sequence and identify the organizational pattern of their sequenced paragraphs with the organizational patterns provided by the class chart (Bailey, 1975; Niles, 1965; Johnson & Myklebust, 1967). Most LD students should then be able to benefit from use of the method described above.

Improving Visual Imagery

The concept of visual imagery has been of interest to reading experts for at least two decades (Durrell, 1955). However, few investigations have been reported in the literature. Recently, Levin (1973) and his associates (Levin, Devine-Hawkins, Kerst, & Guttmann, 1974) have provided information that is of interest to teachers of LD students. They found that instructing students to think of a picture that might be associated with the reading passage aids students who read more than one year below their present grade placement on a reading comprehension task (Levin, 1973). Levin et al. (1974) reported that students who could learn words best when the words were accompanied by pictures could increase reading comprehension when they were instructed to use visual imagery. However, such increases were not found when these same students were instructed to "read the words."

Warner (1977) studied the use of visual imagery to improve reading comprehension with LD junior high school students. Visual imagery as a learning strategy for LD students yielded positive but nonsignificant results. Warner is planning further studies, making use of more frequent teaching sessions.

Questioning Strategies

Questioning strategies have been used for many years in an attempt to guide or involve students in the teaching process. Miller (1973) and Niles (1965) discuss questioning as one of several methods to guide students in comprehension of content areas. Hoover (1976) suggests that questions can be used to increase student participation through the use of volunteers, nonvolunteers, and reciprocal questioning by students.

Questioning is not in and of itself the key to comprehension. Rather, different questions elicit different responses, questions are used most effectively when a person is called upon in class after the question has been stated, and there are differing qualities of questions (Hoover, 1976; Manzo, 1969; Minskoff, 1974). Gallagher (1964, p. 408) identified four types of teacher questions:

1. *Cognitive-memory questions.* Recapitulation or review, giving facts, labels, or definitions, detailing or describing. ("Can you give me the four steps in the Bessemer steelmaking process?")
2. *Convergent thinking questions.* Ask the student for relationships, explanation, reasoning, arriving at conclusions, principles, or inferences. ("What important factors do you think would have changed if the Panama Canal treaty had not been ratified by the U.S. Senate?")
3. *Divergent thinking questions.* Ask the student to create new ideas, generate a number of varied responses, arrive at novel responses through reasoning and inference. ("Describe as many novel uses as you can for a brick.")
4. *Evaluative thinking questions.* Ask students to make judgments on specific criteria, judgments on unspecified criteria, give opinions. ("Based on the information available to you, should Richard Nixon have been impeached by the U.S. Senate?")

These kinds of questions can be further modified by content or sentence structure to fit the questions to the achievement level and abilities of students (Hoover, 1976). Some may also be modified to determine if students can recognize the answer (multiple choice, matching, true-false), recall the answer (short answer or essay), and/or be prompted to recall the answer (fill-in).

Hoover (1976) has shown that questioning by the teacher is ineffective when the teacher does one of the following:

1. Repeats the question. This reinforces students' inattention.
2. Answers his/her own questions. Students see no need in answering or volunteering.

3. Repeats the student's response. This permits students to provide incomplete answers, and
4. Does not listen or maintain eye contact with the responder. This also reinforces (1), (2), and (3). (p. II-71-72)

Teachers can avoid such practices by monitoring their teaching lessons on videotape and correcting poor questioning procedures.

One questioning procedure that has been of interest to the authors and their students is ReQuest (Manzo, 1969). Manzo found his ReQuest procedure was more effective in the enhancement of reading comprehension than the Directed Reading Activity with a group of students ranging in age from seven to twenty-six who were enrolled in a summer remedial reading clinic.

Hori (1977) used a slight modification of the ReQuest procedure as an intervention to enhance the reading comprehension of a small group of junior high school LD students. She concluded that the ReQuest procedure is efficient in increasing reading comprehension as measured by a formal reading test. She implied that the ReQuest method ". . . can be quickly learned by the student and does not require an inordinate amount of teacher time" (p. 38).

The procedure, as it was used by Hori with junior high school LD students, was as follows:

1. Both the student and the teacher used copies of the reading material. Hori used appropriate levels of the Allyn & Bacon *Breakthrough* series.
2. Using the questioning categories outlined by Manzo, the teacher tracked the student through the reading material until the student was able to state the outcome of the passage.
    a. Both the teacher and the student silently read the first sentence.
    b. The student then exhausted the content of the sentence by asking all the questions he or she could generate.
    c. The teacher responded to each question;
    d. The teacher then asked questions based on the structure and content of the sentence.
    e. The student answered the teacher's questions or gave a reason for not being able to.
    f. If the student could not answer the teacher's questions, the teacher provided the responses.
3. For the initial two or three paragraphs of the passage, teacher and student followed the same procedure as in 2.
4. The student was then requested to write a question related to the outcome of the passage. The student answered the question *orally*

when the question was read by the teacher, after the two completed their silent reading of the selection.

Manzo (1969) provides seven question categories, which are illustrative but not mandatory for the teacher when using ReQuest:

1. *Immediate reference*, "What did John call his dog?"
2. *Common knowledge*, "What kind of animal is Lassie?"
3. *Related information*, "Do you know some varieties of dogs?"
4. *Discussion*, "I wonder why some animals make better pets than others?"
5. *Personalized*, "How did your family react to your first pet?"
6. *Further reference*, "What is the average height of a collie?"
7. *Translation*, summary of events and/or evaluation.

Hori (1977) modified these categories by making it mandatory to ask hierarchical questions of the student. Her hierarchy included:

1. *Decoding*, "Why is there an 's' on the end of this word?" or "How do you pronounce the third word in this sentence?"
2. *Literal*, "What color was the car?"
3. *Inferential*, "What do you think will happen?"
4. *Evaluative*, "Did their story convince you that UFO's are real?" (p. 17)

Our suggestion is that the modification of ReQuest used by Hori be applied when intervening with LD secondary students. The modification assures that the teacher will model higher order questions and also ask questions related to word structure and word recognition.

DEVELOPING READING FLEXIBILITY

Students are frequently admonished to read every word carefully, regardless of reading conditions. That this is to be done under all conditions is a myth (Aukerman, 1972). The authors agree with Miller (1973) that students *MUST* vary their reading rate according to (1) difficulty of the material, and (2) purpose for reading the passage.

Most secondary students use inflexible reading rates. They read word by word at approximately 250 words per minutes (wpm). These students will not increase their reading rate unless they have a motive to do so.

Without a motive, students generally see no urgency in increasing the rate (Tinker, 1970).

However, there are some prerequisites that must be met before one can achieve reading flexibility. Tinker (p. 204) lists four:

1. Sight vocabulary (reading recognition).
2. Vocabulary knowledge (word comprehension).
3. Word recognition skills (decoding words).
4. Use of context skills.

These prerequisites are generally satisfied during the primary grades. Therefore, reading flexibility is taught at the beginning of fourth grade and throughout secondary schools.

Several investigators (Della-Piana, 1968; Tinker, 1970; Olson & Ames, 1972; Harris & Sipay, 1975) have postulated reasons for poor reading rate and inflexibility. Some of the most critical reasons are as follows:

1. *Word-by-word reading*. Silent reading is no faster than oral reading. This may be associated with subvocalization, excessive word analysis, slowness in word recognition, and poor word comprehension.

2. *Poor reading habits*, such as regressions, repetitions, losing one's place while reading, excessive eye fixations, finger pointing, and head movements.

3. *Experiential factors*, including infrequent reading, unfamiliarity of concepts, limited breadth and depth of vocabulary, poor study habits (dawdling), vision impairment, and low self-concept.

4. *Factors related to the reading material* may include words or concepts too difficult, material uninteresting to the student, the author's language style or writing structure, factors related to size, clarity, and form of typesetting, factors related to paper and printing format, and type of writing (prose, poetry).

One may assess reading flexibility using formal and/or informal measures. Miller (1973) suggests the *EDL Reading Versatility Test* (Educational Developmental Laboratories) as an appropriate formal measure. The secondary learning disabilities teacher may also wish to use an informal measure of reading flexibility. This can be done by varying the difficulty of reading material from primary to secondary levels and providing students with a purpose for reading the passage. For example:

Reading rate	Reading difficulty	Purpose
1. (skim)	2nd grade - 4th grade	Read for a general impression of the story.
2. (scan)	4th grade - 6th grade	Read to find a place, date, or person's name.
3. (intensive)	3rd grade - 5th grade	Read to find a way one could solve a problem.

Use the first set of reading passages to assess the student's skill in skimming materials, the second set to assess scanning skills, and the third set to assess intensive reading.

One would expect a secondary student without learning disabilities to be able to *skim* the above materials at 600-800 wpm. This same student should be able to *scan* for the information in the second set at 1000+ wpm. Finally, when reading *intensively*, the student should read the material between 200-400 wpm. However, the content of the reading material is critical in arriving at these figures. For example, the intensive reading varies, because 400 wpm is average when students are reading an easy novel and 200 wpm is more related to reading a social studies textbook (Miller, 1973).

One final caution about the above figures: The area of mathematics is not conducive to this reading flexibility measurement. Nearly all mathematics texts require intensive reading to solve problems. Miller (1973) suggests that students must read mathematics problems at 75-150 wpm to obtain the information required to solve the problems.

Comprehension and reading rate are associated, but the degree of association is disputed among investigators (Tinker, 1970; Dechant, 1973). Tinker equates reading rate with comprehension and makes the supposition that reading without comprehension is *not* reading. However, Dechant reports a low positive correlation (r = .30) between reading rate and comprehension in secondary students. In fact, he states that in the areas of math and science there is a low negative correlation between these two reading factors. He categorizes three types of comprehension-rate problems in which a remedy (R_x) can be identified:

1. Decreased rate, decreased comprehension
   R_x — teacher should place emphasis on teaching comprehension skills and *not* reading rates.
2. Increased rate, decreased comprehension
   R_x — same as 1.
3. Decreased rate, increased comprehension

R_x — teacher should place emphasis on teaching reading flexibility and *not* comprehension skills.

He states that problem type 3 is caused by students' lack of confidence, overestimating the difficulty of material, and subvocalizing. Conversely, when problem type 2 is found, it can be associated with readers' superficial attitude toward the material, their skimming or scanning the material rather than reading intensively, poor organization, and underestimating the difficulty of the material (pp. 61-62).

Skimming

When a student skims reading material, it is generally to obtain an impression or general overview of the content. However, this is not the only purpose for skimming. Maxwell (1972-1973) suggests three purposes for skimming: (1) preview skimming, (2) overview skimming, and (3) review skimming.

Students use preview skimming with the thought in mind that the material will be read intensively later. Students preview material to determine the author's organizational style and to get the gist of the story. They are not looking for specific facts or attempting to interpret the material.

Overview skimming is used when students have limited time for reading. They choose to read shortened, simplified, and interpreted material rather than consult the original source. Many digest magazines, such as *Reader's Digest* and *Skill Builder*, encourage overview reading. In this case, students will not read original material at a later time.

Students should also be taught to use review skimming. This type of skimming permits one to reevaluate information accumulated by note-taking and other information-gathering, rather than rereading all the sources. This is a particularly important skill in test preparation.

Scanning

Thomas and Robinson (1972) have identified three levels of scanning. They are:

Level I   — Scanning for a specific point that stands out easily.
Level II — Scanning for an answer to a specific question.
Level III — Scanning for information that will not appear as simple answers to questions.

At Level I, LD students should be taught to look for graphs, tables, and illustrations that provide compressed data, headings and subheadings, words and phrases appearing in boldface or italics. This information is critical for comprehension of the content.

Most texts used in the content areas include review and preview questions that are readily answered, provided the student has completed Level I scanning. These questions are guides to the important factual data included in the passage.

Scanning at Level III is very difficult. In the estimation of the authors, it is not possible to do without intensive reading. This is not a part of teaching scanning, but rather organization. The facts are organized in an outline, and inferences are made on the basis of the facts accumulated or it is determined that critical facts are missing.

Intensive Reading

Intensive reading is used to master the reading content. One student analyzes the author's presentation by studying its syntax, organization, and style. Another student evaluates the details to solve problems. Some students read to answer the questions when, where, who, how, and why. Other students read for thoughts rather than words, to answer questions generated by their own purposes for reading, whether the material is a mathematics problem, a Shakespearean play, or a Robert Frost poem.

The teacher must offer the LD student a purpose for reading the selection that is associated with flexibility. The teaching of flexibility should begin with easy selections and progress to harder material as flexibility is achieved. Students should intermittently be instructed in groups and individually, as advised by Gold (1964).

Mechanical devices to increase reading rate are viewed by experts as either valuable teaching adjuncts or useless technology. We feel that instruments are not essential to student success in this area for two reasons. First, the techniques of skimming, scanning, and intensive reading can be taught adequately without instruments. Having a purpose for reading is more conducive to flexibility than practicing at different reading rates without a purpose for reading.

Second, flexibility is required of students within a single passage. Grayum (1970) reports that "good" readers are flexible in reading a single passage — they read rapidly through sections they judge to be unimportant, uninteresting, and elaborated on. They read slowly through important, interesting, and succinct sections. These readers also reread important sections. None of these procedures was used by "poor" readers. The poor reader reads everything intensively.

In summary, flexibility is determined by the reader's purpose in reading. It cannot be attained without primary level reading skills. Flexibility can be taught! Flexibility is necessary even within single reading passages. No optimal overall reading rate is beneficial without considering reading purpose.

PROMOTING STUDY SKILLS

Pauk (1974) describes a student with excellent vocabulary and reading comprehension skills who failed in his academic pursuits. He reasons that the student lacked study skills to deal with organization of time and ideas, work discipline, retaining and recalling information, and critical reading. These study skills and vocational skills are important for success in school. Specific characteristics of secondary students who are having difficulty in study skills include:

1. Self-concept as a poor reader.
2. Lack of retention.
3. Inability to concentrate.
4. Tendency to give equal stress and value to every word.
5. Searching for the one best way to read.
6. Procrastination and cramming.
7. Reading causing nervousness, restlessness and fatigue (Ephron, 1953).

These factors are critical in view of the classroom instructional procedures usually applied in junior and senior high school that require students to read complex directions, assimilate several outside reading materials with class lectures in a group setting, and to organize these varied materials into main ideas and relevant facts for ensuing written examinations (Murphy, 1972-1973).

Learning disabled adolescents have not generally been introduced to either the concepts or the application of study skills in the elementary grades. Rather, LD students have been instructed in remedial skills to decode words in the resource room. The introduction to study skills has been provided in the classroom during developmental reading instruction sessions. Therefore, the LD adolescent will require a direct introduction to these skills, a description in concrete terms of the relationships between these skills and achievement success, and systematic and continued practice using study skills so they may be effectively learned.

One is faced with a serious limitation in determining which students require the systematic instruction of study skills, because of the limited number of instruments to measure these skills. Of the tests that are available, most are mediocre and tend to measure only locational skills. However, three instruments do appear to have value for LD teachers who are planning to teach study skills:

1. Brown-Holtzman *Survey of Study Habits and Attitudes.* Psychological Corp. (Form H, high school students, grades 9-12).
2. *Ross Test of High Order Concepts.* Academic Press (junior high students, grades 7-9).
3. *Iowa Silent Reading Tests.* Harcourt Brace Jovanovich (Level I, grades 6-9, and Level II, grades 9-12).

The Brown-Holtzman survey contains two subtests, delay avoidance and work methods, which are especially relevant to study skills. Delay avoidance and work methods are described in the subtests respectively as ". . . promptness in completing academic assignments, lack of procrastination and freedom from wasteful delay and distraction" and ". . . use of effective study procedures, efficiency in doing academic assignments, and how-to-study skills" (Brown & Holtzman, 1965, p. 3).

Three sections of the Ross test (Ross & Ross, 1976) appear to hold promise. They are (1) Section III Missing Premises, (2) Section V, Sequential Synthesis, and (3) Section VI, Questioning Strategies. The missing premises section taps students' logic and thought patterns by requiring students to provide a relevant fact to accompany a given fact to draw the conclusion provided by the test maker. Sequential synthesis gives students ". . . a group of statements dealing with a specific topic, 'The Championship Season.'" The statements under this topic are not listed in the proper sequence. Students must read all the statements, determine in what sequence they should occur, and then number the statements in the proper sequence. The questioning strategies section requires students to choose the correct item from among five items on the basis of question groups that provide clues to the relevant attributes of the item.

Part A of the directed reading subtest of the *Iowa Silent Reading Tests* is the measure of choice to tap a student's skills in locating information. It stresses both using the dictionary and locating information in a variety of sources.

Study skills used in reading help students acquire, organize, and retrieve information. These skills are critical for efficient learning in the content areas and must be taught through a variety of techniques and in a variety of settings.

Two major study skills are (1) locational skills, and (2) general organizational skills.

Locational Study Skills

Locational skills always include use of the dictionary. Specific dictionary skills are (1) locating words in alphabetical order; (2) determining the pronunciation of words; and (3) selecting the meaning of words.

Locating words in the dictionary is a skill that can be enhanced by providing students with exercises in arranging words alphabetically. A prerequisite for these activities is student ability to put letters of the alphabet in order automatically. Once students have met 100% criterion in this skill, they are given practice in arranging words that have identical initial consonants or vowels. Then they are asked to arrange words with identical first and second letters, and so on, until they can make the fine discriminations between words that are required if they are to use the dictionary efficiently. These alphabetizing activities should be done in short practice sessions on a daily basis with content vocabulary. Students should have a dictionary available at all times. A validity check of the sequencing skills taught is provided by having students use the dictionary after completing the exercise.

Guide words in dictionaries and other lists must be used to find target words. Students may enjoy locating the guide words that tell on which pages given target words are found. For variety and generalization, students may use telephone directories, student directories, encyclopedias, and almanacs to apply these skills.

The mispronunciation of words can cause embarrassment to most people under some circumstances. When LD students mispronounce words and their peers laugh at them, or snicker, or grimace, the speakers view themselves as inferior and the experience is devastating. Therefore, students in the LD classroom need to learn and practice pronunciation skills. The teacher's initial step in developing these skills is to determine students' skills in syllabication. If students cannot break down words into syllables, learning pronunciation is difficult. A second requirement is sound-blending. The student must be able to blend sounds as a prerequisite to developing pronunciation skills. The skills of syllabication and blending of sounds are taught in the second grade or beginning third grade. If LD students demonstrate these skills, learning pronunciation becomes a matter of learning inflection. In most cases, pronunciation of a word requires knowledge of context to determine the correct pronunciation. Therefore, no word should be studied outside of its context. We are all familiar with words such as *wind* and *read* that are pronounced differently in different contexts.

Learning disabled students must know of accent markings and how to use them. They also must recognize and apply diacritical marks. These skills are best taught individually or in small groups. The words used should be those that students are meeting in their content subjects.

A textbook also may be used to develop locational skills. Each LD student should be taught the major parts of a textbook. Students should be instructed in locating and using a table of contents, the introduction to the text, the index, the glossary, and appendixes. Miller (1973, p. 215) provides an example of questions that must be answered to evaluate LD students' competence in the efficient use of a table of contents:

1. How many parts does this book contain?
2. On what page does Chapter 38 begin?
3. How many chapters does this book contain?
4. Is there a glossary in this book?
5. On what page does the chapter entitled "Radiation Biology" begin?
6. How many sections does Part IV of this book contain?
7. What is Chapter 19 of this book about?
8. What section in this book is about insects?
9. On what page does Chapter 13 begin?
10. On what page does the index begin?

Other questions that may be asked to help students acquire skills that will make books their servants rather than their masters can be generated from a text by Voix, *Evaluating Reading and Study Skills in the Secondary Classroom* (1968).

The use of graphic aids has not been given emphasis in developing the locational skills of most students. Because graphic aids compress a tremendous amount of information into tabular or figure form, they should receive much attention from the teacher of LD students who have reading problems. Summers (cited in Herber, 1965) divides graphic or visual aids into two major areas: (1) maps as visual aids, and (2) charts and diagrams, tables and graphs, pictures and cartoons as visual aids.

The teaching methods to maximize student learning from visual aids include the following:

1. Recognize and interpret separate elements presented in visual aids.
2. Analyze and understand the relationships between elements contained in visual aids.
3. Pose questions and seek answers through the use of visual aids.
4. Make inferences and draw conclusions from visual aids in light of the problem at hand. (Summers, cited in Herber, 1965, p. 100)

Summers presents methods to teach visual aid skills and provides specific unit plans to use with materials resources.

Libraries are important settings in which to apply other locational skills. However, library resources have other qualities that require important but unique skills. Burmeister and Stevens (1974) present a comprehensive discussion of the skills required to use library resources. They separate these skills into two major areas: (1) library organization, and (2) reference aids. Included in these two areas are the following specific skills:

1. Library organization
   a. The Dewey decimal system
   b. The Library of Congress system
   c. The card catalog
2. Reference aids
   a. Periodicals
      (1) Indexes to general and nontechnical magazines
         (a) *Reader's Guide to Periodical Literature*
         (b) Abridged *Readers' Guide to Periodical Literature*
      (2) Specialized indexes
         Indexes that are specific to one field of study or several related fields of study
   b. Books
      (1) Bibliographies classified for student interests
      (2) Bibliographies classified by content areas
   c. General reference aids
      (1) Biographies
      (2) Encyclopedias
      (3) Almanacs
      (4) Atlases
   d. Periodicals with reviews of audiovisual aids

Burmeister and Stevens (1974) suggest four activities to teach skills in the use of library resources. They are, slightly modified, as follows:

1. List from memory the major divisions of the Dewey decimal system. Give exact numbers of important materials in a content area.
2. Name three types of cards for books commonly found in a card catalog.
3. Using a timely topic [of the student's choice] . . . indicate which periodical guide or guides would be useful in locating materials. Using the guides, write a list of twelve current articles that relate to the topic. (The student may use *How to Use the Readers' Guide to Periodical Literature*, New York: H. W. Wilson, rev. ed. 1970, pp. 1-16.)
4. [Have the student] select a content areas topic or theme . . . [and] tell which guides to book selection would be appropriate . . . to use in making book choices. Write a list of twelve appropriate books.
5. Assist the student in designing a content area assignment in which students can use periodical literature, books, general reference works (almanacs, encyclopedias,

encyclopedic biographies, atlases, and dictionaries) and audiovisual aids. [Have the student write out a list of appropriate materials for this use.] (p. 276)

Harris cites two sources of materials for teaching locational skills. They are *Learning to Use a Library* (Columbus, Ohio: Xerox Education Publications, 1973) and *Map and Globe Skills Kit* (Chicago: Science Research Associates, 1977).

General Organizational Skills

Pauk (1974) states that the ability to read does not in and of itself guarantee academic success in school. He then provides characteristics of students with poor study skills and methods to remediate or enhance those skills. Two skill areas deserve major emphasis: (1) scheduling time, and (2) work discipline.

Students experiencing difficulty with scheduling time followed one of two poor organizational patterns. The first pattern is that of applying no schedule to their time under the guise of keeping maximal flexibility. The result of following this pattern is chaos. Students are forever cramming for tests, missing assignment dates, missing appointments, or scheduling competing, simultaneous appointments. We refer to this pattern as "confusion squared." We all recognize this pattern and have followed it at various times, but we have sought to remedy conditions conducive to this style of life.

The second organizational pattern inherently is as poor as the first but may be adopted as a reaction to the first. It is the rigid, minute by minute scheduling of time. Each activity is planned for each hour of the day, many times into five-minute time segments. At first glance, this organizational pattern may appear optimal. However, when one carefully analyzes the situation, the individual functioning under this pattern is spending such an inordinate amount of time planning the schedule that little time remains to meet the work demands of the day.

Pauk (1974) suggests an optional organizational pattern that neither makes the student a slave to time, as the first pattern does, nor a slave to organization, as the second pattern does. He advocates a Time Reminder technique which even omits the word *schedule* from its description. The Time Reminder is simply the use of a 3″ x 5″ notecard on which students jot down both the critical activities that must be performed that day and brief notations of long-term planning activities that must be considered for further reference.

The Time Reminder could easily be adapted for use with LD secondary students. The teacher simply might have LD students turn in a copy of their Time Reminder cards for the following day prior to leaving school. Using this system, the LD teacher can review the activities listed and help students set realistic goals for homework. The LD teacher can also ascertain if LD students have the resources to engage in the activities listed.

It might be of further value to LD students if the teacher evaluated on the following day the activities accomplished at home. This procedure would enable the teacher to reinforce students and provide evaluative feedback on achievements.

Organizing Reading

Notetaking Skills

Underlining is a popular study technique used by postsecondary students when studying textbooks. This practice is not advised for LD students for several reasons. First, in most schools, textbooks are rented, and *all* students are prohibited from underlining under penalty of fine. As a study technique, underlining also encourages short-term memorization rather than integrated comprehension of the topic. That this is true may be seen in the texts of most students using the technique who have underlined profusely, as well as the texts of those who use the technique sparingly but must reread *all* the material to place the underlined material in its proper context.

The present authors would suggest notetaking as a viable alternative study strategy to underlining. Courtney (1965) presents four principles of student notetaking:

1. Students should write the notes in their own words rather than in the author's words.
2. Students should develop a consistent format when notetaking.
3. The notes should show when they were taken and from what source.
4. The notes should be complete and intelligible.

Courtney then provides seventeen strategies to improve student notetaking skills. Here are some examples:

(1) At the beginning of class, the teacher gives the students a mimeographed paper with three or four major points to be covered that day but with ample room for development of points, either in summary or outline form. Time is allotted toward the end of the period to compare and discuss the notes. At the same time, the teacher writes on the board the important items which developed under each point.

(4) . . . the teacher collects students notes without warning. . . . They are graded, returned and discussed.

(9) The teacher requires the students to develop full notes on an entire unit of study.

(13) . . . examine contrasting editorials or articles on the same . . . issue. The students are required to note or outline the opposing points or line of argument and reach an objective conclusion.

(15) . . . students make parallel columnar notes or outlines on their own textual reading, outside reading, laboratory work, and their personal observations or evaluations. (pp. 91-93)

Specific materials that teach notetaking skills are found in many sources. We have found that the sections on "Taking Notes on Written Materials" in *Quest: Academic Skills Program,* developed at the University of Michigan Reading and Learning Skills Center (Cohen, et al., 1973), and "Notetaking" in Carman and Adams (1972) *Study Skills: A Student's Guide for Survival* are helpful resources for the learning disabilities teacher.

Outlining Reading Passages

Outlining long reading passages is a familiar practice to most teachers, but many students are not required to construct outlines to help them organize and understand reading passages better. Outlining *does* help show the essential ideas of a passage.

When one considers outlining as a learning strategy for the LD secondary school student, its importance becomes evident. The outline can be used to help the LD student clarify difficult reading passages by highlighting the specific points the author is making and the organization (major ideas) of the passage. When the outline is completed, it makes an important contribution to the review process. The joint use of the outline and class notes is a powerful aid to learning (Fisher, 1967).

Fisher provides characteristics of a good outline. He states that the outline should be restricted to one topic, for example, the classification of local flora, and that the relationships between the divisions in the outline are clear. He suggests that this clarity can be determined by asking three questions:

1. Does each Roman number (main heading) bring out an important aspect of the topic?
2. Does each subdivision (upper case letter) help to develop its main heading?
3. Do all details (arabic numbers) relating to a (subdivision) appear together and in proper order? (p. 62)

It is not suggested that the outline to be developed from reading passages be expanded beyond the three levels described above. However, this recommendation is not to be applied to the use of an outline for writing. The detailed subdivisions will facilitate writing.

The teacher generally has two options on the type of outline to teach, the topic or the sentence outline. It is recommended that the teacher teach the sentence outline as it "provides a more comprehensive and therefore clearer development of the topic" (Fisher, 1967).

Survey Skills

Many persons writing in the area of reading and Johnson and Myklebust (1964) in learning disabilities have recognized the importance of surveying a passage to provide an organizational set for later intensive reading. Johnson and Myklebust provide the rudimentary skills of surveying. They suggest that a student may ". . . (a) survey main headings, (b) reading for main ideas and (c) reading for thought units" (p. 91). We interpret the third skill of Johnson and Myklebust as "reading for ideas rather than undifferentiated facts."

Johnson and Myklebust provide the skills used in surveying reading passages. However, they do not provide a systematic structure to use when surveying passages. One popular survey method that provides this systematic structure is the SQ3R method and its variations (S. E. Davis, 1970; Aukerman, 1972; Miller, 1973). The SQ3R method consists of five steps, as follows:

1. *Survey* — a rapid preview of the introduction, summary, first sentence in each paragraph, and visual aids provided.
2. *Question* — conversion of each section and subsection title into questions that can be used for future answers.
3. *Read* — rapid reading of the sections and subsections in search of answers to the questions generated in step 2.
4. *Recite* — answers to the questions posed written in the student's own words. The student summarizes each subsection of the passage.
5. *Review* — a written or oral statement of all that has been learned in the passage and the major ideas presented in the passage (Miller, 1973).

In three studies (Donald, 1967; Gruber, 1973; Garty, 1975), the SQ3R strategy was used with nonhandicapped junior high school students. The results showed no significant effects on standardized measures. However, on teacher-constructed tests and criterion measures, the students did show improvement. The results did not give strong support to the strategy even when strong reinforcers were paired with it. No studies were found using the strategy with senior high school students.

Several factors should be considered if the teacher is to use this strategy. First, course materials cues should be provided to LD students using the SQ3R technique (F. P. Robinson, 1946): (1) textbook cues, such as summary sentences, italics and boldface lettering, and enumerative information, (2) classroom cues, such as questions asked by the instructor, definitions, and applications, and (3) cues from previous examinations, including types of questions and format of questions.

Second, Robinson states succinctly that "it is obvious that any technique used must be automatic and simply [in its application] as to be subordinate to the task of reading" (p. 21). If students are so engrossed in following the SQ3R strategy, they may miss the content of the reading passage.

Third, the SQ3R must be individualized for each student. Graham (1976) provides such an adaptation for the survey step. Students should

1. skim the section.
2. read the heading sections.
3. read summary sentences.
4. read topic sentences.
5. interpret graphs and aids.
6. read the picture captions.
7. use any combination of the above techniques. (p. 9)

Finally, SQ3R must be used only with materials that are not above the student's instructional level (Graham, 1976).

Long-Term Storage and Information Retrieval

Three important concepts are involved in long-term storage and retrieval of reading material: (1) recall, (2) retention, and (3) recognition. Kaluger and Kolson (1969) list seven methods to assist in recalling information:

1. Mnenomics.
2. Rehearsal (see Laurita, 1972).
3. Paired association.
4. Active reading, for example, responding to the author's ideas.
5. Review.
6. Using main headings and different typefaces, such as italics and boldface.
7. Chaining.

Students can also recall material more readily if they will review it as soon as possible after reading and reread the notes, outlines, and summaries of the materials they have constructed earlier.

Retention is best enhanced by applying new concepts or ideas to practical problems (Dechant, 1973), such as reading about tennis skills and then actually practicing the skills on the court. The more chances one has to practice the idea in different situations, the better the retention of the concept or idea. The situations include people as well as setting. Retention of a concept is further enhanced by practicing or reviewing the concept or idea with a study group. The group emphasizes attributes of the concept and can provide more examples.

We suggest that an individual can better recognize information that has been read previously by taking trial tests. The trial test should be of the multiple-choice type so that the information to be recognized is available to the student.

To recall, retain, and recognize information requires integrated skills that are not mutually exclusive. Therefore, strategies that have been suggested for recall may also be used to enhance retention and recognition, and vice versa — that is, retention strategies also may be used to enhance recall and recognition.

DEMANDS OF THE CURRICULUM

One excellent way to determine an appropriate learning strategy for meeting the reading requirements of a specific course is to interview both the content teacher and, if possible, the students in the course to determine the reading demands of the course, unit, or topic. Carlson and Keimig (1978) have demonstrated how this is done in a wood technology course. The situation involved an LD student who was to be learning the use of the table saw. The lesson planning was as follows:

Day 1　Student is assigned to read fourteen pages in text as homework and answer ten questions covering the material. The completed answers are to be turned in on Day 2.

Day 2　Student is to listen to a demonstration lecture on the use of the table saw. Several demonstrations of the use of the table saw will be conducted by the teacher.

Day 3　Students are to take a written multiple choice test on the use of the table saw. Upon meeting criteria on the test, the student may then demonstrate the correct use of the table saw.

Day 4　Practice on table saw. Begin project.

This entire unit is based on the student's reading fourteen pages of text and successfully answering the study questions. The question is: How can a student who has difficulty in reading even get beyond day 1?

There are several ways the learning disabilities teacher can help the handicapped student complete this assignment. First, and this is the simplest solution, the teacher can conference with the wood technology teacher to determine if the demonstration lecture will highlight the ten questions and if the test on day 3 will contain questions that are outside the content of the study questions. If the test questions are not outside the content of the study questions, the study questions will be divided into two sets of five each. The first set will be used as a preorganizer, that is, to provide the student with the intent of the selection. The second set will be used as a postorganizer or reinforcer of the content covered in the textbook. The questions then can be orally previewed with the student by the teacher, an aide, or a peer prior to the resource room session on day 1.

MOTIVATION

The popular media have generally presented a distorted picture of the adolescent who attends school. Probably the most biased description of school is carried in flyers distributed by many school systems and especially postsecondary training institutions. The student is described as happy with courses in which the content is presented by teachers who create a classroom milieu of entertaining, social, learning experiences, all this occurring within a structure of formal and informal social-recreational activities that provide the student with a "total learning experience." In reality this description of school is not true. Students are required to work hard to learn.

Some students, including LD students, are not motivated to study, and hold poor attitudes toward their studies. This has probably been caused by repeated failure. These students have not been able to see that hard work in school includes the enjoyment of completing a task successfully. Rather, for them no work, work with a minimal effort, and hard work have all yielded the same effect: failure.

Learning disabled students will require concrete evidence that hard work pays off. We believe that positive reinforcers, both social and nonsocial, are required to change work habits of secondary LD students. We have found that point systems used with LD students are an excellent method of enhancing work attitudes. If the teacher is interested in pinpointing poor work habits and work attitudes, these factors are measured on the Brown-Holtzman survey (1965).

REFERENCES

Aukerman, R. C. *Reading in the secondary classroom.* New York: McGraw-Hill, 1972.

Ausubel, D. P., & Robinson, F. G. *School learning: An introduction to educational psychology.* New York: Holt, Rinehart & Winston, 1969.

Bailey, E. J. *Academic activities for adolescents with learning disabilities.* Evergreen, Colo.: Learning Pathways, Inc., 1975.

Beck, I. L., & Bolvin, J. O. A model for non-gradedness: The reading program for individually prescribed instruction. *Elementary English,* 1969, *46,* 130-135.

Blanton, W., Farr, R., & Tuinman, J. J. (Eds.). *Reading tests for the secondary grades: A review and evaluation.* Newark, Del.: International Reading Association, 1972.

Brown, W. F., & Holtzman, W. H. *Survey of Study Habits and Attitudes* (SSHA). New York: Psychological Corp., 1965.

Bruland, R. A. Learning words: Evaluating vocabulary development. *Journal of Reading,* 1974, *18,* 212-214.

Burmeister, L. E., & Stevens, I. J. Using library resources. In L. E. Burmeister (Ed.), *Reading strategies for secondary school teachers.* Menlo Park, Calif.: Addison-Wesley, 1974.

Carlson, S., & Keimig, J. *The strategies approach to secondary learning disabilities: Learning how to learn.* Presentation at Kansas Council for Exceptional Children, Topeka, March 1978.

Carman, R. A., & Adams, W. R. *Study skills: A student's guide for survival.* New York: Wiley, 1972.

Carroll, L. *Through the looking-glass and what Alice found there.* New York: Random House, 1965.

Cohen, R., King, W., Knudsvig, G., Markel, G. P., Patton, D., Shtogren, J., & Wilhelm, R. M. *Quest: Academic skills program.* New York: Harcourt Brace Jovanovich, Inc., 1973.

Courtney, B. L. Organization produced. In H. L. Herber (Ed.), *Developing study skills in secondary schools.* Newark, Del.: International Reading Association, 1965.

Crawford, E. E. Teaching essential reading skills — vocabulary. In L. E. Hafner (Ed.), *Improving reading in secondary schools.* New York: MacMillan, 1967.

Davis, F. B. The role of testing in reading instruction. In A. V. Olson & W. S. Ames (Eds.), *Teaching reading skills in secondary schools: Readings.* Scranton, Pa.: Intext Educational Publisher, 1970.

Davis, F. B. Psychometric research on comprehension in reading. *Reading Research Quarterly,* 1972, 7, 628-678.

Davis, S. E. High school and college instructors can't teach reading? Nonsense! In A. V. Olson & W. S. Ames (Eds.), *Teaching reading skills in secondary schools: Readings.* Scranton, Pa.: Intext Educational Publisher, 1970.

Dechant, E. *Reading improvement in the secondary school.* Englewood Cliffs, N.J.: Prentice-Hall, 1973.

Deighton, L. C. *Vocabulary development in the classroom.* New York: Teachers College Press, 1959.

Deighton, L. C. Developing vocabulary: Another look at the problem. In A. V. Olson & W. S. Ames (Eds.), *Teaching reading skills in secondary schools: Readings.* Scranton, Pa.: Intext Educational Publishers, 1970.

Della-Piana, G. M. *Reading diagnosis and prescription: An introduction.* New York: Holt, Rinehart & Winston, 1968.

Donald, M., Sr. The SQ3R method in grade seven. *Journal of Reading,* 1967, *11,* 33-43.

Dulin, K. L. New research on context clues. *Journal of Reading,* 1969, *13,* 33-38.

Dunn, L. M., Pockanart, P., Pfost, P., & Bruininks, R. W. The effectiveness of three reading approaches and an oral language stimulation program with disadvantaged children in the primary grades: An interim report after one year of the Cooperative Reading Project. IMRD Behavioral Science Monograph No. 7. Nashville: Institute on Mental Retardation and Intellectual Development, George Peabody College for Teachers, 1967.

Durrell, D. D. *Durrell analysis of reading difficulty.* New York: Harcourt, Brace & World, 1955.

Dykstra, R. *The cooperative research program in first-grade reading instruction.* Minneapolis: University of Minnesota, 1967.

Educational Testing Service. *Sequential Tests of Educational Progress* (STEP), Series 11. Trenton, N.J.: ETS, 1958.

Fareed, A. Interpretative responses in reading history and biology: An exploratory study. *Reading Research Quarterly,* 1971, *6,* 493-532.

Fisher, J. A. *Learning and study skills: A guide to independent learning.* Des Moines, Ia.: Drake University Reading and Study Skills Clinic, 1967.

Frostig, M. Disabilities and remediation in reading. *Academic Therapy,* 1972, *7,* 373-391.

Gallagher, J. J. Meaningful learning and retention: Intrapersonal cognitive variables. *Review of Educational Research,* 1964, *34,* 499-512.

Garty, R. H. *The effect of DRA and SQ3R on immediate and delayed recall of seventh-grade social studies material.* New Brunswick: Rutgers University, The State University of New Jersey, 1975. (ERIC Document Reproduction Service No. ED 108 125)

Gates, A. I. *The improvement of reading* (3rd ed.). New York: Macmillan, 1947.

Gates, A. I., & McKillop, A. S. *Gates-McKillop reading diagnostic tests.* New York: Teachers College Press, 1962.

Gattegno, C. *Teaching reading with words in color: A scientific study of the problems of reading.* New York: Xerox Corp., 1968.

Gibson, E. J. Learning to read. In A. V. Olson & W. S. Ames (Eds.), *Teaching reading skills in secondary schools: Readings.* Scranton, Pa.: Intext Educational Publisher, 1970.

Gibson, E. J., & Levin, H. *The psychology of reading.* Cambridge, Mass.: MIT Press, 1975.

Gold, L. A comparative study of individualized and group reading instruction with tenth grade underachievers in reading. In J. A. Figurel (Ed.), *Improvement in reading through classroom practice,* International Reading Association Conference Proceedings (Vol. 9). Newark, Del.: International Reading Association, 1964.

Goodman, L., & Mann, L. *Learning disabilities in the secondary schools: Issues and practices.* New York: Grune & Stratton, 1976.

Graham, S. E. *SQ3R: Is it an effective technique?* Unpublished manuscript, University of Kansas Medical Center, 1976.

Gray, W. S. A modern program of reading instruction for the grades and high school. In G. M. Whipple (Ed.), *Report of the National Committee on Reading,* Twenty-fourth Yearbook of the National Society for the Study of Education, Part 1. Bloomington, Ill: Public School Publishing Co., 1925.

Grayum, H. S. Skimming in reading: A fine art for modern needs. In A. V. Olson & W. S. Ames (Eds.), *Teaching reading skills in secondary schools: Readings.* Scranton, Pa.: Intext Educational Publisher, 1970.

Gruber, P. M. Junior high boasts super stars. *Journal of Reading,* 1973, *6,* 601-603.

Hafner, L. E., & Karlin, R. A suggested curriculum for teaching reading skills to youth who are reluctant readers. In L. E. Hafner (Ed.), *Improving reading in secondary schools.* New York: Macmillan, 1967.

Harris, A. J., & Serwer, B. L. *Comparison of reading approaches in first-grade teaching with disadvantaged children (The CRAFT Project).* Final Report, Cooperative Research Project No. 2677. New York: Division of Teacher Education, The City University of New York, 1969. (ERIC Document No. 010037)

Harris, A. J., & Sipay, E. R. *How to increase reading ability* (6th ed.). New York: David McKay, 1975.

Herber, H. L. (Ed.). *Developing study skills in secondary schools.* Newark, Del.: International Reading Association, 1965.

Hill, F. G. *A comparison of the effectiveness of Words in Color with the basic reading program used in the Washington Elementary School District.* Unpublished doctoral dissertation, Arizona State University, 1967.

Hoover, K. H. *The professional teacher's handbook: A guide for improving instruction in today's middle and secondary schools* (2nd ed.). Boston: Allyn & Bacon, 1976.

Hori, A. K. O. *An investigation of the efficacy of a questioning training procedure on increasing the reading comprehension performance of junior high school learning disabled students.* Unpublished master's thesis, University of Kansas, 1977.

Johnson, D. J., & Myklebust, H. R. *Learning disabilities: Educational principles and practices.* New York: Grune & Stratton, 1964.

Johnson, H. W. Another study method: Three-level outlining method. *Journal of Developmental Reading,* 1964, *7,* 269-282.

Kaluger, G., & Kolson, C. J. *Reading and learning disabilities.* Columbus, Ohio: Merrill, 1969.

Laurita, R. E. Rehearsal: A technique for improving reading comprehension. *Academic Therapy,* 1972, *8,* 103-111.

Lerner, J. W. *Children with learning disabilities: Theories, diagnosis, teaching strategies.* Boston: Houghton Mifflin, 1976.

Levin, J. R. Inducing comprehension in poor readers. *Journal of Educational Psychology,* 1973, *65,* 19-24.

Levin, J. R., Devine-Hawkins, P., Kerst, S. M., & Guttmann, J. Individual differences in learning from pictures and words: The development and application of an instrument. *Journal of Educational Psychology,* 1974, *66,* 296-303.

Lockmiller, P., & DiNello, M. C. Words in Color vs. a basal reader program with retarded readers in grade two. *Journal of Educational Research,* 1970, *63,* 333-334.

Manzo, A. V. The ReQuest procedure. *Journal of Reading,* 1969, *13,* 123-126.

Maxwell, M. J. Skimming and scanning improvement: The needs, assumptions and knowledge base. *Journal of Reading Behavior,* 1972-1973, *5,* 47-59.

Miller, W. H. *Diagnosis and correction of reading difficulties in secondary school students.* New York: The Center for Applied Research in Education, Inc., 1973.

Mills, D. M. Corrective and remedial reading instruction in the secondary school. In J. A. Figurel, *Reading as an intellectual activity, International Reading Association Conference Proceedings* (Vol. 8). New York: Scholastic Magazines, 1963.

Minskoff, E. H. Remediating auditory verbal learning disabilities: The role of questions in teacher-pupil interaction. *Journal of Learning Disabilities,* 1974, *7,* 406-413.

Murphy, J. F. Learning by testing: A public school approach to learning disabilities. *Academic Therapy,* 1972-1973, *8,* 167-189.

Newland, T. E. Tested intelligence in children. *School Psychology,* 1977, *3,* 1-44. (Monograph)

Niles, O. S. Organization perceived. In H. L. Herber (Ed.), *Developing study skills in secondary schools.* Newark, Del.: International Reading Association, 1965.

Olson, A. V., & Ames, W. S. *Teaching reading skills in secondary schools.* Scranton, Pa.: Intext Educational Publisher, 1972.

Otto, W., & Ford, V. *Teaching adults to read.* New York: Houghton Mifflin, 1967.

Palkes, H., Stewart, M., & Kahana, B. Porteus maze performance of hyperactive boys after training in self-directed verbal commands. *Child Development,* 1968, *39,* 817-826.

Pauk, W. *How to study in college.* Boston: Houghton Mifflin, 1974.

Paulsen, L., & Larmer, N. Using writing to help the poor reader. In H. A. Robinson & S. J. Rauch (Eds.), *Corrective reading in the high school classroom.* Newark, Del.: International Reading Association, 1966.

Pitman, I. J. Learning to read: An experiment. *Journal of Royal Society of Arts,* 1961, *109,* 149-180.

Raygor, A. L. College reading improvement and personality change. *Journal of Counseling Psychology,* 1959, *6,* 211-217.

Robinson, F. P. *Effective study.* New York: Harper Brothers, 1946.

Robinson, H. A., & Rauch, S. J. (Eds.). *Corrective reading in the high school classroom.* Newark, Del.: International Reading Association, 1966.

Ross, J. D., & Ross, C. M. *Ross test of higher cognitive processes.* San Rafael, Calif.: Academic Therapy, 1976.

Science Research Associates. *SRA achievement series* (Multilevel Edition). Chicago: SRA, 1963.

Skinner, B. F. *The technology of teaching.* New York: Appleton-Century-Crofts, 1968.

Smith, H. K. Secondary school programs. a. Research in reading for different purposes. In J. A. Figurel (Ed.), *Changing concepts of reading instruction, International Reading Association Conference Proceedings* (Vol. 6). New York: Scholastic Magazines, 1961.

Smith, N. B. *Reading instruction for today's children*. Englewood Cliffs, N.J.: Prentice-Hall, 1963.

Smith, N. B. Junior high level 1. Reading for depth. In J. A. Figurel (Ed.), *Reading and inquiry, International Reading Association Conference Proceedings* (Vol. 10). Newark, Del.: International Reading Association, 1965.

Spache, G. D. *Diagnostic reading scales* (Rev. ed.). Monterey, Calif.: CTB/McGraw-Hill, 1972.

Strang, R. *Reading diagnosis and remediation*. Newark: Del.: International Reading Association, 1968.

Thomas, E. L., & Robinson, H. A. *Improving reading in every class*. Boston: Allyn & Bacon, 1972.

Tinker, M. A. Uses and limitations of speed of reading programs in school. In A. V. Olson & W. S. Ames (Eds.), *Teaching reading skills in secondary schools: Readings*. Scranton, Pa.: Intext Educational Publisher, 1970.

Tubbs, S. L., & Moss, S. *Human communication: An interpersonal perspective*. New York: Random House, 1974.

Voix, R. G. *Evaluating reading and study skills in the secondary classroom: A guide for content teachers*. Newark, Del.: International Reading Association, 1968.

Wallace, G., & McLoughlin, J. A. *Learning disabilities: Concepts and characteristics*. Columbus, Ohio: Merrill, 1975.

Wapner, I. *The ITA in Lompoc: A longitudinal study*. Paper presented at the International Reading Association, Kansas City, Mo., May 1969. (ERIC Document ED 031-387)

Warburton, F. W., & Southgate, V. *ITA: An independent evaluation*. London: Murray & Chambers, 1969.

Warner, M. M. *Teaching learning disabled junior high students to use visual imagery as a strategy for facilitating recall of reading passages*. Unpublished doctoral dissertation, University of Kansas, 1977.

Wiener, M., & Cramer, W. Reading and reading difficulty: A conceptual analysis. In A. V. Olson & W. S. Ames (Eds.), *Teaching reading skills in secondary schools*. Scranton, Pa.: Intext Educational Publisher, 1970.

Woolman, M. Cultural asynchrony and contingency in learning disorders. In J. Hellmuth (Ed.), *Learning disorders* (Vol. 1). Seattle: Special Child Publications, 1965, pp. 123-168.

WRITING: STRATEGIES AND METHODS

Writing Characteristics of LD Adolescents

Assessing Written Expression Deficits in LD Adolescents

Improving LD Adolescents' Attitudes Toward Writing

The Content Components of Writing

The Craft Components of Writing

Kerrigan's Integrated Method of Teaching Composition

Written Test-Taking Strategies

Significant progress has been made in recent years in understanding the processes involved in language learning. The majority of the work completed pertains to spoken language and to learning to read. Relatively little attention, however, has been devoted to written language. Facility with written expression is a prerequisite for successful performance in the secondary schools and in postsecondary situations. The curriculum in the secondary schools demands that students take notes from lectures, complete essay examinations, and write themes and research reports. Demands for good writing skills in postsecondary situations may be similarly high. For example, writing may be required in applying for college or job placements, as part of an actual work assignment, and in meeting personal needs, such as letter writing. Deficits in written expression can be particularly devastating because the product of the writing act is so visible and permanent.

Irmscher (1972) discusses how many students tend to underestimate the extent to which people are required to write in today's society, and he feels that they ignore the "dependency, inconvenience, and frustration that occur when an individual lacks the capacity and confidence to do a job of writing on his own" (p. 8). Irmscher also contends that to think of writing only in terms of its "most obvious practical uses is to ignore a number of other benefits that can be derived from writing" (p. 8). Specifically, the act of writing is (1) a visible indication of what students know and what they are thinking, (2) a means to organize, control, and direct thought, and (3) an aid to thinking and ideation.

Lerner (1976) contends that "poor facility in expressing thoughts through written language is probably the most prevalent disability of the communication skills" (p. 266). This contention is based on the fact that writing is such a complex skill that it is dependent on reception and comprehension of auditory and visual language forms. Chalfant and Scheffelin

104

(1969) have specified the following as subtasks in the competent use of writing as a means of self-expression: "possess the need to communicate, formulate the message (including sequencing the general content of the message and retrieving the appropriate auditory-language symbols which best express the intent of the communication), retrieve the appropriate auditory-language signals, and produce the appropriate motor movements for producing the graphic symbols" (p. 111).

Myklebust (1965) believes that writing is "man's highest achievement verbally and is achieved only when all of the preceding levels have been established" (p. 6). Kellog (1971) has illustrated the hierarchical relationship among various components of the language arts. It is essential that, prior to mastering the intricacies of written expression, students have some knowledge and expertise in the areas of listening, speaking, reading, spelling, handwriting, punctuation, and capitalization. Difficulties in any of these skills will likely interfere with the normal acquisition and use of written language. (See Figure 4.1)

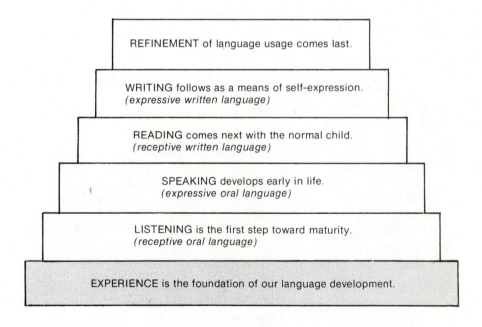

Figure 4.1. Steps in the development of language skills.

From "Listening" by R. E. Kellog, in *Guiding Children's Language*, P. Lamb, Editor. (Dubuque, Iowa: William C. Brown, 1971), p. 118.

Before discussing the reasons for writing failure of LD adolescents, it may be helpful to outline the developmental hierarchy of writing tasks from early childhood through adulthood. Chalfant and Scheffelin (1969) present a sequence of steps involved in the writing act:

1. Scribbling
2. Tracing
   a. connected letters or figures
   b. disconnected letters or figures
3. Copying
   a. from a model
   b. from memory
   c. symbolic and nonsymbolic
4. Completion tasks
   a. figure completion
   b. word completion — supplying missing letters
      (1) multiple choice
      (2) recall
   c. sentence completion — supplying missing word
5. Writing from dictation
   a. writing letters as they are spoken
   b. writing words and sentences
   c. supplying missing word
   d. supplying missing sentence
6. Propositional writing

This chapter focuses on methods for dealing with LD adolescents who are competent in skills 1 through 4 but evidence written expression deficits in tasks related to skills 5 and 6. That portion of the population that is severely or profoundly learning disabled and evidences disorders primarily in skills 1 through 4 probably will require intensive clinical approaches toward improved writing skills. The reader is referred to the work of Johnson and Myklebust (1967) for a discussion of appropriate methods to counteract such deficits.

This chapter will cover seven major topics:

1. Writing characteristics of LD adolescents.
2. Assessment of written expression deficits in LD adolescents.
3. Improvement of LD adolescents' attitudes toward writing.
4. The content components of writing (such as generating ideas, describing, explaining, and drawing comparisons and contrasts).
5. The craft components of writing (such as structuring and organizing themes, vocabulary development, and notetaking).

6. Kerrigan's integrated method of teaching composition.
7. Written test-taking strategies.

WRITING CHARACTERISTICS OF LD ADOLESCENTS

Adolescents with mild to moderate learning disabilities usually demonstrate competence on writing tasks through the fourth step in the Chalfant and Scheffelin (1969) developmental hierarchy. However, they probably had difficulty in earlier stages of language development, for example, in listening, speaking, and reading. They achieved their current level of performance in written expression at a slower pace than their grade-level peers, and their current performance is characterized by poor organization, a limited word pool, a high frequency of mechanical errors (spelling, capitalization, and punctuation), and limited monitoring of writing errors. To compensate for these problems, they (1) learn to depend on classmates for use of their lecture notes, (2) learn to use a tape recorder during class sessions, (3) pass essay examinations by providing answers in outline form or by answering examination questions orally, and (4) keep their written tasks to a minimum whenever possible. While these LD adolescents are less facile than their grade-level peers, they have enough writing skills to warrant intervention in this area without going back to work on prerequisite skills, such as reading, before intervention in writing is undertaken.

A limited number of studies deal specifically with the writing characteristics of LD adolescents. Myklebust (1965, 1973) used the *Picture Story Language Test* to study the writing abilities of normal and exceptional children. This test analyzes three dimensions of written expression: productivity (total words, total sentences, words per sentence), correctness (syntax), and ideation (degree of abstractness or concreteness of expression). Using four different age groups (nine, eleven, thirteen, and fifteen), Myklebust (1973) compared the written language of a reading disabled population with a normal population. The reading disabled group was found to be markedly deficient at all ages in output of written language as measured by total words and total sentences written. In most cases, the reading disability group produced about one-third the output of the control group, suggesting a lack of fluency and a laboriousness in the task of written expression. In the words-per-sentence score, the performance of the reading disability group was similar to the control group at ages nine, eleven, and thirteen; but at age fifteen, the performance dropped markedly. The reading disability group was also deficient on the syntax measures, such as correct use of tense, punctuation, and word order. An interesting trend was noted in syntax facility as a function of age. At nine years of age, the reading

107

disability syntax quotient was seventeen points below average; but at eleven, thirteen, and fifteen, it was only about seven points lower. Thus, deficiencies in syntax are somewhat overcome by age eleven, but like normal readers, the reading disabled group reached a plateau at age eleven and evidenced few gains in syntax thereafter. Finally, the reading disabled group was also retarded in use of abstract meaning — a skill closely associated with language fluency and the size of the word pool available to the student. The ability to use and understand abstractions in communication is of critical importance to adolescents in successfully meeting secondary curricular demands. The fifteen-year-olds were markedly inferior to the normal controls on this index.

The ability to monitor one's performance in writing is critical to good performance. Deshler (1978) has found that LD high school students evidence a monitoring deficit on academic tasks that require their detection of self-generated and externally generated errors. On a creative writing task, for example, LD students detected only one-third of the errors they committed. The control group detected more than twice as many errors as the LD group on the same task. The repercussions of such performance in academic and future employment situations are obvious. Learning disabled adolescents should be made aware of the quality of their performance in written work. They should be taught monitoring strategies and instructed to be selective in their choice of words and sentences when using written expression so as to limit the number of errors committed.

In a study conducted on students in remedial writing classes in a community college setting, Higgins (1975) investigated the composition of the individual sentence and the grammatical relationships among sentences in essays written by college freshmen. A summary of the errors of highest frequency is provided in Table 4.1.

As an extention of his study on the writing characteristics of students, Higgins analyzed instructional materials that were available to teach writing skills. He found that the exercises and skills stressed in these materials usually did *not* correspond with the difficulties experienced by students in written expression. He concluded that most instructional materials are developed without careful consideration of students' instructional needs.

ASSESSING WRITTEN EXPRESSION DEFICITS IN LD ADOLESCENTS

The goal of language arts instruction in writing is to prepare students to be effective communicators of ideas. The initial steps in writing instruction usually include having students dictate stories to teachers. As mechanical skills in handwriting and spelling are acquired, students engage in

TABLE 4.1

Errors of Highest Frequency Occurring and Recurring in College Freshman Essays

Fault	Percentage of all papers in which fault occurred	Percentage of all papers in which fault recurred
Misspelling (excluding homonyms)	83	64
Inappropriate contraction	78	55
Inappropriate use of verb *get*	69	50
Missing commas around parenthetical (including nonrestrictive) element	65	34
Redundancy	64	36
Missing possessive apostrophe	62	21
Misspelling of homonym	57	30
Missing needed comma following introductory element	57	27
Poor subordination or coordination	53	26
Pronoun-antecedent nonagreement or general shift in number	53	16
Inappropriate use of noun *thing*	52	30
Vague pronoun reference	52	11
Run-together sentence (with or without comma)	50	27
Missing needed comma before coordinate conjunction	48	16
Sentence fragment	45	20
Shift in person	45	20
Miscellaneous superfluous comma	44	27
Wrong meaning of word	39	18
Nonparallel structure	38	8
Miscellaneous inappropriate colloquialism	37	13
Word substitution (usually inadvertent; e.g., "He hid it *is* the closet," for *in*)	37	10
Subject-verb nonagreement	36	15
Wrong or missing ending on regular verb form	35	20
Miscellaneous omission of word	35	10
Unidiomatic preposition	33	7
Wrongly included or omitted noun ending (excluding possessive)	31	13

more independent writing activities. By about the fifth grade, most students are able to write well-structured paragraphs. When students fail to reach this skill level, the teacher should assess pupils' written language to ascertain specific areas of difficulty. The teacher must rely on both standardized and informal measures to assess LD students' performance on these writing skills.

The learning disabilities teacher should evaluate a variety of subskills that are necessary for successfully meeting the demands of the secondary curriculum. These skills have been divided into three main categories in an outline adapted from Hennings and Grant (1974): (1) attitude toward writing, (2) ability to generate and deal with ideas on the content, and (3) ability to deal with the mechanical aspects or the craft of written expression. The outline is presented in Table 4.2.

Wallace and Larsen (1978) suggest that the first step in informal assessment of written language is to obtain a representative writing sample from students. This may be secured by asking students to write a story about something that is interesting and motivating to them. For example, students may be shown an intriguing picture to write about or asked to write an account of an event that they have witnessed or participated in. The key consideration is high student motivation so that the best possible samples of their written language are obtained. LD students should be allowed all the time they need to complete the assignment.

The profile form in Figure 4.2 has been developed for use in the informal assessment of groups of students or individuals. The use of such a profile enables teachers to isolate the particular writing problems of students and gain direction for more in-depth analysis of specific deficit areas. Wallace and Larsen (1978) point out that the more mechanical components of written language (punctuation, capitalization, and spelling, for example) lend themselves to objective assessment, but the more abstract components of written expression (content and organization, for example) "must be judged in relation to the student's intelligence, experiential background, and motivation to communicate by written symbols" (p. 397).

There are two diagnostic tests available that have been standardized and may be useful to the teacher in developing educational programs for LD adolescents. These instruments are the *Picture Story Language Test* (PSLT) (Myklebust, 1965) and the *Sequential Tests of Educational Progress* (STEP) (Educational Testing Service, 1958).

The PSLT provides measures of students' written language along three dimensions: (1) *productivity* (total number of words, total number of sentences, and words per sentence), (2) *correctness* (word usage, word endings, and punctuation), and (3) *meaning* (along an abstract-concrete continuum). Scores in each of these areas may be converted into age equivalents,

TABLE 4.2
**Written Expression Skills Requiring Assessment and Intervention
in LD Students**

I. Attitude toward writing
    A. Emotional blocks to writing assignments
    B. Motivation to write
II. Content
    A. Reflection of the world
        1. Description
        2. Reports of happenings
        3. Procedures
        4. Retelling
        5. Summaries
    B. Conception of relationships
        1. Comparison and contrast
        2. Classification
        3. Qualitative analysis
        4. Sequential analysis
        5. Cause and effect
        6. Explanation in terms of supporting principles
    C. Projection of explanatory schemes and designs
        1. Hypothesis
        2. Conceptual schemes
        3. Design: Plan of action
    D. Expression of personal view
        1. Feelings
        2. Preferences
        3. Opinions
        4. Judgment
III. Craft
    A. Structuring paragraphs and themes
        1. Organizing ideas
        2. Sequencing ideas
    B. Vocabulary development
        1. Choosing words to express experiences
        2. Synonyms
    C. Building sentences
        Generating a variety of sentence patterns
    D. Writing questions
    E. Notetaking
        1. From class lecture
        2. From text material
    F. Summaries and paraphrases
    G. Mechanical factors
        1. Punctuation
        2. Capitalization
        3. Neatness
        4. Spelling
    H. Monitoring written expression
        1. Habits of checking for errors
        2. Ability to detect errors
        3. Ability to correct errors
    I. Written test-taking

111

Comments	Designator	Skill Area	
		Emotional blocks Motivation to write	ATTITUDE
		Description writing Relationship writing Explanatory writing Personal views	CONTENT
		Organizing ideas Vocabulary Building sentences Writing questions Notetaking Summaries Punctuation Capitalization Spelling Neatness Monitoring performance	CRAFT
		Test-taking skills	OTHER

Pupil's Name:

Designators: A — performance on grade level
B — performance below grade level, but not critical
C — critical deficit area

Figure 4.2. Profile form for the informal assessment of student writing skills.

112

percentiles, and stanines. The adequacy of the reliability and validity sections of this test have been questioned (Anastasi, 1968), and, therefore, scores from the test should be interpreted with caution.

The items included in the STEP require students to select modifications to correct written passages. Students must identify errors in the items presented and choose more correct alternatives. The subject matter is presented in the form of reports, essays, directions, and the like. Wallace and Larsen (1978) note that while the STEP does not include an analysis of students' own writing, the inclusion of the additional task of selecting appropriate revisions to correct errors may be helpful to the teacher in determining written expression disorders. The STEP includes items that fall into the following five categories:

1. Organization — ordering of ideas, events, facts.
2. Conventions — syntax, word choice, punctuation, and spelling.
3. Critical thinking — detection of unstated assumptions, cause-and-effect relationships and anticipation of the needs of readers.
4. Effectiveness — adequacy of emphasis and development, exactness of expression, economy, simplicity, and variety.
5. Appropriateness — choice of a level of usage suitable to purpose and reader, i.e., using the right "tone" and appropriate vocabulary.

While the reliability and validity of both the PSLT and the STEP have been questioned, each instrument breaks down the writing act into measurable components for the teacher. The basic components tapped by each instrument can serve as guidelines for areas to be *informally* assessed by the teacher. The authors recommend that the teacher read Myklebust's two volumes (1965, 1973) on writing, as they present a thorough discussion of written expression, of disabilities in written expression, and of means of assessing those disabilities.

IMPROVING LD ADOLESCENTS' ATTITUDES TOWARD WRITING

The great complexity of conveying thoughts in writing adequately is understood when one realizes that written language depends on the successful completion of *all* previous stages of language development (Wallace & McLoughlin, 1975). LD adolescents who have not mastered other language skills, such as reading and speaking, are likely to become frustrated and anxious, and even give up when they are repeatedly expected to complete complex writing assignments such as themes, essay examinations, research reports, and class notes. Consequently, the first consideration of the learning disabilities teacher when beginning work with LD adolescents' writing disorders must be to deal with the attitudes of students toward writing. Minimal progress in improving student writing deficits will be made unless anxieties and fears about the writing assignments have been dealt with and students are motivated to write. For example, Steve, an LD student in the eighth grade, had a verbal IQ of 120. He showed good comprehension of reading materials presented by the teacher, and he was quite creative in developing and verbally relating short stories. However, whenever Steve was asked to demonstrate his competence in writing, he would evidence what Drake and Cavanaugh (1970) have called "paralysis of effort." The answers or stories that he could verbally convey to the LD teacher seemed to disappear when he tried to express them in writing. In some classes his anxiety and fear over trying to put his thoughts into writing were so high that he would start to hyperventilate and perspire.

Irmscher (1972) contends that student attitudes toward writing are of first importance. Since writing is primarily a psychological act and not a mechanical skill, the feelings of students must be the major and a first consideration of the learning disabilities teacher.

The following suggestions may help the learning disabilities teacher promote proper attitudes toward writing in LD adolescents:

1. LD adolescents should understand that initially they should be mainly concerned with their ideas and not the mechanical components of writing. While correct capitalization, punctuation, and spelling are important and essential components in effective written communication, they should be reintroduced only after these adolescents feel comfortable in dealing with written assignments. Too frequently, LD adolescents have experienced their greatest failure in trying to achieve perfection in the mechanics of writing at the expense of the expression of their ideas. For LD adolescents who are hesitant to express their ideas in writing, the first goal is to increase productivity. Elbow (1973) suggests that students engage in "freewriting" exercises at least three times a week. This method encourages students simply to write for ten minutes. They are instructed to write as quickly as they can, never to stop to look back, never to correct the spelling of any word, or to even think about what they are doing. The objective is to have students put on paper whatever is in their minds. The only requirement is to never stop during the ten-minute period. Elbow maintains that the major advantage to freewriting is that it does not allow students to edit their work. He contends that the habit of compulsive, premature editing by students inhibits their ability to produce ideas.

Editing is introduced and required of students after they become at ease with putting words down on paper.

2. LD adolescents should be exposed to a broad range of experiences to enhance the pool of knowledge from which they write. Hennings and Grant (1974) indicate that there are three things teachers should do to help students create idea-content for expression in their writing: (a) provide students with first-hand experiences as a base from which to develop ideas; (b) allow students to express their ideas through nonverbal and dramatic activity; and (c) provide students with opportunities to talk about their ideas. Oral sharing of impressions and ideas is a vital first step in the process of translating ideas into the verbal patterns of written expression. Conversation, informal small-group discussions, and informal oral presentations may all be used as means of encouraging LD adolescents to talk about their experiences.

3. Tape recorders can be used to advantage with LD adolescents who are reluctant to write. Initially, students can simply record their impressions on the tape. These statements can then be typed so that students have a written record of their thoughts. On playbacks they can decide how to improve the flow, organization, and presentation of their ideas. At a later date, students may record ideas from a skeletal outline prepared before the recording session to improve the organization and consistency of their presentations.

4. Some teachers have found that students enjoy keeping daily or weekly journals, which also provide them with evidence of how their abilities to use written language improve with practice. Elbow (1973) contends that the most useful thing students can do to improve their facility with writing is to keep freewriting diaries. Again, the activity should be carried on for only ten minutes and should not necessarily be a complete accounting of a student's day, but rather a brief sample for each day.

It cannot be stressed too often how important it is to take this first step in dealing with students' attitudes toward writing. While writing instruction should begin with attitudes and move on to skill development, the teacher should always be sensitive to students' attitudes toward writing assignments. Activities such as those outlined above may have to be used periodically to maintain LD adolescents' motivation and concentration on the writing instruction.

THE CONTENT COMPONENTS OF WRITING

Generating Ideas

Laurence (1972) contends that writing is primarily a semantic and cognitive process. As such, it capitalizes on students' ability to think inductively and on the cognitive skills they already have. In everyday living, older students impose order on information by such means as contrasting, comparing, and categorizing. They also formulate summaries and generalizations about and extrapolate from everyday observations. Therefore, the main focus of activities in written language should be to teach students how to translate their thoughts about everyday observations into writing. Writing should be based on an inquiry method; students should be taught to ask questions, manipulate data, and extrapolate from data. In addition, students should develop the habit of regularly engaging in an "internal dialogue" about their observations.

Irmscher (1972) has specified the basic types of questions students should ask themselves to generate ideas for writing. The teacher should require LD adolescents to ask themselves these questions regularly until asking them becomes an automatic way of responding to situations that are to be written about. The questions, in summary form, are as follows:

ACTION
What happened?
What is happening?
What will happen?
What is it?
ACTOR-AGENT
Who did it?
Who is doing it?
What did it?
What kind of agent is it?
SCENE
Where did it happen?
Where is it happening?
When did it happen?
What is the background?
MEANS
How was it done?
What means were used?
PURPOSE
Why?

The question areas outlined above are by no means exhaustive; instead, they evoke kernel thoughts to be further developed by the students. The teacher must recognize the importance of exposing students to a variety of experiences and of teaching them how to use these experiences and observations actively as the basis for the content of their writing. The detailed answers for the content of writing can come from a variety of sources. Major sources of information that students should be encouraged to rely on are class texts and supplementary reading materials, teacher explanations, demonstrations, and lectures, and television. The application of good listening skills during a class session, for example, will provide students with information stores for writing assignments. Hennings and Grant (1974) suggest that teachers use pictures, titles, objects, music, words, trips, newsworthy events, world and school issues, and content from the sciences and social studies as a means of structuring idea-stimulating activities. Some of these will be discussed below.

Unusual pictures are especially effective as means of triggering ideas for writing. For example, photographs in *The Images of Man* kit (Scholastic Books) have proved highly successful in generating writing from high school students (Deshler, 1978). LD students can bring their unique backgrounds to the situation to produce different ideas. Films, sound filmstrips, or television shows can also stimulate writing. Adams and Klein (1975) have specified some of the merits of using films to teach composition: (1) there is immediacy of impact (students need not rely on detailed out-of-class reading), (2) understanding the film does not depend on reading comprehension, (3) films encourage originality, (4) films hold a natural appeal to students, (5) films can be used for a variety of writing purposes (for example, they can be used as a source of content or for character analysis), (6) the visual nature of films produces a broader range of emotions and reactions, and (7) the teacher can present a wide range of topics at different difficulty levels through films.

A title that catches students' imaginations or relates to something students have experienced may promote writing. The following list is suggestive of areas that may hold appeal for LD adolescents: Tornado Alert, No School Today, Panic, Run for Your Life, Lost in a Crowd.

With LD adolescents, discussions of world, national, and school problems can provide writing ideas. This information allows LD adolescents to confront issues and develop opinions that they can support. Controversial issues in school, such as regulations or quality of cafeteria food, provide the basis for position papers.

In summary, the teacher's primary tasks in this phase of teaching writing skills to LD students are as follows:

1. To convince LD students that in everyday life they deal with the data of their world in relatively sophisticated cognitive terms (such as comparing, contrasting, and ordering) and that writing is the process of translating those thoughts and ideas into words on a page. The teacher should reinforce students for creative thoughts and critical observations.

2. To encourage LD students to ask questions about events. The learning disabilities teacher should serve as a model by asking such questions. Students should be required to ask a set of questions (for example, the ones outlined by Irmscher and given at the beginning of this section) about their observations and they should be reinforced for doing so.

3. To provide LD students with a broad range of experiences so that they will have a source of information from which to write.

Reflecting the World

In reflective content, students attempt to translate their impressions of objects, materials, and events into accurate representations in writing. People tend to observe what they expect and see what they are looking for. Consequently, the teacher should instruct students in what to expect and things to look for. LD students are often passive observers and will need structured guidelines and suggestions from the teacher to increase the productivity of their observations. Here are some strategies and methods for improving some of the written expression skills described in Table 4.2. The authors have attempted to choose representative factors from the table for discussion.

Description

Before LD students can look at specific situations and perceive key elements about which to write, they need a *framework* within which to organize the major attributes. Such a framework will guide the students' observations and will provide the basis of an outline from which to write. Hennings and Grant (1974) suggest that students be taught to develop and use attribute guides (for objects, places, and people to be described). An example of an attribute guide for an object is given in Figure 4.3.

Such a guide structures students' observations and directs their attention to salient features. The teacher should always be concerned about the transfer of this skill from isolated activities or assignments to performances in the regular classroom. To insure this transfer, the teacher should require

Object to be described _____

    Color:

    Shape:

    Size:

        Height, breadth

    Weight:

    Texture:

    Temperature:

    State of motion:

        Speed, evenness, relationship to other things

    Aroma:

    Taste:

Figure 4.3. An attribute guide for describing an object.

students to use the same guide in numerous settings until they have internalized the components of the guide for automatic and independent application. Obviously, the type of framework may vary from one subject area to another and from student to student. It is most important that students acquire the habit of relying on such a framework as an aid in written expression.

Procedures

Various assignments in school require students to describe a sequence of actions or steps; for example, explaining how to carry out an experiment, how to bake a cake, or how to go from one location to another. The first

119

step is for the student to identify the major events involved and the sequence of their happening. One effective way to communicate a given procedure is in a flow diagram. All writing need not be in paragraph form! As LD students are taught to use flexibility in their reading assignments, so they should be taught to use different writing styles for different writing assignments. The objective is clear communication. The flow diagram is particularly advantageous for LD adolescents for the following reasons: (1) it provides a simplified structure within which students can organize their thoughts; (2) the visual diagram serves as a memory aid to students using the information later; and (3) it allows students to use shortened expressions (almost telegraphic expressions) and does not require transitions, and such. Figure 4.4 provides an example of how a flow diagram can be used to describe a sequence of steps clearly and systematically.

Another effective approach to describing procedures is the outline. Outlining is straightforward and clearly illustrates the major steps and sequences of the procedure, as well as the relation of one step to another.

Conceptualizing Relationships

In writing assignments, when the content is reflection, students are involved in presenting an accurate picture of the world as it is. However, with conceptual content, the job is to identify the interrelationships of events, ideas, and so on.

Comparison and Contrast

Comparison is a statement of likenesses and similarities, while contrast deals with differences. Often, in writing, it is necessary to compare *and* contrast, combining information from more than one source. To teach LD students to deal with likenesses and differences, the teacher must provide them with opportunities to recognize common features within differing items, ideas, and events. Laurence (1972) suggests that prior to requiring students to write comparisons and contrasts, they should be able to *identify* statements and questions of comparison and contrast. For example:

1. Jenner and Pasteur are both famous for their work in immunization.
2. A softball is larger than a baseball.
3. How is a drum similar to a telephone?

120

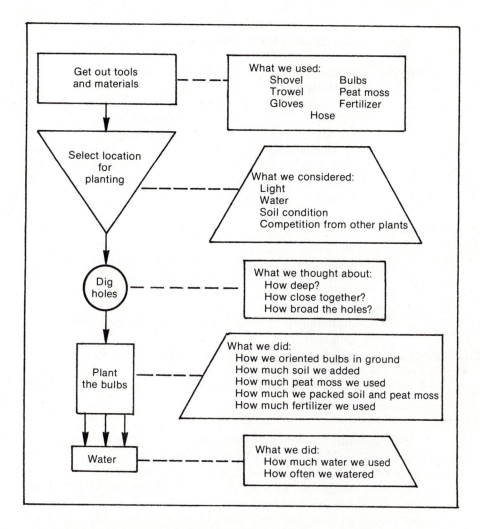

Figure 4.4.   Sample flow diagram of how to plant tulip bulbs.

In another prewriting activity, Laurence (1972) asks students to group statements into two classes: likenesses and differences. In addition, she requires students to learn structure vocabulary that helps students deal with relationships because they know key words and terms of comparison and contrast. The structure vocabulary for this type of writing is provided in Table 4.3.

121

TABLE 4.3
Structure Vocabulary for Comparing and Contrasting

To compare:	similar to	at the same rate as
	similarly	as
	like, alike	just as
	likewise	in like manner
	correspond to	in the same way
	correspondingly	to have _____ in common
	resemble	common characteristics, etc.
	resemblance	to be parallel in _____
	almost the same as	
To contrast:	differ from	unlike
	however	in contrast (to)
	otherwise	in opposition (to)
	still	on the contrary
	nevertheless	on the opposite side
	even so	on the other hand
	dissimilarly	a larger percentage than
	different from	a smaller percentage than
	less than	at a different rate from
	more than	although
	faster than, etc.	while

After the structure has been mastered, Laurence (1972) provides students with a variety of writing exercises to give them practice in applying the concepts of comparison and contrast in isolation before requiring them to do an expanded assignment. One activity involves giving students a set of data about three different airplanes and then asking them to write three questions of comparison, or three statements of contrast that are false according to the data, and so on.

Classification

The act of classification requires students to identify the attributes of an event, object, or group, and determine whether these attributes are similar to those possessed by the whole class of events, objects, or groups. Classification of information is actually a more advanced form of comparison. Requiring LD students to classify information as a prewriting activity is beneficial because it teaches them to look for a structure or organization within data. When this is recognized, the manageability of the information is increased because students have fewer pieces of information to deal with. Some prewriting activities might include giving students a list of twelve words and asking them to classify the words in as many ways as possible (for example, according to function, or color, or other attributes). Laurence (1972) has specified some structure vocabulary for classification, including *main kinds of, significant, primary, minor, similar, contradictory, easily distinguished, classify, divide, unimportant.*

Explanatory Schemes

As thinking becomes more complex, the demands on the student for translating thoughts into writing become increasingly complex. Writing that deals with the projection of explanatory schemes requires that students not only reflect on certain aspects of the world and identify relationships, but also go beyond the data available and propose an explanation for a set of happenings. Subcomponents of this category are hypothesis, conceptual schemes, and a plan of action. As an example, we will discuss the hypothesis.

In a hypothesis, we assume that certain things are true so that we may investigate possibilities. Teachers can give LD students the opportunity to make intellectual jumps so they can learn to hypothesize. One way to get students to go beyond observable facts is to raise unrealistic possibilities for which there are no factual answers (for example, "How would the world change if there were no television?"). Teachers should be aware of a potential problem area for LD students in dealing with hypotheses. Specifically, since certain things are *assumed* to be true when dealing with hypotheses, it is important for the student to realize that any assumptions must be clearly specified. The reader is referred to the chapter on thinking strategies for additional discussion of teaching LD students how to form and apply hypotheses.

Expressing Personal View

Writing can also express personal emotions. However, the writing of personal views uses both facts and opinions. Therefore, the writer has the responsibility of indicating to the reader which statements are facts and which are opinions. Four kinds of personal views are feelings, preferences, opinions, and judgments. Personal opinions will be discussed here.

When students write personal opinions, they may support them with a single statement of reason: "I think we should do _____ because _____."

LD students must be taught that their personal opinions are of value and should be stated. However, they also must realize that stating personal views carries with it the responsibility for identifying logical reasons to support their beliefs. The teacher can help LD students develop the ability to state and support personal views by encouraging them to state their opinions verbally on such issues as school regulations, busing, and drugs. The teacher must always ask the follow-up question "Why?" At the same time, the students should be encouraged to acquire the habit of asking themselves the question "Why?" It is important that students be sensitive to the importance of clearly identifying for the reader what is opinion and what is fact. Some of the structure vocabulary that LD students should learn in relation to the statement of personal opinion is "I think," "seems to me," "in my opinion," "I agree with," "I disagree with," "it's my point of view," "I hesitate to say."

While the strategies and methods presented in this section are not exhaustive, they have been chosen to indicate that learning is facilitated through making the writing act specific and concrete.

THE CRAFT COMPONENTS OF WRITING

Generating ideas for expression through writing is only half of the task for the student. Translating content into a well-organized, clearly articulated passage is the craft of writing. Berke (1971) takes issue with the thesis that "good writing is no more than clear thinking" (p. 251). If this were so, it would only be necessary for students to take courses in logic. While clear thinking is an important and vital first step in writing, it must be accompanied by those skills that can effectively turn what is in the student's head into a visible product on paper. Skills considered important to this end are:

1. Structuring paragraphs and themes.
2. Developing vocabulary.
3. Building sentences.
4. Writing questions.
5. Notetaking.
6. Summarizing.
7. Monitoring written expression.

Regrettably, limited attention has been directed to these components. Lundy (1973) presents an annotated bibliography on remedial English and notes that most of the items listed are "discussion on changing 's' morphemes and little on how to organize and develop writing skills" (p. 269).

Structuring Paragraphs and Themes

The key component to effective written communication is organizing information for the reader. Van Nostrand, Knoblauch, McGuire, and Pettigrew (1978) suggest that nonsensical sentences, disjointed paragraphs, and wandering structure are the major causes of ineffective writing — not poor grammar. Since writing is thinking on paper, the student must manipulate and impose order on data according to logical methods or organization. The ultimate aim of writing should be to have students actively choose the ways in which they impose order on the information they are dealing with (Laurence, 1972).

Kytle (1970) contends that students need specific *prewriting* strategies that can be used to explore their subjects, to discover the limited aspects of their subjects, and to structure and order their thinking. The student should realize that effective writing requires about as much time in thinking and organizing as in the actual writing act. Time spent in prewriting activities is not wasted. Prewriting by analysis is a three-stage process:

1. Exploration through analysis is looking at the subject from as many viewpoints as possible to understand its complexity. This process reveals the necessity of limiting the topic. Students should carry on dialogues with themselves (teachers can do this at first to model for them).
2. After exploring, students must limit the subject. In this prewriting phase, students should continue to break the subject down until they get it to a point where it can be dealt with in confidence.
3. Formulating the thesis through an outline form suggests the specific direction of the paper.

Before addressing the question of organizing information for writing, students should ask themselves the question, "Do I have sufficient information to begin writing?" The teacher can help LD students answer this question by helping them list the ideas and specific examples that will be used in writing. By scanning this list, students can decide if it is complete. If students have enough information, the next question is, "How can this subject best be organized to communicate to the reader?" Van Nostrand et al. (1978) believe that poor writing results from students failing to carry on a dialogue with readers. Writing is not a monologue, and therefore, the reader's perspective must always be considered. Students should also ask themselves, "What is the reader's 'frame of reference'?" "What is the 'organizing idea' (theme) of the paragraph?" "What set of information (facts) should be worked into a paragraph?"

Paragraphs and themes can be organized in a variety of ways. The content should dictate the organization used. Irmscher (1972) has described twelve ways to develop ideas:

1. By defining, elaborating, or restating in different words.
2. By defining and giving examples.
3. By classifying.
4. By summarizing and analyzing.
5. By giving reasons.
6. By presenting facts.
7. By comparing and contrasting.
8. By describing.
9. By narrating.
10. By using an allusion and quoting relevant material.
11. By cataloging details.
12. By developing an analogy or figure of speech.

The arrangement of sentences within a paragraph can also add a degree of organization to students' material. Irmscher (1972) specifies these patterns as (1) from general to particular, (2) from particular to general, (3) alternating order, (4) order of time, (5) order of space, and (6) order of climax.

The effectiveness of an adopted structure or organization for a passage should be evaluated by both student and teacher after the initial writing has been completed. Students should ask themselves the following questions about their work (adapted from Irmscher):

1. Did I tell the reader what I was going to tell him?
2. Are the paragraphs purposeful?
3. Are the paragraphs adequately developed?
4. Are the paragraphs sufficiently varied?
5. Are the paragraphs unified?
6. Are the paragraphs coherent?
7. Is each of the paragraphs needed?

Developing Vocabulary

The vocabulary of many LD adolescents is limited, and hence they are unable to express their ideas and convey their feelings or emotions in a clear, precise, vivid way. The influence of a limited word pool on the complexity of expression has been aptly demonstrated by Myklebust (1965) with his work on the *Picture Story Language Test.* Older students who have low word and sentence productivity scores typically write more concrete-descriptive themes. The teacher who wishes to get a general indication of an LD adolescent's word pool may administer the free association subtest of the *Detroit Tests of Learning Aptitude* (Baker & Leland, 1935). This test simply asks students to name as many words as they can think of. This measure gives an indication of the quality and quantity of their word pool. David, a twenty-one-year-old LD student, for example, named only those objects that he could see in the testing room. Of the words that he produced, only two were abstract (*happy* and *sad*). Vocabulary development was determined to be a high priority area of intervention for David.

Brueckner and Bond (1955) have outlined several vocabulary exercises that are appropriate for LD adolescents. These are as follows:

A. Expanding the vocabulary
    1. Listing words that can be used to convey ideas in a composition about some topic to add interest and color to the language.
    2. Selecting interesting, colorful, important, or new words in what they read in books, stories, and so on.
    3. Discovering and listing synonyms for words, such as *large* and *beautiful.*
    4. Having students discover words built on root words, for example, *care, careful, careless; credible, incredible, creed.*
    5. Discussing the meanings of important prefixes and suffixes, such as *un-, dis-, mal-, mis-, -ful, -ology.*
B. Improving precision of vocabulary
    1. Discussing shades of meanings in synonyms, such as *big, immense; tasty, luscious.*
    2. Classifying words according to categories, such as names of fruits or animals.
    3. Arranging given words on some basis, such as the size implied, for example, *gallon, pint, quart, cup, barrel.*
    4. Discussing appropriateness of words used to convey ideas.
    5. Selecting from among several words the most suitable or appropriate expression, such as *large* or *immense* to describe *house.*
C. Enriching vocabulary
    1. Gathering lists of words that are particularly interesting, colorful, vital, or pleasant.
    2. Trying to restate ideas in different and improved ways.
    3. Learning about the sources of vocabulary.

        4.   Giving synonyms and opposites of words.
        5.   Encouraging creative writing.
  D. Helping children make effective use of the dictionary
  E. Dramatizations

After LD students have completed a writing assignment, they should carefully reread what they have written, specifically evaluating the choice of words. It is important that a separate reading of the passage be devoted to this activity. Key words should be analyzed to determine if they best convey the student's intended meaning.

The use of a clear, precise vocabulary in writing should not be confused with the deliberate use of large or pompous words. Sometimes it is the student's attempt to use big words that stifles production. Flesch (1974) maintains that writing should be composed largely of simple, everyday words. He suggests that writers should avoid using complex words for simple words in most instances. This notion is consistent with the thesis of Van Nostrand et al. (1978) that a major intent of writing is to carry on a dialogue with the reader, and therefore, words that ease communication should be used. Some of the words to be avoided are *utilize* (use), *forward* (send), *indicate* (say), *transpire* (happen).

The reader is referred to the chapter on reading skills for additional suggestions on vocabulary development.

Building Sentences

Writing incomplete and run-on sentences is a common problem with LD students. One of the simplest, most effective techniques for helping students recognize problems that they are having is having them listen to their own writing. The teacher can read a passage back to the student, or the student may read a passage into a tape recorder and listen to it. When the student pauses at the end of a complete thought, the teacher can ask, "Why did you stop there?" Oral exercises help students listen more critically to their writing (Hennings & Grant, 1974).

Simple, telegraphic-type sentences often do not constitute material that is easily read. LD students who have only one sentence pattern (a simple sentence) should be taught how to combine sentences. Example:

(a)   Living things need energy.
(b)   Energy comes directly from the sun.
(c)   Energy comes indirectly from the sun.

          change to:

The energy needed by all living things comes directly or indirectly from the sun. (Laurence, 1972, p. 72)

128

Remember, the purpose is not deliberately to make the writing complex, but to make it readable. In the above example, the student has reworked and manipulated the data to create a clearer, more readable statement for the reader. According to Hennings and Grant (1974), "The ability to carry out some of the higher thought processes implicit in different kinds of idea-content bears some relationship to the ability to handle associated sentence patterns" (p. 140).

Notetaking[1]

The learning disabilities teacher must be able to guide students to attack study material effectively, whether written or dictated, read or heard, and to record the essential ideas for orderly study and use. Three such special skills are (1) outlining — the sequential arrangement of main features of a book, a subject, or a lecture; (2) formal notetaking — the concise but comprehensive statement of essential matter read or heard; and (3) informal notetaking — the brief, spontaneous recording of material to assist the memory or for subsequent reference or development. These skills are organizational output skills and assist students to produce an orderly pattern of material for the purpose of subsequent review and reference. The development of these organizational skills cannot be obtained through sporadic practice, incidental instruction, or isolated drills. A totally involved, systematic program is needed to learn these skills. Students must have much practice and repetition to master notetaking.

Before learning these skills, students should have the prerequisite skills of fundamental language arts (reading, basic written expression skills, and listening ability), familiarity with the vocabulary and technical information being covered, the ability to discriminate and select between main thoughts and details and between what is relevant, interesting, and essential, and what is supplementary. In short, students must be able to write, judge what to put down, and organize it. Before actual writing takes place, they must have abilities in auditory perception. Training in listening and thinking skills precedes instruction in the functional skills necessary for good note-taking (Aaronson, 1975). The basic abilities of the student should be considered before any one method of organization is taught. There is some controversy over whether notetaking interferes with comprehension of lecture material (Castallo, 1976; Peters, 1972). Some say that notetaking interferes with the comprehension of the material and should be used only

---

[1]The material in this section was prepared with the assistance of Edward Pieper, special education doctoral candidate, University of Kansas.

for retrieval of information. The rate of presentation and the density of the information are two variables that affect the type of organization that students will use to remember and comprehend material. Nevertheless, LD adolescents need some organizational structure to help them comprehend classroom discussion and reading materials. In many cases organizational structures aid students who are weak in specific areas. A particular type of organization may help students focus on the main idea or pay closer attention. Before requiring students to take notes or to outline, the teacher should explain the system to be used, demonstrate its use, and closely monitor performance to be sure students are using the notetaking structure agreed upon. To use it successfully, students must practice the procedure to the point of making it an automatic habit if it is to help them in meeting classroom assignments. The following are examples of organizational patterns.

1. *Informal notetaking.* Informal notetaking is spontaneous. The student records oral assignments, directions, major points in class discussion or instruction, or important insights. Accuracy and order are important because this material is usually irretrievable (it is mentioned only once in lecture). Since a major difficulty encountered by LD students is keeping track of homework assignments, it is recommended that students be taught the following technique. They should keep separate assignment notebooks with a separate section set aside designated for each class they are assigned to. During each class period, they carefully record the out-of-class assignment given during that period. At the end of class, students show the teacher what they have written down, and if they have missed any portion of the assignment or misinterpreted it, the teacher can give them immediate feedback. The teacher should be aware of this procedure and insist that students follow it each day.

2. *Formal notetaking.* Formal notetaking involves a deliberate scrutiny of content and the weighing of material in an organized fashion. Some general procedures for students are (1) writing the material in their own vocabulary rather than copying massive quotes: (2) using a consistent format for recording the information, perhaps including a variety of personalized abbreviations or symbols such as w/ for *with* or M for *mountainous*; (3) labeling notes by topic, time, and referent so that they will be intelligible at a later time. There are some advantages in having LD students learn a standard model of notetaking. First, it helps students establish a method for ranking the importance of various elements in what they read or

hear. If students learn to recognize the main idea and the contributing points from which the main idea derives, they can judge how much detail to record in light of the assigned or expected outcome. Gaining this control makes students more efficient learners. Second, the model transforms students from passive readers into active readers who, by necessity, are involved with the print or words. This encourages thinking and comprehension, and contributes to long-term learning. Before committing themselves in writing, students must see relationships and discover meaning. Third, accuracy in notetaking demands that students understand the order and organization of presentation. Notes are a skeletal representation of the material to be learned. By realizing this, they are forced to represent the organization of the material accurately.

To help LD students master notetaking skills in classroom settings, teachers may use the following specific exercises:

1. At the beginning of class, the teacher provides students a mimeographed list of the three or four major points to be covered that day on a sheet with ample room for development of the points, either in summary or outline form. Time should be allotted at the end of the period to compare and discuss the notes. At the same time, the teacher should write on the board important items that were developed under each point.
2. The class may be assigned to write a summary of that day's discussion. The following day the students should review their summaries.
3. The teacher may write the major points of the lesson plan on the board to guide student notetaking.
4. A newspaper article of an expository nature may be read silently or aloud, and students may be alerted to note answers to the specific questions Who? When? Where? How? Why?
5. The teacher gives a carefully prepared lecture with clear verbal clues, using words and phrases such as "Now we will consider the second point," "next," and "above all."
6. To emphasize the necessity of order and selection in notetaking, the teacher allows time at the end of the class period for supervised, purposeful study of the assignment. The students may be required, for example, to pick out the four main points of a section, or the teacher may specify one major topic and have the students note the important supplementary details.

Some exercises that may help LD students master notetaking skills with written texts are the following:

1. SQ3R procedure. *Survey* — Students survey the introductory statement, the headings, and summaries quickly to get the general idea and scope of the assignment. *Question* — Students formulate their own purpose questions. They may use the headings or a question that their survey of the material may have prompted. *Read* — Students read the material to answer the purpose questions. *Recite* — Students pause to relate to themselves the answers to their questions. They may also recall the main ideas of the author's organization of information. *Review* — Students look through the selection to perceive again the organization and basic ideas and to make whatever notes they deem important.

    The SQ3R procedure, although it is a reading comprehension technique, can be incorporated as a writing skill by having students not only mentally go through the steps, but also put down their ideas on paper. The types of skills used in SQ3R are prerequisites for notetaking and summarizing.

2. Outlining skills
    a. Students learn the skeletal form of the outline by direct instruction. The teacher should provide the class with a skeleton outline of some passage to be read and have students fill in only the main topics.
    b. Teachers should demonstrate to the class how to make a skeletal outline, taking major section titles of a chapter as main points, picking out paragraph headings or topic sentences as secondary points, and so on, through the chapter. (It is a serious mistake to assume that LD students have these skills or that merely telling them how to outline is enough.)
    c. In the early stages of outlining, LD students should practice topical outlining, noting only the general headings of what they read. As structure is accurately recorded, they develop full-sentence outlines, using topics only for listing supportive details.
    d. Relationships existing among given facts are demonstrated by drawing parallel columns on the board, one for main ideas or generalizations, the other for details and supporting facts. Arrows can be drawn from one column to the other to emphasize relationships.

3. The two-column method of notetaking requires students to divide their papers into two sections vertically, leaving more space on the right side of the page. This method may be best for combining notes on lectures and written materials. The righthand side of the page may be used for notes from the lecture. Under each major section, students should leave a large space in which to write later notes from texts that cover the major subjects discussed in each section. On the left side students should write a label for each major subject. This helps students recall information and gives them easy access to the notes.

4. Diagrams can help students organize materials from lecture or texts. Graphics have been used effectively in counseling sessions (Nelson & Stadler, 1974) to help students clearly visualize information, see the relationships within the information, and generate alternatives. An example of how a diagram could be used in notetaking is provided in Figure 4.5. In this example, the main topic is revolutions. The key topics are events, places, individuals, and issues. This diagram distills the information and provides students with an additional aid to memory, a visual aid.

   All of these study skills must eventually be woven into the fabric of instruction in the content fields. In other words, if students are to use the skills realistically in the future, they must have ample opportunity to use the skills as part of the class study of content materials. The regular class teacher can aid in student notetaking by presenting material in an organized sequence.

   It is important for the teacher to remember that skills in notetaking must be modeled, practiced, and reinforced if they are to be generalized to regular class settings. The notes that students take in class must be checked by the teacher on a regular basis to insure that LD students are applying appropriate notetaking skills.

5. Walter Pauk from the Cornell University Study Center has suggested some prearranged notetaking formats that have been found helpful. Each format is based on the five Rs of notetaking:

   Record
   Reduce
   Recite
   Reflect
   Review

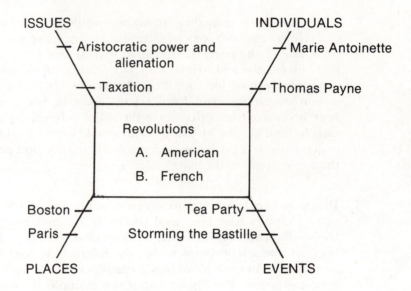

Figure 4.5. Sample diagrammatic aid in notetaking on the subject of revolutions.

The numbers identifying each prearranged format refer to the number of inches of space allowed on the page for each of the steps. The basic formats he suggests are (a) the 2-5-1 format, (b) the 2-6-2 format, and (c) the 2-3-3-2 format, as shown in Figures 4.6, 4.7, and 4.8. The format chosen should be a function of the nature of the subject matter and the student's preference.

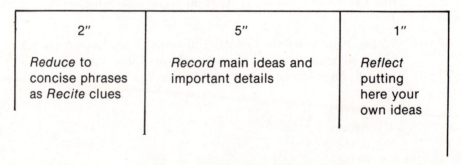

Figure 4.6. The 2-5-1 format.

2"

6"

Reduce to concise phrases as _Recite_	Lecture Notes

Reflection and Synthesis

2"

Figure 4.7.   The 2-6-2 format.

2″	3″	3″
Reduce to *Recite* clues	Textbook Notes	Lecture Notes
	Reflection and Synthesis	

2″

Figure 4.8.   The 2-3-3-2 format.

KERRIGAN'S INTEGRATED METHOD
OF TEACHING COMPOSITION

This section will summarize a teaching method developed by William J. Kerrigan (1974). This method has been used successfully to teach junior high through college students how to write compositions. It has been used with both remedial and regular students, and it combines many of the content and craft factors discussed previously. The reader is referred to *Writing to the Point: Six Basic Steps* by Kerrigan for a complete presentation of the method. The Kerrigan procedure contains factors that are relevant to the needs of the LD adolescent. Specifically, it is a highly structured program; it approaches writing in a step-by-step fashion; and it allows students to interject their own creative ideas and experiences in the writing act.

The goal of the method is to produce well-written themes characterized by the use of (1) a theme sentence that announces its point at once; (2) a topic sentence for each paragraph that is clearly and directly related to the theme sentence; (3) paragraphs that are clearly and directly related to their topic sentences and are well developed; (4) specific examples; and (5) the use of a transitional phrase in the second and third topic sentences to link them to the paragraphs preceding them.

Step One

Write a short, simple, declarative sentence that makes one statement. While it is legitimate for students to write *any* sentence, it is best if they choose a sentence about which something else can be written. For example, "My name is Joe Schumk" is not a very good sentence to choose. "Coal is being used less and less" would be a better sentence because more could be written about that sentence. Kerrigan suggests that for this program the initial sentence (call it sentence X) should *not* be a sentence that is descriptive (tells how something looked) or narrative (tells what happened or introduces a process; tells how to make or do something). Since his program is designed to teach students how to write about relationships of ideas, sentences about ideas should be used. Step One seems very simple, but the advantage of this method for LD students is that it helps them build compositions in steps and gain skill and confidence along the way.

Step Two

Write three sentences about the sentence in Step One that are clearly and directly about the whole of that sentence, not just something in it. A

137

brief explanation of the key words in this step will clarify its intent. First, each of the three sentences must be written about the whole of sentence X, not just a part of it. Students commonly choose one word or phrase in sentence X about which to write all three statements. This does *not* deal with the *whole* idea of the sentence. Secondly, the three sentences must clearly and directly speak about sentence X. The reader wants to know how each sentence is related to the topic sentence. This must be clear to the reader at once. To write sentences in Step Two, Kerrigan suggests that students decide what kinds of questions a reader might naturally ask after reading sentence X.

Step Three

Write four or five sentences about each of the three sentences in Step Two. The four to five sentences written for each of the sentences in Step Two are to be about the whole of each sentence and relate directly and clearly to that sentence, just as the first three sentences were to relate to sentence X.

X I dislike winter.
1. I dislike the winter cold.
2. I dislike having to wear the heavy winter clothing that cold weather requires.
3. I dislike the colds that, despite heavy clothing, I always get in the winter.

X I dislike winter.
1. I dislike the winter cold. It makes me shiver. It chaps my lips. It can even freeze my ears.
2. I dislike having to wear the heavy winter clothing that cold weather requires. I have to wear earmuffs. I have to wear galoshes. I have to wear a heavy coat. I have to wear long underwear.
3. I dislike the colds that, despite heavy clothing, I always get in the winter. They stop up my nose. They give me a cough. They give me a fever. They make me miss school. (p. 26)

This format is to be used throughout the program as it helps students see the relationships of the sentences to each other.

Step Four

Make the material in the four or five sentences in Step Three as concrete and specific as possible. Go into detail. Give examples. Don't ask, "What will I say next?" Say some more about what you have just said. Your goal is to say a lot about a little, not a little about a lot. Sentences X, 1, 2, and

3 are, by their very nature, to be general and even sometimes abstract. But the material in the sentences of Step Four are to become concrete and detailed. Kerrigan contends that good writing consists of details. They are to be supplied here. Students are to try to expand and elaborate on sentences and on words and phrases within sentences. Abstract words are to be concretized. This is an excellent opportunity for LD students to develop their vocabulary skills and writing skills at the same time. For example, given an abstract term, such as *success*, students are to write down as many specific words or terms related to it as they can think of.

Step Five

In the first sentence of the second paragraph and every paragraph following, insert a clear reference to the idea in the preceding paragraph. The obvious purpose of this step is to systematically introduce transitions into the theme. By going through this step, students relate paragraphs to one another just as they related sentences to each other in earlier steps in the program. The reference to "clear" in this step should be noted and implemented as in previous steps.

Step Six

Make sure every sentence in your theme is connected with, and makes clear reference to, the preceding sentence. This step means that the idea of any sentence must be an idea about the sentence just before it. There are several ways that explicit reference can be made to preceding sentences. Kerrigan suggests that the writer (a) repeat in sentence two a word used in sentence one; (b) use in sentence two a synonym of a word in sentence one; (c) use a pronoun in sentence two to refer to an antecedent in sentence one.

In summary, Kerrigan's method of writing development has many advantages for LD adolescents. It is an integrated approach that provides students with a structure within which to write, and yet is clearly flexible enough to allow them to express their thinking and ideas. Obviously, the steps of this approach must be repeated many times before the students gain increased facility in written expression. LD students who have severe spelling problems should be provided with a transcriber during these activities so that they will be able to develop their thinking and ideas and not be penalized because of a mechanical hurdle that would prevent them from communicating through the written medium.

WRITTEN TEST-TAKING STRATEGIES

Written tests are a major requirement of secondary schools. They are given with great frequency in almost all classes, and they follow a variety of formats. Most teachers assume that test-taking skills cannot or should not be taught. As a result, they devote little time to teaching students how to perform well on tests and how to demonstrate their competence over a certain set of materials. We firmly believe that there are some specific strategies that can be taught to students to enhance their performance on written tests. Consequently, it is suggested that LD adolescents be taught these strategies by both the learning disabilities teacher and the regular classroom teacher.

Preparing for Tests

Prior to the actual test, students can do much to enhance their performance on the test. First, students should determine *exactly* what will be covered on the exam. They should ask the instructor these questions: "What material from the lecture notes will be covered?" "What will be emphasized — notes or textbook?" "Will any material be omitted?" "What kinds of questions will be asked — essay, short-answer, true-false?" Finding out exactly what will be covered on the exam and the types of questions that will be asked can often mean the difference between success and failure on tests. LD students can't afford to study material that won't be covered on the exam.

Second, students should try to obtain copies of previous exams given by the teacher. Students who have previously taken the class may have kept copies of past exams, or oftentimes teachers themselves will make available a few copies of previous exams so that students can get an idea of the *types* of questions asked and the topics emphasized on exams.

Third, students should be taught how to set up and follow a study schedule. The major advantage of a study schedule is that it reduces students' dependency on cramming for tests. Cramming is usually a poor way to learn material, and for LD students who may lack proficient reading skills, cramming may not even be feasible. Instead of cramming, LD students should be taught how to review their class notes or reading materials briefly at the end of *each* class session. Frequent review is one of the most effective techniques that students can use to learn material. Material that is not reviewed until just before the exam must be almost totally relearned. This is a highly inefficient method and in many instances may be impossible for LD students to pull off successfully.

Fourth, students should have a complete knowledge of different testing terms, for example, *compare, contrast, illustrate, briefly describe, define, elaborate.* If they understand and follow these directions in the testing situation, students may not do as so many others have done and write a complete page on an item worth two points that requires them to "identify and briefly describe" and then write an equivalent amount for a twenty-point question that asks them to give a "detailed explanation."

Finally, at the end of the study period before an exam, it is important for students to build up a positive mental attitude toward the upcoming test. At this point, it does no good to worry and fret over what has not been accomplished. Instead, students should convince themselves that they will enter the exam with an aggressive attitude, determined to apply what they have learned through studying to the utmost. Many LD adolescents go into exams with fearful, negative, or unmotivated attitudes, which is understandable in view of their previous experiences with exams, but their attitudes often result in poorer test scores than they deserve.

Carman and Adams (1972) have developed a checklist for students in preparing for tests. Parts of this checklist that are most applicable for LD adolescents are provided here:

The Week Before the Exam — "Go" Week

1. Find out exactly what is required for the exam by doing the following:
    a) Ask your instructor what the exam will cover and what kinds of questions will be used. _____
    b) Ask your instructor what, if any, material will be omitted. _____
    c) Make a list of what things you must know, and rank them according to importance. _____
    d) Get copies of previous exams. Your instructor will often be willing to help with this. _____
    e) Talk to friends who have taken the course previously. Get their advice on what to study, what questions to expect, what the test will emphasize. (Very few instructors know their own biases.) _____
    f) Get together a "study group" of some serious students, and fire possible test questions at each other. Make certain the people you select are really interested in studying. _____
2. Organize yourself for maximum efficiency by doing the following:
    a) Eat on schedule all week. _____
    b) Get a normal amount of sleep every day all week. _____
    c) Take time off from your out-of-school job or other activities. _____
    d) Set aside your usual daily activities (TV, dates, hobbies) for *after* the exam. _____
    e) Build up a positive mental attitude by reminding yourself of all the good consequences of succeeding on the exam and recalling past successes. Be positive. Think *up*. _____
3. Learn what you need to know for the exam.
    a) Read the material. . . .
    b) Review it. On each successive review, skip those things you are most sure of. _____

141

c)   Recite. Buttonhole a friend or relative and tell him all about
     it. He'll think you're nuts, but do it anyway.   _____

d)   Review the top priority items again at the last possible minute
     before entering the exam room. (pp. 201-202)   _____

Taking Objective Tests

Objective exams are ones in which the instructor's values and opinions
are not a factor in grading. The most common types of objective exams are
true-false, multiple choice, sentence completion, and matching. These tests
usually require students to choose the best answer or alternative from those
listed. Since not all test questions are well written, it is also necessary for
students to interpret questions correctly and guess what the instructor wants.

Carman and Adams (1972) present a strategy for helping students take
exams. This strategy applies to all exams, not just objective ones. The
system is called SCORER. Each letter in the word stands for an important
rule in test taking.

> *S = Schedule* your time.
> *C = Clue* words.
> *O = Omit* the difficult questions.
> *R = Read* carefully.
> *E = Estimate* your answers.
> *R = Review* your work.

In *scheduling* time during an exam, the student must first consider
the exam as a whole (How many questions? Which questions are easy? Which
are hard?) Time to complete each section must then be estimated. For example, a thirty-minute test containing ten questions permits about three
minutes per question ($30 \div 10$). In estimating time to spend on each question, it is important for students to consider the point value of the various
questions — obviously, those worth more points should be allotted more
time.

Clue words refers to the fact that most exam questions have some
built-in clues. Clue words are particularly revealing in objective exams.
Rarely is something *always* or *never* true or false; thus, when such words
are used in questions, they usually indicate an incorrect answer. On the other
hand, *usually* and *sometimes* are frequently indicative of a correct answer.
The key clue words are *all, some, never, usually, sometimes.*

Omitting or postponing difficult questions until later in the testing
period can markedly affect students' scores. Students should work through
a test like a broken field runner in football: that is, go to the most advanta-
geous spots first (those questions that are easiest to answer). Unfortunately,

many students approach a test like a fullback in football — straight on. Thus, as soon as they encounter a difficult question, they can be stumped for a long time on the test. Carman and Adams (1972) suggest the following procedure:

1. Move rapidly through the test.
2. When you find an easy question or one you are certain of, answer it.
3. Omit the difficult ones on this first pass.
4. When you skip a question, make a mark in the margin (— or ✓). (Do not use a red pencil or pen. Your marks could get confused with the grader's marks.)
5. Keep moving. Never erase. Don't dawdle. Jot brief notes in the margin for later use if you need to.
6. When you have finished the easy ones, return to those with marks (— or ✓), and try again.
7. Mark again those answers you are still not sure of. Change the — to + or ✓ to ✓✓
8. In your review (that's the last R in SCORER), you will go over all the questions time permits, first the ✓✓ , then the ✓ , then the unmarked. (p. 217)

It is important that students *read* the directions for the test and each question carefully and completely. It makes a big difference if a student misreads "Identify the major causes leading up to World War I" as "Identify the major causes leading up to World War II."

To *estimate* on a test has two meanings. First, on test questions requiring problem solving or calculations, students should carefully read the question and roughly estimate what "ball park" the correct answer should be in. Such estimates help students catch careless errors in actual problem solving. The second meaning of "estimate" is "guesstimating," or taking a guess at the correct answers. If students are not penalized for guessing, it is essential that they leave no questions unanswered on an objective exam. After eliminating alternatives and answering all questions that they are sure of, as a last resort, students should take the best guess they possibly can on all remaining questions.

Finally, students should use every minute available to them during a testing session and *review* their answers. Carman and Adams (1972) suggest that students use the following checklist:

1. Return to the double-checked (✓✓) difficult questions. Reread them. Look for clue words. Look for new hints. Then go to the ✓ questions, and finally to the unmarked ones if there is still time.
2. Don't be too eager to change answers. Change only if you have a good reason for changing.
3. Be certain you have considered all questions.
4. PRINT your name on the test. If there are separate sheets, print your name on each sheet. (p. 222)

Taking Essay Tests

Essay exams require students to write detailed and fully developed responses to questions. These tests usually require students to demonstrate a broader understanding of all material covered and of relationships among ideas being tested.

The steps of the SCORER procedure used on objective tests apply equally well to essay tests, with some obvious modifications. A few other strategies have been found helpful for LD students.

Since students will be asked to demonstrate free recall of information, as opposed to recognition recall of information (as on a multiple choice test), students should be encouraged to gain a broad understanding of major ideas and events covered in the material. Essay tests often ask students to discuss several factors and their relation to each other or to an issue. To answer the questions, students must know what the major factors in the text material are. For example, if the test will cover the Great Depression and the text material covers six results of the depression, students should, at the very least, memorize those six results by arranging them in a skeletal outline (maybe using a one-word phrase for each major point). The memory task could be reduced even further, forming a mnemonic phrase or sentence from the words in the outline. To the extent that students can add to the skeletal outline (and memorize the additions), their chances on the test are enhanced.

When the testing session begins, students should be encouraged to not look at the test when it is first handed out, but rather to turn it over on their desks. Before reading any of the exam questions (which may cause them to panic and forget almost everything they have studied), they should quickly jot down the skeletal outlines that they memorized before the test. They then have the outlines available for ready reference throughout the exam session.

Since most LD students have difficulty writing long, detailed answers, they should concentrate on writing down only that information that is most important. One way to do this is to carefully think through and organize an answer before writing it. We encourage LD students to use as much as one-quarter to one-third of the time they have allotted for answering a given question to thinking and organizing. (No writing!) At first, this is hard for students to do. But, to the extent they can follow this practice, their answers will be better organized, and they will usually require fewer words to express the answer (thus, less writing, fewer misspelled words, and sooner!). LD students should also check with the teacher to see if it is acceptable to answer the questions in outline form. If so, they will not have to worry about

144

complete sentences, transitions, and so on, which puts less of a writing load on them.

Just as students are encouraged to take calculated guesses in objective tests, so should they be in essay exams. The skeletal outline jotted down at the beginning of the testing session can often be most helpful. Almost every essay question can, in some way, be related to it. Given that the skeletal outline is adequate to begin with, students should try to relate questions back to that key information.

Since the major purpose of testing should be to allow students to demonstrate their knowledge and understanding of particular materials, the manner in which they demonstrate their competence should match their abilities and style as learners. If students have great difficulty with written expression, essay and short-answer exams unfairly penalize them. LD students and their teacher should negotiate for alternative methods of assessment, such as oral examinations. However, to the extent that LD students must take traditional written examinations, the above strategies should be taught to them.

REFERENCES

Aaronson, D. *Developmental psycholinguistics and communications disorders.* New York: Academy of Sciences, 1975.

Adams, C., & Klein, R. The use of films in teaching composition. *College Composition and Communication*, 1975, *26* (3), 258-262.

Anastasi, A. *Psychological testing.* New York: Macmillan, 1968.

Baker, H. J., & Leland, B. *Detroit tests of learning aptitude.* Indianapolis: Bobbs-Merrill, 1935.

Berke, J. A defense of craft: One response to the Cincinnati conference. *College Composition and Communication*, 1971, *22* (3), 251-255.

Brueckner, L., & Bond, G. *The diagnosis and treatment of learning problems.* New York: Appleton-Century-Crofts, 1955.

Carman, R. A., & Adams, W. R., Jr. *Study skills: A student's guide for survival.* New York: Wiley, 1972.

Castallo, R. Listening guide: A first step toward notetaking and listening skills. *Journal of Reading*, 1976, *19*, 289-290.

Chalfant, J. C., & Scheffelin, M. A. *Central processing dysfunctions in children; A review of research.* Washington, D.C.: U.S. Government Printing Office, 1969. (Monograph)

Deshler, D. D. Psychoeducational aspects of learning-disabled adolescents. In L. Mann, L. Goodman, & J. L. Wiederholt (Eds.), *Teaching the learning disabled adolescent.* Boston: Houghton Mifflin, 1978.

Deshler, D. D., Ferrell, W. R., & Kass, C. E. Error monitoring of schoolwork by learning disabled adolescents. *Journal of Learning Disabilities*, 1978, *11*, 401-414.

Drake, C., & Cavanaugh, J. A. Teaching the high school dyslexic. In L. E. Anderson (Ed.), *Helping the adolescent with the hidden handicap.* Belmont, Calif.: Fearon, 1970.

Educational Testing Service. *Sequential tests of educational progress* (STEP). Series 11. Trenton, N.J., ETS, 1958.

Elbow, P. *Writing without teachers.* New York: Oxford University Press, 1973.

Flesch, R. *On business communications.* New York: Barnes & Noble, 1974.

Hennings, D., & Grant, B. *Content and craft: Written expression in the elementary school.* Englewood Cliffs, N.J.: Prentice-Hall, 1974.

Higgins, J. A. Remedial students' needs vs. emphasis in text-workbooks. *College Composition and Communication,* 1975, *24,* 188-193.

Irmscher, W. F. *The Holt guide to English.* New York: Holt, Rinehart & Winston, 1972.

Johnson, D. J., & Myklebust, H. R. *Learning disabilities: Educational principles and practices.* New York: Grune & Stratton, 1967.

Kellog, R. E. Listening. In P. Lamb (Ed.), *Guiding children's language learning.* Dubuque, Iowa: William C. Brown, 1971.

Kerrigan, W. J. *Writing to the point: Six basic steps.* New York: Harcourt Brace Jovanovich, 1974.

Kytle, R. Prewriting by analysis. *College Composition and Communication,* 1970, *21* (5), 380-385.

Laurence, M. *Writing as a thinking process.* Ann Arbor: University of Michigan Press, 1972.

Lerner, J. W. *Children with learning disabilities: Theories, diagnosis, teaching strategies.* Boston: Houghton Mifflin, 1976.

Lundy, L. Organization follows retrieval. *Man, Society & Technology,* 1973, *32,* 269-271.

Myklebust, H. *Development and disorders of written language: Picture story language test* (Vol. 1). New York: Grune & Stratton, 1965.

Myklebust, H. *Progress in learning disabilities: Studies in the psychoneurology of children* (Vol. 1). New York: Grune & Stratton, 1967.

Myklebust, H. *Problems in learning disabilities* (Vol. 2). New York: Grune & Stratton, 1971.

Myklebust, H. *Development and disorders of written language: Studies of normal and exceptional children* (Vol. 2). New York: Grune & Stratton, 1973.

Nelson, R. C., & Stadler, H. Focus through graphics. *Focus on Guidance,* 1974, *6,* 1-11.

Peters, L. J. *Prescriptive teaching system: Individual instruction.* New York: McGraw-Hill, 1972.

Van Nostrand, A. D., Knoblauch, C. H., McGuire, P. J., & Pettigrew, J. *Functional writing.* Boston: Houghton Mifflin, 1978.

Wallace, G., & McLoughlin, J. A. *Learning disabilities: Concepts and characteristics.* Columbus, Ohio: Merrill, 1975.

Wallace, S., & Larsen, S. C. *Educational assessment of learning problems: Testing for teaching.* Boston: Allyn & Bacon, 1978.

MATHEMATICS: STRATEGIES AND METHODS

Basic Concepts of Mathematics

Mathematics Competencies Needed by LD Students

Characteristics of Students Who are Deficient
in Mathematics Skills

Assessing Mathematics Skills in LD Adolescents

Enhancing Mathematics Skills of LD Secondary Students

5

People use mathematics skills every day of their lives. A person who lacks both a minimal competency in fundamental computation of numbers and the ability to deal with mathematics in problem solving can be taken advantage of by unscrupulous salespersons and lending agents. The LD student must acquire basic competencies in mathematics to deal with business distributors and financial agents. It is not only in the marketplace that learning disabled students will use their skills in mathematics, but also in planning home improvements, balancing checkbooks, and validating paychecks. In fact, mathematics skills are crucial in many situations in adult life.

Several reasons have been offered by Wallace and McLoughlin (1975) to explain mathematics deficits of students with learning difficulties. These reasons range from limited student readiness for the presented concepts and poor teaching methods to students' disinterest and repeated failure. These authors (Wallace & McLoughlin, 1975) have viewed the etiology as focused on behavioral principles. Others (Chalfant & Scheffelin, 1969; Johnson & Myklebust, 1964) have associated the causes of mathematics deficits with the basic psychological processes of memory, spatial relationships, directionality, and receptive language.

These causes have not been adequately separated for computation and verbal problem solving in the long history of the study of students' difficulties with mathematics. It is assumed that poor verbal problem solving, that is, difficulties with word problems, is the result of poor reading and/or a developmental lag in readiness skills. In fact, Lapore (1977) found that when mental age was controlled, educable mentally retarded and LD students made similar types of computational errors. However, it is the opinion of most investigators that a more complex interaction exists among the student, the teacher, and the teaching method and/or materials. Their

148

interaction may involve the student's "ability to solve logical problems through reasoning," the teacher's emphasis on rote learning of the rules of mathematics, and materials that contain only variables that are relevant to the problem rather than some realistically irrelevant variables.

Learning strategies can be used to assist the student and the teacher in the intervention process. Learning disabled students can be taught to use visual imagery, for example, to solve difficult problems at all levels of mathematics. Teachers can also use the banded approach (Brant, 1972) as a classroom management technique. (The banded approach is described on page 171.) Finally, materials that are sequenced in discernible steps will benefit both the learner and the teacher.

However, before such strategies, methodologies, and materials can be introduced, it is important that the teacher have a grasp of the concepts of mathematics, the competencies required by students, and the specific deficiencies that LD students manifest. The following sections provide this information. Upon it is based the rationale for learning strategies to use in teaching mathematics skills to these students.

BASIC CONCEPTS OF MATHEMATICS

The root of our quantitative language, mathematics, is the Hindu-Arabic numeration system. This system consistently groups units called digits into tens. The digits are 0, 1, 2, . . . 9. The grouping is called the base of the number system. In this case, the base of the number system is 10.

Our present system is a place-value system. The numbers increase by the power of 10 from right to left, 9, 90, 900, . . . 9000, . . . 90,000 . . . . Our place-value system also uses this power of 10 to indicate when numbers are decreased from left to right — .9, .09, .009, ...0009. . . . *All* students must demonstrate their knowledge of our number system *before* they can begin to use the rules for combining numbers.

These rules govern both (1) terms of operation and (2) basic axioms. The terms of operation, which are generally familiar to most persons, include addition, subtraction, multiplication, and division.

The basic axioms are not so familiar. Those that appear to have the most relevance to teaching mathematic skills to LD students are (a) commutative property for addition and multiplication, (b) associative and multiplicative property for addition, (c) distributive property for multiplication over addition, (d) multiplicative inverse, and (e) additive inverse. A brief description of each basic axiom will be presented with the use of examples for further clarity.

The commutative property for addition and multiplication is the independence of order of the numbers or numerals. If a and b denote numbers, then $a + b = b + a$, for example $4 + 1 = 1 + 4$. The commutative property for multiplication provides that for all numbers a and b, $a \times b = b \times a$, for example $4 \times 3 = 3 \times 4$. There is *no* commutative property for either subtraction $(4 - 1 = 1 - 4)$ or division $(4 \div 3 = 3 \div 4)$. The student must know that the commutative property is applicable to only *two* of the *four* operations.

The associative property of addition and multiplication states that the numbers are independent of their grouping — in addition, for all of the numbers a, b, and c, then $(a + b) + c = a + (b + c)$; for example, $(4 + 2) + 3 = 4 + (2 + 3)$. The same axiom holds for multiplication. Of all numbers a, b, and c, then $(a \times b) \times c = a \times (b \times c)$; for example, $(4 \times 2) \times 3 = 4 \times (2 \times 3)$. Again, the associative property does not hold for either subtraction, e.g., $(4 - 2) - 3 = 4 - (2 - 3)$, or division, e.g., $(4 \div 2) \div 3 = 4 \div (2 \div 3)$. The conditions are identical to the associative property described above.

The distributive property for multiplication over addition relates the two operations of addition and multiplication. This axiom is stated using the numbers a, b and c, as $a (a + b) = (a \times b) + (a \times c)$. For example, $4 (3 + 2) = (4 \times 3) + (4 \times 2)$. We use this axiom in factoring numbers.

The inverse operation axiom has the greatest applicability for LD students when they are checking their computations for errors. The inverse operations axiom relates to the operations that are opposite in their effects, e.g., addition and subtraction, and multiplication and division. Using the numbers a, b and c, the following statements can be written:

$a + b = c, c - a = b$
$a \times b = c, c \div a = b$
$a - b = c, c + b = a$
$a \div b = c, c \times b = a$

For example:

$4 + 3 = 7$ to check $7 - 4 = 3$
$4 \times 3 = 12$ to check $12 - 4 = 3$
$4 - 2 = 2$ to check $2 + 2 = 4$
$4 \div 2 = 2$ to check $2 \times 2 = 4$

These rules are applied and learned as the student solves problems requiring the use of the operations and axioms.

The experiential basis for teaching numbers, numerals, operations, and axioms is called problem solving. The content of mathematical problem solving includes measurement, money, time, geometry, functions, relationships, deductions, transformations, maps and graphs, computer uses, and mathematical aids.

MATHEMATICS COMPETENCIES NEEDED BY LD STUDENTS

Bell (1973) provides "a short and tentative list of what is 'really' wanted as a minimum residue for everyman from the school mathematics program" (p. 50, Fig. 2). The outline "summarizes my own view of what we *really* want . . . in the minds and guts of people after they have served their required 8, 9, or 10 year sentence in school mathematics classrooms" (p. 49). We think that Bell's outline requires further clarification if it is to be practical for teachers of LD students. We hope that our presentation includes neither information nor concepts that violate the spirit of Bell's conceptual outline.

1. *Uses of numbers not involving mathematical operations.* The best example of this problem is one which simply asks the student to *measure* the outside dimensions of a window frame. It can also include such activities as *counting* pennies or other small matching items found in a jar, ordering coins by size, counting heartbeats for one minute, mixing ingredients of a recipe, and using the Dewey decimal or Library of Congress system.

2. *Efficient and informed use of computation aids.* Students should know how to use an abacus, Cuisenaire rods, models, hand calculators, and cash registers, and should understand the capabilities and limitations of computers.

3. *Relations such as equal, equivalent, less or greater, congruent, similar, parallel, perpendicular, and subset.* The LD student should be able to provide examples of how each of these terms applies to daily living skills. The student should be able to use symbols (< , > , =) in number sentences, such as 14 (< , > , =) 28, or 15 ___ 15. The student should be able to select examples of congruent, parallel, and perpendicular lines from drawings such as the following, which illustrate these relations.

a.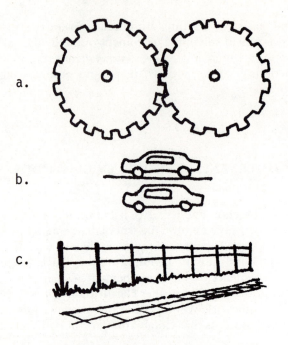

b.

c.

Further, the student should recognize the notation for a proper subset within a number sentence, such as A U B, and draw a Venn diagram of a representative subset relation. For example:

U = (All the juniors in High School Z)
A = (All the boys in junior class)
B = (All the boys in junior class who play football)

Solution:

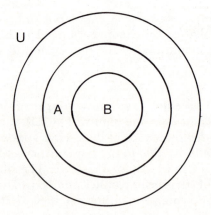

And, finally, the student should be able to identify whether pairs of concepts such as the following are similar or different: (a) sphere and circle, (b) pyramid and triangle, (c) 32°F and 0°C, and (d) six units and one-half dozen units.

4. *Fundamental measurement concepts.* Besides a knowledge of standard and metric units of measure, students should be able to explain why there is a need for the U.S. Bureau of Standards and what its major function is. The student should be able to explain the difference between a "cost estimate" supplied by construction subcontractors, such as electricians, carpenters, and plumbers, and the "actual cost." Besides citing two major benefits of exact measurement, such as measuring quantities rather than guessing when preparing a recipe, the student should provide at least three examples of instrumentation used for standard measurement and two examples of instrumentation for metric measurement.

5. *Confident, ready, and informed use of estimates and approximations.* The usefulness of approximation in problem solving is evident. The student can explain (a) the usefulness of approximating answers when taking a multiple-choice test in mathematics, (b) the benefit of approximation when planning a vacation trip, (c) the benefit of approximating distances when driving both in a crowded city and on a gravel secondary road when following another car, (d) the major advantage of short division when compared with long division, (e) an approximation of the frontage footage of a building site without the use of standard or metric measurement instruments.

6. *Use of variables.* The student must be able to determine the number of variables required to solve mathematics problems. Further, the student should be able to identify excess variables or to determine if there are insufficient variables to solve the problem.

7. *Correspondences, mappings, functions, and transformations.* The student should recognize that graphs, tables, and figures are a compressed mode of describing data. The student can solve problems using both concrete objects and abstract verbal concepts. For examples, a car uses a gallon of gasoline every twenty miles. The car travels 200 miles. How many gallons of gasoline must be replaced after the trip? (One may *actually* pump gasoline into the car until it is filled again.)

8. *Basic logic.* The student uses the following four basic procedures of problem solving:

a. Understanding the problem — focus on information and conditions given in the problem.
b. Planning the problem — select strategies to use in solving the problem.
c. Solving the problem — carry out the plan selected in b.
d. Reviewing the problem and its solution:
   (1) Review the steps taken to solve the problem.
   (2) Apply the steps to a similar problem (LeBlanc, 1977).

9. *"Chance," fundamental probability, ideas, and descriptive statistics.* The student should be able to explain two serious limitations of using trial and error in mathematics. The student can give three practical examples in which probabilities can be used in games of chance, such as bingo, poker, and supermarket "games." The student can identify the appropriateness of the following statement: "The average college student is 20.2 years old and graduated from a high school of 657.5 students," and the inappropriateness of this statement: "The average college student is a farm girl from Macksburg."

10. *Geometric relations in plane and space.* Geometry is used in daily experiences by many people. Measuring house dimensions for painting purposes is a familiar example. An individual may also need to judge the dimensions of a grain storage silo or a water tank.

11. *Interpretation of informational graphs.* The student should be able to read and interpret simple bar and line graphs and figures of unity (circles) subdivided by ratios that represent percentages.

These mathematics skills should be in the repertoire of LD adolescents. If students do not have these skills and if they are not provided in the regular classes, the learning disabilities teacher must teach them. The best approach is for the special teacher and the regular class teacher to plan cooperatively for the competencies to be presented in the regular class to *all* students, including LD students. Cooperative planning such as this can be done as a part of formal curriculum revision or, on a less formal level, between the two teachers. It may be that the regular class teacher will present a concept with an example or two and then the learning disabilities teacher will review the concept and provide several additional examples.

CHARACTERISTICS OF STUDENTS WHO ARE DEFICIENT IN MATHEMATICS SKILLS

It is very difficult to find recent research on the characteristic mathematics skills deficits of LD students. Cawley (1975) has stated:

154

The sad truth of the matter is that there is such a paucity of relevant literature that the notion of being neglected is certainly apropos. (p. 6)

Fernald (1943) listed mathematics deficits under four categories:

1. Lack of skill in fundamentals
   a. basic facts
   b. number combinations
2. Complex situations involving fundamental combinations
   a. addition, subtraction, multiplication, and division
   b. fractions
   c. decimals and percentages
3. Failure to comprehend work problems
4. Blocking of adjustments by ideational or habitual factors or by emotional responses
   a. problem has no connection with child's idea
   b. inattention to variables within problem
   c. affective material of problem affects student's response

How do these four areas relate to our present classification of (1) knowledge of the number system, (2) operations, and (3) axioms? Problems with our number system are not found in Fernald's taxonomy. Rather, a strong case can be made that the operations and axioms account for most mathematics deficits.

Types of Errors

Cox (1975) identifies types of mathematics errors. She defines a systematic error as one that occurs at least three times in five problems that use the same algorithm and in which the error pattern is discernible. In examples a through e, the student added *all* the numbers, indicating a failure to grasp the concept of place value.

a.	12	b.	13	c.	14	d.	15	e.	11
	+11		+12		+13		+14		+11
	5		7		9		11		4

The second type of error is random and occurs in at least three of the five problems, but the error pattern is not discernible. The following are examples of this second type of error; examples f, g, and h are undiscernible errors. This type of error may be made if (1) the student does not under-

155

stand the concept being taught, (2) the student is short of time to solve the problems and believes a solution must be provided, or (3) the student is not attending to the task because of internal (headache) or external (fear of failure) factors.

f.	12	g.	13	h.	14	i.	15	j.	11
	+11		+12		+13		+14		+11
	40		97		79		29		22

The third error type is one in which the student has made a careless error in one or two of the five problems. Examples of this third type might be as follows:

k.	12	l.	13	m.	14	n.	15	o.	11
	+11		+12		+13		+14		+11
	22		25		27		29		22

Type 3 errors occur because of alignment of numbers or not attending to the task as described above. If students check their work, this third type of error is less likely to occur.

Ashlock (1972) has provided a text employing a systematic method for determining if computational errors fall into systematic patterns. The reader is encouraged to use Ashlock's text in the identification of these systematic errors common in mathematics. A cautionary note about Ashlock's system is in order.

Enstrom (1977) found that LD children of elementary school age made errors that, upon either initial observation or attempts to identify them using Ashlock's system, appeared to have no systematic pattern. But after careful analysis, inter-teacher judgment, and discussion with the student, systematic error patterns were identified. Teachers must carefully analyze students' work before concluding that errors are either random or careless. In summary, students' errors in computation are related to both the operations and algorithm required to solve problems. These errors are consistent in their pattern.

Variables That May Affect Mathematics Performance

Lack of intelligence has been suggested as a major factor contributing to mathematics deficits even when chronological age is partialed out in statistical tests (Engelhart, 1932; Goodstein and Kahn, 1973). Cruickshank

(1948) found that students who were labeled mildly mentally retarded performed more poorly than normal students on problems in which there was (1) no superfluous material, (2) only verbal data specific to the problem, and (3) only computation was required, given the algorithm. He also found that on problems of types (1) and (2), the mentally retarded students either guessed at the solutions or used different strategies than did normal students. However, in a concurrent study, Cruickshank (1948) reported that if the mentally retarded students were provided with concrete materials, their performance was similar to their normal peers.

Goodstein and Kahn (1973) analyzed the performances of LD students in grades 4, 5, and 6 in tests of intelligence, reading, and mathematics to identify factors related to mathematics achievement. Using factor analysis procedures, three relatively independent factors emerged: (1) arithmetic computation, (2) intelligence, and (3) reading. Reading as a function of mathematics deficits has been of interest to investigators who have studied verbal problem solving. Linville (1970) suggests that both the vocabulary and the syntactical structure are causes of difficulty. More specifically, Barney (1972, pp. 131-133) stated the difficulties are associated with eight essential variables. They are (1) problem length (narration), (2) narratives with unnecessary or insufficient data, (3) restatement of the problem, (4) punctuation (complex and compound sentences), (5) abbreviations, (6) technical words, such as properties and algorithm, (7) infrequently used words, such as subset and cosine, and (8) words with multiple meanings, such as interest, properties and square.

Blankenship and Lovitt (1976) have identified an additional variable that we feel should be included in the above listing. They identified in LD elementary students a "rote computational habit" (p. 297). They observed these students scanning the problem to obtain numbers rather than carefully reading the problem to determine strategies for solving it. The result is that LD students, including LD adolescents, perform in a manner similar to most low-achieving students in mathematics. They are (1) not persistent in the search for information; (2) use a trial and error problem solving approach, and (3) provide many incorrect answers (Havertape, 1976; Klausmeier & Loughlin, 1961).

ASSESSING MATHEMATICS SKILLS IN LD ADOLESCENTS

The teacher of LD adolescents has three options when selecting a test to measure the mathematics performance of these students. The teacher can (1) use a standardized formal measure, (2) use an informal instrument someone else has developed, or (3) construct an informal instrument specifically to measure the dimensions of the students' apparent problems (Suydam, 1974).

Standardized Formal Measures

We have observed several standardized formal measures used by school psychologists, counselors, and teachers of LD adolescents. They are (1) the *Wide Range Achievement Test*, (2) the *Peabody Individual Achievement Test*, (3) *Key Math*, and (4) the *Stanford Diagnostic Mathematics Test*.

The first three measures are appropriate for surveying areas of mathematics underachievement, but they do not provide the information for developing instructional programming plans. Goodstein's (1975) comments on the *Key Math* are also applicable to the *Wide Range Achievement Test* and the *Peabody Individual Achievement Test*. He stated first that failure on an item does not clearly indicate to the teacher where to begin the remediation program. Second, skill gaps are missing on the subtests. Third, the *Key Math* and, we believe, the other two measures, fail to control for the algorithm in problem solving. Finally, Goodstein observed that mid-range items were lacking on the *Key Math*.

Goodstein noted that the *Key Math* was normalized with average students only. The same is true of the other two measures. Goodstein implies that such normalizing renders these tests inappropriate for assessing mathematics skill performance of LD students. However, the *Key Math* was calibrated using the Rasch-Wright method. Assuming that all conditions of the Rasch-Wright method were met by the *Key Math* developers and that the validity and reliability studies of the *Key Math* predecessor also reflect the reliability and validity of the present version of the *Key Math*, then the test is appropriate for any sampling of students for which the content is appropriate.

Because teachers desire measures that pinpoint objectives, and because items that have been developed from those objectives are included on the measure, we believe that teachers of LD adolescents may be more satisfied with the content of the *Stanford Diagnostic Mathematics Test* (Beatty et al., 1976). However, there are some disadvantages of the SDMT that may limit its usefulness to some teachers.

The SDMT is a group-administered speed test. It takes approximately one hour and forty minutes to administer. It contains items that represent the three test scores of (1) number system and numeration, (2) computation, and (3) applications. The test is multilevel and is divided into concepts and skills for each of the four color-coded levels. The red level measures concepts and skills taught in first and second grades. It is normalized on second, third, and low-achieving fourth grade students. Concepts and skills of third and fourth grades, normalized on fourth, fifth, and low-achieving sixth grade students, are found in the green level. The brown level is normalized on sixth, seventh, and low-achieving eighth grade students. The concepts and skills reach a ceiling at the conclusion of sixth grade. Finally, the blue level contains concepts and skills up to the ninth grade (freshman year) and is normalized on students from eighth grade to community college level. We suggest that teachers use the level most appropriate to the individual LD student's concept and skill development in mathematics. When our teachers used the normalized levels, the basic items were found to range from difficult to impossible for LD students to solve. The information that the teacher wanted was not group comparisons but, rather, instructional programming data. The progress indicator of the SDMT is most important to developing and implementing the individual educational plan (IEP).

A second formal assessment measure that we have found to be useful in determining if students have the grasp of algorithms to assist them in the solution of mathematics problems is the *Ross Test of Higher Cognitive Processes* (Ross & Ross, 1976). Of particular interest is Section VIII, "Analysis of Relevant and Irrelevant Information." This section does not require an assessment of the students' computational skills. Rather, it requires that students select an algorithm and then decide whether the data provided are insufficient, sufficient, or in excess of the amount needed to solve the problem. This measure will provide the teacher with more information if the section is modified. We suggest that the student provide the examiner with the selected algorithm in addition to telling the examiner whether the data are sufficient to solve the problem. This modification provides the examiner with the problem-solving strategy of the student that must be assumed under the standardized directions. An example of this modification would be: Standardized Question: Is there enough information? Answer: Yes. Modified Question: How would you set up this problem to solve it?

The teacher will note that the *Ross* is normalized on gifted and non-gifted students in grades four, five, and six. We have used this measure as a part of the identification procedure for LD sophomores and have found the instrument has functional use in distinguishing LD students from those without learning disabilities. We shall be studying this measure, with our modifications, to determine its reliability and validity with LD secondary students.

Informal Assessment

The informal measures of the mathematical skills of LD secondary students are closely related to methodology, especially task analysis. We shall discuss Cawley's (1975) *Clinical Mathematics Interview* (CMI) and a modification of Manheim's (1971) procedure for solving word problems as assessment procedures.

Task Analysis

Task analysis has been closely associated with behavioral psychology. Glaser and Resnick (1972) succinctly state the educational implications of task analysis:

> For the psychologist concerned with instructional processes . . . the problem of task analysis is a central one. Analytic description of what is to be learned facilitates instruction by attempting to define clearly what it is that an expert in a subject area has learned; for example, what is it that distinguishes a skilled reader from an unskilled one. When this analysis identifies classes of behaviors whose properties as learning tools are known or can be systematically studied, then inferences concerning optimal instructional processes can be formulated and tested. (p. 209)

These tasks can be described through the use of a taxonomy (Bloom, 1956) or a learning hierarchy (Gagne, 1970).

Suppes and her associates (Suppes, 1967; Suppes, Hyman, & Jerman, 1967; Suppes, Jerman, & Brian, 1968) identified three classes of processes when they attempted to task analyze mathematics difficulties. The first class, a transformational process, required the unknown quality to be transformed as the only term right of the equals sign. For example:

Original problem $\quad\quad$ $36 - \square = 6$
The reconstructed problem $\quad$ $36 - 6 = \square$ requires only one
$\quad\quad\quad\quad\quad\quad\quad\quad\quad\quad\quad\quad\quad\quad\quad\quad$ transformation.

A second class of processes requires that the student perform a number of operations to solve the problem. In our example, there would appear to be only one operation:

$$36 - 6 = \square$$

However, this is not the case. It requires the following four operational steps to reach the above result:

Original problem	$36 - \square = 6$
Operation 1	$36 - \square + \square = 6 + \square$
2	$36 = 6 + \square$
3	$36 - 6 = 6 + \square - 6$
4	$36 - 6 = \square$

The final class of processes is memory. Our example required five memory steps. It is evident from the successful solution of the example problem that many sophisticated learners do not identify the processes that are salient to naive learners solving this problem.

Clinical Mathematics Interview (CMI)

Cawley (1975) has recognized the complexity of task analysis. He based his *Clinical Mathematics Interview* on Glennon and Wilson's (1972) taxonomy, which includes the interrelationship of content, behavior, and psychological learning products. Glennon and Wilson do not consider using either a taxonomy (behavior) or a learning hierarchy (psychological learning products) but suggest both should be used concurrently with mathematics curriculum (content).

The CMI is used as a diagnostic procedure that integrates (1) the content of the curriculum, (2) the modes of instruction, and (3) the algorithm or rule the student selects when attempting to solve the problem. Cawley (1975) describes the CMI process as first presenting the student with a relevant computation test. When the student completes the test, the teacher scores the items and sorts them into sets of those solved correctly and those with incorrect solutions.

The second step requires the teacher to ask students about their algorithmic search when they have not solved the problem correctly.

Finally, on a subsequent day, the problem is presented to the students using an alternative mode, such as manipulative objects, oral presentation, or graphic symbols. The student solves the problem using an alternate mode, such as manipulating objects, recognizing the solution from a series of alternatives, orally solving the problem, or using graphs, number sentences, and pictures or line drawings.

The CMI is a functional and structured application of task analysis. It is advocated by the authors of this text because it makes use of the students' learning strategies both in the teaching presentation (input) and in the required student responses (output). This form of clinical teaching meets six of the points listed by Collins (1972, p. 171) as desirable ideas and practices if the transition from assessment to remediation is to remain viable. Collins recommends that teachers do the following:

1. Recognize that not all students need to achieve each instructional objective for any given unit of study.
2. Create learning environments rich in stimuli that are useful for motivating student movement toward attainment of objectives especially selected for that student.
3. Anticipate different learning styles.
4. Make available appropriate instructional material using various media and modes.
5. Judiciously use media to disseminate information and thus free themselves to function increasingly as prescribers, diagnosticians, and consultants during the interactive phase of teaching.
6. Provide for systematic adjustment in plans based on feedback.

For the LD student in the secondary schools, task analysis, as developed within Cawley's CMI model, places major emphasis on the conceptual aspects of mathematics. To a lesser degree it focuses on student reading disabilities as they affect mathematical problem solving. The reader is left to presume the implications of the method for LD students evidencing difficulties in higher mathematics, such as algebra and geometry. It seems to us that CMI can be used to test the student's ability to use rules of higher mathematics.

ENHANCING MATHEMATICS SKILLS OF LD SECONDARY STUDENTS

A Process for Solving Word Problems

The three factors mentioned above (i.e., conceptual aspects of mathematics, reading, and higher levels of mathematics) are considered by Manheim (1971) in his description of a process of solving word problems. Initially, he differentiates between imaginary and real word problems. An *imaginary* word problem includes all the information and formulas required for its solution. The following is an example of Manheim's imaginary word problem:

"The formula for determining the area of a circle is
$$A = \pi r^2$$
If $r^2 = 16$ and $\pi = 3.1416$, find the value of A."

This is *not* a word problem. Students who can focus on the concept and carry out the mathematical computation do not have to depend on reading skills. In reality, the reading is redundant! The imaginary word problem can be used as a diagnostic extension of Cawley's CMI.

Conversely, the *real* word problem is more complex. All the information required to solve the problem is not included in the narration. The algorithm is presumed to be known by the learner. The question is asked in a subject area other than mathematics, e.g., physics, psychology, economics, or biology. An example of a real word problem is the classic train problem (Stone & Mallory, 1936).

A train going east was overtaken in six hours by one leaving the same place two hours later and traveling sixteen miles per hour faster. Find the rate of each. (p. 228)

The example of the train problem is used because (1) it is a familiar word problem that teachers recognize for the frustration it causes, and (2) Manheim (1971) provides a detailed description of its solution.

Students may read the problem and say they understand it. However, if LD students do not know the formula for motion of objects *and* do not know the quantitative language governing the algebraic equations needed to solve the problem, they will not be able to set up the problem for computation. If a teacher questions whether a problem similar to the example above is appropriate for the student, he or she can determine this using the CMI.

Assuming the problem is judged appropriate for LD students, the following procedure can be followed:

Step 1: The student is made aware of a clearly defined problem. The teacher reads the problem orally, and uses questions to make the student aware of relevant information provided in the problem.

Step 2: The student then sets a goal to solve the problem.

Step 3: The student underlines the words in the problem that can be translated into quantitative terms, i.e., distance, time, rate and east.

Step 4: The formula, law, rule, or algorithm is identified from a group of alternatives appropriate to the quantitative terms identified in step 3, including the following: (a) $D = rt$, (b) $A = \pi r^2$, (c) $C = \pi d$, (d) $E = mc^2$, and (e) $E = 90°$. Alternative (a) is the appropriate law.

Step 5: The student then transforms the terms of the law into their numerical values, such as $t = 16$. One should caution the student that there is a use of the law for the first train and for the second train.

Step 6:   The number sentences are written by the student.
Step 7:   The mathematical operations are selected by the student.
Step 8:   The calculations are performed.
Step 9:   The solutions are obtained in quantitative mathematical language, i.e., 32 and 48.
Step 10:   The quantitative solution is translated into the semantic context of the word problem. Hence, the student's goal has been realized. These ten steps are modified and extended from a procedure suggested by Manheim (1971).

After steps 1 and 2 are completed by the LD student, solving the word problem is in order. Manheim (1971) suggests that the learner scan the problem for quantifiable words to satisfy step 3. In the train problem these words are *distance, rate, time,* and *east.* Next the learner must determine by logic which of the four words are relevant to solving the problem.

In step 4 the student eliminates the quantitative word *east* and establishes that the law $D = rt$ contains all the relevant quantifiable words at least once. This general law is then used to solve the problem. In the train problem, the general rule (formula) is:

$$\text{Distance } (D) = \text{rate } (r) \; x \; \text{time } (t)$$

The student orders the rule terms by the formula element and by the numbers of trains (subscripts 1 and 2).

$$D_1 = D_2 \text{ (quantitative value)}$$
$$r_1 + 16 = r_2 \text{ (quantitative and numerical value)}$$
$$t_1 = 6, \; t_2 = 4$$

Then in step 6, number sentences are generated for each of the trains:

$$D_1 = r_1 6$$
$$D_2 = (r + 16) \; 4$$

Steps 7 and 8 require the mathematical calculation of the problem. *It is of paramount importance to the solution that the student isolate the response required to solve the word problem!* In the train problem, the response to be isolated is rate of the two trains. The calculation is as follows:

$$6r_1 = (r + 16)\ 4$$
$$6r_1 = 4r_1 + 64$$
$$6r_1 - 4r_1 = 4r_1 - 4r_1 + 64$$
$$2r_1 = 64$$
$$\frac{2r_1}{2} = \frac{64}{2}$$
$$r_1 = 32$$

Then, retrieving the solution for the categorical ordering for rate done in step 3,

$$r_2 = r_1 + 16$$

and substituting the solution for r_1 one can solve for r_2:

$$r_2 = 32 + 16$$

The quantitative solution of r_2 is

$$r_2 = 48.$$

Having obtained the quantitative solution to the problem (step 9), the student then takes the final step of transforming the quantitative solution back into the original semantic language (step 10): "The rate of the first train is 32 mph and the rate of the second train is 48 mph" (Manheim, 1971).

The generalization of the ten steps provided to the LD student can be extended to a wide range of word problems. The authors of this text found that the procedure was equally applicable in third grade mathematics instruction (Eicholz & O'Daffer, 1968).

For example, a problem in Eicholz and O'Daffer's third-grade *Elementary School Mathematics* states:

> Short stories: time
> Animals, trees, birds, and insects grow old. Exercises 11 through 18 tell how old they sometimes grow. . . .
> 18. An old butterfly: 8 weeks old
>   An old housefly: 6 weeks old
>   How many *days* older is the old butterfly?

Now using the word problem solutions procedure:

Step 1:   Teacher reads problem in its entirety.
    Teacher: How old is the butterfly?
         How old is the housefly?
         What does older mean?
         Can you give the age in days as well as weeks?
         What is the question you need to answer to solve this problem?
         Do you have any questions to help you read this problem?

Step 2:   Teacher: I believe you can solve this problem. Are you ready to solve this problem?

Step 3:   The LD student underlines words that can be translated into quantitative terms: <u>weeks</u> <u>days</u> <u>older</u>.

Step 4:   Alternatives are provided to help the student recognize rules:
    a. Days older = AGE, in days, of older; AGE, in <u>days</u>, of younger
    b. Weeks older = AGE, in weeks, of older; AGE, in <u>weeks</u>, of younger
    c. Months older = AGE, in months, of older; AGE, in <u>days</u>, of younger
    d. Years older = AGE, in years, of younger; AGE, in <u>years</u>, of older

Student chooses alternative a., and converts weeks of age to days.

Step 5:   Butterfly = 8(7) = 56 days
    Housefly = 6(7) = 42 days

Step 6:   The old butterfly is fourteen days older than the old housefly.

Development of Functional Competencies

The generalized procedures just described can be contrasted with procedures of those who advocate teaching functional competencies to the LD student. Using the *Adult Performance Level Project* (Northcutt, 1975) of the University of Texas, advocates have attempted to use a systematic cognitive approach to solving problems presented as competencies. We chose one such competency under the heading of Consumer Economics, "#13 Objective: To determine housing needs and know how to obtain housing and utilities based on those needs" (p. 4).

The first step was relatively simple because the problem appears clear and concise. Step 2 depends on the LD students, but for sake of argument, we shall assume they wish to solve the problem. Step 3 is difficult because of the quantification of terms; housing, in this case, has been considered buying or renting a traditional home. However, other alternatives come to mind, such as mobile homes and vacation homes. We realized that the problem could not be solved because the decisions that are made in step 3 are closely related to an individual's socioeconomic status. We also found that this step required information from economics, architecture, speech and communications, social psychology, sociology, physics, geology, geography, mathematics, and so on. In fact, we felt greater frustration in dealing with this problem than with the previous classic train problem.

The comprehensive model we have advocated in mathematics permits us to use the best of two methodologies: the CMI (Cawley) and a modified and extended procedure patterned on Manheim (1971). Using this model, the LD secondary student can acquire a generalized cognitive strategy in the resource room that can be used in solving both computation and word problems as they are presented in regular mathematics classes, at all levels of mathematics.

Other Methods

Mathematics skills can be enhanced in other ways through use of the learning strategies model that we have proposed. These methods have strengths in specific areas of mathematics, and when used as methods of instruction, they aid in developing the subskills required to solve mathematics problems. The variety of these methods enhances motivation in LD students when they are solving problems.

Identification of Systematic Error Patterns in Mathematics Computation

The first method, when adapted for student self-instruction, enables students to correct their own mistakes in computation. Ashlock (1972) based his methodology on Roberts' (1968) four "failure strategies":

1. Wrong operation: The student attempts to respond by performing an operation other than the one that is required to solve the problem.
2. Obvious computational error: The [student] applies the correct operation, but his response is based on error in recalling number facts.
3. Defective algorithm: The [student] attempts to apply the correct operation but makes errors other than number fact errors in carrying through the necessary steps.

4. Random response: The response shows no discernible relationship to the given problem. (p. 2)

Ashlock uses a semiprogrammed format to instruct teachers that there are consistent error patterns in students' mathematical computations. The errors are shown to be distributed across addition, subtraction, multiplication, and division of whole numbers, common fractions, mixed fractions, decimals, and units of measurement. In addition, Ashlock offers remediation techniques for the specific error patterns.

This method could be adapted for use by LD students as self-instruction. Then, students would be in a position to diagnose their own computational errors and generate their own remediation techniques with minor assistance from the learning disabilities teacher or the regular classroom teacher.

The major limitation of Ashlock's (1972) method is that it cannot be applied to word problems except in a cursory manner. On the other hand, this method is an excellent supplement to Cawley's (1975) CMI.

Charting Independent Student Activities

The second method can also be used by LD students to solve computational problems independently. Close supervision is not mandatory because of this method's structure and the limited reading required of the student. Collins (1972) calls this technique "Charts for independent student activities" (p. 173). This method provides the students with clear, concise directions on how to solve the problem, makes minimum demands on the student's reading competencies, and sequences the task in a highly structured manner. This permits students to solve mathematics problems without becoming frustrated with complicated written directions from which they must determine what is necessary to solve the problem, the sequence of steps required, and the resources available for assistance. An example of this method is provided by Collins (1972, p. 173, Example 1).

Compare:	First step:		Second step:	Solution:
$\frac{2}{3}$ and $\frac{4}{5}$	$\frac{2 \times 5}{3 \times 5}$	$\frac{4 \times 3}{5 \times 3}$	$\frac{10}{15} < \frac{12}{15}$	$\frac{2}{3} < \frac{4}{5}$
$\frac{3}{8}$ and $\frac{2}{9}$	$\frac{3 \times 9}{8 \times 9}$	$\frac{2 \times 8}{}$	$\frac{27}{72} > 16$	$\frac{3}{8} \quad \frac{2}{9}$
$\frac{5}{6}$ and $\frac{3}{5}$				
$\frac{5}{10}$ and $\frac{45}{90}$				

This method uses *fading* techniques to help LD students reach independent problem solving. Students will require a rather thorough knowledge of the concepts before using this method. The fading is accomplished rapidly, and the notation must be understood. This method might be an excellent review or generalization technique than can be used once LD students have shown competence in solving similar problems with assistance.

A variation of the charting methods is the flow chart method (Collins, 1972). The structure and minimal reading are positive aspects of the method. Hatley (1972) presents a simplified PERT chart to describe this method. He uses the example of preparing to give a speech, but one could very easily adapt his method to computational mathematics. The advantage of Hatley's method is that the problem solving does not necessarily have to be linear, as described by Collins (1972). The Computer-Assisted Instruction Program in New York City uses an adaptation of the flow chart method described by Mendelson (1972).

The major limitation of this method is that it requires LD students to be familiar with flow charting. Students who are not familiar with flow-charting can neither "read" the instructions nor order the sequence of the mathematical process.

Learning Activity Packages

The charting and flow chart method might best be used as part of learning activity packages (Collins, 1972). Such packages have developed in the Dade County (Florida) school system for students who are having difficulty with mathematics. Collins (1972, p. 175) presents the following components included in each package:

LEARNING ACTIVITY PACKAGE (LAP)

Student's Unit	Teacher's Commentary
1. Procedure flow chart	1. Introduction
2. Behavioral objectives stated in language student can understand.	2. Prerequisites
	3. Sequence placements
	4. Vocabulary
3. Pretest (situational as well as paper and pencil)	5. Suggested required activities
	6. Objectives correlated with pretest and activities
4. Activities: paper and pencil, audio tapes, films or	7. Comments on evaluation

filmstrips, laboratory experiments, references to textbooks,
magazines, games, puzzles,
drill and practice

8. Posttest (situational as well as
paper and pencil)
9. Keys to tests and activities

The learning activity package is a structured approach to individualized instruction. It permits the teacher to plan activities that capitalize on students' strengths and interests while providing a series of integrated activities to remediate their mathematics deficiencies. This approach has five major advantages that should be considered. First, the learning activity packages can be developed to provide students with the opportunities to use the media, materials, and facilities currently available. Second, the packages can be developed to provide for both individual and group participation. A third advantage is that all teachers' methodologies can be integrated into the packages. Four, if the teachers develop a scope and sequence chart of the mathematics curriculum, a series of short learning activity packages of ten to twelve pages can be used as an alternate to heavy emphasis on the textbook. Finally, the learning activity packages permit teachers to make maximum use of their own ideas and products.

The major disadvantage of the learning activity packages is the amount of time required for teachers to construct the packages and to monitor the progress of students who are working on them.

Another disadvantage is that the packages may be constructed without consideration for the curricular requirements of the content area. If this occurs, students will subsequently fail in areas in which the concepts have not been taught. This disadvantage can be reduced to a minor level if teachers plan adequately before developing the packages.

The Mathematics Laboratory

One method that can be developed with the learning activity package is the mathematics laboratory. Davidson and Walter (1972) have given a detailed description of a mathematics laboratory, including many examples of activities. The integration of the mathematics laboratory with learning packages similar to those described by Collins (1972) has been successfully accomplished at the Sir R. L. Borden Secondary School in Scarborough, Ontario (Strobel, 1972).

The mathematics laboratory is not a physical facility, but rather a method of teaching mathematics. The method makes use of concrete objects, such as geoboards, abacuses, Cuisenaire rods, Diane's Multibase Arithmetic Blocks, Stern Structural Arithmetic Apparatus chips, bottle caps, beads, straws, cubes, and at least fifty other materials. These are used to solve mathematics problems, discover mathematical rules, and/or to illustrate rules of mathematics. Use of the mathematics laboratory emphasizes active student involvement in mathematics problem solving at the concrete level and the maximum use of manipulative skills rather than verbal skills. Because the laboratory is designed to provide for individual strengths and deficits, enhancement of the student's self image is an important outcome (Davidson & Walter, 1972).

The major emphasis of the mathematics laboratory makes it useful for various groups of students (Scott, 1972). The major disadvantage is the minor emphasis on structure. This is a weakness of many other methods advocated by those using the problem-solving approach for teaching students who fail in the traditional curriculum.

The Banded Approach

LD secondary students require structure because of their limited attention spans (Seigel, 1974). One approach that has been suggested is the "banded approach" (Brant, 1972) used in the Baltimore (Maryland) County school system. The example offered by Brant consists of twelve daily lessons broken into three bands each.

Band I is a short activity period of five to ten minutes. During this band, students either review previously attained objectives (competencies) for maintenance or generalization or engage in motivational activities in preparation for Band II. The activity of Band I does not have to be directly related to the instruction provided in Band II.

Band II is the fulcrum of this approach. During this twenty to twenty-five minute period, new concepts are presented to students. Students practice using the concept, and time is allotted for informal assessment to determine if students have achieved the instructional objective. Twenty to twenty-five minutes of sustained instruction is felt to be the maximum period for students enrolled in basic education programs.

Band III time, from five to ten minutes, can be used in two ways. One way is to involve all students in group problem solving. An alternative is to permit students to select individual problem-solving activities that suit their own interests. Many mathematics laboratory activities can occupy students during Band III time (Brant, 1972).

Advantages of the banded approach are that it considers the nature of the task, the number of objectives, and the characteristics of the student. It is flexible enough to permit a greater or lesser number than three bands and to provide alternative activities during each band. It could be useful for integrating grouping procedures and instructional materials (Alley, 1977).

The major disadvantage is that continuity of daily sessions suffers when students are involved in several different activities that relate to different mathematical concepts. A minor disadvantage is that the banded approach requires meticulous lesson planning and an abundance of activities to maintain student interest.

Teachers, Learners, Instructional Procedures, and Materials in Mathematics

Role of the Teacher

Faulk and Landry (1961) found that teachers provide students with different learning strategies than those provided in mathematics textbooks. They asked seventy teachers about their primary mathematics learning strategy and searched for strategies in a mathematics textbook series that covered grades five through seven. The teachers provided fourteen strategies and the investigators identified thirteen strategies in the textbooks. There was no overlap between the two sets of strategies.

A related finding reported by Faulk and Landry was that nearly half of the teachers (n = 34) either taught the students to (1) correctly label the elements of the problem or (2) check their answers. In contrast, they found that approximately half (n = 17) of the identified strategies related to (1) reading problems carefully and (2) selecting the correct process (algorithm) to solve the problem.

It appears to be critical to the skill of LD students in solving mathematics problems for the students to be reinforced by the teacher when they use the strategy provided by the text. At least, the teacher should identify the strategy being advocated by the text, and if the textbook strategy is not used, the teacher should tell LD students so.

Dilendik (1976) reported on the achievement of 336 secondary students after they had viewed a videotape of a teacher presenting ten units, including factual data, on fictitious Indian tribes. The factual data were the basis for a social studies achievement test. Dilendik found that attitude similarity between the teacher and the students did not relate to students' achievement, attitudes, preferences for a teaching method, or opinion of the instructional materials. This finding may have implications both for the teachers' choice of learning strategies and for students' mathematics achievement. The most important variable may be that the strategy is viewed as an essential tool in learning by the students.

Students' Acceptance of Problems

Swenson (1965) reports that students must accept mathematics problems as their own problems to solve rather than as irrelevant problems posed by others to test the students' problem-solving abilities.

Swenson names three conditions that are necessary before students will accept problems as their own:

1. Students must understand the meaning of the problem and its implications.
2. Students must feel confident of their ability to solve the problem.
3. Students must want to know the answer for present or future applications.

Trueblood (1969) met these conditions when he attempted to promote problem-solving skills by using nonverbal problems. Specifically, Trueblood wished to teach students to read an odometer and road mileage markers. His procedure to develop skills as well as student commitment was to (1) focus on the problem and not the reading of the problem, (2) present the problem in flexible and differing contexts, (3) cast the problem within students' real-life experiences, and (4) individualize the problem to capture student interest.

Trueblood used content (reading odometers and road signs) that is highly motivating to most secondary students. The teacher may well be required to use more creativity when teaching other subjects, such as photosynthesis. But the assumption still remains: Students must feel that their efforts to solve mathematics problems have some important ends. The essential elements appear to be that the student feels the problem can be solved and that the solution has application outside the assignment.

Individualization of Mathematics Instruction

If teachers are to individualize mathematics instruction for LD secondary students, we would suggest that they follow these principles developed by Cawley (1975):

Principle I: Arithmetical programs for handicapped children must include activities and instructional sequences that reduce the influence of the chronological age factor in performance.

Principle II: Individualized arithmetic programs for handicapped children must be based on recognition of the principle that successful performance facilitates learning.

173

Principle III: Reduce the fixed frequency system which predominates in most arithmetic programs.

Principle IV: The system must be capable of providing the teacher with qualitative options.

Principle V: Arithmetic programs must be capable of providing instant diagnostic information to the teacher.

Principle VI: The system must be efficient in terms of teacher/learner time and effort.

Principle VII: Arithmetical programs designed to individualize instruction must be developed within the framework of a comprehensive model of instruction. (p. 17)

Principles III and IV appear to us to require further clarification. Pace (1961) has provided clarification for Principle III. He states that students' problem solving is improved in relation to the number of problem-solving opportunities that are provided to them. Thus, Cawley has stated that the problem-solving opportunities must be increased when teaching these skills to students who have deficits in this area. However, Pace has wisely stated that it is not just more solving of one type of problem. Rather, the students require a variety of problems to solve and guidance in using more sophisticated strategies. This latter statement seems to clarify Cawley's fourth principle. We would add one other element that is related to both of Cawley's principles: LD students need various types of problems presented in various contexts to which to apply learning strategies.

Procedures in Problem Solving

Several authors (Earp, 1970; Forase, 1968; Goodstein, circa 1972; LeBlanc, 1977; Sims, 1969; Vos, 1976) have suggested either general or specific procedures to aid in teaching mathematical verbal problem solving. LeBlanc stated four procedures in problem solving:

1. Understanding the problem.
2. Planning the solution.
3. Solving the problem.
4. Reviewing the solution in the context of the problem.

To assist the student in understanding the problem, Forase (1968) suggested that the teacher provide the student with some instructional control over the problem using preorganizers and postorganizers. Pre-organizers are questions posed by the teacher that are given to students before the problem is presented. A preorganizer helps students organize their ideas in relation to the problem. Forase cautions that preorganizers

174

should be general, inclusive questions rather than specific, exclusive questions. Conversely, postorganizer questions posed after students have solved the problem should help them review the solution process, confirm the strategy used in the solution, and provide a hint that ties the solved problem to a forthcoming problem. Learning disabled adolescents will require *both* preorganizers and postorganizers in remediation of their mathematics skills. We base this statement on an investigation of Williams and McCreight (1965) who found that using either all preorganizers or all postorganizers yielded small differences in students' formal test scores. It is only when both preorganizers and postorganizers are used that a difference is apparent.

Earp (1970) lists five subprocedures to facilitate students' ability to understand a problem and plan a solution or solutions. In hierarchical order *and* with slight modification for purposes of clarity, the techniques are as follows:

1. Use a first reading to visualize the situation.
2. Reread the problem to get the essential facts.
3. Note technical vocabulary and/or difficult concepts.
4. Reread the problem to assist in planning the steps for its solution.
5. Reread the problem a third time to check understanding and planned solution.

Rereading the problem will be beneficial *only if* the LD students can visualize the problem situation. Therefore, the problem may have to be read to the students (Goodstein, circa 1972). Vos (1976) suggests that problem situations can be visualized by drawing a diagram, drawing a picture that approximates or verifies the problem situation, constructing an equation or algorithm using the data provided in the problem, classifying sets and subsets of data using Venn diagrams, and/or constructing a figure, table, grid, or chart to organize the data of the problem.

To help the teacher apply these procedures and subprocedures, we suggest consulting Sims (1969), who provides exercises that emphasize the use of learning strategies in mathematics problem solving. If the teacher wishes more structure in assisting students, we suggest the checklist provided by Vos (1976, p. 267). The checklist could be used by students who are having difficulty in finding the solution. Students might apply the checklist before seeking the teacher's assistance.

The procedures and subprocedures suggested above may help LD students solve mathematics problems. However, it may well be that some students still cannot solve problems even with these procedural learning strategies. The teacher should then use materials to represent problem situations. It may be that the student cannot solve the following problem in its symbolic terms:

$$14_x + 15_y - 6_x + 2_y = \square$$

The problem remains difficult when expressed in iconic (pictorial) format. However, if the teacher uses enactive (concrete) manipulative materials, for example, circle = x and square = y, the student is likely to have less difficulty solving the problem.

These three representations of variables can be used in formulating and expressing ideas (Hardgrove & Sueltz, 1969). The two investigators suggest that the teacher use concrete manipulative materials when students cannot conceptualize problems or are being introduced to new concepts. If students are unsure of their conceptualization of problems or are practicing a new mathematics concept or skill, we suggest the initial use of iconic or pictorial materials. Students who are applying newly mastered knowledge of a concept or skill to a group of similar problems will most likely use symbolic representations in terms of mathematical equations or algorithms.

When helping an LD secondary student with mathematics skills, the teacher should make use of all levels of materials. Concrete materials are best used when counting, comparing, or describing objects. Popular concrete materials include clocks, scales, and Cuisenaire rods. Pictorial materials may include photographs, films, graphs, and tables. Generally, pictorial objects are not used to develop a higher level of conceptualization but rather because of the unavailability of concrete objects. In most cases only symbolic materials are used at the secondary level. Learning disabled students who cannot solve the problems provided in the textbook on a symbolic level are generally offered no alternative representations. Therefore, both the learning disabilities teacher and the regular class mathematics teachers must teach various strategies using different levels of object representation with LD students.

REFERENCES

Alley, G. R. Grouping secondary learning disabilities students according to teaching method and material. *Academic Therapy*, 1977, *13*, 37-45.

Ashlock, R. B. *Error patterns in computation: A semi-programmed approach.* Columbus, Ohio: Merrill, 1972.

Barney, L. Problems associated with the reading of arithmetic. *The Arithmetic Teacher*, 1972, *19*, 131-133.

Beatty, L. S., Madden, R., Gardner, E. F., & Karlsen, B. *Stanford diagnostic mathematics test: Brown level.* New York: Harcourt Brace Jovanovich, 1976.

Bell, M. D. The role of applications in early mathematics learning. In J. L. Higgins (Ed.), *Cognitive psychology and the mathematics laboratory.* Evanston, Ill.: Northwestern University, 1973.

Blankenship, C. S., & Lovitt, T. C. Story problems: Merely confusing or downright befuddling. *Journal for Research in Mathematics Education,* 1976, 7, 290-298.

Bloom, B. S. (Ed.). *Taxonomy of educational objectives. Handbook I: Cognitive domain.* New York: McKay, 1956.

Brant, V. Mathematics for basic education (Grades 7-11). In W. C. Lowry (Ed.), *The slow learner in mathematics,* Thirty-fifth Yearbook of the National Council of Teachers of Mathematics. Washington, D.C.: NCTM, 1972.

Cawley, J. F. *Math curricula for the secondary learning disabled student.* Paper presented at a symposium on learning disabilities in the secondary schools, Norristown, Pa., March 1975.

Cawley, J. F., & Fitzmaurice, A. M. *The individualization of instruction: Illustrations from arithmetical programming for handicapped children.* Unpublished manuscript, University of Connecticut, 1975.

Chalfant, J. C., & Scheffelin, M. A. *Central processing dysfunctions in children: A review of research* (NINDA Monograph No. 9, U.S. Department of Health, Education and Welfare). Washington, D.C.: U.S. Government Printing Office, 1969.

Collins, E. A. Teaching styles (Secondary school). In W. C. Lowry (Ed.), *The slow learner in mathematics,* Thirty-fifth Yearbook of The National Council of Teachers of Mathematics. Washington, D.C.: NCTM, 1972.

Cox, L. S. Diagnosing and remediating systematic errors in addition and subtraction computations. *The Arithmetic Teacher,* 1975, 22, 151-157.

Cruickshank, W. M. Arithmetic ability of mentally retarded children: I. Ability to differentiate extraneous materials from needed arithmetical facts. *Journal of Educational Research,* 1948, 42, 161-170.

Davidson, P. S., & Walter, M. I. A laboratory approach. In W. C. Lowry (Ed.), *The slow learner in mathematics,* Thirty-fifth Yearbook of The National Council of Teachers of Mathematics. Washington, D.C.: NCTM, 1972.

Dilendik, J. R. Attitude similarity and the covert curriculum. *Journal of Educational Research,* 1976, 69, 304-409.

Earp, N. W. Procedures for teaching reading in mathematics. *The Arithmetic Teacher,* 1970, 17, 575-579.

Eicholz, R. E., & O'Daffer, P. G. *Book 3, Elementary School Mathematics* (2nd ed.). Menlo Park, Calif.: Addison-Wesley, 1968.

Engelhart, M. D. The relative contribution of certain factors to individual differences in arithmetical problem solving ability. *Journal of Experimental Education,* 1932, 1, 19-27.

Enstrom, J. M. *A training program to teach learning disabled elementary students to monitor their errors in computational mathematics.* Unpublished master's thesis, University of Kansas, 1977.

Faulk, C. J., & Landry, T. R. An approach to problem-solving. *The Arithmetic Teacher,* 1961, April, 157-160.

Fernald, G. M. *Remedial teachniques in basic school stujects.* New York: McGraw-Hill, 1943.

Forase, L. T. Questions as aids to reading: Some research and theory. *American Educational Research Journal,* 1968, 5, 319-332.

Gagne, R. M. *The conditions of learning* (2nd ed.). New York: Holt, Rinehart & Winston, 1970.

Glaser, R., & Resnick, L. B. Instructional psychology. In P. Mussen & M. Rosenzweig (Eds.), *Annual review of psychology* (Vol. 23). Palo Alto, Calif.: Annual Reviews Inc., 1972.

Glennon, V. J., & Wilson, J. W. Diagnostic-prescriptive teaching. In W. C. Lowry (Ed.), *The slow learner in mathematics,* Thirty-fifth Yearbook of the National Council of Teachers of Mathematics. Washington, D.C.: NCTM, 1972.

Goodstein, H. A. *A use of picture materials to facilitate verbal problem-solving.* Unpublished manuscript, University of Connecticut, circa 1972.

Goodstein, H. A. Assessment and programming in mathematics for the handicapped. *Focus on Exceptional Children,* 1975, 7, 1-11.

Goodstein, H. A., & Kahn, H. *A brief inquiry into the pattern of achievement among children with learning disabilities.* Unpublished manuscript, University of Connecticut, 1973.

Hardgrove, C. E., & Sueltz, B. A. Instructional materials. In F. E. Grossnickle (Chair), *Instruction in Arithmetic,* Twenty-fifth Yearbook of The National Council of Teachers of Mathematics. Washington, D.C.: NCTM, 1969.

Hatley, R. U. *Flowcharting, program evaluation and review technique, and critical path method.* Paper presented at an educational research and development training program, University of Kansas, August 1972.

Havertape, J. *Problem solving in the learning disabled high school student.* Unpublished doctoral dissertation, University of Arizona, 1976.

Johnson, D. J., & Myklebust, H. R. *Learning disabilities: Educational principles and practices.* New York: Grune & Stratton, 1967.

Klausmeier, H. S., & Loughlin, L. J. Behaviors during problem solving among children of low, average and high intelligence. *Journal of Educational Psychology,* 1967, *52,* 148-152.

Lapore, A. *A comparison of computational errors between educable mentally handicapped and learning disability children.* Unpublished manuscript, University of Connecticut, 1977.

LeBlanc, J. F. You can teach problem solving. *The Arithmetic Teacher,* 1977, *25,* 16-20.

Linville, W. J. Syntax vocabulary and the verbal arithmetic problem. *School Science and Mathematics,* 1970, *70,* 152-158.

Manheim, J. Word problems or problems with words. In C. W. Schminke & W. R. Arnold (Eds.), *Mathematics is a verb.* Hinsdale, Ill.: Dryden Press, 1971.

Mendelson, M. Computer-assisted instruction in New York City. In W. C. Lowry (Ed.), *The slow learner in mathematics,* Thirty-fifth Yearbook of The National Council of Teachers of Mathematics. Washington, D.C.: NCTM, 1972.

Northcutt, N. *Adult functional competency: A summary.* Austin: Industrial and Business Training Bureau, Division of Extension, The University of Texas at Austin, March 1975. (Mimeo)

Pace, A. Understanding the ability to solve problems. *The Arithmetic Teacher,* 1961, May, 226-233.

Roberts, G. H. The failure strategies of third grade arithmetic pupils. *The Arithmetic Teacher,* 1968, *15,* 442-446.

Ross, J. D., & Ross, C. M. *Ross test of higher cognitive processes.* San Rafael, Calif.: Academic Therapy, 1976.

Scott, J. L. Chicago's attempts to meet the needs of the inner-city child via math labs. In W. C. Lowry (Ed.), *The slow learner in mathematics,* Thirty-fifth Yearbook of The National Council of Teachers of Mathematics. Washington, D.C.: NCTM, 1972.

Seigel, E. *The exceptional child grows up.* New York: Dutton, 1974.

Sims, J. Improving problem-solving skills. *The Arithmetic Teacher,* 1969, *16,* 17-20.

Stone, J. C., & Mallory, V. J. *A first course in algebra* (revised). Chicago: Benjamin H. Sandborn, 1936.

Strobel, L. R. The mathematics laboratory at the Sir R. L. Borden Secondary School. In W. C. Lowry (Ed.), *The slow learner in mathematics,* Thirty-fifth Yearbook of The National Council of Teachers of Mathematics. Washington, D.C.: NCTM, 1972.

Suppes, P. Some theoretical models for mathematics learning. *Journal of Research Development in Education,* 1967, *1,* 5-22.

Suppes, P., Hyman, L., & Jerman, M. Linear structural models for response and latency performance in arithmetic on computer-controlled terminals. In J. P. Hill (Ed.), *Minnesota symposia on child psychology.* Minneapolis: University of Minnesota, 1967.

Suppes, P., Jerman, M., & Brian, D. *Computer-assisted instruction: Stanford 1967-66 arithmetic program.* New York: Academic Press, 1968.

Suydam, M. W. *Unpublished instruments for evaluation in mathematics education.* Columbus, Ohio: The Ohio State University, 1974.

Swenson, E. J. How much real problem solving? *The Arithmetic Teacher,* 1965, October, 426-430.

Trueblood, C. R. Promoting problem-solving skills through nonverbal problems. *The Arithmetic Teacher*, 1969, *16*, 7-9.

Vos, K. E. The effects of three instructional strategies on problem-solving behaviors in secondary school mathematics. *Journal for Research in Mathematics Education*, 1976, 7, 265-275.

Wallace, G., & McLoughlin, J. A. *Learning disabilities: Concepts and characteristics.* Columbus, Ohio: Merrill, 1975.

Williams, M. H., & McCreight, R. W. Shall we move the question? *The Arithmetic Teacher*, 1965, October, 418-421.

THINKING: STRATEGIES AND METHODS

6

Much of the instruction for LD adolescents is directed toward improvement of basic reading or mathematics skills. It is ironic that a discipline devoted to studying dysfunctions in learning has given so much attention to the acquisition of rudimentary skills and so little attention to the development of higher order cognitive processes that are equally important in achieving academic success and life adjustment.

Acquiring efficient thinking and problem-solving strategies is a necessity for the LD adolescent who faces the complex demands of the curriculum and the necessity of preparing for life after high school. Feldhusen and Treffinger (1977) have emphasized the importance of such skills in today's world:

> In an increasingly complex, ever changing, challenging and problem-ridden world, people of all ages have great need to be good creative thinkers and good problem solvers. However, the greatest hope for improving thinking lies with children in school. It is easier to arrange the conditions in school to help children learn how to think than to try to change adults, most of whom are no longer involved in formal education. (p. 4)

Several unwarranted assumptions underlie the field's heavy emphasis on basic skills. One such assumption is that LD students cannot deal with higher order tasks until prerequisite skills have been mastered. However, because LD students possess intellectual abilities within the normal range, they can comprehend and process information at or above their assigned grade level. In many instances, LD students with limited reading skills gain minimal exposure to materials, ideas, and content at their assigned grade level. Only as prerequisite skills, such as decoding ability, are mastered are students exposed to more complex content and ideas.

Another unwarranted assumption is that there is little that teachers can do to alter students' thinking skills. Research on critical thinking and problem solving suggests that students are responsive to such instruction. DeBono (1970) maintains that "lateral thinking can be learned, practiced, and used. It is possible to acquire skill in it just as it is possible to acquire skill in mathematics" (p. 7). Shaver (1962), in reviewing the research on critical thinking, drew the following conclusion:

> Probably the most conclusive suggestion supported by the research reviewed here is that we should not expect that our students will learn to think critically as a by-product of the study of the usual social studies content. Instead, each teacher should determine what concepts are essential — e.g., that of relevance — if his students are to perform the intellectual operations deemed necessary to critical thinking — such as, for example, the formulation and evaluation of hypotheses. Each of these should be taught explicitly to the students. Utilizing what is known about transfer of learning, a further step can be suggested: Situations as similar as possible to those in which the students are to use their competencies should also be set up in the classroom, and the students guided in application of the concepts in this context. (p. 187)

Fraenkel (1973) has adopted the following assumptions about instruction in thinking skills:

- Thinking skills can be taught.
- Thinking involves an active transaction between an individual and the data with which he is working. Data (information) become meaningful only when an individual performs certain cognitive operations upon it. Thus, students must be involved and actively working with data if thinking is to be encouraged.
- The ability to think cannot be "given" by teachers to students. How well an individual thinks depends on the richness and significance of the content with which he works, his own interest and desire to participate in the endeavor, the processes he uses, and the initial assistance he is given in the development of such processes.
- All subjects offer an appropriate context for thinking.
- All children are capable of thinking at abstract levels, though the quality of individual thinking differs markedly.
- Since thinking takes many forms, the specific thinking processes which are being developed should be clearly differentiated in the teacher's mind.
- Precise teaching strategies can be developed which will encourage and improve student thinking. (p. 188)

The authors contend that a major goal of the educational program for LD adolescents should be to help them learn to think, that is, to use information as productively as possible.

The factors included under the general rubric of thinking vary among authors. For our purposes we have attempted to identify those thinking skills demanded by the curricular, social, leisure, and job requirements of the secondary and postsecondary student. Table 6.1 lists those skills.

TABLE 6.1
Thinking Skills

A. General Thinking Behaviors
   1. Observing
   2. Describing
   3. Developing concepts
   4. Differentiating and defining
   5. Hypothesizing
   6. Comparing and contrasting
   7. Generalizing
   8. Predicting and explaining
   9. Offering alternatives
B. Information Organization and Management
   1. Perceiving organization in material
   2. Manipulating materials for organizing
   3. Organizing multiple tasks
   4. Using generalizations as organizers
   5. Using concepts as organizers
   6. Visual imagery
C. Problem Solving
   1. Identifying the problem
   2. Analyzing the problem
   3. Developing options for solving the problem
   4. Decision making
   5. Executing the decision
D. Questioning
   1. Asking questions of materials
   2. Asking different kinds of questions
E. Self-Monitoring of Performance
F. Time Management

For the purpose of this chapter, *thinking has been defined as the process that involves the collection, manipulation, and use of information to solve problems.* This chapter presents methods and techniques designed to improve the thinking skills of LD adolescents. It should be noted that most factors discussed in this chapter cut across other skill areas dealt with in this book.

THINKING CHARACTERISTICS OF LD ADOLESCENTS

Limited research data are available about the thinking characteristics of LD adolescents. Observational data suggest, however, that these students often exhibit ineffective thinking behaviors. Wilcox (1970), for example, has specified some characteristics of LD adolescents that may account for a breakdown in logical thinking. Among these factors are distractibility, inability to sustain attention, breaks in continuity of thought, poor feedback, overlooking or not noticing, poor organization, difficulty in selecting, lack of resourcefulness, and deficient memory.

Havertape (1976) investigated the differences in problem solving between LD and nondisabled junior and senior high school students. He noted that the LD group exhibited perseveration, disinhibition, and qualitatively different approaches in solving problems. Specifically, he found that the learning disabled (1) did not attend appropriately to directions for completing a task and tended to be misled by irrelevant information; (2) seemed to listen attentively to directions, but either could not carry out these directions properly or did not sort out for rehearsal the essential information to be remembered; (3) evidenced random response behavior or impulsive guessing in coming to a problem solution. Havertape concluded that intervention procedures should focus on teaching the adolescent to attend selectively and to respond less impulsively.

Whimbey (1975) found that in problem-solving situations low IQ college students failed to use the abstractions they formed; failed to make systematic comparisons of data; and by lacking the patience for isolating the correct alternative, applied "one-shot" thinking and willingly allowed gaps of knowledge to exist.

The research conducted in the areas of impulsivity, selective attention, and categorization provides some insight into the thinking characteristics of the learning disabled.

Studies of impulsivity have been based on a construct developed by Kagan (1966). This construct refers to the presence or absence of the ability to delay a response until all alternatives have been evaluated. The findings of Keogh (1971) and Hallahan, Kauffman, and Ball (1973) have found that the learning disabled tend to choose the first item that resembles the correct answer without examining all alternatives. Messer (1970) and Walloch and Kogan (1962) found that impulsivity not only leads to errors, but also to social maladjustment.

Studies of attention have been based on the concept of field independence and dependence. Field independence refers to the ability of the individual to attend to relevant stimuli while ignoring the irrelevant. Field dependence refers to the tendency to respond as a whole, rather than selectively. Studies by Keogh and Donlon (1972) and Atkinson and Seunath (1973) found the learning disabled to be more field dependent than the nondisabled.

Learning disabled students generally perform more poorly than their peers in categorizing information. Parker, Freston, and Drew (1975) found that LD students did not use the organization of material in their efforts to recall the material.

The research concerning the problem-solving and thinking strategies of LD students indicates that they are inferior to their peers along a variety of dimensions. The LD students tend to be more distractible and more impulsive. Further, they are less able to attend selectively, to take advantage of organized material, and to shift their attention from one stimulus to another. These deficits underline the importance of considering thinking abilities in programming for the LD adolescent. Specific attention must be given to these behaviors in light of their importance in general school performance.

ASSESSING THINKING SKILLS

The teacher can gain much information about the thinking skills of the LD adolescent through informal assessment procedures and by carefully observing how students perform on other tests such as reading or mathematics. In each of these tests, the students must apply thinking skills, and teacher observation yields valuable information regarding response patterns, risk-taking behavior, and attitude toward problems.

Most of the devices developed to assess thinking are informal in nature. The focus of our discussion will be some of these informal measures. However, in the last part of this section, we will present some formal measures that have been found helpful in assessing thinking skills. The instruments discussed throughout this section are intended to be a representative rather than exhaustive listing of assessment devices.

Informal Measures

An important step in assessing thinking skills is to determine how well grounded the student is in prerequisite skills underlying a particular skill. For example, Thomas and Robinson (1975) list a set of questions that will help the teacher determine a student's readiness to apply problem-solving skills in reading. These questions are presented below. The teacher may want to rate the student on each prerequisite skill, using a scale of 1 to 5, with 5 representing mastery.

1. Does the student know how to narrow the problem to manageable proportions and to state it precisely?
2. Does the student know how to set up reading targets?
3. Can the student locate books and other sources of the desired information?
4. Can the student use a book's table of contents and index as aids in locating information?
5. Can the student scan a passage for information that bears upon the problem?
6. Does the student discriminate between what is relevant to the problem and what is irrelevant?
7. Does the student evaluate what is read — selecting or rejecting after a critical appraisal?
8. Can the student make notes efficiently from a number of scattered sources?
9. Can the student bring the information collected into an orderly presentation?

An informal measure that is easy and relatively quick to administer is a checklist of LD students' perceptions of their thinking ability. A sample instrument is presented below (Williams, 1972). It can be easily adapted by adding items that are unique to a particular situation. In addition to having students complete the instrument, the classroom teacher, learning disabilities teacher, and parents can complete the list. Then these ratings can be compared with those given by the students.

A Second Look at Mental Ability

Activity One

Do you know how to make better use of your mental ability? Respond to the following questions by marking the appropriate box.

	Yes	No	Undecided
1. Do you see yourself as one who likes to work with ideas?	☐	☐	☐
2. Do you believe that there is nothing new — just things you don't know about?	☐	☐	☐
3. Do you regard yourself as a creative person?	☐	☐	☐
4. Do you think that you can learn to become more creative?	☐	☐	☐
5. Do you make an effort to try new things?	☐	☐	☐
6. Do you work with your mind, regardless of the job at hand?	☐	☐	☐
7. Do you find it easy to overcome inertia and start a new task?	☐	☐	☐
8. Do you use your imagination to create ideas of your own?	☐	☐	☐

9.	Do you possess the determination to stick with a task until it is completed?	☐ ☐ ☐
10.	Do you believe in yourself and in your abilities?	☐ ☐ ☐
11.	Do you like the responses you have made to the previous ten questions?	☐ ☐ ☐

Planning means to provide yourself with three essentials of success:

	Agree	Disagree	Undecided
First, setting a goal to achieve something you want; a specific objective.	☐	☐	☐
Second, a plan to reach your goal.	☐	☐	☐
Third, time control; a schedule to save time.	☐	☐	☐

Activity Two

Respond to the following questions by marking the appropriate box.

		Yes	No	Undecided
1.	Do you think you have more mental ability than you use?	☐	☐	☐
2.	Do you think you can better use the mental ability you have?	☐	☐	☐
3.	Do you think you are intelligent enough to be successful in school and work?	☐	☐	☐
4.	Do you think if you reorganized your habits, you could act in a more intelligent manner?	☐	☐	☐
5.	Do you think your level of intelligence affects your state of happiness?	☐	☐	☐
6.	Do you think that motivation plays a role in success?	☐	☐	☐
7.	Do you allow emotional problems to affect your performance?	☐	☐	☐
8.	Do you typically ask yourself or others "Why?" when you don't know?	☐	☐	☐
9.	Do you allow your attitude to affect your performance on tests?	☐	☐	☐
10.	Do you think that emotions affect test scores?	☐	☐	☐
11.	Do you think that your IQ can change?	☐	☐	☐
12.	Do you think that your IQ should keep you from accomplishing your goals?	☐	☐	☐
13.	Do you think that a person with determination will do better in problem-solving situations than one who gives up when faced with a difficult problem?	☐	☐	☐
14.	Do you think that your IQ should limit your choice of career?	☐	☐	☐

From *Motivation for Career Success* by J. C. Williams (Waco, Texas: Education Achievement Corp., 1972) pp. 5-6.

Much of the research in problem solving has assessed the skills of individuals by presenting to them some "classical" problems. These problems usually are challenging and unique in content. Thus, most students are motivated to attempt a solution. Examples of two of these problems are the "Farmer Problem" and the "Prisoner Problem."

Farmer Problem

Once there lived a farmer with four sons. The sons were very jealous of each other and always suspected the father of showing favoritism toward one or the other. So when the time came for the farmer to retire, he was faced with a problem.

He had an odd-shaped piece of land (without buildings) which he decided to divide equally among his sons. Suppose he asked you to divide the piece of land shown below into four parts equal in size and shape, with none left over. Show how you would do this in the following diagram.

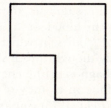

(Answer: Each part has the same shape as the original area, which is three-quarters of a square. Divide each quarter into four small squares, thus making twelve. Each son gets three of them.)

Prisoner Problem

Below is a diagram showing the arrangement of cells in a state prison. One day the prisoner in the cell marked with an X went berserk and was overcome with the urge to kill. So he broke through the wall that separated his cell from the one next to it and murdered the inmate there. This intensified his madness, so he proceeded to break into each cell and kill the prisoner there. After each was dead, he would drop the body and go on to the next. He would never go back into a cell containing a dead body. Every cell contained a prisoner; he never went through a cell without murdering anyone he found there; and he never broke through an outside wall or a corner.

When the authorities finally arrived, he was just killing the last inmate, in the cell marked O. Show on the diagram a path he might have taken to arrive at that cell last.

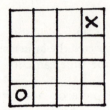

(Answer: He goes to an adjacent cell, kills the prisoner, returns to his own cell, and then proceeds to the other adjacent cell; he continues from cell to cell.)

To analyze problem-solving strategies, the teacher can ask students individually to solve the problem aloud or to give themselves verbal self-directions. There are several studies in which verbalized self-instructions have been examined to study thought processes. Buswell and John (1926) employed this technique to diagnose arithmetic problems. Bloom and Broder (1950) employed the technique in a study of problem solving in college students. Goor and Sommerfield (1975) employed the same technique in a study of problem-solving processes of creative and noncreative students.

While verbalized self-instructions may have some limitations (Bloom & Broker, 1950), they appear to be effective in the *informal* investigation of problem-solving processes. Some authors have emphasized the advantages of this technique. Gogue and Smith (1962), for example, found that verbalization during problem solving facilitated rather than interfered with the process. The students were forced to think of reasons for steps, and this helped them discover general principles.

Fraenkel (1973) has suggested that thinking skills be measured in the context of Bloom's taxonomy (the cognitive domain). The major advantage he sees to using this taxonomy is that the teacher gathers data on all levels and types of thinking (not just students' ability to remember information). The following are sample assessment questions from each of the levels of Bloom's taxonomy as given by Fraenkel:

1. *Memory:* "The revolt of the Pennsylvania farmers who objected to paying excise taxes during George Washington's administration is known as the _____."
2. *Translation:* "Restate the first paragraph of the Declaration of Independence in your own words."

190

3. *Interpretation:* "Below are some statistics relating to education and occupations. You are to judge what conclusions may be drawn from them."
4. *Application:* "In warm weather people who do not have refrigerators sometimes wrap a bottle of milk in a wet towel and place it where there is good circulation of air. Would a bottle of milk stay sweet as long as a similar bottle of milk without a wet towel?"
5. *Analysis:* "We're going to watch a short film on civil rights. The author of the film states that he is arguing neither for nor against the position, but is only describing it. Do you agree? Explain."
6. *Synthesis:* "What hypotheses can you suggest for why people in the tropics seldom develop a high level of civilization?"
7. *Evaluation:* "Examine the conclusions below in light of the selection you just read. Assuming the paragraphs you read gave a fair statement of the problem, which one of the conclusions do you think is justified?" (pp. 297-309)

In summary, the informal measures discussed above are a sample of the kinds of questions and procedures that can be used to assess the thinking skills of LD adolescents. Again, it is most important that the teacher carefully observe and record the behavior of LD adolescents to determine particular response and problem-solving patterns that may indicate the difficulties they are encountering in school.

Formal Measures

Most formal tests available to assess thinking skills are designed to evaluate students' ability to solve formal problems that require some form of right or wrong answer. Unfortunately, few tests are available for some cognitive areas. For example, although most schools spend the majority of the time teaching students information they are expected to memorize, and although memorization is greatly facilitated by the use of mnemonic strategies, tests are not available to assess this skill formally.

The Center for the Study of Evaluation at UCLA completed a major project in 1972 that was designed to identify, organize, and evaluate tests of higher-order cognitive, affective, and interpersonal skills. The reader is referred to the final report, *CSE-RBS Test Evaluations: Tests of Higher Cognitive, Affective and Interpersonal Skills*[1], for a complete listing and evaluation of the instruments identified. Tests are classified along six major dimensions:

1. Information organization and comprehension.
2. Information communication.

---

[1] Copies available from Dissemination Office, Center for the Study of Evaluation, Graduate School of Education, University of California, 405 Hilgard Avenue, Los Angeles, California 90024.

3. Analysis and interpretation.
4. Synthesis and production of new information.
5. Assessment of the reliability of information.
6. Value clarification and decision making.

The tests included in this report focus on the area of cognition beyond memory and specific subject-matter knowledge. A summary of the tests that were located and evaluated is presented in Table 6.2. The meanings of the column headings are as follows:

> *Verbal-semantic* tests involve the processing of language and language-related data. Also included in this dimension are instruments that present pictures rather than verbal content, when the problem cannot be solved by perceptual means but must be dealt with on a verbal-conceptual level.
> *Symbolic* tests include the mental manipulation of numerical, alphabetical, or novel symbol-systems.
> *Figural-spatial* tests deal with items containing pictures and geometric figures in which the cognitive skills are focused on the perceptual characteristics of the figures and not on their meanings or acquired significances. (pp. 14-15)

Table 6.2 reveals that there are several areas in higher-order cognitive skills for which no instruments could be located. Nevertheless, the combination of tests from several separate skills results in activities similar to problem solving and decision making.

TEACHING GENERAL THINKING BEHAVIORS

A variety of techniques can be used to improve adolescents' general thinking behaviors. The work done by Fraenkel (1973), Feldhusen and Treffinger (1977), and DeBono (1967) will serve as the basis for these methods.

Fraenkel

Fraenkel (1973) has suggested that teachers use specific procedures to help students improve their thinking behaviors in the classroom. The operations he proposes are observing, describing, developing concepts, differentiating and defining, hypothesizing, comparing and contrasting, generalizing, predicting, explaining, and offering alternatives. Each is summarized below.

TABLE 6.2
Higher-Order Cognitive Classification Scheme*

Skill	V Verbal—Semantic	S Symbolic	F Figural—Spatial
1. Mnemonic Strategies	V1 (0)	S1 (0)	F1 (0)
2. Cognitive Strategies	V2 (38)	S2 (1)	F2 (1)
3. Cognitive Styles	V3 (56)	S3 (5)	F3 (2)
4. Communication Skills	V4 (13)	S4 (0)	F4 (0)
5. Translation and Interpretation of Ideas	V5 (36)	S5 (34)	F5 (83)
6. Comparing	V6 (31)	S6 (24)	F6 (61)
7. Sequencing	V7 (38)	S7 (64)	F7 (29)
8. Classifying	V8 (58)	S8 (13)	F8 (33)
9. Categorizing	V9 (16)	S9 (3)	F9 (19)
10. Inventing — Ideating	V10 (73)	S10 (12)	F10 (12)
11. Planning	V11 (16)	S11 (5)	F11 (12)
12. Problem-Redefinition	V12 (6)	S12 (1)	F12 (2)
13. Transfer of Approach to New Problems	V13 (1)	S13 (0)	F13 (0)
14. Creating Hypotheses	V14 (1)	S14 (0)	F14 (1)
15. Inferring from Data	V15 (20)	S15 (0)	F15 (0)
16. Deductive Reasoning	V16 (182)	S16 (32)	F16 (48)
17. Evaluating According to Logical Criteria	V17 (43)	S17 (3)	F17 (2)
18. Specifying Judgmental Criteria	V18 (4)	S18 (0)	F18 (0)
19. Sensitivity to Missing, Irrelevant, or Misleading Information	V19 (20)	S19 (1)	F19 (9)
20. Discriminating Statements of Value from Fact	V20 (6)	S20 (0)	F20 (0)
21. Creating Situations to Provide Data for Evaluation	V21 (5)	S21 (0)	F21 (0)
22. Building Theories or Models	V22 (1)	S22 (0)	F22 (0)
23. Valuing (internalizing decisions and plans)	V23 (3)	S23 (0)	F23 (0)

*Parenthesized figures indicate the number of tests located and evaluated for that category.

193

Observing

Since observing is a basic component of thinking, teachers must provide opportunities for students to become involved in as many different kinds of experiences as possible. The teacher's main responsibility is to engage LD students in various experiences and to provide a focus for future activities.

Describing

It is important for students to be able to describe their observations. Teachers should ask open-ended questions about an observation or experience to encourage students to describe and expand their perceptions.

Developing Concepts

When objects, ideas, or events are sorted into meaningful patterns or groupings, students begin to form concepts. Fraenkel suggests that the "teacher's task is to get students to respond to questions which require them to (1) observe a situation (read a book, watch a film, listen to a record, etc.); (2) describe that which they have observed (list items); (3) find a basis for grouping those listed items which are similar in some respect; (4) identify the common characteristics of the items in a group; (5) label the groups they have formed; (6) subsume additional items that they have listed under those labels; and (7) recombine items to form new groups and to create even larger and more inclusive groups." It is important for the students to perform operations for *themselves*, to see relationships that exist among operations, and to recognize alternate groupings. Table 6.3 outlines the questions a teacher may ask to help students in conceptualizing.

Fraenkel offers the following suggestions to help students categorize information:

1. When a category (group) is suggested by students, proceed to identify as many items as possible that fit within it.
2. Encourage students to look for a variety of categories into which *the same* item can be placed. This encourages flexibility of thinking, a quality which a number of theorists have argued plays an important part in cognitive development.
3. Encourage students to combine categories if possible. Thus, items in a category of lesser breadth than another might be included in the broader category.
4. When the meaning of a category is not clear, ask the student who suggested it to explain what he means or to suggest other examples which belong in the category and then state the characteristics which these various examples have in common.

TABLE 6.3
Teaching Strategy for Developing Concepts
(Listing, Grouping, and Labeling)

The teaching strategy consists of asking students the following questions, usually in this order, after they have observed or been otherwise engaged in experience (reading, viewing, listening, or the like).

Teacher Asks	Student	Teacher Follow-through
What do you see, (notice, find) here? (Listing)	Gives items	Makes sure items are assessible to each student. For example: chalkboard; transparency; individual list; pictures; item card; etc.
Do any of these items seem to belong together? (Grouping)	Finds some similarity as a basis for grouping items	Communicates grouping. For example: underlines in colored chalk; marks with symbols; arranges pictures
Why would you group them together? (Explaining)	Identifies and verbalizes the common characteristics of items in a group	Seeks clarification of responses when necessary
What would you call these groups you have formed? (Labeling)	Verbalizes a label (perhaps more than one word) that appropriately encompasses all items	Records
Why? (Explaining)	Gives explanation	Seeks clarification if necessary
Could some of these belong in more than one group? (Recombining—seeking multiple groups for some items)	States different relationships	Records
Can we put these same items in different groups?	States additional relationships	Communicates grouping
Can any groups be combined? (Subsuming)	States additional different relationships	Communicates grouping

From *Development of a Comprehensive Curriculum Model for Social Studies for Grades One Through Eight, Inclusive of Procedures for Implementation and Dissemination,* by Norman E. Wallen, Mary C. Durkin, Jack R. Fraenkel, Anthony H. McNaughton, Enoch I. Sawin. Final Report, Project No. 5-1314, U.S. Office of Education (Washington, D.C., Oct. 1969), p. 17.

5. Encourage students to regroup and relabel all of the items they have listed and previously grouped. Oftentimes this can be done by simply erasing the formed groups but leaving the original list on the board for examination.

6. Realize that in many cases it is by no means necessary to insist upon closure, since the emphasis in concept formation is as much upon the processes involved as it is the content. An open and accepting attitude on the part of the teacher will enable students to offer items that are too difficult to deal with for the time being, or even irrelevant. (p. 197)

Differentiating and Defining

Students need much drill and repetition to gain a solid understanding of a concept. To acquire the ability to differentiate and define concepts, students should be required to compare new examples with examples they already know. Teachers should assist in identifying new attributes, which should then be included in the concept definition. Students should be given a variety of exercises in which they are required to differentiate between examples and nonexamples of the concept. Fraenkel stresses that as concepts become more abstract, teachers should present a varied number of concrete examples to illustrate the abstraction. Table 6.4 summarizes this teaching strategy.

Hypothesizing

Teachers can help students systematically seek information about their world by having them specify hypotheses and then verify them. Hypotheses can provide a great deal of *structure* to the way in which a student deals with information. Fraenkel has suggested a sequence of questions to aid students in hypothesizing. Table 6.5 shows this sequence.

Comparing and Contrasting

An important component in thinking is the ability to compare and contrast information. The understanding of information will be limited unless students can compare and contrast this information with respect to its similarities and differences. Students should always be encouraged to place the information they acquire (through reading, listening, observing, etc.) into an organized form so as to highlight specific similarities and differences. Organizational charts are particularly helpful for accomplishing this. Table 6.6 is an example from a seventh-grade unit on ancient civilizations.

196

TABLE 6.4
Teaching Strategies for Attaining Concepts
(Differentiating and Defining)

Teacher	Student	Teacher Follow-through
Say the word after me[1] (Stating the concept)	Repeats word	Makes sure word is pronounced correctly
This is an . . .[2] This is also an . . . (Gives examples)	Looks at object or listens to description given, or reads statement which illustrates the concept	Checks for any students who may not be able to see or hear
This is not an . . .[2] (Gives non-examples)	Looks, listens to, or reads about new object which is not an example of concept but is similar to concept	Checks again
What characteristics does an . . . possess that enable you to recognize it?	States major attributes which all examples possess	Insures that all attributes are given
Tell me what you think an . . . is (Asks for definition)	States a definition of the concept	Has students write down their definition
Which of these describes[3] an . . . , or is this an . . . (Asks for identification)	Selects from one or more objects or descriptions	Shows additional objects or gives fresh descriptions to test
Show me an . . . (Asks for original examples)	Brings in new examples	Verifies correctness of example

[1]When proceeding deductively, the teacher writes the definition and the key attributes (the defining criteria) on the board initially.

[2]The teacher appropriately identifies each of the examples and non-examples that are presented. (These statements become questions — i.e., "Is this a . . ." when teaching the concept deductively.)

[3]Gradually more complex examples (that is, examples which possess additional defining attributes not originally displayed) should be presented in order to broaden and deepen the student's understanding of the concept's dimensions.

From *Helping Students Think and Value: Strategies for Teaching Social Studies,* by J. R. Fraenkel (Englewood Cliffs, N.J.: Prentice Hall, 1973).

TABLE 6.5
Teaching Strategies for Hypothesizing

Teacher	Student	Teacher Follow-through
What bothers or concerns you about people or the world today? or What kinds of problems are of concern to you? or What are you worried about? etc.	Names problem area	Clarifies responses
Why is that a problem? or Why are you concerned about . . . ? or What about . . . might we investigate? etc.	Identifies and states a precise question or aspect of the problem to consider	Helps get question stated clearly
What causes . . . ? or If . . . continues, then what might occur? etc.	Formulates hypothesis to investigate	Helps get hypothesis stated and available for all to see. Clarifies terms
*Where can we obtain data that might help us come to some conclusions about . . . ?	Locates sources. Gathers data	Suggests additional sources to consult
How can we organize the data we've collected? or How might we group or categorize these data?	Organizes data into relevant categories. Regroups data into sub- and subordinate categories	Suggests additional categories to consider. Helps students place data into appropriate categories
What data can't we use? Why?	Evaluates data as to relevance, accuracy, bias, etc.	Helps determine appropriate criteria by which to judge usefulness of data
What evidence is there to support our hypothesis (or hypotheses)? to refute it? To what extent is it supported or refuted? Should we change our hypothesis (hypotheses) in any way? If so, how? Why?	Considers degree to which hypothesis is supported or refuted. Cites supportive or refuting evidence Modifies hypothesis if necessary. Gives reasons	Asks for evidence. Probes for inconsistencies. Places evidence so all can see Clarifies terms
What can we say about . . . (the problem) in light of the evidence we have obtained?	States generalization (conclusion)	Clarifies terms. Asks for estimate of degree to which conclusion is warranted, and on basis of what evidence

*As the investigation proceeds, it may be necessary to repeat several of these steps. For example, as data are organized, it may become apparent that more information is needed, and thus necessitate further data gathering. Testing the hypothesis against the data may suggest new ways of organizing the acquired information.

From Helping Students Think and Value: Strategies for Teaching Social Studies, by J. R. Fraenkel (Englewood Cliffs, N.J.: Prentice-Hall, 1973).

TABLE 6.6

Example of an Organizational Chart on Ancient Civilizations

People	Resources	Use of Resources	Major New Ideas or Inventions	Purpose or Use of Invention/Idea
SUMERIANS	Clay	Pottery	Cuneiform	Business contracts
	River	Brick buildings	Circle into 360*	
		Writing	Fractions, square root	Study of heavens
	People	Farmers, priests, rulers, slaves, craftsmen, soldiers	Wheeled vehicle	Many fights with neighbors
	Fertile soil	Crops for food, livestock	Ziggurat	Mountains touched heavens of gods
	Date palms	Baskets, ropes	12-month calendar	Study of stars
	Cattle	Leather goods	24-hour day	Gods
	Sheep	Rugs, tapestries	Weights & measures	Trade
		Metal goods	Enameled, baked brick	
		Ivory goods	Keystone	Temples & palaces for arches - no stone
				To keep gold & silver lumps - money
EGYPTIANS	Fertile soil	Crops for food	Hieroglyphics	Accounts for temple and stories of pharaohs
	River	Flax for linen		
		Irrigation		
		Livestock		
	Papyrus	Paper	Paper and ink	For scribes
			Shadoof	Lift water
			Mummifying	Keep soul alive after death
	People	Rulers, priests, slaves, farmers, craftsmen	Stone pyramids	Bury god - pharaohs
			3 seasons of 4 months	
	Stone	Temples, pyramids, palaces	Surveying	When Nile would flood
			Calendar - 12 months	Boundaries after flood
			Shadow clock	Study of heavens
				Tell time - sun god

Continued

199

TABLE 6.6 (continued)

People	Resources	Use of Resources	Major New Ideas or Inventions	Purpose or Use of Invention/Idea
ASSYRIANS	Iron Clay People Horses	Chariots, weapons Books Soldiers, farmers, slaves, rulers	Iron weapons Wheeled rams Horse-drawn chariots Scattering captives First world empire First public library Advertising extreme cruelty	Protection from constant invasion To prevent revolt As a result of war One king liked learning To spread fear
MINOANS	Wood Stone People Water	Palaces Ships Crops for food Sailors, rulers, pottery	Light wells Drainage system Reinforced buildings Bathrooms Bull-vaulting First navy Hot and cold water in houses	Inside-rooms Carry wastes to pits Earthquakes For royalty Bull-worship Trade and protection Comfort

From *Western Civilization: Perspectives on Change,* by Jack R. Fraenkel. Grade Seven, Taba Social Studies Curriculum, Cooperative Research Project OE 6-10-182, U.S. Department of Health, Education, and Welfare, Office of Education, Washington, D.C., 1969 (distributed by Addison-Wesley Publishers, Menlo Park, Calif.), pp. 42-43.

Such a structuring of information separates major from supporting data and provides students with a mechanism for memorizing such data. A major role for the teacher should be to help the students recognize a way to organize the information so as to most clearly delineate similarities and differences.

Generalizing

A critical step in thinking is the ability to form generalizations about available information. The LD student who may receive information in a very laborious fashion, as through reading, may tend to see the information in bits and pieces with little relationship among the parts. Such unrelated information is difficult to process, retrieve, and apply. Fraenkel suggests that the teacher's task is to encourage students to (1) observe two or more incidents; (2) describe what happened in the incidents; (3) explain why they think the incidents occurred as they did; (4) look for similarities and differences; (5) attempt to explain these similarities and differences; and then (6) state a generalization based on the data they have acquired and compared. Teaching students to form generalizations is particularly difficult because they are expected to go beyond the information directly available to them through reading or class lectures. To develop skill in making generalizations, students need many opportunities to go beyond the available information. Initially, students will need a great deal of assistance in drawing inferences, and teachers can provide a model for interpreting data and drawing inferences. While encouraging students to draw generalizations, teachers should at the same time remind them that all generalizations are tentative and probablistic in nature. Teachers play an important role by encouraging students to think about possible relationships that exist and by demanding that students supply supporting data for any generalizations that they draw.

Predicting and Explaining

This step encourages students to apply previously formed generalizations to new information or situations. In essence, this requires divergent thinking on the part of students. Fraenkel suggested that teachers follow a sequence of activities to encourage students to apply generalizations they have formed. Table 6.7 presents this sequence.

TABLE 6.7
Applying Generalizations (Predicting and Explaining)

This cognitive task consists of applying previously learned general-izations and facts to explain unfamiliar phenomena or to infer con-sequences from known conditions. It encourages students to support their speculations with evidence and sound reasoning. The teaching strategy consists of asking the following questions, usually in this order.

Teacher Asks	Student	Teacher Follow-through
(Focusing question) Suppose that a particu-lar event occurred given certain conditions, what would happen?	Makes inferences	Encourages additional in-ferences. Selects in-ference(s) to develop
What makes you think that would happen?	States explanation; identifies relationships	Accepts explanation and seeks clarification if necessary
What would be needed for that to happen?	Identifies facts necessary to a particular inference	Decides whether these facts are sufficient and could be assumed to be present in the given situation
(Encouraging divergency) Can someone give a different idea about what would happen?	States new inferences that differ in some respects from pre-ceding ones	Encourages alternative inferences, requests explanations and neces-sary conditions. Seeks clarification where necessary
If, as one of you pre-dicted, such-and-such happened, what do you think would happen after that?	Makes inferences related to the given inference	Encourages additional inferences and selects those to pursue further

This pattern of inviting inferences, requiring explanations, identifying nec-essary conditions, and encouraging divergent views is continued until the teacher decides to terminate the activity.

From *Development of a Comprehensive Curriculum Model for Social Studies,* by Nor-man E. Wallen, Mary C. Durkin, Jack R. Fraenkel, Anthony H. McNaughton, & Enoch I. Sawin. Final Report, Project No. 5-1314 (U.S. Office of Education, Washington, D.C., Oct. 1969), p. 19.

Offering Alternatives

The teacher must continually expect students to consider additional or different ways to deal with available information. To move students from a literal, unilateral, and concrete level of functioning, they must be constantly encouraged to consider alternative ways of viewing, organizing, and dealing with information. A failure to do this will facilitate the student's uncritical acceptance of the views of others. The types of questions that the teacher can ask to encourage students to offer alternative solutions to situations are the following: "What *else* did you notice?" "Do you see *another way* that some of these things can be organized?" "In what *other* ways are they different?" "What *other* conclusion can you draw?" "What *else* can you suggest?"

Feldhusen and Treffinger

Feldhusen and Treffinger (1977) contend that teachers who decide to emphasize goals that foster thinking skills must take deliberate action to achieve these goals. Some of the methods and techniques that these authors suggest to stimulate creative thinking and problem solving are brainstorming, attribute listing, morphological analysis, and synectics. Each will be summarized briefly.

Brainstorming

Brainstorming is a procedure used to generate ideas or solutions on a given topic. It is a group process in which the emphasis is initially on the *quantity* of ideas generated. The following guidelines should be followed by the teacher who is using the brainstorming technique:

1. All ideas should be recorded. This can be done by using student recorders or tape recorders, or the teacher can record the ideas.
2. The question should be announced in advance so students can prepare ideas for the brainstorming session.
3. Ideas generated are not to be evaluated or criticized during the brainstorming session. (Deferred judgment is the secret of brainstorming.)
4. Following the session, all students should be given a typed list of all ideas generated.

5. Listed items can then be grouped, elaborated on, and evaluated for the purpose of implementation. Brainstorming can be particularly beneficial for LD adolescents who are hesitant to express themselves because of a fear of being judged or evaluated. In the initial stages of brainstorming, wild, imaginative, and unusual ideas are encouraged and accepted without judgment. The group process following the brainstorming session for the elaboration and categorization of ideas can be effective in facilitating group dialogue and problem solving.

Attribute Listing

Feldhusen and Treffinger define attribute listing as a "technique that promotes a clearer view of the qualities, specifications, characteristics, limitations, and attributes of a problem to allow for easy change and the development of new ideas through the changes" (p. 22). Attribute listing can be used on an individual or a group basis and involves the following basic steps:

1. The problem to be solved is specified.
2. A chart in column form should be constructed. In the first column the problem is broken down into components. The characteristics or attributes of each factor are listed in the second column and ideas for improvement or solution to the problem are listed in the third column. (Table 6.8 gives an example of this format.)
3. Following the generalization of ideas, they can be examined, discussed, and prepared for implementation. Attribute listing can be used to stimulate group discussion, story writing, and problem solving.

Morphological Analysis

Attribute listing is based on modifying existing conditions for solutions, whereas morphological analysis focuses on the *combination* of old ideas to produce new ideas. This technique can be used on an individual or a group basis and is a formal way of combining ideas in ways that might be useful in problem solving. This can be a successful thinking technique because it provides a structure within which the students can organize and systematically deal with a problem. The following basic steps are involved in this process:

204

TABLE 6.8
Sample Chart for Attribute Listing

Part or Component	Characteristics or Attributes	Ideas for Improvement
1. The ground surface	1. Grass Blacktop Concrete	1. Need more grass Use artificial turf
2. The placement of play equipment	2. In rows Close together	2. Vary placement Spread out Make game area
3. The baseball diamond	3. At far corner On dirt area	3. Put in grass Stationary bases
4. The swings	4. Very tall Metal chain Wooden seats	4. Need small ones Belt seats better
5. The water fountains	5. One fountain Made of concrete	5. Need more fountains Needs steps
6. The fence around it	6. Very high Chain link Blocks vision	6. Make it lower More open

From *Teaching Creative Thinking and Problem Solving,* by J. F. Feldhusen and D. J. Treffinger (Dubuque, Ia.: Kendall/Hunt Co., 1977).

1. The problem to be solved is specified.
2. A chart is developed. Objects or components that are relevant to the solution of the problem are placed on the horizontal axis and characteristics of those objects or components that are relevant to the solution of the problem (for example, materials) on the vertical axis. For each axis the factors can be generated through brainstorming.
3. The two characteristics are then combined to fill the various cells.
4. Cell combinations are then evaluated and strategies are specified for the solution of the problem or the development of a new product. An example of morphological analysis is provided in Table 6.9.

TABLE 6.9
Sample Chart for Morphological Analysis

Problem: Improving the Classroom Environment Using Common Materials and Available Equipment.

Materials	Floors	Walls	Desks	Tables	Chalkboards
		Components			
Paper	Paper footprints to guide movement	Murals for walls	Paper desk pads for scratch paper work		
Cardboard	Use large pieces of cardboard as room dividers	Partitions study carrels	Use Tri-wall cardboard to build desks	Put card-board boxes on tables for storage	Could get more chalkboards painting black on cardboard
Felt/Cloth	Bring in scraps to sew to-gether to make a classroom carpet	Put up felt/bur-lap strips for display purposes	Make cushions for desk chairs		
Paint		May not be pos-sible to do in some schools	Let each child decorate desk	Have color-coded tables for learning stations	Slate paint on walls, ceiling, boards
Rubber	Old tires for sit-ting in				
Glass		Parti-tions to cut down sound and noise		Glass tops to lay over desks and tables with instructions underneath	
Plastic		Egg carton wall parti-tions are good acous-tic devices			

From *Teaching Creative Thinking and Problem Solving,* by J. F. Feldhusen and D. J. Treffinger (Dubuque, Iowa: Kendall/Hunt Co., 1977).

Synectics

Synectics was developed by Gordon (1961) and is a creative thinking technique that uses analogies and metaphors to help the thinker analyze problems and form different viewpoints. As in attribute listing and morphological analysis, the first step is to specify the problem to be solved. Three types of analogies can be used in synectics: fantasy, direct analogy, and personal analogy. Fantasy analogies allow students to search for ideal and, in many cases, farfetched solutions to problems. After the group has offered a number of solutions, the teacher leads the group in evaluating their ideas to determine which would be most workable. Direct analogy requires students to find parallel problem situations in real life. Personal analogies require students to place themselves in the role of the problem itself. In short, synectics can involve students in imaginative discussions to develop unusual and workable problem-solving strategies.

DeBono

DeBono (1967) differentiates between vertical thinking and lateral thinking:

> Lateral thinking is generative. Vertical thinking is selective. With vertical thinking, one may reach a conclusion by a valid series of steps. . . . But no matter how correct the path may be, the starting point was a matter of perceptual choice which fashioned the basic concepts used. . . . Vertical thinking would then work on the concepts produced in this manner. Lateral thinking is needed to handle the perceptual choice which is beyond the reach of vertical thinking. . . . Lateral thinking enhances the effectiveness of vertical thinking. Vertical thinking develops the ideas generated by lateral thinking. You cannot dig a hole in a different place by digging the same hole deeper. Vertical thinking is used to dig the same hole deeper. Lateral thinking is used to dig a hole in a different place. (pp. 12-13)

DeBono has outlined several lateral thinking techniques, that can be taught to improve students' skills in dealing with information and solving problems. DeBono, emphasizing that such skills can develop only through practice and repetition, describes numerous lateral thinking techniques. Three of these will be summarized.

Challenging Assumptions

Since a primary goal of lateral thinking is to restructure available information, this technique can be used to put information together in an alternative way. In challenging assumptions, one challenges the necessity of

207

boundaries and limits. The purpose of challenging assumptions is *not* to offer better alternatives but simply to restructure existing patterns — assumptions by definition usually escape the restructuring process. The classic problem of the nine dots illustrates the value of this technique quite well. The problem is to link the nine dots using only four straight lines without raising the pencil from the paper. (See Figure 6.1.)

Figure 6.1.   The classic nine dot problem.

The problem seems unsolvable. However, the *assumption* is that the lines must connect the dots and must not extend beyond the boundaries set by the other line of dots. But, if this assumption is challenged, and one goes beyond the boundary, the problem can be solved. (See Figure 6.2.)

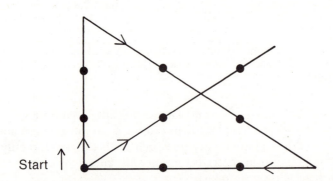

Figure 6.2.   The solution for the classic nine dot problem.

In short, DeBono maintains that many problems become more amenable to solution when one challenges existing assumptions. The point is not to teach students to question all assumptions but simply to recognize the great power of assumptions and the potential value of challenging them so as to look at the data in a different light.

Reversal Method

This technique tends to produce a considerable amount of restructuring of information. The student is encouraged to take things as they are and turn them around, from back to front. It is a provocative rearrangement of information. For example, instead of the teacher giving a test to the students, the students give a test to the teacher. Remember, in lateral thinking the goal is *not* to find the right answer but to achieve a different arrangement of information to encourage a different way of looking at a situation. Students who develop the ability to reverse situations will learn to treat information in a more flexible fashion.

Choice of Entry Point and Attention Area

DeBono defines attention area as the part of a situation or problem that is attended to. The entry point is the part of a problem or situation that is attended to *first*. A student's train of thought may be determined by the choice of entry point. Thus, students should be encouraged to develop skill in picking out and following various entry points to solve problems. Students can readily perceive the consequence of choosing different entry points by listening to a lecture on a person's particular problem. Students are asked to list possible entry points for tackling the problem and to define the entry point used by the person. Choosing a different entry point once again allows students to gain new perspectives on the information at hand.

In summary, the descriptions presented on three lateral thinking techniques have been chosen to illustrate ways in which the teacher can encourage LD students to look at and deal with situations. The mastery of such techniques should increase LD students' ability to cope with the demands placed on them.

TEACHING ORGANIZATIONAL SKILLS

Students' ability to understand, manipulate, and make decisions about information obtained through reading or listening depends on the students' ability to *organize* the material into meaningful segments. Organized material lends itself to such activities as comparing, contrasting, generalizing, memorizing, and recalling. While the value of organizing materials to facilitate thinking is obvious, teachers are quick to point out problems that

LD students have in organizing material. Their organizing problems include the following:

1. LD adolescents have difficulty *perceiving* organization in a set of materials, such as notes from class, class assignments, and the textbook.
2. LD adolescents usually do not appreciate the importance of organizing information.
3. LD adolescents do not realize that information can be manipulated or rearranged to produce an organized structure most consistent with the learner's style of understanding, storing, and using information.
4. LD adolescents have difficulty dealing with an isolated task in an organized fashion.
5. LD adolescents have difficulty dealing with multiple tasks in an organized fashion.

Teaching How to Perceive Organization in Material

The teacher can use the following methods to help LD students perceive organization in material. First, students should be taught how to survey material to get an overview of main ideas and the parameters of the information presented. Most LD students concentrate their attention on specific elements. For example, their approach to reading a textbook is to begin with the first word on the first page of the first chapter without any idea of the major topics and chapter headings in the book. By surveying the chapters in relation to the book as a whole, students can begin to perceive the organizational structure used by the author. This permits LD students to see relationships among topics and ideas more readily and to ask questions about the material and rearrange it as necessary.

Another technique to help LD students perceive the organization of material is to inventory the *amount* of space related to a given topic. For example, the notes taken in a social studies class can be spread out on the floor and arranged in piles according to topic. The number of pages devoted to each topic gives students an indication of the major topics as well as the relative importance of each. Similarly, students can group the pages in the chapter of the text with paper clips according to topic.

The teacher can use questions to help LD students perceive the author's organization of material. Asking questions on a higher level of abstraction than that of the written material can help students identify key topics of organizational referents in material. For example, to help students perceive the organization of a chapter comparing ancient Greece with twentieth-century America, the teacher might ask, "In what ways might ancient Greece and twentieth-century America be compared?" Such questions help LD students see major areas for comparison (for examples, lifestyles, technology, and government) and in turn recognize the major organization of the author.

A large amount of material is presented to students in most secondary classes. If students view the information presented as an endless list of facts that must be learned separately, the task is almost impossible. A major key to successfully mastering and understanding the information is for students to continually look for relationships that will allow them to form generalizations. Once generalizations are made, the students have less information to memorize and their level of understanding is increased. Although generalizations can serve as effective organizers of material, LD students should also be cautioned to look continually for exceptions.

Nevertheless, generalizations can be of value in a number of ways. They can provide a focal point for learning units of information and help determine what is important to emphasize, select, or ignore. In summary, generalizations help keep learners' attention focused on primary rather than secondary matters. Practice in recognizing and stating generalizations should help LD students make wise decisions about the material they will emphasize (Fraenkel, 1973).

Using a structural format to outline material can also help LD students perceive the organization of material. This technique helps students grasp the difference between main topics and supportive information.

Finally, LD students should be taught to use tables of contents, summaries, and overviews of subject matter to determine the organization of material.

Teaching the Importance of Organizing Material

Students will not look for the organization present in information unless they can see the importance of doing so. To help students appreciate the value of trying to organize information, the teacher can use a trial learning game. The game works in this fashion:

LD students are presented with a list of binary digits.

Binary sequence: 1 0 1 1 0 1 0 0 1 0

The students are then asked to memorize the list. After they have tried for several minutes (and their recall has been tested), the teacher shows how much easier the task is if the material is organized in the following way:

Binary sequence: 1 0 1 1 0 1 0 0 1 0
Groups of pairs: 10 11 01 00 10
Labels for pairs: 2   3   1   0   2

Teaching How to Manipulate Information

Let us now consider the failure of LD students to realize that information can be manipulated or rearranged to make it easier to deal with. Students tend to feel that the way material is presented by an author or by the teacher is the only way that information can be organized. If the LD student's style of learning is not compatible with the way in which the material has been organized, that organization probably will not help the student. Teachers can help LD students rearrange information in ways that make it useful for them. Some alternative ways of organizing material are as follows:

1. *According to topics.* For example, a history chapter could be organized according to issues, major events, or people.
2. *According to attributes.* For example, a student who is studying mammals in biology could arrange them according to eating habits, reproduction, mobility, or size.
3. *Along a continuum of simple to complex.* For example, the animal phyla might be organized for study from the simplest one-celled animals to the most complex.

Trial learning games can be used to teach the students how to manipulate information to their advantage. The students are presented with and asked to memorize a list of fifteen random items as in Figure 6.3.

snake, banana, dog, Buick, apple, Oldsmobile, horse,

cherry, lemon, Chevrolet, alligator, orange, elephant,

Dodge, GMC

Figure 6.3.   List of random items to be memorized.

A piece of paper and a pencil should be made available to any student who wishes to use them. After students have spent several minutes trying to learn the list, the teacher can demonstrate how the items can be manipulated and reorganized to make the task easier. One possible rearrangement would be according to the categories of animals, fruit, and vehicles. See Figure 6.4.

Dodge	cherry	elephant
Chevrolet	lemon	horse
Buick	orange	dog
Oldsmobile	banana	alligator
GMC	apple	snake

Figure 6.4. Categorization of random items listed in Figure 6.3.

Another way to arrange the items would be in alphabetical order. See Figure 6.5.

alligator	elephant
apple	GMC
banana	horse
Buick	lemon
cherry	Oldsmobile
Chevrolet	orange
Dodge	snake
dog	

Figure 6.5. Alphabetization of random items listed in Figure 6.3.

Teaching How to Accomplish Single Tasks

A fundamental component to teaching students how to work in a systematic, organized fashion is structure. Jerome Bruner's *The Process of Education* (1960) emphasizes the importance of structure in instruction.

Teaching specific topics or skills without making clear their context in the broader fundamental structure of a field of knowledge is uneconomical in several deep senses.

213

> In the first place, such teaching makes it exceedingly difficult for the student to generalize from what he has learned to what he will encounter later. In the second place, learning that has fallen short of a grasp of general principles has little reward in terms of intellectual excitement. The best way to create interest in a subject is to render it worth knowing, which means to make knowledge gained usable in one's thinking beyond the situation in which the learning has occurred. Third, knowledge one has acquired without sufficient structure to tie it together is knowledge that is likely to be forgotten. (p. 31)

The teacher can help LD students approach tasks in an organized fashion by requiring them to go through a sequence of steps. For example, these steps might be followed in math:

Step 1:   Read the problem.
Step 2:   Decide what information is relevant and what is not.
Step 3:   Estimate an answer.
Step 4:   Work the problem through.
Step 5:   Compare the derived answer with the estimate.
Step 6:   Check your answer.

Flow charts or diagrams of steps to be taken can also help students organize their approach to single tasks. A sample flow chart for working a division problem is shown in Figure 6.6.

Flow charts provide a strong visual representation (image) of the steps to be followed in completing a task and thus aid students in remembering these. Initially, the teacher will want to show the students how to use a flow chart; after they have become comfortable in using it, they can be aided in developing their own flow charts for specific tasks.

Teaching How to Accomplish Multiple Tasks

Learning disabled adolescents are confronted with a broad array of demands in junior and senior high schools. Assignments from different classes require different formats, due dates, and standards, and there is a demand for sophisticated planning and organizing by the student. Teachers report, however, that LD students have great difficulty in this area and are unable to adequately plan for and cope with the varied demands placed on them in school settings. One system, developed by the Navy, called PERT (Program Evaluation and Review Technique) can be used for planning how to complete a set of tasks with different demands within the same time

214

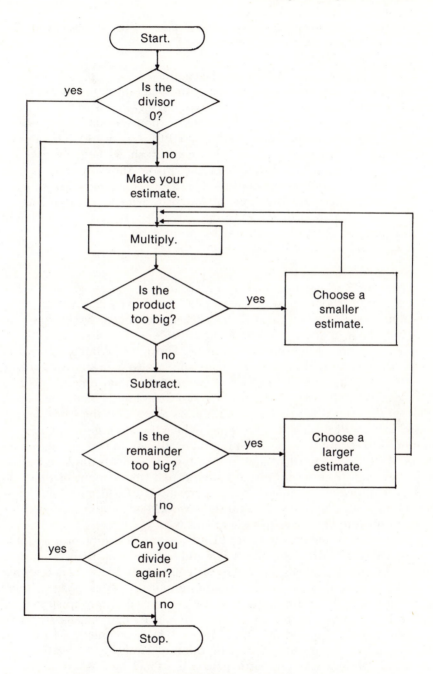

Figure 6.6.   Sample flow chart for solving a division problem.

frame. Uris (1970) advocates the use of PERT for a variety of problems. The basic steps include the following:

1. Listing all tasks that have to be completed.
2. Putting the tasks in the sequence in which they must be done.
3. Estimating the time necessary to complete each task in the sequence (the time can be expressed in minutes, hours, or days).
4. Constructing an arrow diagram (or PERT network). This fourth task is the key step. The PERT network shows how the tasks are interrelated. The direction of the arrows shows how each task relates to the rest of the job. The PERT diagram is constructed by asking three questions about each element in the sequence: (a) What immediately precedes this task? (b) What immediately follows it? (c) What other tasks can be done at the same time?

Figure 6.7 illustrates how the PERT technique was adapted to the task of a high school student preparing for and delivering a speech.

The PERT diagram can tell the teacher and student several things at a glance. First, it shows what tasks must be done first. Second, it reveals the general scope of the entire assignment. Third, it determines the *critical path,* which is the total of the longest consecutive jobs. With knowledge of the critical path, the student can then (1) estimate the total time for the job, (2) identify trouble areas that must be taken care of at the same time as the jobs on the critical path, (3) determine ways to expedite the schedule suggested by the PERT chart. This can be done by allocating more time or resources to certain tasks or becoming more efficient in performing certain tasks. PERT is an excellent tool for helping LD students think an assignment through from beginning to end and plan the amount of time and energy required to complete the assignment. It also demonstrates how several tasks can, in many cases must, be worked on simultaneously if the assignment is to be successfully completed.

As with flow charts, the use of PERT (or a modification of it) requires that teachers carefully model the system and assist students in the beginning stages. As students gain experience in each of the basic phases of developing a PERT system, they should be encouraged to develop these systems independently. PERT techniques can be used effectively in group situations. When PERT is used with a group, students can see that they have responsibilities to the group and that the group can't move on unless each task has been completed successfully. This technique can help students learn to accept group responsibility and to participate as team members — a critical skill for success in many jobs.

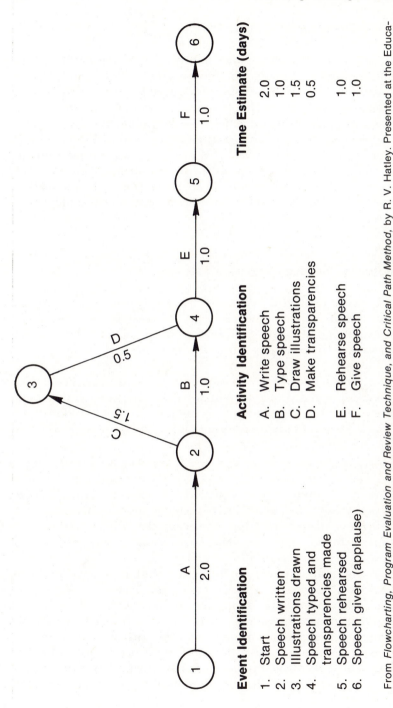

Event Identification

1. Start
2. Speech written
3. Illustrations drawn
4. Speech typed and transparencies made
5. Speech rehearsed
6. Speech given (applause)

Activity Identification

		Time Estimate (days)
A.	Write speech	2.0
B.	Type speech	1.0
C.	Draw illustrations	1.5
D.	Make transparencies	0.5
E.	Rehearse speech	1.0
F.	Give speech	1.0

Figure 6.7. PERT network for delivering a speech.

From *Flowcharting, Program Evaluation and Review Technique, and Critical Path Method*, by R. V. Hatley. Presented at the Educational Research and Development Training Program, University of Kansas, August 1972.

217

TEACHING PROBLEM SOLVING

The importance of secondary students acquiring good problem-solving skills cannot be overemphasized. Not only are these skills demanded by the school curriculum, but they are required for successful adjustment to social and life situations during postschool years. To survive in our increasingly complex society, people need to be able to solve problems on an ongoing and independent basis. Additional strategies for teaching LD adolescents problem-solving techniques are discussed in the chapters on mathematics and social skills. The purpose here is to present some general problem-solving strategies and considerations to be kept in mind by the teacher. In addition, some problem-solving models that apply across content areas will be presented.

Phases in Problem Solving

Patton and Griffin (1973) include the following as phases in problem solving: (1) identification of the problem, (2) analysis of the problem, (3) critical evaluation of possible solutions to the problem, and (4) making a plan of action designed to implement the solution.

1. *Identification of the problem.* The first phase is gaining understanding of the problem. Without this, confusion would result. Distorted perceptions and judgments are typical of LD adolescents. It is difficult to solve a problem that is poorly understood.

2. *Analysis of the problem.* The second phase of problem solving is the analysis of the problem. A problem is the existence of a situation or condition that is not preferred. Problem analysis, therefore, is determining the difference between the present situation or condition and the preferred one. Perceiving, clarifying, understanding, and evaluating personal views and factual information provide insight into the nature of the problem.
    The analysis of the problem can be further broken down into three smaller steps. The first is to determine the scope of the problem. This means establishing the size or extent of the difficulty, giving consideration to the intensity of the perceived need and the amount of emotional investment in the particular problem. The degree of intensity is the degree of dissatisfaction caused by the problem. This stems from one's value system. A person's interest in a problem and feelings concerning the need to do something

about it may not match. However, the critical variable is the person's degree of commitment to solving the problem. The degree of commitment results from one's view of the intensity of the problem and one's emotional investment in the problem; commitment directly affects one's efficiency in implementing a workable solution. The scope of the problem is how large it is, who or what is involved, and what forces are at work. Adequate analysis requires that the forces impelling and constraining change be carefully considered. An optimal solution will neglect neither the impelling nor the constraining forces. In most cases, the best solutions require modification of both forces.

The second small step in the analysis phase is goal setting. Goals should be specific enough so that one will know exactly when they are reached. Goals should be specified in terms of observable events, procedures, or environmental conditions. The problem solver must be able to make a functional commitment to the goals adopted. Goal identification and setting is an area in which LD adolescents are likely to experience difficulty.

The final small step in problem analysis is obtaining relevant, factual information. Students must realize that they need information and they must know where to go to find it. Then they must be able to interpret the information in light of the particular problem. This interpretation depends on the students' analysis of the impelling and constraining forces and on individual value systems.

3. *Critical evaluation of possible solutions to the problem.* Evaluation involves (a) the identification of all possible proposals, and (b) the evaluation of the various proposals. In the first step, it is valuable to identify possible approaches and encourage creativity. Use of a technique such as brainstorming, followed by clarifying and operationalizing the suggestions, would be helpful. The second step represents the beginning of the decision-making process.

There are several criteria to be met in evaluation of possible solutions. First, does each proposal meet the need for change? Each proposal is evaluated in terms of its probable effect on each impelling and constraining force. The second criterion is: Can the proposal be implemented by the individual? The third criterion involves the inherent disadvantages or costs of each proposal. This is similar to cost analysis, which has been popularized by government agencies.

Deciding whether these criteria have been met requires predicting future events on the basis of similar past events. This prediction is based on reasoning. Here, the crux of the reasoning process is the identification of relevant similarities among events. This involves classifying past events according to their relevant characteristics, observing the selected characteristics, and determining the likelihood of similar events occurring under similar circumstances. In this context, inductive reasoning is the process of arriving at generalizations based on observation of selected characteristics of events. Deductive reasoning is the process of using those generalizations to determine whether a predicted event logically follows from the generalizations. Thus, decision making begins with both inductive and deductive reasoning.

4. *Making a plan of action designed to implement the solution.* The final step of problem solving is deciding on the best solution and putting that solution into operation. There are two issues to consider when putting the solution into operation. The first is to develop a plan of action. This involves making a commitment to the plan, identifying specific steps to carry out the plan, determining what resources are needed, providing for potential emergencies, and planning for the evaluation of the solution. The second issue is to mobilize any necessary resources, be they people or objects, that are part of the plan. After the plan of action has been implemented, the predicted change should be accomplished.

There is no doubt that problem solving is a complex cognitive task that involves such psychoeducational processes as attention, perception, discrimination, memory, integration, concept formation, and language. Learning disabled adolescents have shown disturbances in these processes and in verbal and nonverbal thinking, reasoning, and organizational skills. The various phases of problem solving involve all of these processes. Thus, it seems likely that at one point or another in solving a problem, an LD individual will experience a breakdown.

A breakdown may result from disabilities in attention, sequencing, memory, integration, and self-concept. In problem solving, LD adolescents may not be able to select from among the visual, auditory, tactile, and kinesthetic impulses and to attend to one or a limited number at a time. They may experience difficulty remembering or following the sequential steps involved in problem solving. They may not be able to integrate sensory stimuli to establish proposals and to resolve a problem. Students who have experienced continuous school failure have low self-perception and self-confidence (Ross, 1976). LD adolescents often become disorganized, anxious, and insecure in trying to solve problems.

Individual Problem-Solving Styles

A pervading theme in programming for LD students is to carefully match student characteristics with the teaching methodology and instructional materials. This is important in teaching reading and mathematics. It is equally important to match learner characteristics or style and methodology when teaching specific problem-solving strategies. All LD students should *not* be locked into one set strategy.

The necessity for individualizing problem solving is underscored in an article by David W. Ewing (1977). Ewing summarizes the work of McKenney and Keen (1976), who have identified a variety of styles of thinking and problem solving. They have identified the main cognitive styles of *systematic-preceptive* and *intuitive-receptive*. About three-fourths of the people studied used only one style, while the remainder favored one style but did not use it exclusively.

McKenney and Keen (1976) found that most people use their preferred style for *all* problems, rather than switching back and forth between cognitive styles. The researchers note that many problems lend themselves better to one problem-solving style than to others. This leads to the conclusion that in many situations there is an obvious need for people with contrasting styles to work together.

This research has definite implications for instructing the LD adolescent in problem solving. First, due to differences in cognitive style, not all students should be taught to use the same problem-solving procedure. Typical methods are systematic and highly structured and seem to be valued because they follow the scientific method. The intuitive approach is often criticized because it appears to be a hit-and-miss approach. If such an approach yields solutions, it should be reinforced and not criticized. Some instructional efforts may stifle the LD youngster who has an atypical learning style. Teachers should not flippantly put youngsters through a standard scope and sequence of instruction or a given problem-solving model without first considering the potential strength of each individual's cognitive style. A second implication of this research is that since most individuals have unique problem-solving styles, there may be merit in grouping students for instructional purposes in which quite different types of tasks must be completed. Grouping students will bring contrasting problem-solving styles into play.

Goldman and Goldman (1974) have pointed out the advantage of using small groups for problem-solving exercises. They contend that students can learn from each other and the teacher. Many LD students do not attend to relevant elements of the problem, and the group process can promote this attention. The model Goldman and Goldman suggest is a systematic one and may not appeal to those who prefer an intuitive style. However, if it is presented as a *general* set of guidelines, it can facilitate group problem solving. (See Figure 6.8.)

After matching students' cognitive styles with appropriate problem-solving approaches, it is essential that the teacher require students to apply their system until they can use it efficiently and automatically. The steps outlined in Chapter 2 for teaching a specific learning strategy to LD students should be followed carefully.

TEACHING QUESTIONING STRATEGIES

The ability to ask questions is an important skill for LD adolescents to learn. The students must acquire skill in asking different types of questions and must also develop a questioning attitude toward assignments, examinations, and class sessions. To cope successfully with the demands of the secondary curriculum, students must be assertive and willing to ask questions so as to negotiate effectively within the classroom. LD adolescents who use good questioning strategies will enhance their thinking and problem-solving abilities.

Learning disabled students can improve their performance in various situations by asking good questions. Torrance and Myers (1970) have specified the following areas in which such questions can be asked:

1. Questions regarding procedures ("May the answers on the exam be written in outline form rather than in paragraphs?" "Is the final draft or just a preliminary draft due on Friday?")
2. Questions regarding tasks ("Will the test be on the material presented during this last week or during the entire quarter?" "Will the test be all multiple choice?")
3. Questions regarding information ("Is this the right liquid to add to this mixture?" "Is this the screw for adjusting the plane?")
4. Questions regarding understanding ("What is the relationship between these issues and the ones discussed in class yesterday?" "Would you please explain what the author is trying to say on pages 51 through 56?")

Most LD students fail to ask such questions as those posed above for various reasons. Two important reasons are that they haven't been taught how to ask questions and they don't appreciate the value of questions to success in school. However, students also encounter many difficulties because they are not assertive in question asking. For example, LD students

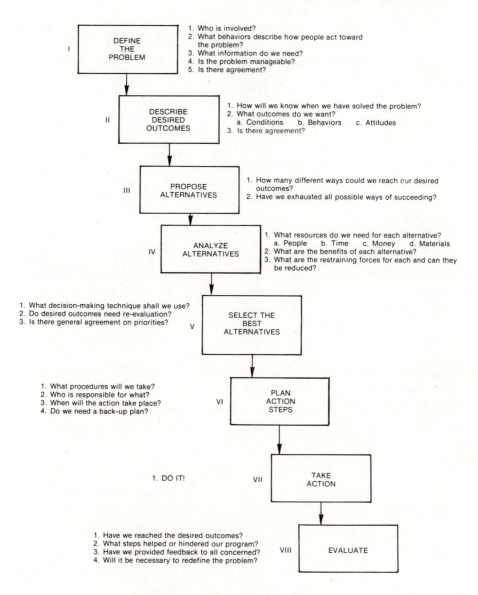

I DEFINE THE PROBLEM
1. Who is involved?
2. What behaviors describe how people act toward the problem?
3. What information do we need?
4. Is the problem manageable?
5. Is there agreement?

II DESCRIBE DESIRED OUTCOMES
1. How will we know when we have solved the problem?
2. What outcomes do we want?
   a. Conditions   b. Behaviors   c. Attitudes
3. Is there agreement?

III PROPOSE ALTERNATIVES
1. How many different ways could we reach our desired outcomes?
2. Have we exhausted all possible ways of succeeding?

IV ANALYZE ALTERNATIVES
1. What resources do we need for each alternative?
   a. People   b. Time   c. Money   d. Materials
2. What are the benefits of each alternative?
3. What are the restraining forces for each and can they be reduced?

1. What decision-making technique shall we use?
2. Do desired outcomes need re-evaluation?
3. Is there general agreement on priorities?
V SELECT THE BEST ALTERNATIVES

1. What procedures will we take?
2. Who is responsible for what?
3. When will the action take place?
4. Do we need a back-up plan?
VI PLAN ACTION STEPS

1. DO IT!
VII TAKE ACTION

1. Have we reached the desired outcomes?
2. What steps helped or hindered our program?
3. Have we provided feedback to all concerned?
4. Will it be necessary to redefine the problem?
VIII EVALUATE

From "Problem Solving in the Classroom: A Model for Sharing Learning Responsibility," by L. C. Goldman and N. C. Goldman, *Educational Technology,* 1974, *9,* 54.

Figure 6.8.   Problem-solving model.

may study hard for a test only to find that two of the chapters studied aren't covered on the exam. Or they may turn on the wrong switch in shop class because they do not know which one is correct and are afraid to ask.

Levels and Types of Questions

Most material written on questioning in education textbooks is directed at teachers (Hoover, 1976; Biehler, 1974; Estes & Vaughan, 1978). This emphasis is well placed, as teachers need to be aware of the importance of good questions and how to ask various kinds. Their good performance will increase students' learning as well as provide them with a good *model* for questioning. It is equally important, however, for students to be aware of different kinds of questions and the importance of asking good ones. Therefore, let us briefly review the various questions that should be asked by *both* teachers and students in a learning situation. Fraenkel's (1973) summary of different levels of questions are presented in Table 6.10. These should be explained to LD students and several examples of each level should be given. Then students should practice identifying the level that a given question belongs to as well as asking questions from each level. For students to feel comfortable in asking questions, they must have many opportunities to do so. By charting the frequency and level of questions that students ask, the teacher can show them how to use questioning more effectively.

Methods for Teaching Questioning

The first step is to provide the kind of atmosphere in the resource room that is conducive to students' asking questions. LD students are often hesitant to ask questions because of their previous experiences in school. Teachers may have ridiculed and belittled questions these students asked. While the learning disabilities teacher will definitely want to shape students' questioning behavior, it is important to convey an accepting attitude, so that students are willing to participate.

The model that the teacher sets for the students cannot be overemphasized. If we want students to ask questions that seek more than factual information, we must ask questions of that type as an example. In chapter 3 the ReQuest reading procedure (Manzo, 1969) was presented. A basic tenet of that approach is that the teacher serves as a model for the student's questioning strategies.

224

TABLE 6.10
Different Types of Questions by Purpose and Student Action Desired

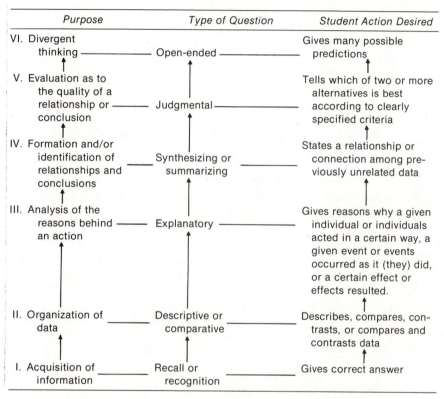

Purpose	Type of Question	Student Action Desired
VI. Divergent thinking	Open-ended	Gives many possible predictions
V. Evaluation as to the quality of a relationship or conclusion	Judgmental	Tells which of two or more alternatives is best according to clearly specified criteria
IV. Formation and/or identification of relationships and conclusions	Synthesizing or summarizing	States a relationship or connection among previously unrelated data
III. Analysis of the reasons behind an action	Explanatory	Gives reasons why a given individual or individuals acted in a certain way, a given event or events occurred as it (they) did, or a certain effect or effects resulted.
II. Organization of data	Descriptive or comparative	Describes, compares, contrasts, or compares and contrasts data
I. Acquisition of information	Recall or recognition	Gives correct answer

From *Helping Students Think and Value: Strategies for Teaching the Social Studies,* by J. R. Frankel (Englewood Cliffs, N. J.: Prentice-Hall, 1973), p. 178.

Some techniques that promise to increase the questioning strategies of students are as follows:

1. Present students with an answer (a concept or a name) and have them ask a set of questions that would allow them to arrive at the correct question for that answer (Fraenkel, 1973).
2. The Ten Questions game can increase both the frequency and types of questions asked by students. The teacher responds only "yes" or "no" to student questions until the problem is solved.

225

3. Torrance and Myers (1970) suggest the use of troubleshooting questions, such as, "Why was this problem so difficult this time and so easy last time?" or "Would this be more a problem of transportation or of communication?"

4. Require students to list the questions that will be *most* critical to ask of the history teacher before the next test.

5. Require students to question themselves about what they'll need to find out before they can begin work on a laboratory or shop project.

6. Present a list of different types of questions (descriptive, explanatory, synthesizing) and have students identify the category to which each question belongs.

7. Suchman (1966) suggests the use of discrepant events (i.e., puzzling incidents or happenings that on the surface don't make sense) about which students are to ask questions of the teacher to unlock the mystery.

8. Students can be taught to use *paraphrasing* to clarify their understanding of what someone has said. Paraphrasing involves restating what another person has said, using one's own words. Students learn to use lead-ins to paraphrasing, such as "I understand you said. . . ."

9. Perception checking is a technique in which the students state their perceptions about the feelings of others. It involves interpreting feelings and can be used to test the climate. Perception checking also allows the other person, such as the teacher, to confirm or correct the student's perception. For example, the student might say, "I get the impression that you are angry with me. Are you?"

In summary, the development of effective questioning strategies in LD students will not occur overnight. Not only must new skills be learned (e.g., how to ask questions at different levels), but students must also assume an active rather than passive stance. They must ask questions that will help them better understand and learn the information being presented and accomplish the required tasks.

SELF-MONITORING OF PERFORMANCE

The role of monitoring, or detecting errors in performance, is crucial for both learning and performance. To acquire a skilled, highly integrated response and to perform in a competent and accurate fashion, one must attend to feedback received. The important role of feedback in learning and performance has been emphasized in the psychological literature, but not in the educational literature. We contend, however, that the ability to monitor (or use feedback) is an important skill that influences the thinking, problem-solving, and decision-making effectiveness of LD students.

Deshler (1974) studied the ability of LD high school students to detect errors in their performance or in the performance of others and found that on measures of creative writing, editing, spelling, and vocabulary, LD students were inferior to their peers in detecting errors. However, LD students did demonstrate skill in detecting and correcting some errors, but they seemed to lack consistent strategies for monitoring their performance.

Learning disabled students must develop techniques to assist in monitoring both written and spoken work. Doing assignments without checking them and responding orally without carefully monitoring content have obvious implications for future employment and life adjustment situations. Adams (1971) has underscored the importance of seeking and using feedback. "Knowledge of results (feedback) is foremost a source of information which results in corrections that eventually lead the subject to a correct response" (p. 122). Certain strategies help LD students monitor their responses more effectively:

Recording Student Responses

Laurita (1972) has outlined a rehearsal procedure for improving reading comprehension. After the teacher has discussed a passage and read it aloud, the student is asked to reread the same paragraph. The student's reading is recorded while the teacher unhesitatingly gives help. When the recording is played back, the student is encouraged to observe the match (or mismatch) between the printed word and the recording of the passage. At each error, the teacher stops the recording, points out the error, and asks the student how it might be corrected. The student is then encouraged to reread the same paragraph to discover the benefits of monitoring the previous attempt.

The tape recorder may also be used to advantage in helping students review their verbal responses, such as answers to oral questions, and monitoring them for errors in pronunciation or logic.

Simulation Activities

The final phase of the SOCS problem-solving technique (discussed on page 268) is a simulation of the selected option. The purpose of simulating solutions is to give students opportunities to *practice* their responses through role-playing activities. During these practice exercises, students can monitor weaknesses in their responses and improve on them. The teacher may have to point out errors in the students' responses or in their logic. In role playing, the teacher can indicate students' errors by posing a response or question that reveals the fallacy of the student's logic. Once students recognize their errors, alternative responses or solutions should be discussed.

Monitoring All Responses

Learning disabled students must acquire a habit of checking their work before turning it in for correction. Despite reminders from the teacher, many students fail to check their work. Some techniques to help students check their responses more carefully are as follows:

1. Teachers should not *assume* that LD students know how to monitor their responses. Time should be spent demonstrating how to check different types of assignments, including key areas where errors are most likely to be made. For example, one strategy for checking spelling in writing assignments is to proofread the passage backward. If it is proofread from left to right, the reader uses context clues and meaning and tends to overlook errors in spelling. By reading backward from right to left, the student cannot rely on context clues.

2. A certain portion of each work session should be set aside for checking work. For example, a student who is answering questions for a history assignment and has thirty minutes to work on the assignment should set aside seven to ten minutes for monitoring the completed work. Most assignments require *more than* one proofing. The history assignment may be read one time to check for spelling errors and a second time to determine if any key ideas have been omitted.

3. Some teachers have successfully used point systems to encourage LD students to check their work. Points are awarded to students who carefully check the assignment. Points are taken from students who turn in work containing careless errors that they should have caught through careful monitoring.

4.   The teacher can help LD students focus on errors that they have made by giving general rather than specific feedback. For example, in checking a theme for spelling, the teacher may put a mark in the margin next to the line in which the error occurs. When the paper is returned, the student locates the exact error that has been made. Thus, much of the responsibility for monitoring performance remains with the student. Similarly, suppose a student who listed certain attributes of an object omitted several. The teacher may indicate that a certain number of attributes have been omitted. The student should then try to complete the list independently before returning it to the teacher for rechecking. If the teacher merely filled in the missing items on first grading the assignment, the student would have no practice in monitoring the work — the teacher would have assumed that responsibility.

5.   LD students should be encouraged to be selective in making responses so as to avoid as many errors as possible. For example, in a creative writing assignment, students should use words and sentences that they have learned to use correctly. On the other hand, students should not be so selective as to inhibit expression and should adjust their selectivity according to the requirements of each assignment.

6.   Students can improve their monitoring ability if teachers give appropriate feedback. Teachers usually learn in education courses that feedback is most effective if it is given as soon as possible *after* students respond or perform. This is true, but it is only half of the story! It is equally important to give feedback right *before* the next response or performance. For example, suppose that on Monday a student was asked to write a short theme and turn it in for grading. The teacher should try to return the corrected copy to the student on Tuesday (or as soon *after* the performance as possible). If the student is asked to write another theme on the following Monday, the teacher should *precede* the assignment with some feedback. This would consist of a reminder of specific errors that occurred on the previous assignment. Such feedback *before* the next assignment is begun will reduce the repetition of errors.

TIME MANAGEMENT

Learning disabled adolescents have difficulty managing their time appropriately (Wilcox, 1970). Assignments are repeatedly unfinished due to a combination of a lack of skills and poor work habits. Drake and

Cavanaugh (1970) describe LD adolescents as experiencing time panic when they realize how much work they have to do and the limited amount of time at their disposal. LD students also experience time perception difficulties, as evidenced by their inability to adhere to time schedules, such as making it from one class to another on time (Deshler, 1978). In short, LD students manifest time-related problems in the following areas: (1) lack of awareness of time, slow work speed, and (2) poor time management. There are techniques for increasing time awareness and work speed. A first step is to have LD students recognize the importance of time as a variable in their life. As students move from elementary to secondary schools, the work load increases considerably. To cope with the curriculum requirements, the effective use of time is essential for the LD student who has not mastered basic academic skills.

Procedures for Increasing Time Awareness

Because much of their instruction emphasizes task *accuracy* and *correctness,* LD students often do not place appropriate value on time as a factor. To emphasize the importance of time and to increase students' awareness of it, the following procedures have been found to be effective:

1. *Make time a criterion in assignment completion.* Most criteria for achieving instructional objectives relate to percentage or number of correct responses. For example: "Given ten problems on compound interest, Chuck will correctly answer eight problems in written form." Such requirements may be supplemented with a time component — for example, "Given ten problems on compound interest, Chuck will correctly answer eight problems in written form in thirty minutes." The time requirements specified in instructional objectives should be at a level that will press LD students to produce at their maximum. If too much time is allotted, students may not apply themselves efficiently. Too little time may produce anxiety and result in a decrease in accuracy. In instances, however, when students' work habits are highly laborious and deliberate, it may be appropriate to sacrifice some accuracy for improved time. For example, an LD student who works very slowly and who is overly concerned with accuracy may correctly complete all problems *attempted* (e.g., two of three, or 100 percent of those attempted on an assignment with ten problems, or 20 percent of

the total). The end results are considerably short of a passing grade. If, on the other hand, the student's work speed increases to a point at which all ten problems are completed with only 50 percent accuracy (that is, five of ten correct), the end result will be better.

2. *Use time clocks, stopwatches, and other timing devices.* Many LD resource rooms require students to check in at the beginning of each class period and to punch the time clock at the beginning and completion of specific assignments. Stopwatches and other timepieces can effectively motivate students to increase productivity. In conjunction with these devices, students should be encouraged to graph the time they spend on specific assignments by using a simple bar graph or plotting time and accuracy on the same graph. Again, the purpose of such procedures is to increase students' awareness of time and to increase their productivity.

3. *Change assignments on the basis of time.* Students often work on assignments until completed, and only then do they change tasks. For certain types of assignments, there are advantages to long, sustained work sessions on one assignment. However, in many cases, there are advantages to changing tasks on a regular and frequent basis as a function of *time* and not task completion. For example, a student who has assignments to complete in three subject areas (A, B, and C) may work in twenty-minute blocks, shifting from A to B after twenty minutes and from B to C after the next twenty minutes, and so on. By changing subject matter every twenty minutes, the student experiences new material and a frequent change of pace. For some LD students, such a schedule is effective because it prevents boredom with a given subject or assignment. The key to such scheduling is to have the tasks for each time segment *well* organized and prepared so no time is wasted in changing tasks.

4. *Reward effective use of time.* All students value free time in which they can become involved in unstructured activities of their choice. Obtaining free time can be made contingent on the effective use of time for assigned tasks. Students can be placed on a reward system that grants them free time if they have met an agreed on criterion for completing a certain amount of work in a given time.

Techniques for Improving Time Management

The concept of time management has become increasingly popular in recent years (MacKenzie, 1974; Lakein, 1973). As society becomes increasingly complex, the choices that individuals must make have increased tremendously. In essence, when choices of activities are made, people are deciding how to spend the limited amount of time at their disposal. Since LD students are part of this increasingly complex society, they too should be very concerned with how they manage their time. LD students who have limited skills or who have to apply compensation procedures often spend more time completing certain tasks than their peers. Careful time management is particularly crucial for LD students.

Some time management techniques that teachers can present and practice with LD students include the following:

1. *Write down things that you have to or want to do.* This step forces LD students to specify the complete set of activities that demand their attention. It requires students to avoid generalities about how much work they must do. When the list is completed, the tasks often appear much more manageable than the nebulous activities existing only in the student's imagination.

2. *Set priorities for the tasks on the list.* Lakein (1973) suggests using an ABC priority system, that is, assigning an A to those items on the list that have high value, a B to those items of medium value, and a C to those of low value. Items marked with a A should be given the *most* time and should be done first. Taking account of time and the urgency of the items, they can be broken down further, so that A items become A-1, A-2, A-3, and so on. Teachers can teach LD students how to do this by using a hypothetical example (list of typical tasks of a high school student) and working the example through so that students can see that different tasks have different values and that a task of little value is not worth a big effort. This activity is very important, as LD students often fail to differentiate between tasks in importance.

3. *Set short-term and long-term goals.* All time management systems require people to define their lifetime goals. Lakein (1973) suggests that the goals be written down in three major categories: (a) lifetime goals, which are rather broad and may be quite inclusive; (b) three-year goals, which become much more specific; and (c) six-month goals. Individual goals provide a context in which to make decisions about activities and time management. Students should

compare the priority ratings (A, B, or C) given to the items on their task list with their goals list.

4. *Keep a time log.* For at least one whole day, at fifteen-minute intervals, students are to note what they have done. This step requires honesty and is to include all activities, including snack and bathroom breaks and phone calls.

5. *Analyze the time log.* The time log can be analyzed in a variety of ways. One way is to analyze the percentage of time spent in different kinds of activities (for example, 20 percent spent on breaks, 32 percent spent in studying). Or the time log may be analyzed according to the percentage of time spent on planned activities. This step clearly reveals to students how they spend time. Based on the results of this activity, the percentage of time spent on certain activities can be reallocated.

6. *Help students become aware of their personal time traps.* This step also requires that students be candid in analyzing their habits. Teachers should refrain from immediately telling students what they think are students' time traps. It is much more meaningful if students discover these for themselves. Teachers can ask leading questions or can suggest general time areas that the student might consider. When the time traps are identified, they should be *written down*. The teacher and students can then discuss specific ways to overcome time traps.

7. *Make a plan.* Several plans or schedules should be used, ranging from general overview schedules, such as a semester calendar on which students record the days on which important things are due, to specific schedules, such as daily or hourly schedules of events. The advantages of using such schedules are (a) they provide a structure for LD students, and (b) they require students to write down tasks. The format of time schedules can vary considerably, but the basic components should include the task and the time allotment. Scheduling requires much practice, and it is an activity that teachers should both demonstrate and do with LD students. LD students should be encouraged to keep these basic schedules: (a) a semester schedule or calendar that they can survey periodically and tell at a glance what major activities they must plan for; (b) a weekly schedule that specifies major requirements and blocks off enough time for completing those requirements; (c) a daily checklist (possibly a 3″ x 5″ card) on which the student can record tasks to be completed during that day. The LD student can practice making schedules by spending the first five minutes in the resource room preparing a time and task schedule for that hour. The process

233

of making schedules encourages students to observe more closely how they function as learners. It also requires students to think more closely about the demands of given tasks and what is necessary to meet those demands.

REFERENCES

Adams, J. A. A closed-loop theory of motor learning. *Journal of Motor Behavior*, 1971, *3*, 111-149.

Atkinson, B. R., & Seunath, O. H. M. The effect of stimulus change on attending behavior in normal children and in children with learning disabilities. *Journal of Learning Disabilities*, 1973, *9*, 569-573.

Biehler, R. F. *Psychology applied to teaching.* Boston: Houghton Mifflin, 1974.

Bloom, B., & Broder, L. J. Problem solving processes of college students. *Supplementary Educational Monographs*, 1950, *73*, 1-31.

Bruner, J. S. *The process of education.* New York: Vintage Books, 1960.

Buswell, G. T., in cooperation with J. Lenore. Diagnostic studies in arithmetic. *Supplementary Educational Monographs* (Vol. 30). Chicago: University of Chicago Press, 1926.

DeBono, E. *New think.* New York: Basic Books, 1967.

Deshler, D. D. *Learning disability in the high school student as demonstrated in monitoring of self-generated and externally generated errors.* Unpublished doctoral dissertation, University of Arizona, 1974.

Deshler, D. D. Psychoeducational characteristics of learning disabled adolescents. In L. Mann, L. Goodman, & J. L. Wiederholt (Eds.), *Teaching the learning disabled adolescent.* Boston: Houghton Mifflin, 1978.

Drake, C., & Cavanaugh, J. Teaching the high school dyslexic. In L. E. Anderson (Ed.), *Helping the adolescent with the hidden handicap.* Belmont, Calif: Fearon, 1970.

Estes, T. H., & Vaughan, J. L. *Reading and learning in the content classroom.* Boston: Allyn & Bacon, 1978.

Ewing, D. W. Discovering your problem-solving style. *Psychology Today*, 1977, 69-71.

Feldhusen, J. F., & Treffinger, D. J. *Teaching creative thinking and problem solving.* Dubuque, Iowa: Kendall/Hunt, 1977.

Fraenkel, J. R. *Helping students think and value: Strategies for teaching the social studies.* Englewood Cliffs, N.J.: Prentice-Hall, 1973.

Gogue, R. M., & Smith, E. C., Jr. A study of the effects of verbalization on problem solving. *Journal of Experimental Psychology*, 1962, *63*, 12-18.

Goldman, L. C., & Goldman, N. C. Problem solving in the classroom: A model for sharing learning responsibility. *Educational Technology*, 1974, *9*, 53-58.

Goor, A., & Sommerfield, R. E. A comparison of problem-solving processes of creative and non-creative students. *Journal of Educational Psychology*, 1975, *67*, 495-505.

Gordon, W. J. *Synectics.* New York: Harper & Row, 1961.

Hallahan, D. P., Kauffman, J. M., & Ball, D. W. Selective attention and cognitive tempo of low achieving and high achieving sixth grade males. *Perceptual Motor Skills*, 1973, *36*, 579-583.

Havertape, J. F. *The communication functions in learning disabled adolescents: A study of verbalized self-instructions.* Unpublished doctoral dissertation, University of Arizona, 1976.

Hoover, K. H. *The professional teacher's handbook: A guide for improving instruction in today's middle and secondary schools.* Boston: Allyn & Bacon, 1976.

Kagan, J. Reflection-impulsivity and the general dynamics of conceptual tempo. *Journal of Abnormal Psychology*, 1966, *71*, 17-24.

Keogh, B. Hyperactivity and learning disorders: Review and speculation. *Exceptional Children*, 1971, *38*, 101-110.

Keogh, B., & Donlon, G. McG. Field dependence, impulsivity and learning disabilities. *Journal of Learning Disabilities*, 1972, *5*, 331-336.

Lakein, A. *How to get control of your time and your life.* New York: New American Library, 1973.

Laurita, R. E. Rehearsal: A technique for improving reading comprehension. *Academic Therapy*, 1972, *1*, 103-111.

McKenney, J. L., & Keen, P. G. W. How managers' minds work. *Harvard Business Review*, 1976, *52*, 14-21.

Manzo, A. V. ReQuest procedure. *Journal of Reading*, 1969, *13*, 123-126.

Messer, S. The effect of anxiety over intellectual performance on reflection-impulsivity in children. *Child Development*, 1970, *31*, 723-735.

Parker, T. B., Freston, C. W., & Drew, C. J. Comparison of verbal performance of normal and learning disabled children as a function of input organization. *Journal of Learning Disabilities*, 1975, *8*, 386-393.

Patton, B. R., & Griffin, K. *Problem-solving group interaction.* New York: Harper & Row, 1973.

Ross, A. O. *Psychological aspects of learning disabilities and reading disorders.* New York: McGraw-Hill, 1976.

Shaver, J. R. Educational research and instruction in critical thinking. *Social Education*, 1962, *26*, 16.

Suchman, J. R. Inquiring workshop: A model for the language of education. *The Instructor*, 1966, *76*, 33, 92.

Thomas, E., & Robinson, A. *Improving reading in every class: A sourcebook for teachers.* Boston: Allyn & Bacon, 1975.

Torrance, E. P., & Myers, R. E. *Creative learning and teaching.* New York: Dodd, Mead, 1970.

Uris, A. *The executive deskbook.* New York: Van Nostrand Reinhold, 1970.

Walloch, A. M., & Kogan, N. *Modes of thinking in young children.* New York: Holt, Rinehart & Winston, 1962.

Whimbey, A. *Intelligence can be taught.* New York: Dutton, 1975.

Wilcox, E. Identifying characteristics of the NH adolescent. In L. E. Anderson (Ed.), *Helping the adolescent with the hidden handicap.* Belmont, Calif.: Fearon, 1970.

Williams, J. C., *Motivation for career success.* Waco, Texas: Education Achievement, 1972.

7

SOCIAL INTERACTION: STRATEGIES AND METHODS

Development of Social Skills

Social Development of the LD Adolescent

Assessing the Social Skills of LD Adolescents

Teaching Social Skills to LD Adolescents

7

The social skills development of LD adolescents is critical. They must develop social skills to the level that they become integrated into a peer group. The peer group will shape LD adolescents' behavior to the demands of present societal values and technology. The peer group offers LD adolescents a sounding board for new ideas, coping skills, and affective relationships.

Most readers have known adolescents who did not associate with a peer group because of physical proximity, choice, or skills. These persons relate to adults, younger children or siblings. Adolescents reared on farms or in isolated settings may temporarily lack the social skills that make them acceptable for peer group membership. However, as the number and variety of their experiences increase, these adolescents become more readily accepted by the peer group.

Other adolescents who choose interests that are markedly different from the common interests of the peer group follow one of two social courses. Some become shy, reticent, and retiring in peer groups, but develop intense relationships with persons in their field of interest. Others develop the social skills of more sophisticated adults and come to be rejected by peers, who call them "snobs" or "little professors."

Neither of the two aforementioned groups is of great concern to the learning disabilities specialist. Rather, it is the adolescents who have had opportunities to interact with peers and share common peer group interests, but who simply use social skills inappropriately (Siegel, 1974). For example, the LD student who says to another student, "Didn't you try out for the play? I don't see your name in the cast. I thought they chose anybody who wanted to be in the play. They asked John to be in it and he didn't even try out." How does the second student answer this question? Probably the student doesn't answer the question, but reacts negatively ("Stuff it!") or ignores the LD student.

This LD student needs help! Intervention is as important in the area of social skills as it is in the area of cognitive skills (Kronick, 1976). If LD youngsters fail in their peer relationships during adolescence, their adult life may be as seriously hampered by this lack of skill as would be the inability to read, solve mathematics problems, or write a letter of application. However, the social skills of the child and the adolescent with learning disabilities have received minimal attention. Lack of social skills has never been included as a manifestation of learning disability by any federal definition to date (PL 94-142, November 29, 1976). In the past, investigators have considered lack of social skills a manifestation of learning disability (Siegel, 1974; Kronick, 1976; Johnson & Myklebust, 1964), but the only investigator to date who has shown any sustaining research interest in the area has been Bryan (1972, 1974, 1976). Currently, the strong implied relationship between learning disability and juvenile delinquency has focused professional attention on social manifestations of disability, particularly in the adolescent LD.

DEVELOPMENT OF SOCIAL SKILLS

Erikson's Eight Stages

The development of social skills is a complex process. One may choose from several taxonomies to clarify this development. We have chosen Erikson's (1950) developmental hierarchy as a context within which to structure social skills. The stages are:

1. Trust.
2. Autonomy.
3. Competence and confidence.
4. Accomplishment.
5. Identity.
6. Intimacy.
7. Parental and community responsibility.
8. Integrity.

A brief explanation of each stage reveals the skills that are associated with that stage.

Trust

The first stage in the lifelong quest for self-actualization is trust. It has been said that this stage culminates in the infant's being able to manipulate persons and objects, primarily through the use of language and psychomotor skills. During this first stage, the infant is dependent on others. The infant first learns the comfort of having primary needs met by a care-giver. In most cases, the initial care-giver is the mother. With development, the infant learns that the care-giver can also provide comfort for secondary needs, such as social and environmental stimulation. It is at this stage that infants learn that trust can be reciprocal. The infant gradually forms interpersonal trust with care-givers by use of smiles, language, postural relaxation, and simple motor acts. However, this reciprocal trust between care-giver and child may be disturbed. The infant may not seek out the care-giver. Rather, the infant may become either tense and rigid or lethargic and limp upon coming into contact with the care-giver. The next developmental stage, autonomy, will be affected by the nature and type of trust relationship that has grown up between the infant and the care-giver.

Autonomy

The onset of the child's autonomy is well recognized by parents of young children. The stage begins in the second year. Gesell and his associates (1956) popularized this stage as "the terrible twos." Young children begin to discard objects of all types. (Parents of our acquaintance refer, in their frustration, to their two-year-old as "the plumber's friend," due to the focus of their child's discarding behavior.) Along with discarding, children begin discovering and exploring. The most frequent word in the vocabulary of both parents and child is "No."

This stage culminates in self-identification ("Jackie go!" or "Jackie no go!"). This statement is made with all the affect associated with feelings of autonomy.

If the child is not permitted to develop an autonomous self, it will affect his or her language, and social and affective relationships with others. The reader may have met some twins who have not developed autonomous selves. Failure to do so may result in an unhealthy symbiotic relationship.

Competence and Confidence

Between the ages of four and six, children begin to interact with peers and play cooperatively. The peer group is undifferentiated by competence

("We are having fun."). Competence develops as children engage in activities ("I helped make cookies.").

Confidence is instilled in children by the approval of parents, the completion of a project, or the effects of the peer group. Children are other-oriented for evidence of their success or failure. They do not focus on the strengths or weaknesses of individual members of the group.

Children who have difficulties at this stage do so because they disrupt the group rather than participate in it. Such children may not be flexible enough to "play" in these unorganized activities. Overorganized children who may have a difficult time during this period may respond very well during the ensuing stage.

Accomplishment

Once children enter school, accomplishments of a cognitive and psychomotor nature are demanded of them. Earlier stages required children only to "play the game." Now, the outcome of the game, whether it be solving mathematics problems or playing baseball, is important. One now "wins" or "loses," and by how much also becomes important.

Children are encouraged to master tasks. A child who is not competent may be chosen for an activity *only* if *all* children must be included in the selection process. Children become acutely aware of their strengths and weaknesses in relation to the standards set by parents, peers, and teachers. They will not enter into activities in which they feel incompetent, but will eagerly enter into those activities for which they feel qualified. One special note about the standard-setting groups named above: The competition for meeting standards in formal, school-oriented, cognitive and psychomotor activities is more intense than it is in informal neighborhood activities. That is to say, school-oriented activities generally require greater competence for entry than informal neighborhood activities that take place after school or on weekends. The neighborhood peer group activities generally include some younger and older children and, at times, opposite-sex peers. This group requires flexibility of entry-level standards to function. Thus, the child with marginal skills may receive a great deal of satisfaction from neighborhood activities.

Children whose skills are far below the entry standards for school activities are often referred to special services, such as special self-contained classrooms for the learning disabled, mentally retarded, emotionally disturbed, or physically handicapped. As the neighborhood groups recognize other children's severe incompetence, they then apply school standards to their own selection process — "He can't play, he's LD." As a result, children's incompetence in cognitive skills may be generalized by their peers to all skill areas, whether they be cognitive, affective, or psychomotor. Consequently, these children may not be chosen to enter into peer activities, even though they are competent in the activities or have achieved mastery of a desirable skill. Children also may be left out of activities because they do not have enough confidence to penetrate the group.

Identity

Students in secondary school spend a great deal of time thinking about their futures — choosing a vocation, choosing a partner, planning to acquire possessions and have adventures, such as buying a car or a stereo and going on trips. Thus, students plan ahead, and they may make many errors in judgment in this new cognitive act if they do not receive supportive guidance. Certain conflicts will occur between students and authority figures if authorities seek to direct the students' activities or dismiss student planning as "dreaming." It is well for adults to remember that during this thinking time students practice the long-term planning required if they are to function adequately as adults. If parents provide everything that their children wish for and direct all their planning, students will not have an opportunity to plan and select options to achieve their goals. On the other hand, parents who put down their children's plans and options for reaching goals will reap the same results as the directing parents.

All planning is based on student perceptions of their mastery of skills. Interests and perceived mastery are nearly synonymous to youngsters. For example, if one suggests vocations by title only to these students, they will judge vocations by social prestige and select occupations based on ideal conditions and skills rather than real conditions and skills. One must discuss with students the skills involved if they are to make realistic vocational choices. In general, students can explore an occupational cluster and the skills required for competence in a vocation when they are still in a comprehensive high school. This is one important contribution of career/vocational education.

Students who feel they are not competent do not plan well for the future. Students with low self-esteem need more professional counseling to help them seek out future vocations and partners than do students with adequate self-esteem.

Intimacy

Young adults who have successfully completed each preceding stage now actively seek a partner. In previous stages young adults have developed trust in others and self-identity as individuals and as members of a group based on their cognitive, affective, and psychomotor skills. During the intimacy stage they test their skills in sharing goals and caring for another's needs. This requires extreme trust and the ability to deal with social relationships without giving up one's own identity. Society does not provide the young adult with much training for this stage. Rather, the models it provides are romanticized to such an extent that using logic in the mate selection process is discouraged.

What if a young adult chooses *not* to select a partner? Society deals harshly with this individual. There are few informal situations in adult life to which single persons are invited or in which they are encouraged to participate with couples. Society offers few models of single persons in adult life. In general, society demands that a person secure a partner upon successful completion of the intimacy stage. The adage, "No matter how crooked the pot, there is a lid to fit it," reinforces the universality of this statement.

There are persons who find a partner but who are unprepared to develop an intimate relationship with that partner. These individuals are unable to share and care, and still maintain their identity. Some persons may remain locked in this relationship and feel trapped, with no way out. Others break the relationship and reevaluate their identity and goals. On the basis of this insight, they either seek to establish a more fulfilling relationship with another partner or choose to remain single. Finally, there are persons who break the relationship with their partner and do not go through a period of insightful reevaluation. These persons generally run through numerous partner relationships that are not satisfying to themselves or their partners.

One final point must be made about broken intimate relationships. Some people feel pressured to justify their separation from a partner when discussing the relationship with other people. However, they need not do this, since it is only the need to respond to society's demand for establishing a relationship with a partner that is lasting.

Parental and Community Responsibility

During the parental and community responsibility stage, adults derive satisfaction from their vocation, family, and community. It is generally assumed that if one does not enjoy one's vocation, family, and community, one is either immature or disturbed. There has been little written about the developmental skills of adulthood. However, one writer, Sheehy (1977), has attempted to provide some direction and describe developmental skills of adulthood in her book *Passages*. This book is both an insightful and reflective step in the study of adult life. The reader is encouraged to at least scan the text to note the complexity of the developmental skills of adulthood.

Present society is changing, so much so that the prospects of parental and community responsibilities as conceptualized by Erikson (1950) nearly three decades ago have been dramatically affected. Technology also makes different demands on adults. Several examples come to mind. First, adults do not choose one vocation for life any longer. Experience has shown that the adult may pursue three or four vocations in a lifetime. Second, parenting is a choice today, and not a demand. Finally, community involvement and pride are less important today in view of the mobility of the population and the dissatisfaction or apathy toward community governments. For these and other reasons, it is impossible today to establish criteria by which to judge competencies at this life stage.

Integrity

The persistent question to be answered during this stage in life is, "Was it all worth it?" This question relates to the accomplishments of the individual and to that person's relationships with partner, peers, and children. At this stage, one is assumed to have the perspective to survey the developmental tasks of life and make a rational decision. Until recently, society has required that all persons must face this question at age sixty-five and then retire into oblivion as nonproductive and unneeded individuals in society.

However, there is nothing either magical or logical in facing this question at sixty-five. Some persons face it at thirty-five or forty. Others, such as Abraham, Toscanini, and Picasso, died after long lives, having apparently never asked the question. Seemingly, they assumed productivity was to last throughout their lifetime. The Gray Panthers is one group of older citizens currently striving to uphold this same concept of lifelong productivity. Perhaps they will realize their goals when society recognizes the resources available in aging persons and stops emphasizing youth as the standard of productivity and the criterion of self-esteem. Sheehy (1977) appears to have provided the seed for establishing other values, criteria, and standards. It remains for others in society to nourish the seed in the search for the developmental skills of integrity.

Adolescence as a Developmental Stage

Adolescence provides an opportunity to further development of skills learned at earlier stages. Some adolescents require further practice to perform to criterion the skills for coping with identity. It is not sufficient to be "old enough" to attain the social competencies required of adolescents by society. Junior and senior high school are two types of settings in which adolescents attain these required social skills. These two settings offer vehicles for social learning that are different from those available in the elementary school. Several more readily apparent social vehicles in large comprehensive secondary schools are more content areas, diverse groups of students, teachers with differing interests. These social vehicles give the secondary student more opportunities to identify with different individuals, groups, and activities.

The question is often raised, "What can we give students in small rural schools?" There may be greater opportunities to develop social skills within the small rural school than within the large urban school. In the small rural secondary school, the resources of *all* students are required to form an interest club or engage in a school activity. Conversely, in the large school, students are subtly selected from among the most competent to form an interest club or engage in a school activity. In the large school, the average or near average students find it difficult to develop social skills in junior and senior high school clubs and activities. In fact, at one large school, it was reported that if a student could find just one friend, it would confirm the student's adequate social skill development. If this is the general case with nonhandicapped students, one can easily see the implications that size of school must have on the development of social skills of LD adolescents.

Developing social skills of the adolescent is an important goal. Some social competencies are further developed to strengthen peer group ties or to help students cope with tension. Other competencies are taught for the pleasure they give the individual. Adolescents often need the security of the peer group to cope with the tension that exists between their parents and themselves. However, adolescents also need the social skills required to become independent from the peer group when its demands and customs do not satisfy the adolescent's own needs (Vernon, 1971).

Maslow's Hierarchy of Needs

Maslow (1962) has developed a hierarchy of needs that require specific social skills of the individual at each level:

1. Physiological needs
2. Safety
3. Love
4. Self-esteem
5. Esteem of others
6. Self-actualization (Maslow, 1962)

To each of Erikson's (1950) stages, one may apply Maslow's (1962) need hierarchy. Using this paradigm, the teacher can better understand the goals that are necessary to satisfy specific needs of students at the respective stages of social development. The teacher can then identify skills required by adolescents to meet the higher needs within each stage. A scope and sequence plan for social skill development could then be constructed as an informal means of assessment and as a guide to curricular and instructional direction in this area. At this time, no such scope and sequence plan has been developed for adolescents or for any other group.

SOCIAL DEVELOPMENT OF THE LD ADOLESCENT

Reclassification of Social and Cognitive States

Several persons in the field of learning disabilities have focused on the social skills of the LD adolescent (Kronick, 1975, 1976; Siegel, 1974; Drake & Cavanaugh, 1970). Kronick has spoken of the social status change of adolescents when they are reclassified from nonhandicapped to handicapped. Once students are classified as LD, social expectations change. Ms. Luci Johnson Nugent stated to participants attending the Kansas Association of Learning Disabilities in Wichita, Kansas (October 22, 1977), that "stupid" was the word she used to describe herself until she was sixteen years old. "By labeling myself as stupid and incompetent, I no longer had to try to succeed. I could give up and find some peace" (*Lawrence Journal World,* October 22, 1977, p. 9). This self-evaluation of her competence reclassified Ms. Nugent cognitively as a nonlearner and caused other persons to reclassify her socially in the same way. Other persons did not expect her to attain cognitive or social competencies at a rate expected of her peers. When she gave up, she did not have to develop her social skills to meet her low expectations based on her low cognitive status.

Conversely, social deficits can affect cognitive skills (Karnes, McCoy, Zehrback, Wollersheim, & Clarizio, 1962). Karnes et al. reported that underachieving, academically talented students may have a hostile, rejecting father and consequently manifest poor social adjustment. Underachievement is not only associated with father's behavior, but also with parents who are unaccepting of the child and who are authoritarian in their management of the child. This type of underachievement results from external classification of the child as acceptable or not acceptable by the parents of the child. Parental labeling is in direct contrast to Ms. Nugent's self-labeling. Ms. Nugent chose to lower her aspirations for cognitive achievement at specific stages. In parent-labeling, it is the parents who have failed to provide the child with opportunities to obtain cognitive skills or have demanded higher levels of skills than the child can hope to achieve. In both labeling situations, the ends are the same, but the means are radically different.

In the case of secondary LD students, social skills can be negatively affected by either self-labeling or parent-labeling. It also appears that any significant person in the child's environment who is hostile, rejecting, and authoritative in managing the LD child can externally limit the child's cognitive and social competencies.

Classification of LD Adolescents' Social Skills

The following list is a compilation of terms used by various writers to describe the social characteristics of LD students (Bradfield, 1970; Drake & Cavanaugh, 1970; Lehtinen-Rogan, 1971; Siegel, 1974; Thompson, 1970; Wilcox, 1970):

1. Low motivation.
2. Gullibility.
3. Aloneness.
4. Perseveration.
5. Aversiveness.
6. Low ego status (depression, low self-esteem, guilt).
7. Supersensitivity to external cues (overconcern with the way others feel about them and how they are approached and treated).
8. Paralysis of effort (extreme difficulty in starting a task involving reading, writing, and spelling).
9. Ambivalence over intelligence and dependence (they think they are subnormal mentally and are sensitive about becoming dependent on others).
10. Suggestibility (prey for unscrupulous leaders).
11. Emotional lability.

12. Poor concentration.
13. Overreaction to stimuli.
14. Demanding with other persons.
15. Poor social judgment.
16. Lack of awareness of social impact on others.
17. Goof-offs (don't pay attention, distract others).
18. Lack of resourcefulness (inflexible, unimaginative, unable to see optional solutions).

Alley, Deshler, and Warner (1977) have surveyed secondary learning disabilities teachers to determine which of the listed characteristics best discriminate LD secondary students from nonLD students (nonhandicapped as well as mentally retarded and other special students). They found that the most discriminating characteristics were "ambivalence over intelligence and dependence on others" (Drake & Cavanaugh, 1970). There is a surprising correspondence between our preliminary findings and the self-classification label Ms. Nugent applied to her own competence. However, the critical, limiting phrase in Ms. Nugent's description is ". . . until she was sixteen years old." It was at that point that she changed her self-classification to that of a person who would raise her cognitive and social needs levels. She took the opportunities provided in adolescence to further develop earlier learned social and cognitive skills that helped her cope with her identity crisis.

In the preceding discussion we have tried to show the importance of social status and social skill development for LD adolescents and the relationship between social skills and cognitive achievement. Also, we have listed the social characteristics that LD adolescents manifest after a sustained period of academic failure and after experiencing negative self-evaluation or peer-adult evaluation. Erikson (1950) was optimistic when he postulated that during the identity stage (i.e., adolescence) students can reevaluate the skills developed during earlier stages and further develop these skills to better cope with the identity crises of adolescence. Professionally, our time panic as learning disabilities teachers is that adolescence may be the last developmental period that LD students have for restructuring because adult settings usually do not provide opportunities for developing and practicing social skills supposedly learned at earlier stages.

ASSESSING THE SOCIAL SKILLS OF LD ADOLESCENTS

Currently, there are no formal assessment instruments that specifically identify either the developmental stages postulated by Erikson (1950) or the needs hierarchy of Maslow (1962). Until such instruments are developed, we suggest that teachers use the following measures, both formal and informal, to assess various aspects of social competence. These measures evaluate LD students within the social setting of the secondary school:

1. *Tennessee Self-Concept Scale* (Fitts, 1964).
2. *Modified Ohio Social Acceptance Scale* (Rucker, 1968).
3. Scope and hierarchy of LD students' curricular choices.
4. Frequency of contacts with school counselors and administrators.
5. An inventory of educational program satisfaction.

A brief description of each measure and its use may help the reader identify the specific qualities that make the measure appropriate in this context.

Tennessee Self-Concept Scale

The *Tennessee Self-Concept Scale* is a 100-item self-evaluation instrument that purports to measure perceptions in the six areas of Family Self, Moral-Ethical Self, Personal Self, Physical Self, Self-Criticism, and Social Self. Fitts (1964) uses a five-point Likert-type scoring procedure for the scale. This measure permits the teacher to obtain comprehensive information about LD students' self-evaluations across several social settings.

Modified Ohio Social Acceptance Scale

The *Modified Ohio Social Acceptance Scale* (OSAS) is also a sociometric, Likert-type measure used to determine social position of students in the classroom setting. The directions for administering the OSAS were originally written for elementary children. The OSAS results were to be discussed with each child (Fordyce, Yauck, & Raths, 1946). Rucker (1968) modified the directions to make them appropriate for junior high school students. The modified version requires that the results of the measure be kept confidential. This Modified OSAS provides a mean social position for each student as evaluated by peers. The instrument gives the teacher some measure of LD adolescents' social skills among their peers.

Scope and Hierarchy of LD Students' Curricular Choices

The scope and hierarchy of curriculum offerings selected by LD students also should be evaluated. This is an unobtrusive, informal measure of the range and depth of the scholastic interests of LD students and their penetration of the various social subsystems of the school, such as literary arts, fine arts, practical arts, social sciences, physical and biological sciences, physical education, and communication. It can also provide an index of the effect of cooperative planning among the various content area teachers at the junior and senior high school levels. This information permits the learning disabilities teacher to evaluate LD students' range and depth of interests, as well as the content teachers' perceptions of the limits of educational opportunities that should be made available to LD students. The teachers' evaluations can be determined by comparing the differences between the choices made by the students and the schedules approved at registration. Final class schedules should not be used because of course conflicts and class closings, which reflect unavoidable circumstances.

Frequency of LD Students' Contacts with School Counselors and Administrators

The counseling and administration use index is also an unobtrusive, informal measure of LD students' demands for services. When applying this index, the learning disabilities teacher must determine whether LD student contacts were voluntary or occurred by request of school personnel or parents. A simple frequency count of contacts is all that is required for this measure. A comparative frequency count should also be made for groups of nonhandicapped peers of LD students. A more formal procedure could be developed that would include (1) the reason for the referral, (2) the source of the referral, (3) the disposition of the referral (no action, continued contact, further referral to school psychologist, mental health center, and so on). The LD teacher can then compare the use of counseling and administrative services by LD students with a baseline group.

Inventory of Educational Program Satisfaction

The *Educational Program Satisfaction Inventory* (EPSI), an instrument to measure the level of student attainment and satisfaction of LD students and their parents with the students' program in senior high school, is in the developmental stage. No specific instrument has been found to measure student satisfaction and attainment in the school program. We encourage readers to experiment and develop scales or inventories of school satisfaction. Oyler (1978) has suggested that exceptional students and their parents be asked: "What is one important skill your (son/daughter) has obtained in the resource room? How is the skill used in the regular class?" The answers to these questions would be included in the formal evaluation of the student's progress and the program's objectives. The authors of the EPSI hope to develop the instrument to obtain information that will help learning disabilities teachers make program decisions based, in part, on student satisfaction with the several components of the program and the school curriculum.

The measures described provide the teacher with gross estimates of LD students' evaluations of their own social and cognitive competence and of their peers, and school personnel evaluations of the LD students' social and cognitive competence. Few measures are available that comprehensively measure the social skills of adolescents. Those measures that are available will be revised and refined as more data are gathered on LD adolescents (Bryan, 1974). Perhaps the reason why so little attention has been given to this area by learning disabilities investigators is our limited knowledge about social skills among all secondary students.

TEACHING SOCIAL SKILLS TO LD ADOLESCENTS

Several authors (Kronick, 1975, 1976; Behrmann, 1975; Siegel, 1974) have named social skills of LD adolescents that should be of concern to teachers, parents, and LD students. We wish to identify several major social skill areas so that the educator will have a comprehensive view of the dynamics and methods of teaching these skills. However, we do not wish to identify so many social skill areas of major and minor importance that one could not operationally differentiate between them. Based on this rationale, we selected two major areas: (1) self-awareness skills and (2) social relationships skills. Each of these areas is described in detail, and specific teaching methods are suggested to redirect or enhance student competence in these specific areas. Finally, we discuss the teacher as a surface counselor to LD students.

Two Factors Related to the Teaching of Social Skills

Two key factors related to the social skills of LD adolescents must be considered before one can discuss specific social skill areas and the interventions to be initiated. First, not all LD secondary students lack social skills. In fact, some LD students have used their superior social skills to

251

compensate for deficits in cognitive or psychomotor skills. A current issue in the field of learning disabilities is the apparent strong relationship between LD students and juvenile delinquency. A recent study by the Department of Justice (1977) provides evidence that "one fourth of the juvenile delinquents in institutions tested by GAO consultants evidenced primary learning problems" (p. 1). The GAO report specifically states that the cause and effect of this finding is uncertain at this time. However, in the context of the present chapter, *all* LD students are *not* juvenile delinquents and *all* juvenile delinquents are *not* learning disabled.

Second, LD students may manifest incompetence in social skills in various ways. DeHirsch (1963) described two patterns of social skill problems in LD adolescents:

Group A — Good intellectual performance, immaturity, passivity; articulate, avid readers showing poor school progress
Group B — Low frustration tolerance; explosive behavior

There are, no doubt, other patterns of social behavior manifested by LD adolescents. More investigative work is needed to delineate these and other behavior patterns prevalent among LD adolescents. With these two principles as guides, we shall proceed with our discussion of self-awareness and social relationships.

Self-Awareness Skills and How to Teach Them to LD Adolescents

Description of Self-Awareness Skills

Erikson (1950) states that the goal of adolescents in the identity stage is development of the ability to view themselves as unique individuals in their own right. Their motives, values, and interests are separated from those of the peer group to which they belong. This "self-typing" is the primary goal of adolescence, but it is not complete until adolescents can demonstrate stability in behavior in various settings, such as the classroom, at formal and informal peer functions, at home, and on the job (Mussen, Conger, & Kagan, 1969). Adolescents must then consciously develop an identity. The resulting identity protects them from threats of failure, anxiety, and depersonalization (Vernon, 1971). Identity development may not be completed until well into adulthood.

Characteristics of LD Adolescents with Inadequate Self-Awareness Skills

In educational systems we generally use the terms *self-awareness*, *self-esteem*, or *self-concept* to describe the identity development of students. Kronick (1976) suggests several consequences of interaction between LD students whose self-awareness skills are inadequate and their peers, parents, and teachers, who react with evasion, conversation-directing comments, humoring, and underreaction to forestall the natural social outcomes of LD students' inappropriate behavior. Kronick (1976) says:

1. The LD person who has an unclear image of self receives less truthful or confirming feedback.
2. The LD person who may have difficulty perceiving and assessing affect (Wiig & Harris, 1974) receives distorted information between affect and ideas.
3. The LD person who has trouble perceiving the situational gestalt, and individual and group images and is too concrete to reconcile ambiguity, receives an ambiguous message concerning the (social) situation or group (interaction) image.
4. The LD person lacks the perception to perceive this (message) as pseudo-communication so that he patterns his own communication from it. Consequently, this may be one of the reasons his communication is unclear, shallow, and lacks appropriate affect.

Behaviors Affected by Inadequate Social Awareness Skills

The problems associated with school achievement, given these four behavioral manifestations, may occur because LD adolescents are unrealistic in the goals set for themselves. One result of setting unrealistic goals is that LD students may overestimate their abilities and select materials, courses, and activities that are not possible for them to master. In an effort to attain these goals, students may resort to cheating or devote all their energies to striving for one unattainable goal to the detriment of all other activities. Conversely, LD students may underestimate their goals and select goals that require minimal energy.

Identity problems of the LD adolescents may well affect their study skills. Learning disabled students may diminish their efforts by studying too little or block their energies by either studying too late (cramming) or "freezing" during an examination (Berry, 1975). Schneider and Turkat (1975) reviewed the literature relating self-esteem to academic performance. They found that ". . . subjects with high self-esteem are less accepting of failure and threatening experiences" (p. 128). In the same vein, if students show positive affect, it will facilitate their information retention (Dilendik, 1975). The effect of "good" behaviors is an increase in student-teacher interactions (Kester & Letchworth, 1972). On the other hand, it can be postulated that LD students are more accepting of failure and threatening

253

experiences, have debilitating memories, and, because they perform fewer "good" behaviors, have fewer student-teacher interactions. Some evidence is available (Bryan, 1974; Bryan, Wheeler, Felcan, & Henck, 1976) to support this postulation in the elementary grades.

Teachers' Options for Redirecting and Enhancing
Student Self-Awareness in the Classroom

What can the teacher do to redirect or enhance the self-esteem of LD adolescents? The first and most obvious answer would be to refer LD students for psychiatric intervention. This option is clear, and the service to LD adolescents is direct, but the results of such referrals have met with limited success (Nichol, 1974). Nichol followed a group of 252 students who manifested academic difficulties and were subsequently referred to a psychiatric facility for counseling. From a representative sample of these clients, he found that for only 50 percent of the youngsters seen at the facility was there any record of the contact in the school folder. For the students who had psychiatric evaluations in their school folders, only one-half of the evaluations were judged helpful by school personnel. In view of these findings, the psychiatric referral to redirect or enhance LD students' self-esteem should be considered only one option, and probably not the first option selected by the teacher. Other options for the learning disabilities teacher include:

1. Prescriptive teaching.
2. Directed writing (composition) activities.
3. Identifying sources of failure and threats to success.
4. Rap sessions.

The teacher may also refer LD students to the school counselor, who may use a wide variety of counseling techniques to assess and to redirect and enhance student self-esteem. We shall discuss several methods to be used in the classroom and describe various counseling methods that the teacher may use concomitantly.

Prescriptive teaching option. Page (1970) suggests that LD students' self-esteem can be enhanced by using prescriptive teaching in cognitive areas. This is an indirect but effective method (McDonnell, 1975). The rationale for this is that LD students must become aware of their competencies across many skill and content areas, both social and cognitive. Once students are aware of their many strengths and weaknesses, they can make more realistic evaluations of their competencies and enhance their self-esteem through competent performances on specific tasks. For example, an LD student may state, "I can do well on listening skills assignments, but I am a poor organizer of my time." Prescriptive teaching provides teachers with evidence of student performance that confirms or denies student self-evaluation and provides affective feedback to the student on cognitive skill development. This method also limits the possibilities for pseudocommunication between student and teacher. Once students are able to redirect their self-esteem as it relates to academic tasks, their self-esteem in social interactions will be enhanced.

Lerner (1976) has developed a prescriptive teaching procedure. She calls the procedure the Clinical Teaching Cycle (p. 105), and states that clinical teaching "implies that the teacher is fully aware of the individual student's learning style, interest, shortcomings and areas of strength, levels of development and tolerance in many feelings, and adjustment to the world" (p. 106). This implication has not been thoroughly investigated, and until definitive evidence is forthcoming, teachers teach social skills directly as part of the learning disabilities curriculum (Rabinovitch, 1962).

Directed writing activities. A second option is the use of a daily activities journal to develop students' awareness of their strengths and weaknesses. The journal can be structured by the teacher to focus students' attention on strengths or weaknesses. We suggest that the teacher direct students to write about at least one daily instance of positive feelings or action and one instance of negative feelings or action. If students cannot think of one positive feeling or action, have them describe positive means to overcome or circumvent the negative feeling or action. From this structured journal the teacher can learn about students' criteria for their strengths and weaknesses. No grade is given for this activity. Rather, reinforcing or supportive statements are made in the journals, which are then returned to the students. Generally, in a week's time, the activity is established and the journals are kept as daily logs, which the teacher monitors less frequently. The journals must be turned in each week to determine if students are including both positive and negative feelings and actions. The directed writing activities method is also untested in relation to improving LD students' self-esteem.

Identifying sources of failure and threats to success. A third technique, suggested by Felton and Davidson (1973), is teaching students the concept of locus of control and then teaching them to apply the concept to situations in school, home, and community. The concept of locus of control states that LD students who feel they are primarily controlled from outside themselves report that their fate, the conditions in their life, or other persons are responsible for what happens to them as a result of their own behaviors. These LD students do not readily accept responsibility for the consequences of their behavior. They may well say, "I don't want to attend regular classes because the teachers are always unfair and none of the kids in there are friendly."

Conversely, LD students whose primary control is internal report that they are solely responsible for the consequences of their behavior. They accept much or all responsibility, and they may well say, "I don't want to attend regular classes because I can't do anything in those classes, and I am so dumb that nobody likes me."

The statements of these two types of students must be analyzed. Perhaps the best way to determine if the locus of control is where the student perceives it to be is to ask for group opinion. In class discussions of students' problems, peers often resolve the issues by confirming or denying the student's view of the situation. Discussions might best be held with a school counselor in attendance who will help students cooperatively identify the source of their problems. Role playing has been used effectively to increase students' awareness of situations and possible solutions that do not negatively affect the self-esteem of LD students. Flowers and Marston (1972) suggested a College Bowl format that has been shown to increase self-esteem of low-achieving students. This format may be used to deal with social as well as cognitive question-and-answer problems.

An alternative to the locus of control method for improving the self-esteem of LD students has been reported on by Kroth (1973). He suggests the use of a Q-sort to measure the discrepancy between the students' perceptions of how they view their behavior as it exists and how they view their behavior as they wish it would be. Kroth and his students have developed a Q-sort on observable behaviors in the classroom. Kroth then targets behaviors that students wish to change and helps them shape the desired behavior through operant conditioning techniques. At the conclusion of the shaping sessions, Kroth readministers the behavioral Q-sort to determine if students perceive change toward the targeted behavior. This method could be modified for use with secondary students. Work on such a Q-sort has begun at the University of Kansas.

Rap sessions. Another method that learning disabilities teachers can use to help students gain a clearer perception of their behavior and the consequences of their behavior is the rap session. Loughmiller (1971) offers three excellent guidelines for teachers conducting rap sessions:

1. Distinguish between what can be and cannot be discussed at the beginning of the rap session.
2. Determine when discussion methods of any kind are appropriate and inappropriate.
3. Determine your [the learning disabilities teacher's] leadership style and emphasize your leadership strengths. (p. 73)

The first guideline should not be considered a control on the topics of discussion, such as sex education, drug education, or grades. Rather, this guideline limits the discussion to issues for which there are no right or wrong answers. Discussion of questions for which there are factual answers (for example, "When does third hour begin?") should be, in Loughmiller's view, eliminated from the discussion. This type of question does not stimulate thinking. We disagree with Loughmiller when the class discussions include LD students. Disabled students may not be aware of factual information that is readily available to nonhandicapped students because LD students have limited peer contacts (Bryan & Wheeler, 1972; Bryan, Wheeler, Felcan, & Henck, 1976). However, we do not feel that the giving of factual information should be the sum and substance of the rap session. A good mixture of factual and problematic questions may well increase LD students' self-awareness of their behavior and lead to the development of more positive self-esteem.

Loughmiller's second guideline is one of practical concern to learning disabilities teachers. There will be times when group discussion is not appropriate. When a new topic is introduced, certain background information is required before students can discuss the topic adequately. At this time, the teacher or resource person needs to provide factual information to the whole group and delineate the issues that surround the topic. Without such background, students will arrive at inappropriate assessments of the question or underestimate its options or ramifications.

Each learning disabilities teacher has a predominant leadership style. It may be authoritarian, which is best suited to the teaching of factual information, or it may be facilitative, which is more suited to group problem solving. The teacher should ask a counselor to sit in on selected sessions to help the teacher identify his or her leadership style. If the counselor has a different leadership style, teacher and counselor might well share in the conduct of the rap sessions (Loughmiller, 1971).

Once the learning disabilities teacher has started the group sessions and tries to follow Loughmiller's guidelines, a familiar concern soon arises. The group appears to be disinterested, and discussion of topics is thereby limited. In most cases, the teacher discontinues the rap sessions. Loughmiller provides seven "discussion liveners" that may help the teacher extend discussion of topics that have not been covered adequately or that teacher and students feel are important. These are as follows:

257

1. Pose problems that are specific, concrete, and challenging, and as close as possible to the experiences of the group.
2. If there is strong disagreement among members, direct the confrontation to a noncommittal option without offering a judgmental opinion to the group. Clarify the similarities and differences among the options.
3. Summarize a group member's comment or suggestion if some group members do not understand the person's intent or reasoning. Ask if the summary accurately reflects the person's thoughts. The teacher can also synthesize several members' discussion points.
4. Be alert to subtle signs of interest from the more subdued members of the group. This is very difficult and takes a lot of practice, but if some members monopolize the session, those who are not participating will quickly lose interest.
5. Supplement the rap sessions with resources. Films, experts, and field trips add immeasurable interest to the rap sessions.
6. Be sensitive to differences between silences that indicate the topic has been exhausted and those that mean the group members are attempting to develop new options. The best technique is simply to say, "Have we presented all the options and their differences for this topic?"
7. Tie in unrelated discussions of members to the topic being discussed. This seems appropriate in discussion groups of LD students. LD students must reaffirm the topic at hand. The teacher may say, "Do you agree or disagree with Tom or Mary?" "Why?" This procedure makes the LD student aware of the direction of the discussion and confirms that the student is providing irrelevant information or feelings for the situation.

In addition to the above methods, there are many formal counseling and psychotherapeutic methods advocated to help individuals develop self-awareness and self-esteem. Two of these formal methods are best used by appropriately trained counselors or psychologists: (1) transactional analysis (Harris, 1969), and (2) reality therapy (Glasser, 1969).

Guidelines for Teachers

Helping LD students develop awareness of their social behavior and its consequences and more positive self-esteem is the responsibility of the learning disabilities teacher. Several methods have already been suggested.

Perhaps the best advice we can give the learning disabilities teacher is the following set of guidelines:

1. Provide an authentic climate of warmth and concern. This climate enhances student trust in you as an accepting person.
2. Be aware of the differences between students' value systems and your own. Do not attempt to change the student values by admonishment ("Oh, I would *never* . . . and you shouldn't either!").
3. Clearly state your limits of confidentiality. To say *"Everything* you tell me is confidential"* may be as dangerous to you as it is to the student.
4. Refer students with problems that are beyond your competence to handle to more highly trained school specialists, such as counselors, psychologists, nurses, and social workers.
5. Actively listen to the student. Provide both verbal clues, through techniques such as paraphrasing and summarizing, and nonverbal clues, through techniques such as head-nodding and eye contact.
6. Take written notes for recall and documentation of important facts and possible solutions.
7. Give students feedback.
   a. State the information in plain language, and support it with facts. (NOT: You have low ego functioning. RATHER: I don't think you feel you are important to girls at this high school. You said, "I can't get dates" and "I tried to talk to Jennifer and she said, 'I don't want to date you'.")
   b. Be specific in your remarks. (NOT: You'll grow out of it. RATHER: Jennifer's rejection is very important to you, but now perhaps we should talk of other girls who may date you.)
   c. Give feedback, using care not to alienate the student (NOT: Jennifer probably thinks you are weird because she does not know you. RATHER: Jennifer probably does not know you well enough to accept you as a date.)
   d. Don't use the words "right," "wrong," or "You should."
   e. Give your opinion *only* if it is asked.
   f. End each session with a positive remark, even if it is no more than, "I look forward to speaking with you again."

Social Relationships

Peers are very important to both handicapped and nonhandicapped adolescents. In fact, Anthony (1973) stated that extroversion (seeking out friends) developmentally increases from age seven until about thirteen or fourteen. This socialization process is enhanced when adolescents join or are selected for school teams, attend parties, and spend time at summer or winter camps.

The conversation of most adolescents is centered on social relationships. They ask such questions as, "Does she or he like me?" "Who will I ask to the dance?" "Who's going to be at the game?" These are all indicators of the desire and pressure to develop and maintain social relationships.

Peer groups are also important to adolescents. Schwebel (1973) aptly stated:

> Groups are powerful. . . . They erode self-respect, stifle intelligence and cripple decision making competency. . . . [Conversely, they can] restore self-respect. They free intelligence and release the capacity to order one's own life. (p. 39)

Building Trust

Any group that is to have positive effects on its members must first build trust in each member. How does one build other people's trust? Tubbs and Moss (1974) suggest three methods: (1) cooperation, (2) communication, and (3) self-disclosure. Games that require cooperation to win are valuable tools for teaching the concept of personal trust among group members. Tubbs and Moss (1974) describe in detail one such game, "Prisoner's Dilemma." Another game that applies the principle of interpersonal trust is called "Get What You Can" (anonymous, circa 1974). This second game is like the first in that it vividly demonstrates in its results that persons tend to compete with one another, *even* when it is to their advantage to cooperate!

Verbal and Nonverbal Communication

When persons communicate with one another, they develop trust in each other. However, communication must be within a supportive climate or it will increase distrust. Gibb (1961) lists six climates supportive of communication:

1. Description.
2. Problem-orientation.
3. Spontaneity.
4. Empathy.
5. Equality.
6. Provisionalism.

Supportive communication is not limited to spoken language alone. Active listening, as described in the chapter on listening skills, is also important to increase interpersonal trust. Listening includes both verbal and non-verbal communication.

Nonverbal communication is complex, according to Galloway (1974). Wiig and Harris (1974) studied LD adolescents' perception and interpretation of nonverbal affective states. They found that LD adolescents were less able to identify affective states correctly than were their achieving age-peers. The LD adolescents made more substitutions when labeling nonverbal expressions of emotion and, of particular note, LD students substituted positive emotions for those judged negative by both the investigators and the achieving peers. This finding suggests that LD adolescents require formal training in judging and evaluating nonverbal communication if they are to be more trusted by peer group members.

Learning disabled students can compensate for their trust deficit. However, to do this, they must use powerful verbal communication with group members, (Galloway, 1974) or make use of powerful nonverbal communication techniques such as eye contact (Breed & Colaiuta, 1974). Breed and Colaiuta found that college students who maintained visual contact with the instructor comprehended more material from a lecture. A decrease in comprehension was noted in students whose eyes strayed to other persons or objects in the classroom, and they engaged in more blinking behavior than students who maintained eye contact with the instructor.

Learning disabled adolescents should be trained to (1) provide supportive verbal communication climates, (2) engage in active and empathic listening, and (3) judge and use nonverbal communication in ways that instill trust in chosen group members. The best setting for this type of teaching is a discussion period during which the teacher and other LD students provide a supportive climate for the LD student who is changing or developing these skills.

Self-Disclosure

Trust between group members in any social relationship is increased when group members disclose information about themselves to each other. In fact, when one member increases self-disclosure, there is a reciprocal effect on other members to increase their self-disclosures. As members become involved in self-disclosure, they all learn more about themselves as a group (Tubbs & Moss, 1974). The Johari Window (Luft, 1969) is a model for describing the self-disclosure process.

We are not advocating indiscriminate use of self-disclosure in groups. We are advocating that groups develop authentic social relationships rather than "cocktail party" relationships. LD students must be taught authentic use of self-disclosure, which will improve their interpersonal relationships and trust among group members. Luft (1969) lists five important characteristics of self-disclosure that must be considered when teaching its use:

1. It is a function of the ongoing relationship.
2. It occurs reciprocally.
3. It is timed to fit what is happening.
4. It concerns what is going on within and between persons present.
5. It moves by small increments. (pp. 132-133)

Self-disclosure is best taught in the same climate and setting we previously described for the teaching of communication skills. A contrived setting, unlike the one described by Lufts, will most likely damage the persons involved or take on a comic atmosphere.

Redirecting and Enhancing Social Relationships of LD Adolescents

Social relationships are also effected by the social behavior of the persons involved in the relationships. At the beginning of this chapter, we enumerated the many negative social behaviors that are emitted by LD adolescents. This is a major management problem for teachers and LD students. Any one or a combination of these negative social behaviors performed by LD students can negatively affect their social relationships among handicapped and nonhandicapped peers.

Two Management Systems

We shall consider negative social behaviors and their subsequent redirection or enhancement under two management systems (Dreikers, Greenwald, & Pepper, 1971; Krumboltz & Krumboltz, 1972). Both of these approaches have their unique strengths. Dreikers, Greenwald, and Pepper provide a rationale for the specific types of social behaviors emitted by students, and Krumboltz and Krumboltz provide definitive management techniques for teachers redirecting or enhancing LD student behavior.

Dreikers, Greenwald, and Pepper system. Dreikers et al. (1971) state that students have goals toward which specific behaviors are directed. They

262

list four goals of behavior: (1) attention, (2) power, (3) revenge, and (4) inadequacy. These four goals may be met by either positive or negative behaviors. For example, students may receive attention for useful efforts and accomplishments or for disruptive behaviors that produce scolding, reprimands, and threats from the teacher. In a like manner, students may seek power by attempting to subdue others, either by demanding or fighting; in contrast, they may achieve power by leadership, election, or persuasion.

Revenge is a goal that is obtained by performing irrational behaviors. Students may demand preferences that are unfairly applied. The reason for demanding these preferences is not based on target goals. For example, revenge behavior is clearly in evidence when a student who fails a test for which she or he did not study demands to be given another test because the teacher was unfair. It is nearly impossible to focus the student's attention on the rational target behavior — not studying for the test. It would be difficult to apply behavior analysis techniques to this revenge situation.

When students feel inadequate, their goal is to protect themselves against the demands of the situation. As in the case of revenge, it is difficult to emit positive behaviors that meet the goal. However, some behaviors emitted for self-protection may appear to be positive, but are actually negative in consequences. For example, there are students who appear to be ambitious but who will not participate in tasks or activities unless they can prove superiority over all other participants. Dreikers et al. label this behavior "overambition"; that is, these students can't do as well as they want to do. Also, students may not be competitive because they cannot do as well as others. Finally, students also may perform inadequately because of pressure; for example, they do not do as well as their capabilities would suggest. As a result of feeling inadequate, students often try to (1) demonstrate superiority in simple, elected tasks, (2) withdraw from tasks, or (3) make self-defeating or discouraging remarks related either to the tasks or to themselves. Associated with feelings of inadequacy are poor work habits and uncooperative behaviors (Dreikers et al., 1971).

As one reviews the behavioral characteristics of LD secondary students, the goals in order of their occurrence are: inadequacy, attention, power, and revenge. This hierarchy should be the order of priority for the teacher who is trying to redirect and enhance LD students' behavior. In our estimation, Krumboltz and Krumboltz (1972) provide behavior management techniques that are most appropriate in redirecting and enhancing secondary LD students' social behaviors.

Krumboltz and Krumboltz system. Using the Krumboltz and Krumboltz (1972) management system, one must determine if LD students know how to perform the behaviors necessary to be judged adequate in an activity, such as saying "Hi" to an opposite-sex peer who is not a classmate. If the answer is "No," students must be taught to develop this new behavior. Krumboltz and Krumboltz suggest four techniques: (1) backward chaining, (2) modeling, (3) cueing, and (4) successive approximation. One or more of these techniques may be appropriate to both the target behavior and the situation. For example, backward chaining may be employed by introducing the LD student to the target peer while that peer is having a conversation with another student. This approach is direct, but may interfere with another technique we wish to use in this situation, that is, having the LD student observe the extended conversation for its modeling value. Effective use may be made of peer models in developing the social relationships of LD students.

Another technique that can be used to develop a new behavior is cueing. Cueing requires that some discriminating event occur just prior to the target behavior. Cueing events for the target behavior of saying "Hi" may include waiting outside the target peer's classroom, attending the same function or activity as the target peer, dialing that peer's phone number, or conversing with a friend of the target peer as that peer approaches. Cueing simply means to be in the right place at the right time (Tubbs & Moss, 1974).

Probably, the least anxiety-producing technique to develop this new behavior is successive approximation. Using this technique, the student is reinforced for saying "Hi" to same-sex resource room peers, opposite-sex resource room peers, same-sex nonhandicapped peers, opposite-sex nonhandicapped peers, and finally, the target peer. It may take several days to several months before the LD student can shape his or her behavior to meet the target behavior criterion. If the teacher and student elect to use successive approximation techniques, common sense is the best measure of the student's rate of progress.

But, alas, in most cases the problem is not that LD students do not have appropriate target behaviors in their repetoire. Rather, LD students display aversive personalities, withdrawing tendencies, and poor social judgment, which means that students must reduce the rate at which they perform these socially inappropriate behaviors before they can redirect themselves toward socially appropriate behaviors.

Categories of Social Relationships

Persons who are accepted by peers are individuals who enhance the self-esteem of their peers (Tubbs & Moss, 1974). Behavioral characteristics of individuals are strong indicators of their social relationships. Individuals are most likely to fall into four categories, based on their predominant behavior. They may best be described as (1) accepted, (2) neglected, (3) rejected, or (4) withdrawn (Conger, 1973). A brief description of each category follows:

1. Adolescents of both sexes who are *accepted* by their peers are perceived as liking other people and being tolerant, flexible, and sympathetic; being lively, cheerful, goodnatured, and self-confident without being conceited; and possessing initiative, enthusiasm, drive, and plans for group activity.
2. The adolescent who is ill-at-ease and lacking in self-confidence and who tends to react to his discomfiture by timidity, nervousness, and withdrawal is likely to be *neglected or unknown* by his/her peers.
3. The adolescent who reacts to his/her discomfiture by compensatory overaggressiveness, conceit, or demands for attention is likely to court *active dislike and overt rejection.*
4. The adolescent who is self-centered and unable or unwilling to perceive and act to meet the needs of others, who is sarcastic, tactless, inconsiderate, and contributes little to the success of group efforts is likely to receive little overt consideration in return [an *unneeded* person]. (p. 304)

The reader must remember we are discussing acceptance by peers, not popularity. Popularity demands more characteristics than acceptance characteristics. To be popular among peers requires physical attractiveness, generosity, and affection, in addition to the qualities that foster peer acceptance. In the same vein, certain characteristics of rejection are more salient than others. Self-centeredness, arrogance, conceit, dogmatism, obnoxiousness, pushiness, and insincerity are qualities that heighten the possibilities of peer rejection (Tubbs & Moss, 1974).

Where should LD adolescents be categorized in Conger's (1973) system? If we draw some implications from the findings of Bryan et al. (Bryan & Wheeler, 1972; Bryan, Wheeler, Felcan, & Henck, 1976) at the elementary level, then our best estimate is that most LD adolescents are overtly rejected by peers. Fewer LD students at the secondary levels would be viewed as unneeded, covertly rejected, or unknown. In practice, if one were to ask junior and senior high school students if they knew certain LD students, the majority of these students would answer "Yes." But these students would tend not to be friends with the LD students because of peer pressure. Of those LD students who are unknown to peers, one can assume that they have not developed the social skills to interact with peers. These LD students are fearful and anxious in social situations.

Diminishing Inappropriate Social Behaviors

Most rejected LD secondary students exhibited inappropriate social behaviors. Krumboltz & Krumboltz (1972) list three methods for eliminating or reducing the rate of socially inappropriate behaviors: (1) satiation,

(2) elimination of rewards, and (3) reducing aversive conditions as behavior improves (negative reinforcement). If an LD student is interrupting discussion among peers or teachers, Krumboltz and Krumboltz suggest that the behavior manager attempt to answer the following questions:

1. Is this behavior so bad that it cannot be tolerated?
2. Can I arrange natural conditions so that the student is not rewarded for the inappropriate behavior?
3. What would I like the student to be doing instead of this current behavior?
4. What have I tried before that included all three possibilities suggested above?

The first question relates to the satiation principle. In most cases of disruptive behavior in the classroom, the satiation principle cannot be used. Applying the satiation principle, the teacher would set conditions so that the inappropriate behavior would occur many times in a short period of time; that is, the LD student would interrupt the presentation many times, and soon the interrupting behavior would decrease.

We have seen the satiation principle used only once to diminish interrupting behavior. In this case, the teacher provided the LD student with a tape recorder and earphones and directed her to a study carrel where she would not disturb other students. The student was then told to say "Mrs. Jones" each time she heard the word *and* on a fifteen-minute tape. The teacher reported later that it took four sessions over a two-day period before the student was not interrupting during class sessions. After the fourth session, she sought recognition by raising her hand as was the custom among other class members.

The principle of extinction is similar to satiation. When using extinction, the teacher would permit the student to continue to interrupt the presentation, but the behavior would not be reinforced. Extinction is difficult to control in a classroom because *any* attention by any class member or the teacher will reinforce the interrupting behavior.

The question about what competing appropriate behavior can be substituted for the inappropriate behavior must be considered carefully. Having students raise their hands to speak is not a competing behavior for those who talk out. Students may raise their hand and simultaneously say "Mrs. Jones." Teachers may think they are reinforcing students for raising their hands, while students may not be discriminating the behavior for which they are being reinforced. The competing appropriate behavior must be such that the inappropriate behavior cannot occur simultaneously. Calling on students when they appear to be ready to interrupt is an example of competing behavior. Students must respond to the teacher rather than the teacher to the students. This principle is called the *incompatible alternatives principle*. It is most effective in small groups such as the learning disabilities resource room. It is rarely effective in a large regular classroom.

Now suppose you, as the learning disabilities teacher, have answered the fourth question posed by Krumboltz and Krumboltz in a way that suggests you have exhausted the first three alternatives. Only at this point do you consider the negative reinforcement principle. This principle functions in a complex manner, and it is the last resort in behavior management. Negative reinforcement is often confused with aversive conditions. However, when using negative reinforcement, the teacher reinforces the student by avoiding aversive conditions. An aversive condition might be taking points away from students for inappropriate behavior in the classroom. The use of negative reinforcement in the case of our talking-out student would be that points would not be taken away if she did not interrupt the teacher's presentation. We have found that neither students nor teachers conceptualize the negative reinforcement principle well. In practice, we have found that aversive conditions paired with positive reinforcement in a management system are the most effective techniques for reducing or eliminating disruptive behavior. For example, if the teacher uses a point management system, points are taken away for inappropriate interruptions on a frequency basis and points are awarded for no inappropriate interruptions on an interval-time basis, for example, every ten minutes. In junior and senior high school we advocate the use of a point management system, with tangible rewards provided at the end of each week based on number of points. There is some support for the use of a point system as an effective method of increasing appropriate academic and social behavior (McDonnell, 1975). McDonnell (1971) used a point system with learning problem students ages twelve to sixteen for improving academic achievement and appropriate social behavior. After using the point system for seven months, he found increases in achievement, motivation, study habits, social behaviors, and peer relationships in *both* the special class and the regular classroom settings.

Developing Social Problem-Solving Skills through Surface Counseling

The most effective strategy in any counseling process is the one that allows students to gain skills for independent functioning. Consequently, surface counseling is conceptualized as a problem-solving and decision-making process that initially involves both teacher and students and ultimately students by themselves. It is assumed that advanced training as a counselor is not necessary for a teacher who assists LD adolescents through surface counseling. The very term *surface* implies that the procedures used tend to be first-line-of-defense techniques for problems that do not involve severe emotional or psychological problems. Students whose problems require the services of a trained counselor or social worker should be referred to those professionals for help.

When fulfilling the role of surface counselor, the learning disabilities teacher will perform several functions, including the following:

1. The teacher must first make students aware of effective strategies for problem solving and decision making, and *then* teach them how to apply appropriate strategies. There is a variety of problem-solving paradigms that can be used for a wide range of problems. Two paradigms that have been used with effectiveness with secondary LD populations are the SOCS system (Roosa, 1974) and Feldhusen's system (1973). Each outlines a series of steps for the student to apply in solving problems. The steps of the SOCS system are identifying (1) the situation or problem, (2) the options for solving the situation, (3) the consequences or possible outcomes of each option, and (4) simulation of the chosen option prior to its actual implementation. The Feldhusen model is similar in intent, but is more detailed. It consists of the following steps: (1) sensing that a problem exists, (2) defining the problem, (3) clarifying the problem, (4) guessing causes, (5) judging if more information is needed, (6) noting relevant details, (7) using familiar objects in unfamiliar ways, (8) seeing implications, (9) picking solutions, and (10) verifying solutions.

   Once a model is chosen that meets the needs of LD adolescents, it should be explained and demonstrated to them until it becomes a technique that they can apply independently and habitually in problem solving. Problem-solving models can be used on a one-to-one basis and in small or large groups. Glasser's (1969) use of the classroom meeting as a social problem-solving meeting and Friedman's (1973) use of the "magic circle" are examples of how these strategies can be used to advantage in group settings.

   To teach problem-solving skills effectively, the teacher should be aware of some problems often evidenced by LD students in problem-solving situations. Havertape (1976) has noted LD adolescents' perseveration, disinhibition, and qualitatively different approaches to problem solving. Whimbey (1976) has noted that low IQ college students failed to use abstractions, failed to make systematic comparisons of data, lacked the patience for isolating correct alternatives and resorted to "one-shot" thinking, and willingly failed to bridge gaps of knowledge in their own thinking. Knowing these characteristics of poor problem-solvers should heighten the teacher's awareness in working with LD students.

2. It is important that the teacher serve as a good model for LD students, in problem solving and decision making. Good modeling includes: demonstrating a positive attitude, approaching problems with confidence, and applying sound approaches and reasoning in handling the problems in one's own life.

3. Another function of the teacher should be to encourage students to make value judgments about what they are doing or have done that contributes to their own problem. While much of the problem-solving process involves an objective analysis of external factors, part of the process must be personalized. Students must be taught to recognize how they are a part of their own problem and, as such, they must make a commitment to change their behavior so as to effect a solution to the problem.

4. Finally, the teacher should help students adopt a proper "response approach" to problems. At one extreme, this includes encouraging students to inhibit initial responses and refrain from snap judgments. At the other extreme, the teacher should encourage some rational risk-taking behavior. For students who impulsively guess or who place little value on reasoning as a way to solve problems, the teacher may have them attempt to solve a problem out loud. Following students' explanations, a correct explanation of the problem is given so that students may compare their responses and see how their solutions and approaches differed from the ideal. For students who give up easily or are very conservative in their approach to problems, rewards and encouragement should be given for guessing at solutions based on students' hunches.

To effectively apply surface counseling, which in essence encourages LD adolescents to make decisions and solve problems, the teacher must establish a proper atmosphere in the learning disabilities classroom. The following factors are necessary if the teacher is to create an atmosphere that is conducive to surface counseling with LD adolescents.

1. *Order and structure.* An organized classroom reduces student uncertainty and creates a feeling of control of one's environment. Order and structure in a classroom help students more readily identify variables and events to which they must react or over

which they may exercise control. Rules that determine the nature of classroom and school operation should be formed by both staff and students. Once established, however, rules should be consistently enforced and relaxed only when students demonstrate enough maturity to perform without them. Glasser (1969) maintains that reasonable rules are part of a thoughtful problem-solving education.

2. *Recognition of student decision-making and problem-solving capabilities.* Gaining independence is important to LD adolescents — both personally and socially. One of the frequently cited goals of secondary education in general and special education in particular is to teach youngsters enough skills so that they can function independently. Certainly, all self-supporting adults have repertoires of skills that they can apply independently. On the other hand, each individual undertakes a variety of tasks that demand the assistance of someone else. In other words, none of us is *completely* independent. Instead, successful adjustment to adult living requires both independent action and dependence on others in various situations. Dyer (1972) suggests that in today's world the wisest course of action is not complete independence or complete dependence, but rather a posture called *interdependence*. Interdependence is having the ability to determine when to be independent from others and when to move toward a position of collaboration with others. LD adolescents should be encouraged to assess their abilities under present circumstances to determine if independent or dependent action is called for. Determining when to be independent and when to be dependent requires skill, practice, and experience. These youngsters should be required to make such decisions regularly in school activities, and they should be taught to assess the consequences. For example, if the choice is dependence, they should decide *who* is the best person to ask and *how* to ask that person to help.

Learning disabled students often develop close relationships with special education teachers. The individual attention they receive and the success they experience in the special class setting may account for these feelings. Such relationships are challenging to teachers because of the problems they may raise. Specifically, special teachers must beware of making youngsters too dependent on them, and thus inadvertently discouraging student efforts to function with other teachers or in other settings. The teacher should strive to strike a balance between fostering a strong relationship with students in which they feel accepted and successful, and yet encouraging students to operate independently.

270

3. *Recognition that change is not easy.* Most decisions and attempts to solve problems involve change on the part of the individual. Change is particularly difficult when it involves behaviors or affective styles that are habits. Furthermore, when a person makes a change, it is accepted by some and resisted by others; this may cause internal conflict. Often, changes meet the expectations of some persons and violate the expectations of others. Consequently, while the need for and direction of change may be intuitively logical, its implementation may be considerably more complex.

4. *Knowledge of the key components in helping relationships.* Dyer (1972) maintains that the bases for effective working relationships with others are understanding and meeting other people's needs, values, and expectations, and communicating acceptance to persons being helped. For a teacher to understand the unique needs, values, and expectations of each LD adolescent requires careful observation and a high degree of sensitivity. The teacher's success in a helping relationship is largely a function of how well these unique factors are understood. Constructive action over time is based on the teacher's ability to communicate feelings of acceptance both verbally and nonverbally.

REFERENCES

Alley, G. R., Deshler, D. D., & Warner, M. *A Bayesian approach to the use of teacher judgment of learning characteristics in identification of students with learning disabilities at the secondary level.* Paper presented at the Annual International Convention, Council for Exceptional Children, Atlanta, Georgia, 1977.

Behrmann, P. The four R's: Reading, 'riting, 'rithmetic, and respect. *Journal of Learning Disabilities,* 1975, *8,* 555-556.

Berry, R. G. Special feature: Fear of failure in the student experience. *Personnel and Guidance,* 1975, *54,* 190-203.

Bradfield, R. J. Preparation for achievement. In L. E. Anderson (Ed.), *Helping the adolescent with the hidden handicap.* Belmont, Calif.: Fearon, 1970.

Breed, G., & Colaiuta, V. Looking, blinking and setting: Non-verbal dynamics in the classroom. *Journal of Communication,* 1974, *24,* 75-81.

Bryan, T. Peer popularity of learning disabled children. *Journal of Learning Disabilities,* 1974, *7,* 621-625.

Bryan, T., & Wheeler, R. Perception of children with learning disabilities: The eye of the observer. *Journal of Learning Disabilities,* 1972, *5,* 484-488.

Bryan, T., Wheeler, R., Felcan, J., & Henck, T. "Come on dummy": An observational study of children's communication. *Journal of Learning Disabilities,* 1976, *9,* 661-669.

Conger, J. J. *Adolescence and youth: Psychological development in a changing world.* New York: Harper & Row, 1973.

DeHirsch, K. Two categories of learning difficulties in adolescents. *American Journal of Orthopsychiatry*, 1963, *33*, 87-91.

Departments of Justice & Health, Education and Welfare. *Learning disabilities: The link to delinquency should be determined, but schools should do more now.* GGD-76-97, March 4, 1977.

Dilendik, J. R. Teacher-student attitude similarity and information retention. *American Education Research Journal*, 1975, *12*, 405-414.

Drake, C., & Cavanaugh, J. R. Teaching the high school dyslexic. In L. E. Anderson (Ed.), *Helping the adolescent with the hidden handicap.* Belmont, Calif.: Fearon, 1970.

Dreikers, R., Greenwald, B., & Pepper, F. *Maintaining sanity in the classroom.* New York: Harper & Row, 1971.

Dyer, W. G. *The sensitive manipulator: The change agents who build with others.* Provo, Utah: Brigham Young University Press, 1972.

Erikson, E. H. *Childhood and society.* New York: Norton, 1950.

Feldhusen, J. F. *Teaching problem solving skills: Development of an instructional model based on human abilities related to efficient problem solving* [Final Report, Project 2E051 Grant No. OEG 5720042 (509)] Lafayette, Ind.: Purdue University, 1973.

Felton, G. S., & Davidson, H. R. Group counseling can work in the classroom. *Academic Therapy*, 1973, *8*, 461-468.

Fitts, W. H. *Tennessee self-concept scale*, 1964.

Flowers, J., & Marston, A. Modification of low self-confidence in elementary school children. *Journal of Educational Research*, 1972, *66*, 30-34.

Fordyce, W. G., Yauck, W. A., & Raths, L. A. *Manual for the Ohio Guidance Tests for the elementary grades.* Columbus: Ohio State Department of Education, 1946.

Friedman, P. *Developing children's awareness through communication.* Lawrence, Kan.: Extramural Study Center, 1973.

Galloway, C. M. Nonverbal teacher behaviors. A critique. *American Educational Research Journal*, 1974, *11*, 305-306.

Gesell, A., Ilg, F. L., & Ames, L. B. *Youth: The years from ten to sixteen.* New York: Harper, 1956.

Gibb, J. R. Defensive communication. *Journal of Communication*, 1961, *11*, 141.

Glasser, W. *Schools without failure.* New York: Harper & Row, 1969.

Harris, T. A. *I'm OK — You're OK: A practical guide to transactional analysis.* New York: Harper & Row, 1969.

Havertape, J. *Problem solving in the learning disabled high school student.* Unpublished doctoral dissertation, University of Arizona, 1976.

Johnson, D. J., & Myklebust, H. R. *Learning disabilities: Educational principles and practices.* New York: Grune & Stratton, 1964.

Karnes, M., McCoy, G. F., Zehrback, R. R., Wollersheim, V., & Clarizio, H. F. *The efficacy of two organizational plans for unachieving intellectually gifted children.* Champaign, Ill.: Champaign Community Unified Schools, 1962.

Kester, S. C., & Letchworth, G. A. Communication of teacher expectations and their effects on achievement and attitudes of secondary school students. *Journal of Educational Research*, 1972, *66*, 51-55.

Kronick, D. *What about me? The L.D. adolescent.* San Rafael, Calif.: Academic Therapy, 1975.

Kronick, D. The importance of a sociological perspective toward learning disabilities, *Journal of Learning Disabilities*, 1976, *9*, 115-119.

Kroth, R. The behavioral Q-sort as a diagnostic tool. *Academic Therapy*, 1973, *8*, 317-330.

Krumboltz, J. D., & Krumboltz, H. B. *Changing children's behavior.* Englewood Cliffs, N.J.: Prentice-Hall, 1972.

Lehtinen-Rogan, L. E. How do we teach him? In E. Schloss (Ed.), *The educators' enigma: The adolescent with learning disabilities.* San Rafael, Calif.: Academic Therapy, 1971.

Lerner, J. W. *Children with learning disabilities: Theories, diagnosis, teaching strategies* (2nd ed.). Boston: Houghton Mifflin, 1976.

Loughmiller, G. Keep the session alive. *Instructor*, November 1971, 73.

Luft, J. *Of human interaction.* Palo Alto, Calif.: National Press, 1969.

Maslow, A. *Toward a psychology of being.* New York: Van Nostrand, 1962.

McDonnell, M. K. Bridging the achievement gap in negative learning adolescents. In J. Arena (Ed.), *The child with learning disabilities: His right to learn.* Proceedings of the 8th Annual Conference, Association for Children with Learning Disabilities, Chicago, 1971.

McDonnell, M. K. *The comparative effects of teacher reinforcement of self-esteem and of academic achievement on affective variables and achievement of learning disabled children.* Unpublished doctoral dissertation, University of Southern California, 1975.

Mussen, P. H., Conger, J. J., & Kagan, J. *Child development and personality* (3rd ed.). New York: Harper & Row, 1969.

Nichol, H. Children with learning disabilities referred to psychiatrists: A follow-up study. *Journal of Learning Disabilities,* 1974, 7, 118-122.

Oyler, R. H. Comment at Protection in Evaluation Procedures Criteria study panel. Washington, D.C., May 10-11, 1978.

Page, W. The disabled learner learns. In L. E. Anderson (Ed.), *Helping the adolescent with the hidden handicap.* San Rafael, Calif.: Academic Therapy, 1970.

Rabinovitch, R. D. Dyslexia: Psychiatric considerations. In J. Money (Ed.), *Reading disability: Progress and research needs in dyslexia.* Baltimore: Johns Hopkins Press, 1962.

Roosa, J. Situations, options, consequences and simulation (SOCS). Cited in P. Graubard & H. Rosenberg, *Classrooms that work: Prescriptions for change.* New York: Dutton, 1974.

Rucker, C. N. *Acceptance of mentally retarded junior high children in academic and non-academic classes.* Doctoral dissertation. University of Iowa, 1968. (University Microfilms No. 68-973)

Schneider, D. J., & Turkat, D. Self-presentation following success or failure: Defensive self-esteem models. *Journal of Personality,* 1975, *43*, 127-135.

Schwebel, M. Groups for the educationally distraught. *Educational Technology,* 1973, *13*, 39-44.

Sheehy, G. *Passages: Predictable crises of adult life.* New York: Bantam Edition, 1977.

Siegel, E. *The exceptional child grows up.* New York: Dutton, 1974.

Thompson, A. Moving toward adulthood. In L. E. Anderson (Ed.), *Helping the adolescent with the hidden handicap.* Belmont, Calif.: Fearon, 1970.

Tubbs, S. L., & Moss, S. *Human communication: An interpersonal perspective.* New York: Random House, 1974.

Vernon, M. D. *Human motivation.* New York: Cambridge University Press, 1971.

Whimbey, A. Getting ready for the testor: You can learn to raise your IQ score. *Psychology Today,* 1976, *9* (8), 27-29, 84-85.

Wiig, E. H., & Harris, S. P. Perception and interpretation of nonverbally expressed emotions by adolescents with learning disabilities. *Perceptual and Motor Skills,* 1974, *38*, 239-245.

Wilcox, D. Guidelines for parents. In L. E. Anderson (Ed.), *Helping the adolescent with the hidden handicap.* Belmont, Calif.: Fearon, 1970.

LISTENING: STRATEGIES AND METHODS

Listening has been largely neglected in most elementary and secondary schools in spite of the demands of school curriculums and subsequent job and social situations for good listening skills. Teachers often assume that listening skills develop independently of instruction. The acquisition of these skills is particularly critical for LD adolescents because they typically experience difficulties in reading and writing. Good listening skills can help students compensate for deficits in these areas. For example, if poor reading skills limit the amount of information students can acquire through reading textbooks, *good* listening skills can help them gain a maximum amount of information from class lectures. Similarly, poor writing skills may prevent students from taking complete notes during classroom lectures but using effective listening techniques may compensate for this. On the other hand, *poor* listening skills may precipitate or accentuate deficits students may have in reading, speaking, and writing. Listening, therefore, is an important instructional area for the LD student. The following points elaborate on the reasons why.

First, the curriculum demands of secondary schools place heavy requirements on listening skills. A study by Wilt (1950) indicated that students spent about two and one-half hours of a five-hour school day in listening. Interestingly, this was about twice as much time as teachers estimated that students spent in listening. While Wilt's study was done in elementary classrooms, it is reasonable to assume that the time spent by secondary students in listening activities is at least as high because of the increased use of the lecture method of teaching. Furthermore, as students enter the secondary school, their language environment becomes more complicated — stories are longer, directions are more complex, subtle meanings are used more frequently, and the demands for critical listening are greater. Therefore, students need to acquire and apply listening skills of a higher order. This is particularly true for LD adolescents since they may lack fluent reading skills. In some cases, it may be more productive to shift the intervention emphasis to developing and refining listening skills so that LD students can more effectively meet the demands of the secondary curriculum.

Second, a great deal of time is spent each day by adolescents and adults in listening activities. Much of our information dissemination is accomplished by television and radio. Use of the telephone has reduced the amount of written correspondence and, for the adolescent, represents a major means of developing and maintaining social relationships. The early and much quoted study by Rankin (1930) found that Americans spent 30 percent each day speaking, 16 percent reading, 9 percent writing, and 45 percent listening. Markgraf (1957) found that high school students listened approximately 46 percent of the time during an average school day; 66 percent of this time was spent listening to the teacher. (In English class, 97 percent of the time was spent listening to the teacher.)

Third, there is a tremendous demand for good listening skills in both social and job situations. The degree to which one is accepted by a group is, in large part, a function of one's ability to receive verbal and nonverbal messages. Many jobs require that a large amount of time be spent listening to supervisors. It is essential to pay attention to instructions, explanations, and even reprimands to achieve job success.

Fourth, there is considerable evidence to indicate that instruction in listening leads to improvement in listening performance. This has been demonstrated for students of widely different age levels. Experimental groups of college freshmen, for example, who have received systematic training in listening have in many cases obtained significantly higher scores on listening comprehension tests than control groups who haven't received such training (Bird, 1953; Brown, 1954; Childers, 1970). The training usually consisted of instruction and activities on how to listen. The improvement in listening comprehension has been found to be appreciable in below average listeners (Bird, 1955; Erickson, 1954). Similar improvement has been noted with groups of high school students (Lewis, 1956) and junior high students (Pratt, 1956). Many of the studies designed to teach listening skills have often noted gains in related communication skills as well (e.g., speaking).

UNDERSTANDING AND DEFINING LISTENING

Listening is traditionally defined as a language arts skill in which spoken words are translated into meaning. The emphasis is usually placed on the meaning of the spoken words. However, effective listening extends far beyond merely attending to and comprehending the spoken word (the linguistic channel). Listening also involves attending to and comprehending *nonverbal* messages (the nonlinguistic channel). To make wise intervention decisions that will improve the listening skills of LD students, the teacher must have an understanding of the broad array of factors involved in communication.

Channels of Communication

For students to be effective listeners, they must attend to messages that come in a variety of forms. Wilkinson, Stratta, and Dudley (1974) speak of different channels of communication through which the message can be delivered to the listener. Among these channels are the linguistic, the paralinguistic, the visual, and the kinesic.

The Linguistic Channel

Linguistic communication consists of words and phrases, as well as the noise made in uttering them. Comprehension of information from the linguistic channel depends largely on the listener's vocabulary skills. For secondary students, understanding multiple meanings of words becomes important. For example, to the young child, the word *party* connotes a gathering of friends to celebrate a birthday. However, an older student needs to understand the meaning of the word *party* in expressions such as "political party" or "third party" (legal meaning). Thus, vocabulary work should be emphasized with secondary LD students. In addition to teaching multiple meanings of words, students should be taught the vocabulary *unique* to particular subject areas to facilitate their understanding of the information presented in class lectures. It is imperative that this vocabulary work *precede* the class lecture.

The Paralinguistic Channel

Paralinguistic communication comprises those factors that run alongside (*para-*) the language. Tone of voice, loudness or softness of delivery, quality of the speaker's voice, speed of speaking, and pauses and hesitations in delivery are all paralinguistic properties of the message. Speakers communicate the true intent of their messages by using paralinguistic factors. For example, to emphasize certain points, speakers may raise their voices or may pause for listeners to reflect on the information just delivered. If the listeners attend to these factors, their comprehension of the information being delivered is greatly increased. LD students should learn the importance of these factors and practice interpreting their meaning in lecture situations. Tape recordings of class lectures, or presidential speeches can be used for this purpose.

The Visual Channel

Visual communication imparts information related to the appearance of the speaker. Often a speaker's appearance influences the listeners' first impressions and provides clues regarding the message. Clothing and hair style may put a speaker into certain stereotypes. For example, a hippie's sandals and long hair are as much badges of identity as is a soldier's uniform. Using information received through the visual channel, listeners often form expectations about the content of the message even before it is delivered. Such prejudgments should, of course, be made with caution. Wilkinson et al. (1974) report how information gained through first impressions can be misleading:

> . . . an experiment whereby the photographs of criminals were mixed up with photographs of virtuous citizens, and people were asked to judge which was which. The results were nearly always the same: Acid bath killers and necrophiliacs appeared to many people to be virtuous citizens, whilst clergy of blameless life were frequently picked out as convicted murderers. (p. 32)

The Kinesic Channel

Kinesic communication relies on body movements such as posture, facial movements, eye movements, expressions, gestures, and the arrangement of the limbs. These nonverbal components of communication are important to the speaker in conveying the message. Certain points can be emphasized and others strengthened through use of the kinesic channel. All speakers have unique gestures and body movements, and listeners must attend to these carefully to grasp their meaning and importance. For example, one speaker may point a finger when making an important point, whereas another speaker may point a finger throughout an entire speech without the pointing being related to what is being said. In the first instance, the gesture conveys meaningful information to the listener; in the second, the gesture is habitual and meaningless as it does not help the listener discriminate between important and less important information. Kinesic information may also be unique to certain groups or subgroups,

279

and to the extent that listeners are sensitive to these differences they will better understand the message conveyed. In Japanese culture a smile is the accompaniment to any social act; it does not mean that the person is pleased. "It has been remarked that had the Americans been able to interpret the 'Japanese smile' of the emissaries who talked to them before Pearl Harbor, they might not have been lulled into a false sense of security" (Wilkinson et al., 1974, p. 3).

Differences in Spoken and Written Language

There are several differences between spoken and written language. An understanding of these basic differences helps the practitioner assess and intervene in listening skill development. Wilkinson et al. (1974) summarized these major differences, including the following:

1. Organization — In general, the organization of written material is much tighter than that of spoken language. Written pieces are usually carefully sequenced and well structured, whereas spoken language communications are often filled with parenthetical statements or afterthoughts.
2. Redundancy — Spoken passages usually contain many more words than written passages. Words are often repeated in speech, particularly nouns. This is done to make sure that the listener gets the point. For example, "This horse that I'm going to tell you about" may be used in speaking, whereas "This horse" is quite adequate and would probably be used in writing.
3. Reciprocity — Speakers usually include words or phrases in their speaking to get feedback from those being addressed. Such words or phrases as "you know," "see what I mean," or "you see" aid the sensitive speaker in determining how well the audience is getting the message. Much of the audience's response is nonverbal: puzzled looks, yawns, shuffles, nods of agreement. Written language does not involve this reciprocal relationship between the author and the reader.
4. Punctuation — In written expression, punctuation is based on the idea of the well-formed sentence. It is up to the reader to determine whether to go on reading or to review to gain greater understanding. The reader has sole responsibility for adding proper emphasis to the printed message. However, in speaking, pauses rather than punctuation marks are used. Pauses serve to pace the information so that it is not presented too fast for the listener. Because pauses

often come at key points to emphasize information being presented, listeners' nonverbal feedback to the speaker may affect the pauses used.

5. Grammar and idiom — Written messages are often more complex and concentrated than corresponding spoken version messages. Since less formal phraseology is used in speaking than in writing, speaking reduces the vocabulary load on the receiver. Spoken language is less concentrated and allows the listener more time to reflect on information just presented and to prepare for information that will follow.

6. Written language can be read at any pace desired, and the reader can go back over the material if it is necessary. On the other hand, the pace of spoken language is determined by the speaker, although the listener can affect this pace by indicating a lack of understanding.

Listening skills have been categorized in a variety of ways ranging from simple to increasingly complex. For our purposes, we have attempted to identify those listening skills demanded by curriculum, social, leisure, and job requirements of the secondary and postsecondary student. The outline presented in Table 8.1 represents an adaptation of several taxonomies of listening (Wilt, 1964; Russell & Russell, 1959; Early, 1954). It should be noted that "attending to nonverbal communication" is presented as a factor that goes across all areas listed in the taxonomy. It has been presented accordingly to emphasize its critical importance in the listening act. To exclude nonverbal factors and the broad array of components they represent (gestures, pauses, eye movements) would be to ignore listening as a total communication process. As we will see later in this chapter, LD adolescents can become far more effective listeners if they learn to attend to such nonverbal factors.

LISTENING CHARACTERISTICS OF LD ADOLESCENTS

Little specific information about the language capabilities of LD adolescents is available. That which does exist generally places greatest emphasis on reading, with less attention given to listening, speaking and writing (Deshler, 1978). Observational data suggest, however, that LD adolescents often exhibit ineffective listening habits and skills. Drake and Cavanaugh (1970), for example, have postulated that LD adolescents' fear of failure, feeling of mental subnormality, and reduced motivation to achieve within the classroom accounts, in part, for their poor listening performance. While researchers have found evidence that listening is a

TABLE 8.1
Listening Skills

1. Understanding words, concepts, and building a listening vocabulary
2. Understanding sentences and other linguistic elements of language
3. Auditory memory
4. Listening Comprehension (literal)
   a. Understanding the relationship of details to main ideas
   b. Following directions
   c. Following the sequence of the message
   d. Listening for details
   e. Listening to a question with an intent to answer
   f. Repeating what has been heard
5. Critical Listening* (evaluative/inference)
   a. Recognizing absurdities
   b. Recognizing propaganda
   c. Correct me
   d. Finishing stories
   e. Distinguishing between fact and opinion
   f. Distinguishing between emotive and report language
   g. Detecting bias and prejudice
   h. Evaluating speaker's argument
   i. Drawing inferences and making judgments
   j. Understanding sales pressure
   k. Recognizing repetition of the same idea in different words
6. Appreciative Listening
   a. Listening to visualize
   b. Listening for rhythms of speech
   c. Recognizing tone and mood
   d. Appreciating speakers' style
   e. Interpreting character from dialogue
   f. Understanding effect on listeners of speaker's vocal qualities and gestures
   g. Understanding effect of audience on listener's reactions

*Critical listening has been included in this outline of listening skills because many authors in the listening field have done so. It could logically be included under thinking skills because it includes the processes involved in thinking — namely, persuasion, evaluation, problem solving. The methods discussed in chapter 6 on thinking skills are applicable to critical listening deficits.

separate skill (Spearritt, 1962; Clark, 1972), these same researchers point out the close relationship between listening and general language abilities of students. Therefore, the results of studies on the general language functioning of LD students may indicate why they encounter difficulties in successfully applying listening skills.

Though not specifically studying LD adolescents, Loban (1976), in a longitudinal study of language abilities, described three groups of subjects at all grade levels, kindergarten through twelfth grade. The following conclusions regarding the differences between the high- and low-proficiency subjects seem to relate to the problems LD students may encounter in listening. "The less effective subjects' vocabulary was meager; and as listeners they did not focus on relationships or note how main ideas control illustrations or subordinate ideas . . . " (pp. 70-71). The low-proficiency subjects were those identified by teachers as less skillful in oral language, and it is probable that their characteristics resemble those of LD adolescents. Those students who used language most effectively (high-proficiency group) achieved higher scores on tests of listening. Loban also found that in both oral and written language, students in the low group used shorter sentences, less elaboration, fewer clausal constructions, and more restricted vocabulary.

Characteristics of Poor Listeners

Authors who have attempted to differentiate good listeners from poor listeners suggest that poor or ineffective listeners usually possess a set of incorrect listening habits. Nichols and Stevens (1957), for example, through years of listening research on high school and college students, have identified behaviors common to poor listeners. These seem to be ones that LD adolescents are vulnerable to.

1. *Calling the subject dull.* The poor listener readily finds a subject "too dry" and uses this as an excuse to wander off on a mental tangent. LD adolescents may be particularly prone to call subjects "dull" because of experiences of failure in the classroom. It is a convenient rationalization to say, "I've heard that stuff before" rather than to apply oneself to the listening task. Also, it is often popular (or at least acceptable) with the peer group to criticize aspects of school instruction.

2. *Criticizing the speaker.* The poor listener readily finds fault with the way the speaker looks, acts, and talks. An obsession with such factors takes attention away from the message.

3. *Getting overstimulated or emotionally involved.* Listening efficiency is greatly sacrificed when listeners fail to control their emotions. Emotional involvement may distort or interfere with the acquisition of important information. Evaluation should be withheld until comprehension is complete. The speaker's point of view should be understood before it is accepted or rejected.

4. *Listening only for facts.* Poor listeners concentrate most attention on facts. Consequently, they acquire only a few facts because they have no context or framework within which to interpret and store facts. In addition, poor listeners tend to avoid critical analysis and evaluation of the message. Of course, there are situations that require fact listening; however, students must learn to be selective in the application of various listening behaviors. The most effective behavior may often be to listen for the main ideas and use these as connecting threads to give sense and a context to the whole presentation.

5. *Trying to outline everything.* Poor listeners often spend too much time and attention trying to write down what is covered in a lecture. Notetaking should not interfere with listening and should be used only as a means of recording key concepts or ideas. The listener should attempt to stand back from the message to see the major points being conveyed and to avoid getting lost in a sea of facts.

6. *Wasting the differential between speech speed and thought speed.* It is estimated that students can process over 400 words per minute, whereas a lecturer usually speaks at the rate of 150 words per minute. With thought speed being so much greater than speech speed, there is a tendency for the listener's mind to wander.

7. *Listening only to what is easy to understand.* Because of low motivation, a history of failure, or the habit or prematurely calling a subject uninteresting, students may listen only to those things that make a minimum number of demands on them.

8. *Letting emotion-laden words get in the way.* This bad habit refers to a listener's own reaction to certain words. Such words as *principal, graduation,* and *test* have emotional connotations, and a listener who reacts to these words, regardless of their context, may distort the message.

9. *Becoming distracted.* Poor listeners are easily distracted and may even create disturbances that interfere with their own listening efficiency. Failure to adjust to distractions or to compensate for them is common among poor listeners.

10. *Permitting personal prejudices or deep-seated convictions to impair comprehension and understanding.* Barker (1971) points out that this bad habit presents significant barriers to efficient listening.

Variables That Affect Listening

In a review of the literature, Barker (1971) identified several variables that are associated to a moderate or high degree with listening skills. The major findings are summarized below.

1. *Age.* The primary age-related variable is attention span. Young children have considerably shorter attention spans than young adults. However, to the extent that one's attention span is limited, listening effectiveness is reduced. In general, children older than twelve or thirteen begin to prefer reading to listening because they can read at their own pace (usually faster than the speaker talks), and reading is purely an act of "reading to learn." This may not be the case for LD adolescents, who often have a history of prolonged failure and frustration with reading, who are still "learning to read," and cannot read at a rapid pace.

2. *Motivation and interest.* Considerable research has established the relationship between motivation and listening effectiveness. Listening is related to the learning process, and this research has established a positive relationship between motivation and learning. For example, students who know they will be tested on a certain section of a class lecture may have increased motivation to learn the material when it is presented. On the other hand, knowing that a test will follow the presentation of the material may increase the student's anxiety and thus adversely affect test performance. Interest and attitudes are closely related to motivation and, therefore, relate to listening effectiveness; that is, the more interesting the material is, the more likely it is that students will listen.

3. *Scholastic aptitude and achievement in high school.* Listening relates moderately to scholastic achievement and somewhat more to scholastic aptitude, but the relationships seem primarily a function of intelligence rather than pure listening skills.

4. *Verbal ability.* There is a moderate relationship between verbal ability and listening. Students who score higher on reading tests than listening tests also tend to score higher on language sections of IQ tests than on tests involving listening skills.

5. *Vocabulary size.* Most data suggest a relationship between vocabulary size and listening comprehension. Research also indicates that effective listening skills help to strengthen a listener's vocabulary.
6. *Organizational ability.* There is limited research in this area. Existing studies suggest, however, that persons who can organize materials mentally tend to listen more effectively.
7. *Reading comprehension.* In situations where material is easy to comprehend, students prefer listening to reading. In situations where the material is difficult to comprehend or the conditions for listening are not favorable, students prefer reading.
8. *Listener fatigue.* An inverse relationship between listener fatigue and listening ability has been found; that is, the more fatigued listeners are, the less able they are to listen effectively.

ASSESSING LISTENING SKILLS

An assessment of listening skills should consider three major components: (1) the listening characteristics of the student, (2) the speaking and communication characteristics of the teacher, and (3) the interaction between the listener (student) and the speaker (teacher). Several attempts to measure these factors have been made. However, there has been considerable controversy regarding the evaluation of listening because of disagreement concerning the definition of listening, the factors that are critical to listening success, and the ways in which to measure listening skills adequately.

Evaluating Listening Characteristics of Students

Some of the specific standardized tests available to measure listening are the following:

Brown-Carlsen Listening Comprehension Test. New York: Harcourt, Brace & World, 1955.

Sequential Tests of Educational Progress (STEP) (Listening subtest). Princeton, N.J.: Educational Testing Service, 1958.

Detroit Tests of Learning Aptitude (Subtests: Auditory Attention Span for Unrelated Words, Auditory Attention Span for Related Syllables, Oral Directions). Indianapolis: Bobb-Merrill, 1935.

Durrell Listening-Reading Series, Intermediate Level. New York: Harcourt, Brace, & World, 1956.

Peabody Picture Vocabulary Test. Circle Pines, Minn.: American Guidance Service, 1959.

Two of the most widely used tests are the subtest on listening in the *Sequential Tests of Educational Progress* (STEP) and the *Brown-Carlsen Listening Comprehension Test.* The STEP subtest is designed to provide a measure of general achievement in listening comprehension for grades 4 through 12. It measures literal comprehension (finding the main idea, finding significant details, determining the sequence of ideas, and understanding denotative meanings), interpretive comprehension (implication of ideas and details, interrelationship among ideas and connotative meanings), and evaluation and application skills (judging validity of ideas, judging sufficiency of details, criticizing organization, judging mood and effect, and recognizing intent). The material that the teacher reads aloud is of several different types, including directions, explanations, expositions, narrations, arguments, persuasions, and aesthetic materials.

The *Brown-Carlsen Test* is considered more appropriate for diagnostic purposes than is the STEP test. It was developed for use in grades 9 through 13 and measures auditory recall, following directions, recognizing word meanings, and comprehending lectures. In addition to measuring listening directly, this test also measures memory span and reasoning, which Spearitt (1962) has shown to be highly correlated with listening comprehension.

Both of these tests have received mixed reviews and reactions from communication scholars and teachers. Most criticisms have been focused on the validity of the tests (whether they are really testing listening ability or some other trait such as intelligence, aptitude, or hearing). Wilkinson, Stratta and Dudley (1974) have been most critical of these tests, particularly the *Brown-Carlsen,* on the grounds that there are certain essential differences in the nature and function of spoken and written language. These differences have been stressed earlier in this chapter. In all the listening tests a *written* language passage is read aloud to determine the student's listening ability. Wilkinson et al. (1974) argue that students being tested should be asked to listen to the type of material they would naturally encounter in a listening task — that is, spoken language. An example of an item from the *Brown-Carlsen Test* illustrates their point:

> Listen to this statement: "Place the two braces marked A on the diagram in the slot marked D on the shelf. Insert them an inch and one-half, then place the shelf against the wall and fix it in place with four screws marked C on the diagram. The number of inches the braces are to be inserted in the shelf is . . ." (Form BM, Part A, Immediate Recall)

It is highly unlikely that oral directions would ever be given like that. Further, anyone giving such instructions orally would phrase them so as to stress the information considered important, rather than present a mass of undifferentiated details. Also, the information would be supported by nonverbal information such as gestures and demonstration.

An additional criticism of these listening tests is that they present information in isolation. Critics have argued that effective listening depends on the context within which the information is presented. Without the context the listener has a much more difficult task to interpret the information presented.

Wilkinson et al. (1974) have attempted to improve on some of the shortcomings of traditional listening tests. Their test materials are published by Macmillan Education (London) under the title *Schools Council Oracy Project Listening Comprehension Tests*. Test batteries B and C are appropriate for the adolescent population. These tests are on tapes, but since the tests have been standardized on a United Kingdom population, they may have limited application to American students (because of the British accent). However, the principles that were followed in constructing these tests are worth noting for the teacher who wishes to develop informal measures of listening. First, the tests consist of "spoken" language and not "written" language. Second, the information is presented in a context, such as a telephone conversation, and not in isolation. Third, the material presented was from "natural" conversations.

Test batteries B and C each consist of a number of tests designed to measure comprehension of various spoken materials. The tests that have been included in the batteries are:

1. *Tests of content.* These are designed to measure the ability to follow and to understand a piece of fairly informal exposition.
2. *Tests of contextual constraint.* These are designed to measure the ability to infer missing parts of a conversation from what is actually heard.
3. *Tests of phonology.* These are designed to measure the ability to understand differences in meaning brought about by different emphases in speech.
4. *Tests of register.* These are designed to measure the ability to detect the appropriateness of the spoken language used in various situations.
5. *Tests of relationship.* These are designed to measure the ability to detect the relationships existing between people from the language they employ.

Even though many existing standardized and teacher-made listening tests have been justly criticized on several points, it is still desirable to attempt to measure listening skills. The teacher should carefully consider the above comments on available instruments, and if the tests are used, the results should be interpreted in light of these potential shortcomings. If informal instruments are constructed, the principles outlined by Wilkinson et al. (1974) should be followed.

Assessing Speaking Characteristics of the Teacher

Evaluation of listening problems *should not* be confined to assessment of student factors. The conditions that exist in students' immediate surroundings, the listening model presented by classroom teachers, and the teaching habits and style of classroom teachers that foster or impede effective listening should be analyzed. For example, to assess these factors, teachers may want to ask themselves questions such as the following (Russell & Russell, 1959):

1. What kinds of listening do I do myself?
2. In the classroom, am I usually talking or do I often listen?
3. Do I encourage students to listen so that they speak more than a single word in response to a question?
4. Do I ask thought-provoking questions which require attentive listening and auding?
5. Are students developing the ability to carry on a class or group discussion more independently than they did previously?
6. When I give oral directions, do I prepare the pupils for what is to come and then avoid repetition?
7. Do I make sure that the purposes for listening are clear to each student?
8. Do I relate good listening habits to all classroom activities?
9. Do I plan a variety of auding activities, not only for word study but also for appreciation and for different types of comprehension?
10. Do I collect some tangible evidence of growth in auding abilities during the school year — evidence about the speaker, the listener, and the kind of message being conveyed? . . . (pp. 18-19)

Other dimensions of the teachers' speaking and delivery styles that should be analyzed are the following:

1. *Nonlinguistic communication.* Does the teacher make effective use of gestures, eye contact, pauses?
2. *Preorganizers.* Does the teacher present an overview that stresses the major points of the material to be covered?
3. *Organization.* Does the teacher present information in a logical, organized fashion?
4. *Pace.* Does the teacher present the information at varied paces — slowing down for important points and repeating them for emphasis?
5. *Examples.* Does the teacher use examples to illustrate points and give concrete examples of abstract information?

Determining Interaction Between Student and Teacher

To be complete, the assessment of listening must consider the interaction between students and teachers, since effective listening involves much more than hearing and interpreting spoken words. The feedback that listeners provide to the speaker, such as confirming nods or expressions of disinterest, often affects the reaction of the speaker to the listener. Observations should be made that provide answers to such questions as: Does the teacher make or avoid eye contact with the students? Do students demonstrate an interest in what the teacher is saying by verbal participation? Do students demonstrate interest through positive nonverbal feedback?

TEACHING LISTENING STRATEGIES

Of the four language arts — reading, writing, speaking, and listening — listening has been given the least attention. This is unfortunate at a time when technical advances in radio, television, telephones, and recording equipment have tended to put greater emphasis on this essential aspect of communication. The ability to listen, and to listen with understanding, has been taken too much for granted.

The teacher who is committed to teach listening skills to LD adolescents should be aware of some general concerns and proposed guidelines in teaching these skills. First is the recognition by students, learning disabilities teachers, and regular classroom teachers that listening is a critical language arts skill. Its importance is underscored when students have such reading deficits that they cannot acquire much information through that channel. Writing deficits that prevent students from taking notes in class place additional demands on listening as a means of acquiring information. Students should be made aware that good listening skills are important and that listening, like any other skill, can be improved and, therefore, must be practiced. Second, an important consideration in planning instructional activities is to remember that listening skills should not be assessed or taught in isolation. The relationship of listening skills to other language arts activities must be continually emphasized. For example, a student who is encountering difficulty in reading a textbook should be shown how important it is to be an active listener during class sessions and how to use the information from lectures in selectively reading passages from the text. Similarly, students should be taught how to correlate the information they may take in notes from class lectures and from outlining key portions of the text. It is imperative that the interrelationships between information sources and information acquisition skills be taught to students. Students should be encouraged to use various language arts skills so as to minimize forgetting. Finally, it is most important to recognize the importance of providing students with activities that are as "natural" as possible — that is, activities that emphasize spoken rather than written language. A variety of media is available for teaching listening strategies. Tape recorders, videotapes, television, radio, and role playing have all been used to advantage. The application of some of these will be discussed later.

For purposes of discussion, the listening strategies described here will be related to the demands placed on LD adolescents in secondary school lecture situations. The lecture has been chosen because it is one of the most popular methods of presenting information in secondary schools. It is important to note, however, that most strategies presented below are appropriate in other contexts, such as listening in social situations. We have organized these strategies under three major headings: first, those that can be applied prior to the listening act, or *prelistening* strategies; second, those that can be applied *during* the listening act; and finally, those that can be applied *after* listening to promote retention and recall of information presented.

Prelistening Strategies

At the root of most methods or strategies for improving listening effectiveness are two factors. First, incorrect listening habits must be avoided (see the section on characteristics of poor listeners). Second, one must be motivated to learn through listening and to take an active rather than a passive approach to listening tasks. As a first step in developing effective listening strategies, it is important for LD students to be made aware of the difference between good and poor listening habits. An effective approach is a simulation activity in which LD students listen to two videotaped class lectures (about fifteen to twenty minutes in length) on similar topics. Prior to presenting each videotape, tell the students that they will be asked some comprehensive questions on the material presented. During the first videotape presentation, allow students to use their typical listening approach to class lectures. Prior to the second presentation, give students a few strategies to use (for example, relate the proposed topic to previous experiences or instruction they have had, have them look for the main ideas in the presentation, encourage them to ask questions during the lecture to clarify their understanding — the teacher can provide answers). Following each presentation, ask a few comprehension questions and have students relate their understanding of each presentation. The teacher and LD students should then discuss which listening task was easier and which one enabled students to learn more. This activity can motivate students to change their current listening habits and to acquire strategies that will serve them better in the classroom.

Some prelistening strategies that have been found effective for LD adolescents are the following, which have been adapted from the work of Nichols and Stevens (1957), Barker (1971), and Taylor (1964).

Being Mentally Prepared to Listen

The listener must prepare mentally for a listening session by reviewing notes from previous lectures, relating text material to subjects to be discussed in class, and noting the content of the topic of discussion in relation to other topics discussed throughout the semester. In short, if students have a "set" for the information to be presented and are somewhat familiar with the topic, their learning will be more efficient and their retention will be greater. In addition to cognitive preparation, students should also have a strong purpose for listening. Motivation adds considerably to understanding and retaining information. Each of these factors can be stressed individually through specific prelistening activities. For example, teach students how to quickly review notes and materials from previous lectures shortly before the new lecture by having them skim their notes and identify three to five main points or questions that they feel the teacher stressed. When the learning disabilities teacher has determined the particular teaching style of the students' classroom teachers and the strategies that LD students should follow in prelistening, these can be summarized and put into an abbreviated format for the students to refer to prior to each class period. An example would be the following:

Review notes and materials from previous class.
Read materials related to today's class.
Relate lecture topic to other topics.

These steps should be stressed by the teacher until they become an automatic part of students' prelistening repertoire.

Being Physically Prepared to Listen

Students should be shown the importance of being prepared to listen physically as well as mentally. They should learn to be selective in choosing a seat in the classroom. Usually, when students choose seats toward the

292

front of the room, they are forced to concentrate more on the material being presented. They are also in a better position to interact with the teacher both verbally and nonverbally. Oftentimes, the teacher feels that underachieving students who sit in the back of the classroom are saying (nonverbally) that they are not interested in the class or in its activities. Therefore, choosing a seat near the front of the class not only tends to increase students' concentration during lectures, but also subtly communicates to the teacher that "I do care about this class and what I can learn from it."

Another aspect of physical preparation is coming to each class session with appropriate materials. Specifically, students should always bring their textbooks and workbooks so that they can check teachers' references to these materials. Commonly, teachers refer to a diagram in the text. Without a text to follow, the student can lose a great deal of information. Students should also be prepared with pencils, pens, and notetaking materials. As with the steps that students should follow to prepare mentally, the learning disabilities teacher can develop a brief checklist for students to go through before reporting to each class to insure that they have the necessary materials. Students might write this checklist on 3″ x 5″ cards and keep them in their pockets.

Gaining the Necessary Vocabulary

This component has been isolated to emphasize its importance as a prelistening strategy. Educational psychologists have found that it is very difficult for students to learn *both* vocabulary and concepts at the same time. Students are often confronted with this task when listening to a lecture on a new topic. Because of an unfamiliar vocabulary, students' understanding and retention of a lecture may be greatly reduced. Therefore, as a prelistening strategy, they should familiarize themselves with the key vocabulary words that will be used in the upcoming lecture. Most of this vocabulary is rather technical in nature and usually is contained in the students' textbook.

Listening Strategies

A variety of learning strategies may be used by students to increase their listening effectiveness. Eight of these strategies are discussed here.

293

Listening for Organizing Cues

An important area of investigation during the past fifteen years has been the examination of organizational processes that have been found to play an important role in learning and retaining verbal material. This research has concluded that with virtually all learning tasks, students organize to *some* degree the material to be learned. However, the extent and success of these organizational strategies appear to be partially a function of the degree to which the individuals deliberately try to organize information presented to them *and* the degree to which the materials presented are well organized (Hall, 1971). These findings have many implications for students who want to obtain maximum information through listening.

There are several cues that the student should learn to use to indicate how the teacher is organizing the information being presented. First, many teachers present a skeletal outline on the chalkboard of the material to be covered. This information is critical and should be previewed and studied before class begins. These outlines provide students with key reference points, as well as an organizational overview of the material. Students should be encouraged to copy this outline verbatim in their notes. Second, LD adolescents should be taught to listen for *verbal organizational cues* given by teachers. For example, a teacher might say, "Our topic will be discussed under three major headings. . . ." Verbal cues are also provided by introductory statements in which the teacher gives an *overview* of the information to be presented. Third, *sequences* of information can be arranged according to time, space, position, degree, or some other relationship. Deliberately sequencing information helps students create a larger structure or framework into which bits of information can be placed, thus aiding retention and making possible maximum use of the information.

In addition to looking for organizational cues, LD students should be taught to reorganize or index material that is presented in a loosely or poorly organized fashion. *Mental reorganization* is a technique that works most effectively with material that is low in meaningfulness. For example, when presented with long series of symbols (for example, chemical symbols) or words (for example, bones in the hand and arm), students may regroup or recode them to bring tighter organization to the task. Taylor (1964) advocates that students *index* information that is presented. In indexing, students assign relative values to pieces of information, look for main ideas and supporting details, separate the relevant from the irrelevant, and, in short, create a mental outline by ranking the information according to importance.

Finally, by *making comparisons,* students note similarities and differences in the information presented. This process allows students to find relationships between facts and to perceive additional relationships by categorizing information.

Listening for Verbal and Nonverbal Cues

Speakers use both verbal and nonverbal cues to emphasize important points. Students should be taught what some of the frequently used verbal and nonverbal cues are. Frequently used verbal cues include "in summary," "as a result," "a key point," and "last but not least." In addition, verbal cues include voice inflection, voice emphasis, variation in speaking pace, and repetition of certain information for emphasis. Frequently used nonverbal cues include eye contact, gestures, varied body positions (for example, standing up when an important point is made), facial expressions, and pauses between words, phrases, or thoughts. Each speaker has a unique style of delivery and individual mannerisms. It is important for students to be sensitive to these differences among individuals. Videotapes or televised lectures can be used to teach LD students how to identify verbal and nonverbal cues. As a first step the teacher and students should view the videotapes together for the purpose of identifying these cues. The advantage of videotape is that it can be stopped and replayed to locate specific cues students may have missed or to point out how a certain cue relates to information later in the lecture. At first the videotapes should be rather straightforward, with the speaker giving obvious cues. As LD students gain in their ability to listen for these cues, the complexity of the taped presentations should be increased. To promote transfer of this strategy to the regular class setting, LD students should identify unique mannerisms and speaking styles of their various teachers.

Listening for Main and Supporting Ideas

Being able to identify main ideas is of critical importance in listening. LD adolescents are frequently unable to differentiate main ideas from supporting details and to ignore irrelevant information. Activities that can be used to teach LD students to find the main idea include the following:

1. Have students listen to a short selection and suggest a title.
2. Tell a short story and have students summarize it in one sentence.
3. Give three statements, one containing a main idea and two containing subordinate ideas. Have students identify each statement.

4. Have students listen to a class presentation on videotape and identify the main ideas. In the beginning, students should be presented with a worksheet from which they can choose the main idea. Students should discuss why each of the other choices is *not* a main idea (too general, too specific, irrelevant, or inaccurate).

In learning to identify main ideas, students should also be encouraged to listen for organizing cues and the verbal and nonverbal cues that have been discussed previously.

Questioning for Clarification

Students must be taught questioning strategies that can be used to help them clarify their understanding of material presented in class. Students must come to recognize that questioning is an important way to accomplish this. There are various strategies they can use. First, students should be aware that the most appropriate times for raising questions are during a pause or between discussion points. Students should be encouraged to hold their questions so as not to interrupt a point that the teacher is trying to make. Also, by waiting and listening intently to what the teacher is saying, the question may be answered. On the other hand, students should not hold their questions so long so that they cannot understand the material being presented. Students should also be taught to ask questions in a polite, unoffensive manner using an appropriate tone of voice. It is definitely to students' advantage if the teacher does not misinterpret their questions as attempts to put the teacher down or to be a smart aleck. Questions need not always be verbal. LD students should also be taught how nonverbal communication can indicate to the teacher that they need clarification. For example, a puzzled look, a wrinkled brow, or a slight scowl can sometimes cause the teacher to repeat a given point. Finally, students should be taught the value of taking a few minutes with the teacher after class to clarify or confirm their understanding of the material. A one-to-one situation is sometimes less threatening than asking a question in front of the entire class. Students can also take this opportunity to show the teacher their notes on a confusing point so the teacher can gain some indication of their level of understanding.

In the resource room, videotapes or tape recordings of class lectures can again be used to advantage. As students listen, they can practice questioning strategies with the teacher or a peer tutor. Teachers or tutors can give students feedback about the appropriateness of their questioning strategy or its timing.

Seeking and Using Feedback

Feedback is vital in any learning situation. It is particularly important for effective listening. Barker (1971) has discussed several types of feedback. Listener-to-listener feedback suggests that the response of an individual listener often provides important information that may affect the behavior of others. Certain variables seem to increase the probability that a listener will be affected by feedback from other listeners. One variable is an awareness of the feelings of other listeners (e.g., they are bored). Another is the value a listener places on group membership. If a majority of group members exert pressure for conformity, listeners who feel socially inadequate will be more likely to conform.

A listener can use feedback to control some aspects of the speaker's behavior. Students should be made aware that feedback may be beneficial or harmful to the teacher-student relationship. Feedback from students can be given both verbally (including yawns, groans, etc.) and nonverbally (including facial expressions and body positions). The major purpose of giving feedback to the teacher is to indicate how effectively the message is coming through. Students who are sensitive to the feelings of a teacher and provide positive feedback will probably be favorably perceived by the teacher. Feedback can be positive or negative; using both types helps improve interpersonal communication. Students should be aware that feedback to teachers can provide critical information about students' understanding of material and play an important role in developing positive student-teacher relationships.

Applying Memory Strategies

LD adolescents can be taught strategies that will facilitate storage of the material being listened to. Three strategies will be described here: rehearsal, visual imagery, and coding and clustering. To apply these strategies effectively, students must be *actively* involved in listening. *Rehearsal* is repeating to oneself information one has just heard to promote its retention. Rehearsal is a most appropriate strategy to use in listening because of the differential between speech speed and thought speed. As indicated earlier in this chapter, students can process information more than twice as fast as a teacher can speak. This time differential can be used productively or unproductively. Unproductive use is letting one's mind wander. Rehearsal is a productive use of this time differential. For example, if a science teacher is discussing three main characteristics of blue stars, students should briefly repeat each characteristic to themselves after the description has been given and the teacher is making a transition to the next characteristic. The rehearsal should be done without looking at any notes, if possible. Usually, the rehearsal would consist of merely repeating the major idea of each characteristic. The major advantage of using a rehearsal strategy during a lecture is that the student gains multiple exposure to the information (Levin & Allen, 1976). The most potent learning variable is practice, and rehearsal is a form of practice occurring close in time to the learning situation. Another rehearsal technique is skimming over notes just taken during the differential time. Rehearsal has the added advantage of clarifying information so that students might better understand what has been presented as well as anticipate what will be presented next.

Visual imagery is a phenomenon that is easy to demonstrate. Simply imagine your room at home when you were growing up — where the furniture was located, etc. Experiments on the use of visual imagery as an organizational and memory strategy suggest that it is a useful technique (Paivio & Csapo, 1973; Levin & Allen, 1976). Its effectiveness is highly dependent on the task and the materials. Usually, the more concrete the task, the more effective visual imagery is as a memory strategy. Much of the information presented in secondary classrooms is concrete enough for visualization. Imagery strategies can be used in a variety of ways. One popular technique (Paivio, 1971) is to have students image a familiar room, such as their kitchen. As concepts or pieces of information are presented in the lecture, students image them at different locations in the room. For example, if the biology teacher lectures on the ten animal phyla, students would systematically image each phylum at a different location. The one-celled animals might be imaged in the sugar bowl, the amphibians in the sink, and so on. Another popular approach is to use an associational device that has high imagery value. An example of an association device is rhyming words, such as one-bun, two-shoe, three-tree, four-door. . . . As points are made in a lecture, they are sequentially imaged according to the associational device. For example, if the shop teacher is explaining the four steps to adjust the gauge on a coping saw, the student could image each point in an associational device. Thus, the first point for adjusting the gauge could be imaged between the two parts of a hamburger bun (one-bun), the second point could be imaged in a shoe (two-shoe), and so forth.

Clustering and coding information is another memory strategy that can be used to increase listening effectiveness and recall. Certain information lends itself to clustering and subsequent coding. For example, if the history teacher summarizes eight major causes of the Civil War, students may more effectively deal with the information by clustering the causes under three headings (economic, political, social). Thus, instead of having to deal with eight separate and isolated pieces of information, they have clustered the information into three major, related areas. The information may be further reduced by coding it with mnemonic devices. For example, each separate cause that is listed may be so arranged that the first letter of the first word in each cause combines to spell a certain word (COAL). Thus, to recall the four causes, students would merely have to remember the mnemonic COAL and what each letter stands for.

Concentrating During the Presentation

Since there is a great difference between thought and speech speed, listeners should use that extra time efficiently. Specifically, they may anticipate the next point, identify supporting material, identify the organization of the material, and review previous points. This last item is very important. For information to become retained and useful, it must be internalized. This internalization demands conscious effort on the part of the speaker. Students mistakenly think that they will retain information for a long period of time after hearing it only once. On the contrary, unless students consciously review the information, a significant portion of it will be forgotten.

Taking Notes

LD students who have to rely primarily on listening (as opposed to reading) to obtain information will be aided if they can take a few notes during lectures. Specific techniques for notetaking are discussed in the chapter on written expression, but Lewis and Nichols (1965) have specified some considerations in taking notes to facilitate listening: (1) Determine if notes will be helpful. Not all situations dictate the use of notes; but if students can't rely on their memory to recall such information as announcements, they should make a written reminder. (2) Decide the most effective kind of notes to take. Notes may consist of complete outlines, partial outlines, or key words. The type of system should be determined by the situation and the students' ability to take notes and not lose main ideas presented by the teacher. (3) Notes should be clear and brief. (4) Notes should be reviewed as soon after the class period as possible. The sooner and more frequent the reviews, the better the retention.

Postlistening Strategies

The follow-up activities that LD students engage in after the class has ended are *extremely* crucial in helping them maximize their understanding, retention, and use of the information presented in class. These postlistening or *review strategies* consist of the components discussed below.

First, students should develop a strategy for reviewing the information presented in the lecture *as soon after* the class as possible. To the extent that information is reviewed immediately, forgetting is reduced. Ideally, students' written and mental notes should be reviewed right after class. At the latest, students should review the notes every evening. (Incidentally, reviews conducted close to the actual presentation take little time because students are familiar with the material. Reviews conducted only before tests are much more time consuming because students are unfamiliar with the material.) Unfortunately, most students do not review their notes until the night before a test. This practice requires students to relearn almost totally the information presented in class.

Second, as LD students review their notes, they should carefully add information that they did not have an opportunity to record in class. This step is important because the writing/spelling problems LD students experience prevent them from taking comprehensive notes. If their limited notes are not reviewed shortly after the presentation, it becomes almost impossible to supplement them. At this point, students should also attempt to correlate the information presented in class with the information in the text. This requires nothing more than recording the numbers of the pages in the text that correspond with certain sections of their class notes.

Third, another review strategy is for students to question themselves to confirm their understanding of the information presented in class. If they have several unanswered questions, they should seek assistance *immediately*. If the difficulty is not resolved, it may multiply until it is beyond hope. LD students should have in mind a set of people and means by which they might gain assistance. In addition to going back to the classroom teacher, they might also ask to borrow notes from friends or classmates to see if their notes contain answers to their questions.

Fourth, an important review strategy is for students to draw a set of summary statements or conclusions from each lecture presented. This activity requires students to go beyond the information presented and to put it in their own words. Summarizing causes students to go through the material closely and to practice working with it.

Finally, right before the beginning of the next class session, students should skim their notes once again as a prelistening activity to prepare for the new information to be presented. By doing so, they can more readily relate the new to the old information.

Although strategies presented in the above discussion may appear rather laborious and demanding, our experience with LD adolescents suggests that only through the deliberate application of strategies that require a great deal of repetition, questioning, and active participation can LD students become effective listeners who can benefit from the material presented in the regular classroom.

SUGGESTIONS FOR COOPERATIVE PLANNING

Cooperative planning between the regular class teacher and the learning disabilities teacher on behalf of students with listening deficits is very important. Since the degree of listening effectiveness experienced by LD adolescents is related to the teacher's communication characteristics, the regular class teacher should be made aware of listening problems of students and the strategies they have been trained to use.

The regular class teachers can often greatly increase their effectiveness in communicating with a class by simply modifying a few of their standard procedures. Certain techniques have been developed for application in the regular classroom. They have been designed to improve students' learning of content and to increase students' general language facility, but will not take time away from content teaching. Two techniques are presented as possible suggestions that learning disabilities teachers might make to regular class teachers for the purpose of improving student learning of content. These procedures are seen as being beneficial to not only LD students, but to *all* students within a given class. These techniques have been described by Cunningham and Cunningham (1976).

Directed Listening Activity

Directed listening activity is an adaptation of directed reading activity. Cunningham and Cunningham (1976) suggest three stages: a readiness stage, a listening-reciting stage, and a follow-up stage. Activities at each stage include the following:

1. The Readiness Stage
    a. Establish motivation for the lesson.
    b. Introduce any new or difficult concepts.
    c. Introduce any new or difficult words.
    d. Set purposes for listening.

2. The Listening-Reciting Stage
   a. Students listen to satisfy the purposes for listening set during readiness.
   b. The teacher asks several literal and inferential questions that relate to the purposes set during readiness.
   c. The students volunteer interpretive and evaluative comments about the lesson. Some class discussion may ensue.
   d. If there are errors or gaps in the students' understanding of the lesson, the teacher directs the students to relisten to certain parts of the lesson.
3. The Follow-Up Stage
   a. The teacher provides opportunities for and encourages students to engage in activities that build on and develop concepts acquired during the lesson. These may include writing, reading, small group discussions, art activities, . . . (pp. 27-28)

The next example of using a directed listening activity also is provided by Cunningham and Cunningham (1976):

Mrs. Jason teaches an eighth grade math class. She introduced the basics of the metric system with a directed listening activity. After establishing motivation for the lesson by explaining that our nation will soon be adopting this measurement system, Mrs. Jason introduced the words liter, gram, and meter, and the concept of volume. She set purposes for listening by asking the students to listen for answers to the following questions: How did the meter originate? Which is larger — a liter or a quart? a meter or a yard? a gram or an ounce?

During the listening-reciting stage, Mrs. Jason described an American trying to survive in Paris. As he traveled and shopped he discovered some relationships between American units and metric units. Mrs. Jason then questioned the students to see that they had fulfilled the purposes set for listening and provided further explanation where necessary.

As a follow-up Mrs. Jason distributed metric-converter slide rules and the student converted yards to meters, quarts to liters, and ounces to grams. (p. 28)

Guided Listening Procedure

This technique is an adaptation of Manzo's (1975) guided reading procedure. The purpose is to increase long-term recall. This procedure should be used once every two or three weeks. The teacher presents a ten- to fifteen-minute speech on tape or by lecture and then takes the class through the following steps:

1. The teacher sets the major purpose: "Listen to remember *everything.*"
2. The teacher lectures, reads, or plays a recorded selection. If the teacher is lecturing, she records her lecture.
3. The teacher reminds the students that she asked them to listen to remember everything. She then writes everything they remember on the board. (She may have two students perform this task.) During this stage the teacher accepts and writes everything the students contribute. She makes no corrections and asks no questions.
4. The teacher reads everything listed on the board, directing the students to look for incorrect or missing information.
5. The students listen again to the tape, record, or reading to correct wrong information and obtain missing information.

6. The information on the board is amended and added to as needed.
7. The teacher asks the students which ideas on the board seem to be the main ideas, the most important ideas, the ones they think they should remember for a long time. She marks these items.
8. Now that the students have mastered the literal level of the selections, the teacher raises any inferential questions she feels are vital for complete understanding.
9. The teacher erases the board and tests short-term memory with a test that is not dependent on reading or writing skills. (Oral true-false or multiple-choice items will do.)
10. Test long-term memory with a similar test containing different items several weeks later. (Manzo, 1975, p. 290)

REFERENCES

Barker, L. L. *Listening behavior*. Englewood Cliffs, N.J.: Prentice-Hall, 1971.

Bird, D. E. Teaching listening comprehension. *Journal of Communication*, 1953, *3*, 127-130.

Bird, D. E. Developing literate listening. *Oral aspects of reading*, Proceedings of the Annual Conference on Reading. Chicago: University of Chicago Press, 1955.

Brown, D. P. Auding as the primary language ability. *Dissertation Abstracts*, 1954, *14*, 2281-2282.

Childers, P. R. Listening is a modifiable skill. *The Journal of Experimental Education*, 1970, *38*, 132-137.

Clark, M. L. *Hierarchical structure of comprehension skills*. Hawthorn, Victoria: Australian Council for Educational Research, 1972.

Cunningham, P. M., & Cunningham, J. W. Improving listening in content area subjects. *NASSP Bulletin*, December, 1976, pp. 26-31.

Deshler, D. D. Psychoeducational characteristics of learning disabled adolescents. In L. Goodman, L. Mann, & J. L. Wiederholt (Eds.), *Teaching the learning disabled adolescent*. Boston: Houghton Mifflin, 1978.

Drake, C., & Cavanaugh, J. Teaching the high school dyslexic. In L. C. Anderson (Ed.), *Helping the adolescent with the hidden handicap*. Belmont, Calif.: Fearon, 1970.

Early, M. J. Adjusting to individual differences in English: Listening. *Journal of Education*, 1954, *137*, 17-20.

Erickson, A. G. Can listening efficiency be improved? *Journal of Communication*, 1954, *4*, 128-132.

Hall, J. F. *Verbal learning and retention*. Philadelphia: Lippincott, 1971.

Levin, J. R., & Allen, V. L. *Cognitive learning in children: Theories and strategies*. New York: Academic Press, 1976.

Lewis, T., & Nichols, R. *Speaking and listening: A guide to effective oral-aural communication*. Dubuque, Iowa: William C. Brown, 1965.

Loban, W. *Language development: Kindergarten through grade twelve* (Research Report No. 18). Urbana, Ill: National Council of Teachers of English, 1976.

Manzo, A. V. Guided reading procedure. *Journal of Reading*, 1975, 7, 287-291.

Markgraf, Bruce R. *An observation of study determining the amount of time that students in the tenth and twelfth grades are expected to listen in the classroom*. Unpublished master's thesis, University of Wisconsin, 1957.

Nichols, R. G., & Stevens, L. A. *Are you listening?* New York: McGraw-Hill, 1957.

Paivio, A. *Imagery and verbal processes*. New York: Holt, Rinehart & Winston, 1971.

Paivio, A., & Csapo, K. Picture superiority in free recall: Imagery or dual coding? *Cognitive Psychology*, 1973, *5*, 176-206.

Pratt, E. Experimental evaluation of a program for the improvement of listening. *Elementary School Journal*, 1956, *56*, 315-320.

Rankin, Paul T. Listening ability: Its importance, measurement and development. *Chicago Schools Journal*, 1930, *12*, 177-179.

Russell, D. H., & Russell, E. F. *Listening aids through the grades*. New York: Bureau of Publications, Teachers College, Columbia University, 1959.

Spearritt, D. *Listening comprehension — a factor analysis*. Melbourne: G. W. Green, 1962.

Taylor, S. E. *Listening*. Washington, D.C.: National Education Association, 1964.

Wiig, E. H., & Semel, E. M. Productive language abilities in learning disabled adolescents. *Journal of Learning Disabilities*, 1975, *8*, 578-586.

Wilkinson, A., Stratta, L., & Dudley, P. *The quality of listening*. London: Macmillan Education, 1974.

Wilt, M. E. The language of listening and why. In V. Anderson (Ed.), *Readings in the language arts*. New York: Macmillan, 1964.

SPEAKING: STRATEGIES AND METHODS

Speaking Characteristics of the LD Adolescent

Speaking Deficits and Oral Communication Problems

Developing Speaking and Oral Communication Skills

9

Learning disabled students must continue to develop their oral language skills while progressing through the secondary schools. The development of these skills is important to both social and academic achievement.

One need only walk the halls of any junior or senior high school to recognize the social implications of speaking. Without speaking skills, especially for informal speech, students may experience limited social acceptability. The connotative meanings of words are learned in these settings, as are colloquialisms and subtle meanings. Speech must be fluent and inflections appropriate. These skills are learned from peers, and informal speech can influence peer acceptance. Informal speech is generally shaped and approximated by extended face-to-face contact and telephone conversations with friends.

In a similar fashion, secondary students use more formal speaking skills in the content classrooms, such as social studies, home economics, and health. Although speaking demands vary according to subject and classroom, it is important when students are called on by the teacher to be able to deal appropriately with the situation. The importance of the utterance appears to be negatively related to the frequency of the teacher's demands. For example, if a teacher calls on the student for an answer only once or twice a week, the spoken response and quality of response probably are more important to the teacher than if the student is called on once or twice a day.

The speaking skill problems of LD adolescents may affect both their social and academic progress. If students have poor peer relationships, mild speaking problems can be magnified because of the failure to acquire informal speaking skills from the peers. If the LD youngster's responses are viewed as confused or inadequate by the content teacher, the student is often called on less frequently. In view of the importance of both informal and formal speaking requirements in social and academic contexts, attention should be given to this aspect of a youngster's performance.

SPEAKING CHARACTERISTICS OF THE LD ADOLESCENT

Speech Development in Adolescents

There is a paucity of information either of an observational or research nature on the development of speech during adolescence. It appears, however, that the following four areas of speech are evident from observational and clinical data:

1. *Rapid vocabulary growth in formal speech:* Giving a speech; organizing and participation in discussion groups; and following parlimentary procedure.
2. *Use of speech across a variety of formal and informal conversations:* Talking with a counselor; talking to peers of an approaching event, interviewing for a job.
3. *Increased knowledge of standard formal and informal English usage:* Meeting requirements for a speech class; attending "rap sessions."
4. *Sophisticated use of total communication with a value of the standards of clarity and consistency:* Using parlimentary procedure as a part of conducting an organized club or interest group. (Warriner, Renison, & Griffith, 1965, p. 409)

These four areas are largely the responsibility of the teacher of English in junior and senior high schools. The amount of time spent on these areas usually depends on the training of the teacher — that is, literature vs. composition. In addition, development of speaking skills must compete with the development of writing skills. Finally, the emphasis on the lecture method of content presentation in secondary school classes does not afford many opportunities for the LD student to enhance speaking skills.

Speaking Deficits in LD Adolescents

Halpern, Darley, and Brown (1973) postulate the following four types of oral communication problems: word finding, motor planning, confused language, and general retardation of language development. We would add a fifth type of oral communication problem — cognitive/socialization problems.

Word-finding Problems

Students with word-finding problems are described as:

... often voluble and rapid-fire talkers. Their sentences appear to be hanging in mid-air. There is little structure to their verbal output; they tend to ramble on. One observes an unusual number of fillers such as "em," "you know," etc., as well as omissions of words or even sentences. ... [They] simplify phonemic clusters and telescope

307

words in both speech and spelling. They run their words together in writing exactly the way they do in speaking. . . . [and have] difficulties with organization. (DeHirsch, 1975, p. 64)

Associated with their word finding problems, these students also experience problems with syntax. They often use sentences in speaking that are simpler and shorter than those produced by their peers. An example of such a sentence is one produced by a junior in high school when asked to define the word *unicycle*. This particular student stated, "It's a different thing you ride."

Other associated errors in oral speaking include (1) word substitutions, (2) circumlocutions, (3) high-frequency use of low-information words, (4) omissions, (5) perseveration, (6) atypical intonation patterns, and (7) cluttering.

Examples of each type of oral speaking error are as follows:

1. Word substitutions
    a. Phonemic substitution, e.g., *steam* for *stream*
    b. Contextual substitution, e.g., *pony* for *horse*
2. Circumlocutions, e.g., "You know what I mean . . . it's red . . . you write with it . . . it has an eraser . . . oh yes, . . . a pencil."
3. High-frequency use of low-information words, e.g., *somebody, somewhere, anywhere*
4. Omission of words from sentences, e.g., "They got the whatcha call it fixed" for "They got the windshield wiper fixed."
5. Using a word from a previous sentence in the new context of the subsequent sentence, e.g., "They won the game. He scored the game." (should have been *touchdown*)
6. Using atypical intonation patterns, e.g., voice pitch is inappropriate for declaratory (statement), exclamatory (strong feeling), imperative (request), and/or interrogative (question) sentences.
7. Using rapid, jerky, and stumbling speech without anxiety, e.g., "r-r-river"

Other oral communication deficits related to word-finding problems include poor auditory attention span and the inefficient use of learning strategies to acquire and retrieve information.

Motor-planning Problems

Motor-planning problems manifest themselves by difficulties in producing phonemes (sound elements of words) or a sequence of phonemes.

Classroom teachers may have mistakenly viewed students who manifested this problem as having difficulty in syllabification (decoding) and/or sound blending, rather than considering the motor planning that is involved in syllabification and sound blending.

Confused Language

The third type of oral communication problem is confused language. Severely disturbed persons with this type of problem manifest errors of reasoning, short-term memory deficits, and spatial and time orientation problems. This problem is also called a thought disorder in clinical psychology and psychiatry and is a classic symptom of childhood psychoses, i.e., autism and schizophrenia (Davison & Neale, 1974). This type of communication problem, which has been associated with the severely disturbed inpatient, has not been noted in LD students.

General Retardation of Language Development

The fourth type of oral communication problem identified by Halpern, Darley, and Brown (1973) is general retardation of language development. The investigators suggest that general intellectual impairment (mental retardation) is the primary source of this type of oral communication problem. Ingalls (1978) describes the language deficits of the educable mentally retarded as follows:

> The more serious types of language difficulty with the retarded are problems of vocabulary and a general lack of fluency. Both the expressive and receptive vocabularies of retarded children are more limited than those of their nonretarded peers, and this means that they have more difficulty understanding what is said to them and they have more difficulty putting their thoughts into words. As a result, their speech is more repetitive and less varied. This problem may be compounded by the fact that many mildly retarded children come from families where language is not used very much at home except to communicate basic feelings and wants. . . . These children may have had little experience in trying to communicate ideas to people or presenting logical arguments. (p. 366)

Cognitive/Socialization Language Problems

These language problems come from a deviation in language structure and/or meaning. A problem can result in both speech and language difficulties. Tubbs and Moss (1974) include an example from Whorf (1956) of a language-thinking problem that could be related to speaking:

> For example, people would be very careful around barrels labeled "GASOLINE," but would smoke unconcernedly around barrels labeled "EMPTY GASOLINE BARREL," though the fumes in the empty barrels were more likely to ignite than the actual gasoline. (p. 135)

Relating this situation to a speaking problem, a person may say, "It's OK to smoke around these barrels because there is no gasoline in them." If one person misperceives the situation, cognitively reasons that conditions are safe, and relays this information to another person who has appropriately perceived the situation, then a cognitive/social problem may be said to exist between the two persons.

Speech is an important function for persons to socially communicate "who they are" and "where they are coming from." In fact, the Whorfian hypothesis (1956) presumes spoken language is a strong determiner of a person's experience of the world. Certainly one can experience the world without oral speech, for example, as the deaf person does. However, a person who is relating experiences orally needs to have their reality confirmed or disconfirmed by a listener.

Prerequisites to appropriate speaking are adequate awareness of situations and problem-solving skills. How does the LD student acquire adequate awareness of situations and use problem-solving skills? The generally acceptable methods involve having many experiences and discussing these experiences and their meaning with other persons. The problem is not a speech problem per se, but rather a speech-related problem that we call a cognitive/socialization problem.

This problem becomes extremely important to the adolescent's development during secondary school. The peer group serves an important function of providing both confirming and disconfirming feedback to the student. In the halls of any secondary school building, conversation among students ranges from nonverbal greetings, such as hand waving, smiles, and back-slapping, to talk of future plans, exchange of opinions about classes and persons, or animated discussion on some topic of interest.

A second group of students, *not* engaged in these social communications, may be (1) preoccupied with their own thoughts, (2) uncomfortable in the social situation, or (3) alienated by the group. Many LD students are part of this second group. These students are either preoccupied with their own thoughts or socially uncomfortable as a part of the group. The effect is that LD students often do not share their thoughts and experiences and have them confirmed or disconfirmed by their peers during school hours.

However, social interaction with peers or friends is not limited to school interactions. Social interaction occurs during phone conversations. If LD

310

adolescents do not engage in this important means of socialization, the consequences of limited oral communication at school are compounded.

Secondary students need close friends to mutually confirm or disconfirm experiences and ideas. If LD students do not develop these close identification ties with a friend, a third important source of feedback to their cognitive/social language is unavailable.

SPEAKING DEFICITS AND ORAL COMMUNICATION PROBLEMS

Learning disabled students often manifest verbal behavior that may maximize communication problems. The student's oral communication does not convey the intended idea and, because of this, the listener is likely to miss the meaning of the utterance. This miscommunication can affect the social relationships of the learning disabled, especially if their families and peers are highly verbal (Kronick, 1974).

Oral Communication Problems of LD Adolescents

There is a paucity of empirical evidence about the speaking deficits of LD adolescents. The major investigative focus has been on reading, with minor attention to written and oral expression (Clark, 1978).

Wiig and Semel (1975), in a study of oral language deficits specific to LD adolescents, found that these youngsters displayed more difficulty when defining words and formulating sentences and slower reaction times when recalling opposites than their academically achieving peers. These findings provide limited but empirical support that the LD adolescent displays word-finding and cognitive/socialization problems. The motor-planning problems associated earlier with the undifferentiated age group of LD persons may also be present when one considers the delayed reaction times of the LD adolescents in Wiig and Semel's (1975) study. Future investigation will be required to provide both definitive evidence of these speaking problems and to isolate motor-planning problems from word-finding and cognitive/socialization problems. Until the future investigations provide a clearer direction, the assessment of LD adolescents *must* include study of word-finding, motor-planning, and cognitive/socialization problems.

Assessing Oral Communication Problems of LD Adolescents

The hypothetical case presented below is an indication of how sub-tests of existing formal instruments can be used to assess speech functioning. The hypothetical case is used because formal tests that are now available are not totally adequate for precise measurement of the speaking skills of LD adolescents.

First, the learning disabilities teacher may administer the *Peabody Picture Vocabulary Test* (PPVT) (Dunn, 1965) to provide a gross measure of the student's receptive vocabulary. The teacher could determine the student's verbal fluency by administering the *Free Association Test* of the *Detroit Tests of Learning Aptitude* (Detroit) (Baker & Leland, 1967). A comparison of these two scores will permit the teacher to compare the relative differences between the two measures when viewing the student's percentile standing. For purposes of this chapter, the teacher will be looking for a discrepancy that suggests intervention to correct a word-finding problem.

If the discrepancy is found to exist, the teacher should then administer the *Social Adjustment B* test and the *Likenesses and Differences* test of the *Detroit*. The *Social Adjustment B* test is a measure of vocabulary definitions of words that are familiar in the social community context. This test provides the teacher with information as to the levels of spoken language the students use and the quality of their verbal expression. The *Likenesses and Differences* test provides similar information, but it also measures the degree of abstraction of the student's verbal expression.

The teacher then may proceed to determine if the student is having difficulty with syntax. Although the measures described above will provide some information, more specific data are required to pinpoint the problem. This assessment process is made somewhat less time consuming because of investigative studies by Brown and Fraser (1963), Lackner, (1968), Menyuk (1971), Menyuk and Looney (1972), and Scholes (1970). They found that elicited imitation of sentences approximates the student's underlying language competence. Using this rationale, syntax problems of oral language could be identified using the *Auditory Attention Span for Related Syllables* test of the *Detroit* as an informal measure. The major disadvantage of this test is that memory is a strong factor in the student's performance on the latter portion of the test. The teacher should determine where the student is having difficulties imitating the modeled sentences. Consistent errors are the most important factor for remediation purposes.

Finally, oral speaking errors may be assessed with three informal measures. The first measure requires the teacher to provide the student with an interest checklist, including items such as camping, football, volleyball, and sewing. A good source for such a checklist is the list of 4-H projects available from a county extension agent. Select some of these projects, and ask the student to tell you about them. This provides a context in which the teacher can sample the student's extended spontaneous speech. This discussion should be tape-recorded for future scoring of oral communication errors.

The second informal measure is an adaptation of the *Auditory Attention Span for Related Syllables* test of the *Detroit*. The teacher tapes a recording and pairs correct and incorrect models of sentences for thirty of the forty-three sentences. Examples of oral communication errors provided earlier in this chapter may be used by the teacher in constructing this informal measure. For the remaining thirteen sentences the teacher pairs two correct model sentences. The thirteen no-error pairs are randomly selected from the forty-three sentences to control for the student's guessing. Once the informal measure is completed, the student listens to the sentence pairs and notes on a separate sheet of paper whether the pairs are the "same" or "different." After completing this aspect of the test, the teacher then discusses each sentence pair with the student to determine if the student recognized the error and can now correct the sentence.

Perhaps an example of this second informal measure, the modification of the *Detroit,* is needed. For example, consider the following sentence:

"My car has a tape deck."

It could be used as an identical replication:

"My car has a tape deck." (pause) "My car has a tape deck."

Question — Are the two sentences the same or different? (If the student says "Different," the teacher says, "How are they different?")
In the same manner the two sentences may have subtle differences:

"My car has a tape deck." (pause) "My car, it has a tape deck."

The same questions follow as above. However, this second pairing is a comparison of two structurally different sentences. One can make changes in phonemic, contextual, syntactic, or semantic elements of the phrase. Using assessment procedures similar to the example provided, the teacher can assess the student's monitoring and signal-detection skills and use this information in intervening with oral speaking errors. The testing should be done within the classroom rather than an unfamiliar setting such as the nurse's room or principal's office.

DEVELOPING SPEAKING AND ORAL COMMUNICATION SKILLS

Four important strategies can be used in developing speech skills in the LD adolescent:

1. Wait time.
2. Rehearsal.
3. Recognizing the social impact of the LD adolescent's speech on listeners (Warriner, Renison, & Griffith, 1965).
4. Surface counseling.

A commonsense adage, which has been attributed to Abraham Lincoln, states, "I would rather keep my mouth shut and be thought a fool than to open it and remove all doubt." Wait time involves pausing a few seconds and organizing one's thoughts before speaking. Warriner et al. (1965) remind the teacher to teach students that "... clear thinking precedes clear speaking" (p. 403). LD students should be encouraged to wait until they have organized their thoughts before speaking. Token systems of reinforcement can be used by the teacher to reward students for inhibiting their responses for the purpose of planning and organizing.

Rehearsal is another strategy that adolescents can learn to use in both informal and formal speaking situations. Rehearsal involves the following steps:

1. The students should think through the situation thoroughly and should ask the following questions:
   a. Is the information to be spoken based on opinion or fact?
   b. If it is fact, upon what basis was it determined — own experience, hearsay, circumstance, noted authority?
2. Students should then discuss what they want to say with friends, parents, or teachers and ask for feedback.
3. The students should modify what they are going to say, based on the feedback they receive.
4. They should then ask, "How might I say what I'm going to say to be most effective?" A major factor here is the order of events to be expressed. Determine the order and then rehearse or memorize the main thought.

This sequence should be sufficient for most situations. However, in formal speaking situations, such as giving a speech, accepting an award, or giving a public announcement, students should be encouraged to use an outline. Then they should practice in front of a mirror and before *anyone* who will take the time to listen to the speech. Never write out the speech word for word! An example of writing out dialogue word for word was used when a friend of one of the authors was in high school and using the telephone for making dates. The friend had a response for contemplated questions or responses to be made by the girl he had called to ask for a date. The system worked well if the girl followed the script, but this rarely occurred. In all but one case, the author's friend abruptly terminated the phone call because his script did not provide for the girl's question. Only at the suggestions of a sensitive classmate was the author's friend able to discontinue the charade.

A third strategy is for the teacher to help students recognize the social impact of conversation on listeners. Discourage students from engaging in long, extended monologues in social discussions. Persons who do this are generally viewed as egocentric and boring. LD students should be taught that they can keep their peers interested by their enthusiasm, eye contact, and by systematically asking for feedback from members of the group by using names — "Do you agree with Miss Jones, Jim?" LD students should be taught never to put down group members by sarcasm or ridicule. Students who use these tactics should be cautioned that their arguments are probably weak or have no sound basis. If a conversation turns into a heated argument, students should try to stay calm. Not doing so is a dead giveaway for being "uptight." The voice tone becomes staccato, facial expressions become more animated, and rate of speaking increases. Students who cannot control their emotions should be cautioned not to say anything further until the subject changes or the group disbands (Warriner et al., 1965).

The learning disabilities teacher also must use some of the surface counseling techniques described more fully in the chapter on social interaction. Specifically, the teacher must assume the responsibility to describe the behavior observed, react to the behavior, and relate how this behavior is affecting the peer group. For example:

> Tom, during the class discussion today you broke in with a comment unrelated to the subject when Kim was making an important point. As I remember it, Kim was talking about how main points of a passage can be important for recall, and you said something like, "Do we have an assembly next week?" I was concerned because Kim was not anxious to make the point again, and I could tell by the expressions on the other students' faces that they were upset by the inappropriateness of your remark. What could you have done rather than interrupt Kim?

It may be that Tom will be unable or unwilling to look for an option. If this occurs, the teacher can provide one or more options with their associated consequences. Teachers may have to use this surface counseling strategy frequently with students who are unaware of the impact of their communication behavior.

Word-Finding Methods

Assisting LD students in using the correct word is critical to all teaching. This naming process must be systematically taught, using a uniform procedure. Berry and Eisenson (1956) suggest five steps to establish the naming process using concrete objects. The steps are described on the basis of using an object as the focus of training. However, with modification a similar sequence can be established that includes Tanck's (1969) three instructional strategies to teach naming, using pictures, or sounds as the focus of the training. We suggest the following procedure, which is a modification of the Berry and Eisenson (1956) training.

1. The function of the object is demonstrated; then the object is named.
2. The student is asked to repeat the name of the object after the teacher says it.
3. The name is incorporated into a short sentence, which is spoken by the teacher with emphasis on the key word.
4. The student repeats the sentence.
5. The student writes the sentence and underlines the key word.
6. The student generates a new short sentence using the key word.
7. The following day, the student is asked to generate a sentence using the key word, and the teacher demonstrates the concept represented by the key name.
8. The teacher makes intermittent records of the student's spontaneous speech to chart the frequency of use of the key word in the classroom.
9. The teacher augments the key word and concept when teaching new key words and concepts.
10. The teacher makes intermittent records of the student's spontaneous speech to chart the frequency of the key word across classroom settings.

Some examples of exercises that can be used here are the Twenty Questions game, naming objects in a picture, discussion of concrete objects (Lerner, 1976), the Categories game (Lerner, 1976), and expanding sentences (I went to the circus and found . . .).

Correcting Problems of Syntax

Remediation of students' word-finding problems is only part of the learning disabilities teacher's function in teaching oral language. The teacher must also deal with students who have problems with syntax — that is, stringing words together to provide meaningful units of thought. Teachers can teach students to generate sentences that are longer and more grammatically complex using the teaching strategies of Lerner (1976). She suggests that the teacher provide the students with two basic kernel sentences and assist the student in transformation of the two sentences by combining them into a more complex single sentence as in the following example:

> Kernel sentence: I saw two girls in the hall.
> Kernel sentence: I was on my way to English class.
> Transformation: I saw two girls in the hall while I was on my way to English class.

It may be that students will need practice in learning to transform declaratory sentences into exclamatory, imperative, or interrogative sentences. This practice permits students to produce sentence variations systematically (Lerner, 1976). The following is an example of this activity:

Declaratory sentence		*Exclamatory sentence*
I will receive an A in history.	to	I will receive an A in history!
Imperative sentence		*Interrogative sentence*
I must receive an A in history.	and	Will I receive an A in history?

Lerner (1976) also provides a method to combine vocabulary-building skills within the sentence formulation strategy. She calls this "substitution to form sentences" (p. 232). Using this method, the teacher provides the student with the kernel sentence, such as "It was so cold and rainy that I put on my *winter* coat." Students can substitute other words for *winter — rain, heavy, wool, all-weather*. This exercise provides students with a greater verbal facility in choosing the most appropriate word for the intended meaning. The teacher can extend this approach by using a thesaurus to provide various synonyms.

Some students may not be ready to engage in the activities for formulating sentences as suggested above. These students need to spend time individually with the teacher to learn prerequisite skills. The teacher may begin by (1) modeling simple but grammatically correct sentences for the student, then (2) having the student repeat the sentences that have been modeled by the teacher, and (3) writing the sentences in the student's practice workbook so the student can rehearse them for practice on the following day.

Once the student has mastered the sentences, on the second day the teacher should use those sentences when teaching the activities requiring these prerequisite skills.

Oral Speaking Practice

The third major responsibility of the teacher when teaching oral communication skills is to provide ample opportunities for LD students to practice these skills. All students will benefit from this structured activity, but oral speaking practice is a necessity for students who make the oral communication errors described earlier.

This activity must not be construed as simply a practice session without concern for errors. In fact, just the opposite is true. During the practice sessions, the teacher observes the student's role communication and notes errors to the student. All oral communication errors noted earlier as characteristic of LD students are considered with other grammatical errors, and errors of logic are pointed out to the student. The teacher may also provide students with tape-recorded samples of their oral communication. Using the tape recorder, students can monitor their own errors with the help of the teacher. Students may also benefit from monitoring the oral communication of other students. Another useful activity is to require students to note examples of good speakers and good total communication (verbal and nonverbal) on videotape.

The following activities for practicing oral communication are provided by Lerner (1976):

1. Oral language activities
   A number of activities can be used to promote practice in the use of oral language and speaking. These include: conversations; discussions; radio or television broadcasts; show and tell sessions; puppetry; dramatic play; telephoning; choral speaking; reporting; interviewing; telling stories, riddles or jokes; book reports; and role playing.
2. Comprehension
   Ask questions that require [students] to think and formulate responses. What are three ways you would improve school spirit? Why is it easier to make a dress shorter than it is to make it longer? How could a student petition be used to abolish the closed lunch hour?
3. Tell me how . . .
   . . . you choose a vocation, get to the football field, develop a class schedule for next year, drop a class, etc. Also tell me why tickets are required for basketball games. Tell me, where do we get late slips?
4. Finishing stories
   Begin a story and let the [student] finish it. For example: Betty went to visit her boyfriend at Northwestern University. When the plane landed at O'Hare Airport, Betty could not find her boyfriend and . . . (p. 232)

Planned Class Discussions

A method of teaching LD adolescents that has implications for *all* secondary teachers is the planned use of class discussions. The importance of class discussions for *all* secondary students, including LD students, has been described earlier. However, class discussions are not an intuitive part of teaching; they must be carefully planned. Hoover (1976) provides a lesson plan on which teachers can model their own lessons.

ILLUSTRATION OF DISCUSSION OUTLINE

I. Useful in biology, general science, and health classes
   Unit: Microorganisms
   Concept: Respiratory diseases are transmitted in many ways
   Problem: How can the transmission of respiratory diseases by minimized?
   Sample Analysis Questions:
      1. What are some common respiratory diseases?
      2. What are airborne microorganisms?
      3. How are they transmitted?
      4. Why is the problem more important today than in the past?
   Some Possible Solutions to Consider:
      1. Pass strict laws on air pollution
      2. Require inoculations against disease
      3. Require regular chest X-rays. (Hoover, 1976, pp. 111-120)

The teachers should be aware that there are limitations to planned class discussions. Hoover (1976) identified five limitations:

1. If the class is not prepared on the subject, discussion is fruitless as a learning method.
2. The teacher must control the discussion to insure that it does not digress from the subject and concept.
3. The teacher must be able to tolerate different perspectives.
4. The teacher must be prepared for unexpected results and have a tolerance for ambiguity.
5. The goals the teacher had planned to meet are not assured.

We believe that the potential benefits of class discussion are great enough to tolerate the inherent limitations of the method.

Other Methods

Other methods of promoting oral communication skills include:

1. Enrolling LD students in speech courses in secondary schools.

2. Instigating a required general course in communication that includes the teaching of total communication skills.
3. Training counselors in the importance of the link between speech, thinking, perception, and socialization.
4. Conveying to parents the importance of the telephone as a socialization vehicle for secondary students.

REFERENCES

Baker, H. J., & Leland, B. *Detroit Tests of Learning Aptitude.* Indianapolis: Bobbs-Merrill, 1967.
Berry, M. F., & Eisenson, J. *Speech disorders: Principles and practices of therapy.* New York: Appleton-Century-Crofts, 1956.
Brown, R., & Fraser, C. The acquisition of syntax learning. In C. Cofer & B. Musgrave (Eds.), *Verbal behavior and learning: Problems and processes.* New York: McGraw-Hill, 1963.
Clark, R. *An integrated language intervention program for learning disabled adolescents.* Unpublished manuscript, University of Kansas, 1978.
Davison, G. C., & Neale, J. M. *Abnormal psychology: An experimental clinical approach.* New York: Wiley, 1974.
DeHirsch, K. Cluttering and stuttering. *Bulletin of the Orton Society,* 1975, *25,* 57-68.
Dunn, L. *Peabody picture vocabulary test.* Circle Pines, Minn.: American Guidance Service, 1965.
Halpern, H., Darley, F. L., & Brown, J. E. Differential language and neurological characteristics in cerebral involvement. *Journal of Speech and Hearing Disorders,* 1973, *38* (2), 162-173.
Hoover, K. H. *The professional teacher's handbook: A guide for improving instruction in today's middle and secondary schools* (2nd ed.). Boston: Allyn & Bacon, 1976.
Ingalls, R. P. *Mental retardation: The changing outlook.* New York: Wiley, 1978.
Kronick, D. Some thoughts on group identification: Social needs. *Journal of Learning Disabilities,* 1974, *7,* 144-147.
Lackner, J. A developmental study of language behavior in retarded children. *Neuropsychologia,* 1968, *6,* 301-320.
Lerner, J. W. *Children with learning disabilities: Theories, diagnosis, teaching strategies* (2nd ed.). Boston: Houghton-Mifflin, 1976.
Menyuk, P. *The acquisition and development of language.* Englewood Cliffs, N. J.: Prentice-Hall, 1971.
Menyuk, P., & Looney, P. A problem of language disorder: Length versus structure. *Journal of Speech and Hearing Research,* 1972, *15,* 264-279.
Scholes, R. On functors and contentives in children's imitations of word strings. *Journal of Verbal Learning and Verbal Behavior,* 1970, *9,* 167-170.
Tanck, M. L. Teaching concepts, generalizations, and constructs. In D. M. Fraser (ed.), *Social studies in curriculum development: Prospects and problems,* Thirty-ninth Yearbook. Washington, D.C.: National Council for the Social Studies, 1969.
Tubbs, S. L., & Moss, S. *Human communication: An interpersonal perspective.* New York: Random House, 1974.
Warriner, J. E., Renison, W., & Griffith, F. *English grammar and composition* (Rev. ed.). New York: Harcourt, Brace & World, 1965.
Whorf, B. L. *Language, thought and reality.* Cambridge, Mass.: MIT Press, 1956.
Wiig, E. H., & Semel, E. M. Productive language abilities in learning disabled adolescents. *Journal of Learning Disabilities,* 1975, *8*(9), 578-586.

320

APPENDIX

INSTRUCTIONAL MATERIALS FOR THE LEARNING DISABLED ADOLESCENT

APPENDIX

The majority of time that LD adolescents are in the resource room is spent working with "special education" instructional materials. To increase the probability that these materials will meet the students' instructional needs, Wilson (1978) contends that the choice of materials should be made in light of (1) curricular variables, (2) student variables, and (3) teacher variables. Selecting and using materials without considering each of these factors often results in a mismatching of materials and student needs.

Due to the limited time available to teachers in the secondary schools to address the instructional needs of the LD adolescent, it is critical that the selection and application of instructional materials be systematic and well directed. Therefore, this appendix discusses how to select and analyze instructional materials for LD adolescents and presents a representative listing and analysis of materials that have been used with LD adolescents under a learning strategies approach.

The reader should refer to chapter 2, in which the authors described the *use* and *role* of instructional materials within the learning strategies approach.

SELECTION OF INSTRUCTIONAL MATERIALS

Let us further describe each of the components of the curriculum/student/teacher triad presented by Wilson (1978), since these factors singly and in combination must be considered in selecting instructional materials for LD adolescents.

Curriculum variables are those factors that make up the information presented to students through the instructional materials. Since the learning strategies approach operates primarily out of a resource room, the selection of materials must be largely determined by the strategies that youngsters need to adjust to the demands of the regular classroom. Since a learning strategies approach is basically content-free (relative to the regular curriculum), materials should be selected primarily to teach learning and coping strategies. The materials should not focus on delivery of the content that is taught in the regular classroom. (This is not to say, however, that multiple-level texts and materials that aid the classroom teacher in delivering content should not be purchased; they should be. But these materials should be purchased for regular education and used primarily in the regular classroom.) In short, in considering curriculum variables, the teacher attempts to select instructional materials that will best bridge the gap between youngsters' deficiencies and the demands of the regular classroom. Thus, under a learning strategies approach, these materials are *not* considered an end in themselves but rather a means to an end (that is, adjustment and success in the regular curriculum).

Student variables represent the unique needs of the student, which must be considered in the selection of materials. The student needs that Wilson finds most critical are the current level of functioning and the most immediate educational demands. Other factors to consider are students' physical, social, and psychological characteristics; their ability to work independently and in groups; their interest level and motivation; and their past history of success and failure with specific materials.

Finally, teacher variables must be considered in the selection of instructional materials for LD adolescents. Frequently, these variables are not even considered in materials selection (for example, when a central special education office orders materials for an entire district without teacher input). Kass (1972) has underscored the importance of the teacher in the link between the student and the material: "It may be that the mediation between subject variables on the one hand and methods and materials on the other is accomplished by the teacher. The mechanism which allows the teacher to match the two is the teacher's philosophical conception of the curriculum for learning disability children" (p. 208). Thus, the teacher's philosophy in terms of method and approach to be used in instruction must be considered. Equally important are the training background of the teacher and the time constraints placed on the teacher.

While the list of variables outlined by Wilson is not exhaustive, it is indicative of the broad array of factors that should be considered by the teacher in selecting instruction materials.

ANALYSIS OF INSTRUCTIONAL MATERIALS

In recent years with the passage of PL 94-142, public school services for LD adolescents have been increasing markedly, thus creating a great demand by teachers for instructional materials for use with these students. This demand is being met by publishing companies with an onslaught of materials that are said to be designed for use with LD students. With a broad array of materials to choose from, the teacher should adopt some guidelines and criteria for analyzing materials before purchasing them.

There are several sets of guidelines that have been developed for the analysis of instructional materials (Ensminger, 1970; Van Etten, 1970; Bleil, 1975; Brown, 1975; Watson & Van Etten, 1976). Wiederholt and McNutt (1977) have acknowledged that each contains some valuable guidelines that can be applied to all instructional materials for analysis, although none is designed specifically for analysis of materials for the LD adolescent.

Wiederholt and McNutt, therefore, have proposed a set of guidelines for analyzing materials that consists of two major components: static evaluation and dynamic evaluation. The purpose of static evaluation is to obtain information that can be used in making a decision whether to purchase or implement a given material. Dynamic evaluation is designed to gather information on an instructional material that is currently being used to determine if it should be altered or discontinued.

According to Wiederholt and McNutt, the key elements to consider in conducting a static evaluation on materials are the following:

1. *Relevance* — Teachers should consider whether the objectives of the materials have practical applicability and relevance to the present and/or future needs of the students; and whether the student has an understanding of the importance of the objectives and the materials.
2. *Readability* — Teachers should determine the readability level of the instructional materials. A variety of formulas are available for this purpose. The teacher is cautioned not to rely on the estimate given by the publisher as it is often inaccurate. If a desired material is written on a too high reading level, the teacher should determine if it would be possible to modify the reading level of the material.
3. *Language of the material* — The appropriateness of language within the material should be analyzed. The language may be composed of words and sentences that are either too complex or too simple for particular students. The background and concept

development of the students must be matched with the language of the program.

4. *Prerequisites* — The teacher should determine what prerequisite learning skills or behaviors are required to use the instructional material. Prerequisites may be of three general types: content prerequisites, skill prerequisites, and experiential background prerequisites.

5. *Motivation* — This is a major consideration because of the history of failure and often low level of interest evidenced by LD adolescents. It is critical to consider the type of reinforcement that is suggested and/or contained within the instructional material as well as the interest level suggested by the illustrations and types of exercises.

Dynamic evaluation should be a continual concern of the teacher, as materials should be evaluated to determine their effectiveness when used by students. Four techniques are outlined by Wiederholt and McNutt for conducting dynamic evaluation of instructional materials.

1. *Pre/Posttesting* — Criterion-referenced testing is recommended over norm-referenced testing as one means of determining the extent to which identified objectives have been met. Norm-referenced tests usually do not include sufficient items to determine what a student has accomplished over time, whereas criterion-referenced tests can be designed to reflect the specific objectives taught to the student.

2. *Analytic Teaching* — The application of those teaching methods that allow the teacher to analyze a student's behavior within an instructional situation is called analytic teaching. Characteristics of analytic teaching methods are (a) the students must be systematically observed using the materials, (b) the students' responses must be recorded and analyzed according to some specified frame of reference, and (c) the interpretation of these results should affect the future use of the materials.

3. *Observation* — Observation is viewing and interpreting students' behavior while they are engaged in using a particular material. Observation can be rather informal when the teacher merely notes a student's behavior as it occurs; or it can be highly structured with a specific format for recording behaviors in relation to the materials.

4. *Interviews* — This form of dynamic evaluation involves discussing with the students their perceptions of the materials being used.

Is is also suggested that other teachers be interviewed to solicit their input on the value of the instructional materials currently being used.

None of these dynamic evaluation techniques described above is intended to stand alone in the analysis of instructional materials. Instead, teachers should use a combination of these procedures to determine the effectiveness of a given instructional material in facilitating gains in student performance. Finally, Wiederholt and McNutt, while acknowledging that following their system or any worthwhile materials analysis system is time consuming, conclude that "unfortunately, however, there are few shortcuts to defensible professional practices" (p. 139).

In conjunction with the analysis procedures outlined by Wiederholt and McNutt, the present authors recommend that the teacher seriously consider the work of Virginia Brown (1975) in materials analysis. Brown has developed a Q-sheet (question sheet) for use in analyzing materials. The Q-Sheet consists of thirty-one questions and a number of subquestions or statements that help in the evaluation, comparison, and selection of materials. Each query is followed by a brief description to help teachers apply the question and determine the answer. Brown's list is rather comprehensive in its approach and can be most instructional for the teacher who has not had a great deal of experience in analyzing instructional procedures. A sampling of some of the questions and subquestions are presented below. The reader is referred to Brown's original work for the complete Q-Sheet.

Item 7. Is there evidence of any psychological principles of instruction which are content free?
— Look for reference to the systematic use of stimulus control, reinforcement, rate of introduction, set induction, etc.
Item 14. How independently can the material be used?
— If independence of use is recommended, is there a systematic program to teach the child *how* to use materials independently?
— How is progress in work habits or independence to be monitored?
Item 20. Have there been any attempts to determine readability or learner interest?
— What processes have been used and are the results available?
Item 21. What is the comparative cost of the program?
— An attempt should be made to estimate the cost-effectiveness of the program.
Item 24. What are the target populations for whom the materials were developed?
— If the population characteristics are stated, it is easier to access the potential relevance of the materials to your population of interest. (pp. 412-415)

Regardless of the set of analysis guidelines adopted, the teacher must consider the importance of systematically analyzing all materials used. The instructional time lost through the application of inappropriate or ineffective materials cannot be regained in the case of the secondary student.

INSTRUCTIONAL MATERIALS FOR LEARNING STRATEGIES — A REPRESENTATIVE LISTING

The following list of selected materials represents the types of instructional materials currently used in secondary learning disabilities services that are following a learning strategies approach. We are not necessarily endorsing the materials described in the following pages but are presenting them as an indication of how teachers have attempted to operationalize the learning strategies approach through their selection of instructional materials.

READING

Title: Action Libraries
Author: Varies per title
Publisher: Scholastic Book Services
Copyright date: 1971-1976
Approximate cost: $39.50 kit (4 copies, 5 titles) (in 1976-1977)
                              1.80 book
                              12.50 spirit masters (50)
Format: Book
Reading level: Libraries 1 & 1A — Grade 2.0-2.4
                         Libraries 2 & 2A — 2.5-2.9
                         Libraries 3 & 3A — Grade 3.0-3.4
                         Libraries 4 & 4A — 3.5-3.9
Interest level: Grades 7-12
Specific instructional skills: Reading development and enrichment

Title: The American People: Part I, Part II
Author: Henry G. Dethloff & Allen E. Begnaud
Publisher: Steck-Vaughn
Copyright date: 1976
Approximate cost: $1.68 each (in 1976)
Format: Workbook
Reading level: Lower reading level
Interest level: Grade 7 to adult
Specific instructional skills: Word study, reading comprehension, written self-expression,
                         test-taking skills.

Title: Archie Multigraphic Kit
Publisher: Archie Enterprises
Copyright date: 1975
Approximate cost: $45.50 (in 1975)
Format: 10 different comic books (3 copies each), 6 copies of questions per book, 2 answer
                cards per book, 10 follow-up lessons (4 stories per book)
Reading level: Grades 3.5-5.5
Interest level: Junior and senior high
Specific instructional skills: Sequence, main idea and detail, inference, draw conclusions,
                                character analysis, figurative language, description, cause/effect,
                                fact/opinion, relevant detail

READING

Title: Be Informed Series (Units 1-20)
Publisher: New-Readers Press
Copyright date: Varies from 1968-1976 (some units revised)
Approximate cost: $25.00 for all 20 units bound, $.85 per unit (in 1977)
Format: 8″ x 11″ bound units
         20 units total
Reading level: Grades 5-6
Interest level: Grade 9 to adult
Specific instructional skills: Reading comprehension, word study, writing, listening, grammar skills

Title: Breakthrough Series
Author: William D. Sheldon, Nina Woessner, Warren Wheeloch, George Mason, & Nicholas J. Silvaroli
Publisher: Allyn & Bacon
Approximate cost: $1.68-$2.40 per book (in 1977)
                  .90 teacher's guide
                  8.25 spirit masters
Format: Short paperback books
Reading level:

Grade Level	Number of Books
1	2
2	6
3	3
4	3
5	3
6	3
7	2

Interest level: Grades 7-12
Specific instructional skills: Vocabulary development, reading comprehension

Title: CLUES
Author: Adrian B. Sanford & Kenneth R. Johnson
Publisher: Educational Progress Corporation
Copyright date: 1976
Approximate cost: $350.00 kit (trays 1, 2, 3) (in 1976)
Format: Tape and workbook magazine
Reading level: Grades 2-5
Interest level: Grades 5-12
Specific instructional skills: Word analysis and comprehension

Title: Contact Series
Publisher: Scholastic Book Services
Copyright date: 1976
Approximate cost: $99.50 per unit (16 in all) (in 1977)
Format: 31 books, 31 logs, LP record, filmstrip, teacher's manual per unit
         3 basic series — Communication and the Media, The Individual, Society
Reading level: Grades 4-6
Interest level: Grades 7-12
Specific instructional skills: Reading, writing, discussion, decision making

READING

Title: Countries and Cultures
Publisher: Science Research Associates
Copyright date: 1977
Approximate cost: $77.95 (in 1977)
Format: 120 4-page reading selections
            120 skill cards
Reading level: Grades 4.5-9.5
Interest level: Junior and senior high
Specific instructional skills: Reading comprehension

Title: Croft Skillpacks, Level II
Author: Marion McGuire & Marguerite Bumpus
Publisher: Croft
Copyright date: 1976
Approximate cost: $24.50 each (in 1976)
Format: Booklets, 14-16 pages in length
            Literal and interpretive skills, 7 units
            Analytic and critical skills, 5 units
Reading level: Grades 4-6
Interest level: Grades 4-9
Specific instructional skills: Reading comprehension skills in four areas: literal, interpretive,
                                    analytic, critical

Title: Dimension in Reading Series: Manpower and Natural Resources
Publisher: Science Research Associates
Copyright date: 1977
Approximate cost: $109.00 (in 1977)
Format: 300 four-page reading selections; kit package
Reading level: Grades 4-12
Interest level: Senior high to adult
Specific instructional skills: Stimulate interest in independent reading

Title: Double Action
Author: Karen S. Kleiman, editor
Publisher: Scholastic Book Services
Copyright date: 1976-1977
Approximate cost: $139.50 (in 1976-1977)
Format: 4 books (2 unit books, play anthology, short story anthology), posters, 2 records,
            teacher's guide
Reading level: Unit Book 1 — Grade 3.0-3.4
                   Unit Book 2 — Grade 3.4-3.9
                   Short Story
                   Anthology — Grade 3.0-3.9
                   Play
                   Anthology — Grades 3.2-4.5
Interest level: Grades 7-12
Specific instructional skills: Main idea, specific details, word attack, vocabulary, inference

329

READING

Title: Forward, Back and Around
Author: Robert G. Forest
Publisher: Curriculum Associates
Copyright date: 1976
Approximate cost: $4.95 (in 1977)
Format: 60 activity cards, 1½" x 3"
Reading level: Grades 5-8
Interest level: Grades 5-12
Specific instructional skills: Vocabulary development, lateral thinking

Title: GO Reading in the Content Areas
Author: Harold Herber
Publisher: Scholastic Book Services
Copyright date: 1974-1975
Approximate cost: $ 2.50 test (in 1976-1977)
                    12.50 spirit masters (50)
                    5.00 teacher's guide
Format: Workbook
         5 books: Levels 4, 5, 6, 7, 8
Reading level: Book 4 — Grades 2.0-4.0
                Book 5 — Grades 2.5-5.0
                Book 6 — Grades 3.0-6.0
                Book 7 — Grades 4.0-6.5
                Book 8 — Grades 4.0-7.5
Interest level: Upper elementary to junior high (possibly senior high)
Specific instructional skills: Basic word analysis, comprehension, reasoning skills

Title: Key Ideas in English: Levels 1, 2, 3
Author: Joseph N. Mersand, consulting editor
Publisher: Harcourt Brace Jovanovich
Copyright date: 1974
Approximate cost: $ 3.96 workbook (in 1977)
                    75.00 spirit masters and key
                    .45 key
Format: Workbook (one page per lesson)
Reading level: Grades 4-6
Interest level: Upper elementary and junior high
Specific instructional skills: Grammar, mechanics, usage

Title: Language Lab
Author: Ed Radlauer
Publisher: Bowmar
Copyright date: 1977
Approximate cost: $155.50 (in 1977)
Format: Softbound book, cassette or record, workbook for 3 units
Reading level: Grades 3-5
Interest level: Grades 7-12
Specific instructional skills: Reading, language, dictionary skills, research skills

READING

Title: Multiple Meanings
Author: Robert G. Forest
Publisher: Curriculum Associates
Approximate cost: $12.95 (in 1977) (Precise Word Kit is included)
Format: 100 cards, 1½″ x 3″
Reading level: Grades 4-6
Interest level: Grades 5-12
Specific instructional skills: Develop practice with meanings of words and their multiple
                                definitions

Title: New Streamlined English Series
Author: Frank C. Laubach, Elizabeth Mooney Kirk, & Robert S. Laubach
Publisher: New Readers Press
Copyright date: 1977
Approximate cost: See below
Format: 5 skill workbooks, grades 1-5 $1.40-$2.00
         Correlated readers, grade 5
         Supplementary reading materials
             (2 books with some exercises)
         Teaching aids: check-ups
                          crossword puzzles
                          flashcards
         Teacher's manuals for skill books $2.00-$3.25
         One of everything was approximately $45.00 (in 1977)
Reading level: Grades PP-5
Interest level: Grade 7 to adult
Specific instructional skills: Phonic word attack skills

Title: News for You
Publisher: New Readers Press
Copyright date: 1977
Approximate cost: 8¢ per week (in 1977) (min. order 8 weeks)
Format: Weekly 4-page tabloid newspaper, pub. for 50 weeks each year
Reading level: A edition, grades 3-4   B edition, grades 4-5
Interest level: Grade 7 to adult
Specific instructional skills: Reading comprehension skills

Title: Pal Paperback Kit
Publisher: Xerox Education Publications
Copyright date: Varies per kit
Approximate cost: $39.95 each (in 1977)
Format: Paperback books (18 titles per kit, 3 copies of each)
Reading level: Beginning Pal — Grades .5-2.5
                 Kit A — Grades 1.5-3.5
                 Kit A plus — Grades 2.5-4.5
                 Kit B — Grades 3.5-5.5
Interest level: Grades 5-12
Specific instructional skills: Recreational reading, comprehension skills

READING

Title: Picto-cabulary Series
Publisher: Dexter and Westbrook, Ltd.
Copyright date: 1976
Approximate cost: (in 1976)

Basic Word Set A	36 titles (1 copy each)	$70.00	Suggested grade 1 & 2 Spec. ed. Adult basic ed.
Words to Eat	6 titles (3 copies)	36.95	Grades 3-5
Words to Wear	6 titles (3 copies)	36.95	Grades 3-5
Words to Meet	6 titles (3 copies)	36.95	Grades 3-5
Set III	6 titles (3 copies)	36.95	Grades 5-9
Set 222	6 titles	36.95	Grades 5-9

Format: Illustrated booklets and spirit masters
Reading level: See above
Interest level: See above
Specific instructional skills: Increase vocabulary

Title: Precise Word
Author: Robert G. Forest
Publisher: Curriculum Associates
Approximate cost: $12.95 (in 1977) (Multiple Meaning Kit is included)
Format: 80 cards, 1½″ x 3″, sequenced from easy to hard
Reading level: Grade 7 to adult
Interest level: Grades 5-12
Specific instructional skills: Development of *precise* meanings of words

Title: Read and Reason Activity Cards
Author: Maxine Steck
Publisher: Frank Schaffer
Approximate cost: $3.95 (in 1977)
Format: 8½″ x 5″ cards
Reading level: Grades 3-4
Interest level: Elementary to junior high
Specific instructional skills: Language arts activities: antonyms, synonyms, grammar

READING

Title: Reading Incentive Program, Lab 20
Author: Ed & Ruth Radlauer
Publisher: Bowmar
Copyright date: 1971
Approximate cost: $737.00 (20 kits)
                                    37.00 (each kit) (in 1976-1977)
Format: Book (10 copies), filmstrip, cassette or record, and skill development.sheets
              (8 per book)
Reading level: Grades 3-5
Interest level: Elementary to senior high
Specific instructional skills: Vocabulary development

Title: The Reading Practice Program
Publisher: Harcourt Brace Jovanovich
Copyright date: 1973
Approximate cost: $75.00 (in 1977)
Format: 200 task cards, criterion-referenced pretests and posttests
Reading level: Grades 4-5
Interest level: Upper elementary and junior high
Specific instructional skills: Decoding, vocabulary, sentence study, comprehension

Title: Reading Success Series
Publisher: Xerox Education Publications
Copyright date: 1977
Approximate cost: $.60 each (in 1977)
Format: Six-booklet series (32 pages each)
Reading level: Grades 2-4
Interest level: Junior and senior high
Specific instructional skills: General reading skills

Title: Reading, Thinking, and Reasoning
Author: Don Barnes, Arlene Burgdorf, & L. Stanley Wenck
Publisher: Steck-Vaughn
Copyright date: 1976
Approximate cost: $1.26 each (in 1976)
Format: Workbook (6 books)
Reading level: Grades 1-6
Interest level: Junior high
Specific instructional skills: 40 skills in 3 main areas — analysis, synthesis, evaluation

READING

Title: Reading/Thinking Skills
Author: Dr. Ethel S. Maney
Publisher: Continental Press
Copyright date: 1976
Approximate cost: $.56 each (in 1976)
Format: Workbook
Reading level: Grades 1-6 (2 books per grade)
Specific instructional skills: Study skills, specific reading skills

Title: Skillbooster Series
Author: Sandra M. Brown
Publisher: Modern Curriculum Press
Copyright date: 1975-D; 1977-EF
Approximate cost: $1.08 each (in 1977)
Format: Softbound workbooks
Reading level: Grades 4-6 (D-F)
Interest level: Junior and senior high
Specific instructional skills: Building word power, increasing comprehension, working
                                with facts and details, organizing information, using references

Title: Specific Skill Series
Author: Richard A. Boning
Publisher: Barnell Loft, Ltd.
Approximate cost: $1.40 per book
                   2.25 for spirit master books (in 1976)
Format: Booklet (56 available)
Reading level: Grades 1-7
Interest level: Varies per book
Specific instructional skills: Sounds, follow directions, use context, locate answer, get facts,
                                get main idea, draw conclusions, sequence

Title: The Spice Series: Anchor, Vol. 1, Vol. 2
Publisher: Educational Service
Approximate cost: $5.25 (in 1977)
Format: Duplicating masters
Reading level: Vol. 1: grades 4-6   Vol. 2: grades 6-8
Interest level: Junior and senior high
Specific instructional skills: Varies according to specific book

READING

Title: Sprint Libraries
Author: Varies with book
Publisher: Scholastic Book Services
Copyright date: Varies per library
Approximate cost: $29.50-39.50 kit (4 copies of 5 books) (in 1976-1977)
                              1.30-1.80 book
                              12.50 spirit masters
Format: Book (32-96 pages long)
            Spirit masters
Reading level: Libraries 1 & 1A — Grade 2.0-2.4
                  Libraries 2 & 2A — Grade 2.5-2.9
                  Libraries 3 & 3A — Grade 3.0-3.4
                  Libraries 4 & 4A — Grade 3.5-3.9
Interest level: Grades 4-9 (4-6)
Specific instructional skills: Comprehension and word attack skills

Title: Study Skills for Information Retrieval: Books 1, 2, 3, 4
Author: Donald L. Barnes & Arlene Burgdorf
Publisher: Allyn & Bacon
Copyright date: 1974
Approximate cost: $2.22, $2.43 Teacher's Edition (in 1977)
Format: Paperback workbook
Reading level: Grades 4-6
Interest level: Grade 5 to adult
Specific instructional skills: Alphabetizing, dictionary skills; library work; use of encyclo-
                                   pedia; read and interpret maps, charts, graphs, and data;
                                   organize and write reports

Title: Systems for Success: Book 1, Book 2
Author: R. Lee Henney
Publisher: Follett
Copyright date: 1976
Approximate cost: $2.82 (in 1976)
Format: Workbook
Reading level: Book 1 — Grades 0-4, Book 2 — Grades 5-8
Interest level: Grade 7 to adult
Specific instructional skills: Book 1:   Reading, writing, spelling, computation, English
                                           skills
                              Book 2:   Comprehension, vocabulary, spelling, practical
                                           computations, effective communication

READING

Title: Target Programs
Author: Henry A. Bamman, program director; authors vary per kit
Publisher: Field Enterprises Educational Publications, Inc.
Copyright date: Varies per kit
Approximate cost: $190.00 (in 1973)
Format: Tape and worksheets with 12 study skill cards per kit
          Red — audio-visual description
          Yellow — phonetic analysis
          Blue — structural analysis
          Green — vocabulary I
          Orange — vocabulary II
          Purple — study skills
Reading level: Blue, green, orange, purple — Grade 4+
Interest level: Red and yellow — elementary
               Blue, green, orange, purple — Grade 7 to adult
Specific instructional skills: See above

Title: Troubleshooters I
Author: Patricia Ann Benner, Virginia L. Law, & Joel Weinberg
Publisher: Houghton Mifflin
Copyright date: 1975 edition
Approximate cost: $1.74 each, 8 for $9.48 (in 1978)
                  Teacher's edition, 8 for $10.47
Format: Workbook
Reading level: Varies with book
Interest level: Junior high
Specific instructional skills: Word attack, spelling, punctuation, vocabulary
                              Book 1 — Sound out
                                   2 — Sound off
                                   3 — Spelling action
                                   4 — Word attack
                                   5 — Word mastery
                                   6 — Sentence strength
                                   7 — Punctuation power
                                   8 — English achievement

Title: Troubleshooters II
Author: Patricia Ann Benner, Virginia L. Law, & Joel Weinberg
Publisher: Houghton Mifflin
Copyright date: 1975 edition
Approximate cost: $1.80 each, 6 books for $7.50 (in 1978)
Format: Workbook
Reading level: Varies with book
Interest level: Junior high
Specific instructional skills: Vocabulary, spelling, specific reading skills
                              Book 1 — Word recognition
                                   2 — Vocabulary
                                   3 — Spelling and parts of speech
                                   4 — Reading rate and comprehension
                                   5 — Reading in specific subjects
                                   6 — Reading and study skills

READING

Title: Turning Point
Author: Varies per book
Publisher: McCormick-Mathers
Copyright date: 1975
Approximate cost: $87.60 (in 1977)
Format: Paperback book, 62 duplicating masters (4 each of 10 books) (16 stories)
Reading level: Grades 1.8-3.1
Interest level: Junior and senior high
Specific instructional skills: Main ideas, using details, making inferences, sequencing

Title: Vocabulary Improvement Practice
Author: Donald D. Durrell, Helen A. Murphy, Doris V. Spencer, & Jane H. Catterson
Publisher: Harcourt Brace Jovanovich
Copyright date: 1975
Approximate cost: $27.00 (in 1977)
Format: 160 cards at 4 levels: A, B, C, Challenge
Reading level: Grades 4-12
Interest level: Grades 7-12
Specific instructional skills: Vocabulary growth, classification of words

Title: West Word Bound Book
Author: Rambeau & Rambeau
Publisher: Economy
Copyright date: 1976
Approximate cost: $1.35 (in 1977)
Format: Workbook
Reading level: Grades 2*-6
Interest level: Grade 6 to adult
Specific instructional skills: Word attack, comprehension, study skills

*Manual

Title: World of Vocabulary
Author: Sidney J. Rauch, Zacharie J. Clements, & Alfred B. Weinstein
Publisher: Learning Trends (Globe Book Company)
Copyright date: 1977
Approximate cost: $2.25 each (in 1977)
Format: Workbook, 20 lessons of 10 words each
Reading level: Bk. 1 — Grade 3, Bk. 2 — Grades 4-5, Bk. 3 — Grades 5-6, Bk. 4 — Grades 6-7
Interest level: Grades 7-12
Specific instructional skills: Vocabulary development

WRITING

Title: Be Informed Series (Units 1-20)
Publisher: New Readers Press
Copyright date: Varies from 1968-1976 (some units revised)
Approximate cost: $25.00 for all 20 units bound, $.85 per unit (in 1977)
Format: 8″ x 11″ bound units
          20 units total
Reading level: Grades 5-6
Interest level: Grade 9 to adult
Specific instructional skills: Reading comprehension, word study, writing, listening,
          grammar skills

Title: Contact Series
Publisher: Scholastic Book Services
Copyright date: 1976
Approximate cost: $99.50 per unit (16 in all) (in 1977)
Format: 31 books, 31 logs, LP record, filmstrip, teacher's manual per unit
          3 basic series — Communication and the Media, The Individual, Society
Reading level: Grades 4-6
Interest level: Grades 7-12
Specific instructional skills: Reading, writing, discussion, decision making

Title: Continuous Progress in Spelling
Author: Read, Allred, & Baird
Publisher: Economy
Copyright date: 1977, revised
Approximate cost: $99.90 kit (in 1977)
Format: 16 placement tests, 16 levels of words, delayed recall tests (8″ x 11″ cards)
Reading level: Grade 2-adult
Interest level: Grade 7 to adult
Specific instructional skills: Spelling

Title: English for Everyday Living
Author: Sally Shapiro Pallati & Nell Stiglitz Reitman
Publisher: Ideal
Copyright date: 1976
Approximate cost: $7.00 (in 1977)
Format: Hardback text
Reading level: Grades 4-6
Interest level: Junior high to adult
Specific instructional skills: Language arts, writing

WRITING

Title: Flub Stubs (Prescriptive Task Cards to Improve Writing Skills)
Author: Cheryl Brown
Publisher: Creative Teaching Press
Copyright date: 1975
Approximate cost: $5.95 (in 1976)
Format: Task card
Reading level: Grades 3-4
Interest level: Elementary and junior high (possibly senior high)
Specific instructional skills: Grammar skills, including capitalization, punctuation, verb
agreement, plurals, homonyms

Title: Language Exercises Books
Author: Mabel Youree Grizzard & Annie L. McDonald
Publisher: Steck-Vaughn
Copyright date: 1976
Approximate cost: $1.50 (in 1976)
Format: Workbook
Reading level: Grades 1-8
Interest level: Varies per book
Specific instructional skills: Traditional grammar

Title: Lessons in Paragraphing
Author: Jean N. Alley & Elaine B. Dohan
Publisher: Curriculum Associates
Copyright date: 1976
Approximate cost: $22.95 (ten-pack) (in 1977)
Format: Workbook (88 pages)
Reading level: Grades 5-6
Interest level: Grades 7-12
Specific instructional skills: Develop paragraph writing ability through the use of main
ideas, topic sentences, clinchers, sentences of detail;
paragraph styles are developed: enumerative, sequential, cause
and effect, comparison and contrast

WRITING

Title: The Outlining Kit
Author: Herbert D. Hill, Jr. & Joan McKenna
Publisher: Curriculum Associates
Copyright date: 1977
Approximate cost: $24.95 (in 1977)
Format: 108 lesson cards, 6″ x 9″
Interest level: Grades 5-12
Specific instructional skills:

1. Selecting a topic from subtopics
2. Selecting a topic for subtopics
3. Sorting items into 2 groups and listing in outline form
4. Sorting items, selecting topics, listing in outline form
5. Sorting 3 groups, outlining
6. Sorting 3 groups, selecting topics, outlining
7. Organizing 3 simple outlines, given subtopics
8. Completing a 2-topic outline
9. Selecting topics, completing outline of 2 groups
10. Completing outline for 3 topics
11. Selecting topics, set of 3-part outline
12. Finding subtopics for topic and outline form
13. Making outlines of stories
14. Writing stories and reports using outlines provided

Title: Story Starters, Intermediate
Author: George N. Moore & G. Willard Woodruff
Publisher: Curriculum Associates, Inc.
Copyright date: 1975
Format: $5.80 (in 1977) 32 activity cards
Format: 32 activity cards, 5″ x 8″
Reading level: Grades 4-5
Interest level: Grade 5 to adult
Specific instructional skills: To present the first line of a composition and probing questions to assist paragraph development

Title: Systems for Success: Book 1, Book 2
Author: R. Lee Henney
Publisher: Follett
Copyright date: 1976
Approximate cost: $2.82 (in 1976)
Format: Workbook
Reading level: Book 1 — Grades 0-4, Book 2 — Grades 5-8
Interest level: Grade 7 to adult
Specific instructional skills: Book 1:   Reading, writing, spelling, computation, English skills

Book 2:   Comprehension, vocabulary, spelling, practical computations, effective communication

340

WRITING

Title: Thirty Lessons in Notetaking
Author: Jennifer & Alex Pirie
Publisher: Curriculum Associates
Copyright date: 1975
Approximate cost: $17.95 (ten-pack) (in 1977)
Format: 48-page skillbook
Reading level: Grades 4-6
Interest level: Grades 7-12
Specific instructional skills: Principles of notetaking

Title: The Write Thing: Ways to Communicate
Author: Raymond E. Lemley
Publisher: Houghton Mifflin
Copyright date: 1978
Approximate cost: $94.47 per level (A & B) (in 1978)
Format: Multimedia approach — posters, photoprints, cassette, booklet to write in
Interest level: Junior and senior high
Specific instructional skills: Topic sentence, word choice, narration, dialogue

MATHEMATICS

Title: Basic Essentials of Mathematics: Part 1, Part 2
Author: James T. Shea
Publisher: Steck-Vaughn
Copyright date: 1976
Approximate cost: $1.44 each (in 1976)
Format: Workbook
Reading level: Grades 5-9
Interest level: Junior high to adult
Specific instructional skills: Part 1 — Four fundamental operations with whole numbers,
                                    common fractions, decimals
                              Part II — Percent, measurement, ratio and proportion, simple
                                    equations

Title: Computational Skills Development Kit
Author: Charles M. Proctor, Jr. & Patricia Johnson
Publisher: Science Research Associates
Copyright date: 1977
Approximate cost: $108.50 (in 1977)
Format: Kit with exercise cards
Interest level: Junior high to adult
Specific instructional skills: Basic operations of whole numbers, fractions, decimals,
                              percents

MATHEMATICS

Title: Experiencing Life Through Mathematics
Author: Usher & Bormuth
Publisher: Pawnee Publishing
Copyright date: 1977
Approximate cost: $2.85 per volume, $4.50 TE per volume (in 1977)
Format: 2 volumes
Reading level: Grades 5-6
Interest level: Senior high to adult
Specific instructional skills: Basic operations with whole numbers, fractions,
                    mixed numbers, decimals, percents

Title: Figure It Out: Book 1, Book 2
Author: Mary C. Wallace
Publisher: Follett
Copyright date: 1976
Approximate cost: $1.23 (in 1976)
Format: Workbook
Interest level: Grade 7 to adult
Specific instructional skills: Book 1 — Add, subtract, multiply, divide, money measurements
                    Book 2 — Fractions, decimals, rounding off, estimating

Title: Fun & Games with Mathematics: Activity Cards, Intermediate — Junior High
Author: Haugaard & Horlock
Publisher: Prentice-Hall Learning Systems
Copyright date: 1975
Approximate cost: $4.95 (in 1977)
Format: 5″ x 8″ cards appropriate for duplication
Interest level: Intermediate and junior high
Specific instructional skills: Increase math skills and creative thinking

Title: Good Times Again with Math
Author: Ronald Kremer
Publisher: Prentice-Hall
Copyright date: 1975
Approximate cost: $5.95 (in 1977)
Format: 8½″ x 11″ booklet appropriate for reproduction
Interest level: Multilevel (through adult)
Specific instructional skills: Math-centered activities

MATHEMATICS

Title: Good Times with Math
Author: Ronald Kremer
Publisher: Prentice-Hall
Copyright date: 1977
Approximate cost: $5.95 (in 1977)
Format: 8½″ x 11″ booklet appropriate for reproduction
Interest level: Multilevel
Specific instructional skills: Math skills, critical thinking

Title: Math Mystery Theatre
Publisher: Imperial International Learning
Copyright date: 1975
Approximate cost: $170.00 (in 1977)
Format: 12 tapes, 12 filmstrips, 48 spirit masters, 12 lessons, cartoon format
Interest level: Upper elementary and junior high (grades 7 & 8)
Specific instructional skills: Addition, subtraction, multiplication, division, factoring,
least-common multiples, fractions (4 computations)

Title: Money Makes Sense
Author: Charles H. Kahn & J. Bradley Hanna
Publisher: Fearon
Copyright date: 1973
Approximate cost: $2.00 (in 1975)
Format: Text-workbook
Reading level: Grade 2.3 (Spache)
Interest level: Depends on student; can go as high as adult
Specific instructional skills: Addition, coin recognition, relative value of coins and
one-dollar bill

Title: SLAM (Simple Lattice Approach to Mathematics): Addition
Author: Susan James & Louise Pedrazzini
Publisher: Prentice-Hall
Copyright date: 1976
Approximate cost: $4.95 (in 1977)
Format: 8½″ x 11″ reproducible workbook
Specific instructional skills: Addition

Title: SLAM (Simple Lattice Approach to Mathematics): Subtraction
Author: Susan James & Louise Pedrazzini
Publisher: Prentice-Hall
Copyright date: 1976
Approximate cost: $4.95 (in 1977)
Format: 8½″ x 11″ reproducible workbook
Specific instructional skills: Subtraction

Teaching the Learning Disabled Adolescent

MATHEMATICS

Title: SLAM (Simple Lattice Approach to Mathematics): Multiplication
Author: Susan James & Louise Pedrazzini
Publisher: Prentice-Hall
Copyright date: 1975
Approximate cost: $4.95 (in 1977)
Format: 8½″ x 11″ reproducible workbook
Specific instructional skills: Multiplication

Title: SLAM (Simple Lattice Approach to Mathematics): Division
Author: Susan James & Louise Pedrazzini
Publisher: Prentice-Hall
Copyright date: 1975
Approximate cost: $4.95 (in 1977)
Format: 8½″ x 11″ reproducible workbook
Specific instructional skills: Division

Title: Sports in Things: High Interest Math Series
Publisher: Educational Insights
Copyright date: 1973, revised 1974
Approximate cost: $2.95 per package (7 for $19.95) (in 1977)
Format: Task cards (10) plus answer card
        9″ x 6″   Add-subtract 0-20
                        Add-subtract   0-100
                        Add-subtract   0-5000
                        Multi-divide   easier
                        Multi-divide   harder
                        Fractions
                        Decimals and percent
Reading level: Grade 5
Interest level: Elementary to senior high
Specific instructional skills: Basic math computations, fractions, decimals, percents

Title: Steps to Mathematics, Books 1 and 2
Publisher: Steck-Vaughn
Copyright date: Recently revised
Approximate cost: $1.35 each (in 1976)
Format: Workbook
Reading level: Book 1 — Grades 1-2
                 Book 2 — Grades 3-4
Interest level: Junior high to adult
Specific instructional skills: Fundamental operations (addition, subtraction, multiplication, division) with whole numbers

MATHEMATICS

Title: Using Dollars and Sense
Author: Charles H. Kahn & J. Bradley Hanna
Publisher: Fearon
Copyright date: 1973
Approximate cost: $1.80 (in 1974)
Format: Workbook
Reading level: Grade 3.0 (Spache)
Interest level: Elementary through adult
Specific instructional skills: Subtraction, multiplication, and division of money problems;
                                   making change

Title: Winning Touch
Publisher: University Publishing
Copyright date: 1975
Approximate cost: $5.00 (in 1975)
Format: Game board and number chips
Interest level: Junior and senior high
Specific instructional skills: Increase knowledge of multiplication facts

THINKING

Title: Basic Thinking Skills
Author: Anita Harnadek
Publisher: Midwest Publications
Copyright date: 1976
Approximate cost: $2.50 per book, $7.95 dup. master (in 1977)
Format: 11 books or duplicating masters
Reading level: Middle to upper elementary
Interest level: Upper elementary and junior high
Specific instructional skills: Analogies A
                                   Analogies B
                                   Analogies C
                                   Analogies D
                                   Antonyms and synonyms
                                   Antonyms, synonyms, similarities and differences
                                   Conservation, paths
                                   Miscellaneous, including transitivity and same person or not
                                   Patterns
                                   Think about it
                                   What would you do?
                                   True to life, or fantasy?

THINKING

Title: The Productive Thinking Program: A Course in Learning to Think
Author: Martin V. Covington, Richard S. Crutchfield, Lillian Davies, & Robert M. Olton
Publisher: Merrill
Copyright date: 1974
Approximate cost: $140.00 (in 1977)
Format: 15 booklets (5 copies each) modified cartoon format
Reading level: Grades 4-5
Interest level: Grades 5-9
Specific instructional skills: Discovering and formulating problems; organizing and
                                processing information; generating ideas; evaluating ideas

Title: A Programmed Introduction to the Game of Chess
Author: M. W. Sullivan
Publisher: Behavioral Research Laboratories
Copyright date: 1972
Approximate cost: $4.46 (in 1972)
Interest level: Junior and senior high
Specific instructional skills: Essentials of chess logic and reasoning

Title: Reading, Thinking, and Reasoning
Author: Don Barnes, Arlene Burgdorf, & L. Stanley Wenck
Publisher: Steck-Vaughn
Copyright date: 1976
Approximate cost: $1.26 each (in 1976)
Format: Workbook (6 books)
Reading level: Grades 1-6
Interest level: Junior high
Specific instructional skills: 40 skills in 3 main areas — analysis, synthesis, evaluation

Title: Reading/Thinking Skills
Author: Dr. Ethel S. Maney
Publisher: Continental Press
Copyright date: 1976
Approximate cost: $.56 each (in 1976)
Format: Workbook
Reading level: Grades 1-6
Specific instructional skills: Study skills, specific reading skills

THINKING

Title: Thinking Skills Development Program II
Author: Louis Raths, Jack Wassermann, & Selma Wassermann
Publisher: Benefic Press
Approximate cost: $147.00 (class set of 30) (in 1977)
Format: 240 skill development cards
        60 self-help cards
        30 nonconsumable student reference books
        12 filmstrips
        2 cassettes
Reading level: Grades 5-6
Interest level: Grades 6-9
Specific instructional skills: Observing, looking for assumptions, collecting and organizing data, comparing, classifying, hypothesizing, criticizing, interpreting, imagining, coding, problem solving, summarizing

Title: Thinklab I
Author: K. J. Weber
Publisher: Science Research Associates
Copyright date: 1974
Approximate cost: $54.50 (in 1977)
Format: 125 puzzle cards (4 each) plus additional manipulative items
Reading level: Grades 3.5-9.0+ (20-40 cards per grade level)
Interest level: Grade 3 to adult
Specific instructional skills: Object manipulation, perception and creative insight, perceiving image patterns, logical analysis

SOCIAL INTERACTION

Title: Alcohol: Facts for Decisions
Author: Gail Lichtman
Publisher: New Readers Press
Copyright date: 1974
Approximate cost: $1.25 (in 1977)
Format: 40-page soft-cover booklet
Reading level: Grade 6.4
Interest level: Junior and senior high
Specific instructional skills: Basic facts for students; topics for class discussions

Title: Beginning Values Clarification
Author: Sidney B. Simon & Jay Clark
Publisher: Pennant Press
Copyright date: 1975
Approximate cost: $3.95 (in 1976)
Format: Paperback book (182 pages), resource book for teachers
        33 units
Reading level: For teacher use
Interest level: Grade 7 to adult
Specific instructional skills: Dealing with affect

SOCIAL INTERACTION

Title: Building Safe Driving Skills
Author: Patrick Kelley
Publisher: Fearon
Copyright date: 1972
Approximate cost: $4.35 student test (in 1974)
                             7.20 chapter tests
                             1.20 teacher's guide
Format: Clothbound book, 16 chapters
Reading level: Grade 3.0 (Spache)
Interest level: Grade 9 to adult
Specific instructional skills: Basics of good driving skills, motorcycles, planning a
                 trip, car ownership and maintenance

Title: Choices: Organizing and Teaching a Course in Personal Decision Making
Author: Joan Kosuth & Sandy Minnesang
Publisher: Pennant Educational Materials
Copyright date: 1975
Approximate cost: $34.95 (in 1976)
Format: 26 learning activity packages and teacher's guide
Interest level: Grade 9 to adult
Specific instructional skills: Directs students in personal decision making

Title: Civics
Author: Lee J. Rosch & Grant T. Ball
Publisher: Follett
Copyright date: 1976
Approximate cost: $7.80 text or booklets (7) (in 1976)
Format: Textbook or seven unit booklets
Reading level: Grades 6-8
Interest level: Grades 7-12
Specific instructional skills: Content commonly taught in citizenship courses

Title: Deciding for Myself: A Values-Clarification Series
          Clarifying My Values — Set A
          My Everyday Choices — Set B
          Where Do I Stand? — Set C
Author: T. Paulson
Publisher: Winston Press
Copyright date: 1974
Approximate cost: $2.52 per set
                             3.96 leader guide (all sets in 1) (in 1975)
                             10 8-page units per set
Interest level: Grade 6 to adult
Specific instructional skills: Practice in values clarification

SOCIAL INTERACTION

Title: Discovery Kit
Publisher: Scholastic Book Services
Copyright date: 1976
Approximate cost: $169.50 (in 1976)
Format: 8 15-min. sound filmstrips (records or cassettes); 30 logbooks, teacher's guide
Interest level: Grades 7-10
Specific instructional skills: Students learn about a variety of jobs, probe job-related problems, and use productive thinking regarding their own goals and interests

Title: Drugs: Facts for Decisions
Author: Roger Conant
Publisher: New Readers Press
Copyright date: 1976, revised
Approximate cost: $1.25 (in 1977)
Format: 32-page soft-cover booklet
Reading level: Grade 5.6
Interest level: Junior high to adult
Specific instructional skills: Factual information on drugs

Title: Getting a Job
Author: Florence Randall
Publisher: Fearon
Copyright date: 1968
Approximate cost: $2.01 (in 1974)
Format: Text-workbook, 8″ x 11″
Reading level: Grade 3.6 (Spache)
Interest level: Grades 9-12
Specific instructional skills: Life survival skills related to careers, jobs, and wages

Title: How to Register and Vote
Author: K. Baer
Publisher: New Readers Press
Copyright date: 1972
Approximate cost: $.35 (in 1977)
Format: 16-page pamphlet, 8½″ x 5½″
Interest level: Senior high
Specific instructional skills: Specific information on mechanics of registering and voting

SOCIAL INTERACTION

Title: Jerry Works in a Service Station
Author: Jewel M. Wade
Publisher: Fearon
Copyright date: 1967
Approximate cost: $1.20 (in 1974)
Format: Text-workbook
          8 chapters with exercises
Reading level: Grade 2.2 (Spache)
Interest level: Grades 9-12
Specific instructional skills: Language arts skills, vocational skills

Title: You, The Police, and Justice
Publisher: Scholastic Book Services
Copyright date: 1976
Approximate cost: $99.50 (in 1976)
Format: Anthology (31 copies), logbooks, posters, teacher's guide
Reading level: Grades 4-6
Interest level: Grades 9-12
Specific instructional skills: To provide a variety of reading experiences for exploring the
                                 relationships between laws and people

Title: Making It on Your Own
Author: Jack Hyde, Robert Smith, & John Travis
Publisher: Mafex Associates
Copyright date: 1977
Approximate cost: $58.95 for 10 books, 4 poster sets, guides
                    25.00 for 10 books, guide (in 1977)
Format: Text, transparencies, teacher's guide, posters
Interest level: Grade 9 to adult
Specific instructional skills: Basic skills of survival

Title: Occupations 1 & 2
Author: 1: Caroline Blakely, editor; 2: Dennis Schroeder, editor
Publisher: New Readers Press
Copyright date: 1: revised 1975; 2: 1974
Approximate cost: $1.60 each (in 1977)
Format: Book
Reading level: 1 — Grade 6.7; 2 — Grade 6.3
Interest level: Senior high
Specific instructional skills: Career orientation

SOCIAL INTERACTION

Title: Out of Work
Author: Stephen Ludwig
Publisher: New Readers Press
Copyright date: 1975
Approximate cost: $1.50 (in 1977)
Format: Booklet
Reading level: Grade 6.8
Interest level: Senior high to adult
Specific instructional skills: For out-of-work reader who needs help getting training and
getting a job

Title: Planning Meals and Shopping
Author: Ann Weaver
Publisher: Fearon
Copyright date: 1970
Approximate cost: $1.65 (in 1974)
Format: Text-workbook
Reading level: Grade 2.5 (Spache)
Interest level: Grades 7-12
Specific instructional skills: Plan meals, budget money, make shopping lists, compare
prices, store food

Title: Real People at Work
Author: Varies with book
Publisher: Changing Times Education Service
Copyright date: 1975
Approximate cost: $1.65 per title (in 1975)
Format: Booklet, 10 titles per level
Reading level: Series A — Grade 2L
                        B — Grade 2M
                        C — Grade 2H
                        E — Grade 3L
                        F — Grade 3M
                        G — Grade 3H
Interest level: Grades 2-12
Specific instructional skills: Career awareness, reading practice

Title: Rules and Rights: Juveniles Have Rights, Too
Author: Judge Roy W. Seagraves, H. B. McDaniel, & B. A. Truce
Publisher: Fearon
Copyright date: 1973
Format: Workbook, 12 units, with realistic story and followup activities to reinforce legal
processing
Interest level: Grades 7-12
Specific instructional skills: Positive attitudes toward law; student rights and
responsibilities

351

SOCIAL INTERACTION

Title: Scope Magazine
Publisher: Scholastic Book Services
Copyright date: 1976
Approximate cost: $2.40 per subscription per year (in 1976)
Format: Periodical, weekly (24 issues)
Reading level: Grades 4-6
Interest level: Junior and senior high
Specific instructional skills: Reading practice, writing, related language skills

Title: Tell It Like It Is: The Un-Game
Publisher: Pennant Educational Materials
Approximate cost: $8.50 (in 1976)
Format: Game board, pawns, die, deck of special cards (one for adolescents and adults,
        one for children)
Interest level: Grade 4 to adult
Specific instructional skills: Communications problems

Title: Values Clarification: A Handbook of Practical Strategies for Teachers and Students
Author: Sidney B. Simon, Leland W. Howe, & Howard Kirschenbaum
Publisher: Hart Publishing
Copyright date: 1972
Approximate cost: $3.95 (in 1974)
Format: Paperback book; 79 strategies for values clarification
Interest level: Elementary to adult
Specific instructional skills: Communications, values clarification

Title: The World of Work
Author: Kay Koschnick & Stephen Ludwig
Publisher: New Readers Press
Copyright date: 1975, revised
Approximate cost: $1.50 (in 1977)
Format: Book
Reading level: Grade 6.4
Interest level: Senior high
Specific instructional skills: Introduces variety of jobs to reader; covers language of want
                    ads, tips in job interviewing; fringe benefits, unions and
                    workers' rights

SOCIAL INTERACTION

Title: You Can Change the Law
Author: Judge Roy M. Seagraves, H. B. McDaniel, & B. A. Truce
Publisher: Fearon
Copyright date: 1973
Approximate cost: $2.00 (in 1974)
Format: Text-workbook, 12 units
Interest level: Grades 7-12
Specific instructional skills: Positive attitude toward the law; rights and responsibilities
       as citizens

LISTENING/SPEAKING

Title: New Horizons in English
Author: L. Mellgren, M. Walker, J. A. Upshur (consulting editor)
Publisher: Addison-Wesley
Copyright date: 1973-75
Approximate cost: $1.86-$2.37 books (in 1976)
       $2.70 teacher's guide
       $66.00 3-reel tapes
       $56.10 6 cassettes
       $ .99-$1.20 workbooks
Format: 6 softbound texts, workbooks, audio forms
Interest level: Older students and young adults
Specific instructional skills: Word structures, vocabulary development,
         concept development

Title: Pride in Language, Books 1, 2, 3
Author: William Rosch, Gene Orland, Deborah K. Osen, & Stephen Sloan
Publisher: Random House
Copyright date: 1975
Approximate cost: $4.56 hardback $6.57 teacher's edition (in 1975)
       3.42 softback   1.77 workbook
Format: Hardbound or softbound book
Reading level: Grade 4
Interest level: Junior high
Specific instructional skills: Critical thinking, listening and speaking, writing,
         observing language, grammar

GENERAL MATERIALS

Title: Action Biology
Author: Stanley L. Weinberg & Herbert J. Stoltze
Publisher: Allyn & Bacon
Copyright date: 1977
Approximate cost: $8.97 $5.22 teacher's guide (in 1977)
                        1.47 per unit, 1974 series
Format: Book (1977)
        7 units (1974)
Reading level: Slow learner, poor reader
Specific instructional skills: Career development, reading skills, math skills

Title: American Adventures
Publisher: Scholastic Book Services
Copyright date: 1976
Approximate cost: $2.25 text (in 1976)
                    2.50 teacher's guide
                    9.95 spirit masters
Format: Small booklets approximately 180 pages in length, 4 in series:
        I   A Nation Conceived and Dedicated
        II Old Hate — New Hope
        III Between Two Wars
        IV Yesterday, Today, Tomorrow
Reading level: Grades 4-6
Interest level: Junior and senior high
Specific instructional skills: Provides American history material in high-interest
                                low-vocabulary presentation; improves reading skills through
                                gradual increase in difficulty and practice in reading

Title: Individualized Science Investigation Series
Author: Educational Research Council of America
Publisher: Allyn & Bacon
Copyright date: 1974
Approximate cost: $12.70 worktext (set of 5) (in 1977)
                    99.00 topic area units (30 students)
                    other components per kit
Format: Phase A — worktext
        Phase B — units in kit form
Reading level: Grade 5+
Interest level: Grades 7-12
Specific instructional skills: Science information development, 4 units per year, minimum

354

GENERAL MATERIALS

Title: A Modified History of the United States
Author: Ardelle Manning & Caroline Wood
Publisher: Ardelle Manning Productions
Copyright date: 1977
Approximate cost: $4.25 (in 1977)
Format: Workbook
Reading level: Grade 3
Interest level: Junior and senior high
Specific instructional skills: Material for low-level reading in U.S. history

Title: Pathways in Science
Author: Joseph M. Oxenhorn & Michael N. Idelson
Publisher: Globe Book
Copyright date: 1976
Approximate cost: $2.25 (soft-cover) (in 1976)
                              3.75 (hard-cover)
Format: Soft-cover or hard-cover; 3 series, 4 books per series
Reading level: Grades 5-6
Interest level: Grades 7-12
Specific instructional skills: Earth science, chemistry, physics, biology

REFERENCES

Bleil, B. G. Evaluating educational materials. *Journal of Learning Disabilities*, 1975, *8*, 12-19.

Brown, V. A. A basic Q-sheet for analyzing curriculum materials and proposals. *Journal of Learning Disabilities*, 1975, *8*, 407-416.

Ensminger, E. E. A proposed model for selecting, modifying, or developing instructional materials for handicapped children. *Focus on Exceptional Children*, 1970, *1* (9), 1-9.

Kass, C. E. Methods and materials in learning disabilities. In N. D. Bryant & C. E. Kass (Eds.), *Leadership training institute in learning disabilities* (Vol. 1). Tucson: University of Arizona, 1972.

Van Etten, C. *Materials selection guide*. Olathe, Kansas: Select-Ed., 1970.

Watson, B. L., & Van Etten, C. Materials analysis. *Journal of Learning Disabilities*, 1976, *9*, 408-416.

Wiederholt, J. L., & McNutt, G. Evaluating materials for handicapped adolescents. *Journal of Learning Disabilities*, 1977, *10*, 132-140.

Wilson, J. Selecting educational materials. In D. D. Hammill & N. R. Bartell (Eds.), *Teaching children with learning and behavior problems*. Boston: Allyn & Bacon, 1978.

INDEX